D1739446

Perspectives on Development in the Middle East and North Africa (MENA) Region

Series editor

Almas Heshmati, Sogang University, Seoul, Korea (Republic of)

This book series publishes monographs and edited volumes devoted to studies on the political, economic and social developments of the Middle East and North Africa (MENA). Volumes cover in-depth analyses of individual countries, regions, cases and comparative studies, and they include both a specific and a general focus on the latest advances of the various aspects of development. It provides a platform for researchers globally to carry out rigorous economic, social and political analyses, to promote, share, and discuss current quantitative and analytical work on issues, findings and perspectives in various areas of economics and development of the MENA region. Perspectives on Development in the Middle East and North Africa (MENA) Region allows for a deeper appreciation of the various past, present, and future issues around MENA's development with high quality, peer reviewed contributions. The topics may include, but not limited to: economics and business, natural resources, governance, politics, security and international relations, gender, culture, religion and society, economics and social development, reconstruction, and Jewish, Islamic, Arab, Iranian, Israeli, Kurdish and Turkish studies. Volumes published in the series will be important reading offering an original approach along theoretical lines supported empirically for researchers and students, as well as consultants and policy makers, interested in the development of the MENA region.

More information about this series at http://www.springer.com/series/13870

Almas Heshmati · Haeyeon Yoon
Editors

Economic Growth and Development in Ethiopia

 Springer

Editors
Almas Heshmati
Department of Economics
Sogang University
Seoul
Korea (Republic of)

Haeyeon Yoon
Department of Economics
Sogang University
Seoul
Korea (Republic of)

and

Jönköping International Business School
Jönköping University
Jönköping, Jönköpings Län
Sweden

ISSN 2520-1239   ISSN 2520-1247   (electronic)
Perspectives on Development in the Middle East and North Africa (MENA) Region
ISBN 978-981-10-8125-5   ISBN 978-981-10-8126-2   (eBook)
https://doi.org/10.1007/978-981-10-8126-2

Library of Congress Control Number: 2018939929

Printed on acid-free paper

This Springer imprint is published by the registered company Springer Nature Singapore Pte Ltd. part of Springer Nature
The registered company address is: 152 Beach Road, #21-01/04 Gateway East, Singapore 189721, Singapore

Contents

Part IV   Human Capital and Firm Growth

Contributors

Hassen Azime Department of Public Finance, Institute of Tax and Customs Administration, Ethiopian Civil Service University, Addis Ababa, Ethiopia

Jonse Bane Department of Economics, Addis Ababa University, Addis Ababa, Ethiopia

Mekonnen Bersisa Economics at Department of Economics, Ambo University Woliso Campus, Woliso, Ethiopia

Yonatan Desalegn Economics Department, Addis Ababa University, Addis Ababa, Ethiopia

Tufa Garoma Department of Development Economics, Rift Valley University, Addis Ababa, Ethiopia

Selamawit Gebreegziabher Department of Economics, Addis Ababa University, Addis Ababa, Ethiopia

Tsegaye Mulugeta Habtewold Department of Economics, College of Business and Economic, Addis Ababa University, Addis Ababa, Ethiopia

Almas Heshmati Department of Economics, Sogang University, Seoul, Korea; Jönköping International Business School, Jönköping University, Jönköping, Sweden

Guta Legesse Department of Economics, Addis Ababa University, Addis Ababa, Ethiopia

Gollagari Ramakrishna School of Graduate Studies, Ethiopian Civil Service University, Addis Ababa, Ethiopia

Getu Tigre Department of Economics, Addis Ababa University, Addis Ababa, Ethiopia

Haeyeon Yoon Department of Economics, Sogang University, Seoul, Korea

Abbreviations

ADF	Augmented Dickey–Fuller
AERC	African Economic Research Consortium
AEU	Adult Equivalent
AIC	Akaike Information Criterion
ANOVA	Analysis Of Variance
ARDL	Autoregressive Distributed Lag
ATE	Average Treatment Effect
CA	Cluster Analysis
CPI	Consumer Price Index
CSA	Central Statistical Agency
DHS	Demographic and Health Survey
DTR	Direct Tax Revenue
ECM	Error Correction Model
ESDP	Education Sector Development Program
ESR	Endogenous Switching Regression
FA	Factor Analysis
FAO	Food and Agriculture Organization
FDI	Foreign Direct Investments
FE estimation	Fixed Effect estimation
FE model	Fixed Effect model
FGT	Foster–Greer–Thorbecke
FIF	Farmer Innovation Fund
FIML	Full Information Maximum Likelihood
FTC	Farmer Training Center
GDP	Gross Domestic Production
HGF	High-Growth Firm
HQ	Hannan–Quinn
ISIC	International Standard Industry Classification
ITR	Indirect Tax Revenue
KM	Kernel Matching

KM	Kernel Method
LCA	Latent Class Analysis
LDC	Less-Developed Countries
LM	Lagrange Multiplier
LPE	Law of Proportionate Effect
MCA	Multiple Correspondence Analysis
MoARD	Ministry of Agriculture and Rural Development
MOFEC	Ministry of Finance and Economic Cooperation
MOFED	Ministry of Finance and Economic Development
MZM	Money Zero Maturity
NBE	National Bank of Ethiopia
NGO	Non-Governmental Organization
NLFS	National Labor Force Survey
NNM	Nearest Neighbor Matching
OLS	Ordinary Least Squares
PCA	Principal Component Analysis
PSM	Propensity Score Matching
PSU	Primary Sampling Unit
RESET	Ramsey Regression Equation Specification Error Test
RM	Radius Matching
SB	Standardized Bias
SCB	Schwarzbirth information criterion
SEM	Structural Equation Model
SNP	Safety Net Program
TLU	Tropical Livestock Unit
UNDP	United Nations Development Program
VECM	Vector Error Correction Model
WFP	World Food Program

List of Authors

Abafita, J.
Abbas, Q.
Abdon, A.
Abdulai, A.
Abduselam, A. M.
Abu, G. A.
Acemoglu, D.
Achtenhagen, L.
Acs, Z.
Adamu, J.
Addis, Y.
Adebayo, A. J.
Adekambi, S. A.
Adetola, A.
Admassie, A.
Adnan, A. S.
Afzal, M.
Ahmad, N.
Ahmad, U. G.
Ahmed, M.
Akben-Selcuk, E.
Akinboade, O. A.
Alemayehu, A.
Alemayehu, G.
Alemu, M.
Alemu, G.
Alemu, Z. G.
Alene, A. D.
Al-Fawwaz, T. M.
Ali, M.
Ali, S.

Alkire, S.
Allingham, M.
Allison, P. D.
Alm, J.
Alsadiq, A. J.
Alshahrani, S. A.
Ambel, A. P.
Anderson, K.
Andreoni, J.
Angrist, J. D.
Apablaza, M.
Appleton, S.
Araar, A.
Arenius, P.
Arrow, K. J.
Asfaw, M.
Asfaw, S.
Ashenfelter, O.
Assefa, A.
Aterido, R.
Atkinson, A. B.
Ayenew, T.
Azime, H.
Babatunde, R. O.
Bahaddi, T.
Bahadur, K. L.
Bahl, R.
Balagtas, V.
Balema, A. A.
Balihut, A.
Balihuta, A.
Ballon, P.
Banerjee, A. V.
Bargicho, S.
Barnes, H.
Barnum, H.
Barro, R. J.
Barron, D. N.
Bates, R. H.
Bayo, F.
Becerril, J.
Becker, G. S.
Becker, S. O.
Bedad, B.
Been-Lon, C.

Bekele, H.
Belshaw, D.
Berenger, V.
Bergman, M.
Berihun, B.
Berisso, O.
Bersisa, M.
Besley, T.
Biaou, G.
Bigsten, A.
Binns, T.
Biratu, Y.
Birru, Y. A.
Bleaney, M.
Bleaney, M. F.
Blundell, R.
Bobek, D. D.
Bokanga, M.
Bose, N.
Bourguignon, F.
Braithwaite, V.
Bravo-Biosca, A.
Brouwer, P.
Bruck, T.
Brüderl, J.
Brundin, E.
Bwalya, R.
Byron, R. P.
Caliendo, M.
Card, D.
Carneiro, P.
Catao, L. A. V.
Cavoli, T.
Chakravarty, S.
Chang, J. J.
Chang, T.
Chang, Y.
Chen, S.
Chenery, H.
Chilonda, P.
Chitonge, H.
Chowdhury, N. M.
Chu, H. P.
Chung, K.
Clover, J.

Coad, A.
Collier, P.
Costa-Dias, M.
Coulibaly, J. Y.
Cowell, F. A.
Cummings, R. G.
Dagsvik, J. K.
Das, S.
Datt, G.
Daunfeldt, S. O.
Davidsson, P.
Deaton, A.
Debebe, H.
Decancq, K.
Dejuan, A.
Delmar, F.
Demssie, M. W.
Denning, G. L.
Dercon, S.
Desalegn, Y.
Di Falco, S.
Diagne, A.
Diamond, P.
Dibben, C.
Ding, S.
Ditimi, A.
Dixon, A.
Doagostino, R. B.
Donaldson, D.
Dressler, S. G.
Dridi, J.
Dridi, M. J.
Du, J.
Duaz, D.
Duclos, D. S.
Duclos, J-Y.
Dufalo, E.
Durevall, D.
Durnecker, G.
Easterly, W.
Eiely, F.
Elert, N.
Elizabeth, F.
Erard, B.
Esquivel, G.

Estrada, G. B.
Evans, D. S.
Faltermeier, L.
Fan, S.
Faridi, R.
Feder, G.
Feinstein, J.
Fekadu, B.
Feleke, S.
Filtoussi, J.
Fischer, C. M.
Fisman, R.
Fjeldstad, O. H.
Fleurbaey, M.
Foster, J.
Foster, J. E.
Freeman, J.
Fris, P.
Gartner, W.
Gebreegziabher, S.
Gebreeyesus, M.
Geland, T.
Gemmell, N.
Geoghegan, J.
Gertler, P. J.
Getahun, T.
Ghosh Roy, A.
Gilligan, D.
Gisore, N.
Gladwin, C.
Goedhuys, M.
Goldsmith, A.
Gomes, J. F.
Gordon, P. F.
Green, W. H.
Greer, J.
Griffin, K.
Grimm, L. G.
Guandong, B. Y.
Gujarati, D. N.
Gupta, S.
Habtewold, T. M.
Haddad, I.
Hageman, A. M.
Hagos, A.

Haile, H. K.
Hailemariam, T.
Hajara, B.
Hallward-Driemeier, M.
Halvarsson, D.
Hannan, M. T.
Haque, M.
Harriss, B.
Hart, M.
Haughton, J.
Hayami, Y.
Heckman, J.
Heckman, J. J.
Heggstad, K. K.
Heinemann, F.
Henderson, A.
Henrekson, M.
Hentschel, J.
Heshmati, A.
Hiagne, A.
Hirru, A.
Hishe-Gebreslassie, G.
Hoddinott, J.
Holly, A.
Hölzl, D.
Hölzl, W.
Hosmer, D. W.
Hossain, M.
Hossain, M. A.
Hsin-Yi, L.
Hsu, M.
Hua, Y.
Huergoa, E.
Huerta-Pineda, A.
Hulme, D.
Humphreys, J.
Hungerford, T.
Hyuha, T.
Ichimura, H.
Ichino, A.
Jabbar, M.
Jaleta, M.
Jaumandreu, J.
Jiang, C.
Johansson, D.

Johnson, O. E. G.
Jones, N.
Jonse Bane, J.
Joshi, R. D.
Jung, S.
Just, R. E.
Kakwani, N.
Kalio, A.
Karim, M.
Kassie, M.
Kastlunger, B.
Kebede, B.
Kelliher, C. F.
Kelsey, J.
Ketema, T.
Keynes, J. M.
Khandker, S. R.
Kiani, A.
Kibet, I.
Kibrom, T.
Kilmer, I.
Kim, K.
Kim, T.Y.
Kimenyi, M. S.
Kiprop, S.
Kirchler, E.
Kirchler, L.
Klasen, S.
Kling, J. R.
Kneller, R.
Kocher, M. G.
Köhlin, G.
Kok, J.
Kopeinig, S.
Krishnan, P.
Krueger, A. B.
Kudhlande, G.
Lamartina, S.
Lanjouw, P.
Laveesh, B.
Layard, R.
Le Pfau
Lee, L. F.
Lee, M.
Lemeshow, S.

Levine, R.
Lipper, L.
Livingstone, I.
Loaning, I. J.
Loderer, C.
Loenin, J. L.
Loening, L. J.
Loganathan, N.
Lokshin, M.
Lopez-garcia, P.
Lugo, M. A.
Lury, D. A.
Lutkepol, H.
Luttmer, E. F. P.
M'Amanja, D.
Maasoumi, E.
Maddala, G. S.
Maggino, F.
Mahjoub, E.
Mahmoodi, E.
Mahmoodi, M.
Manaloto, E. Q.
Manda, D. K.
Maniquet, F.
Maniquet, F.
Mannaf, M.
Mansouri, B.
Manyong, V.
Mark, M.
Markowsk, M.
Martinez, S.
Martinez-Vazquez, J.
Matchaya, G.
Maxwell, D.
Maxwell, S.
Mcclelland, G. H.
McKay, A.
Mckee, M.
Mclennan, D.
Mebta, P.
Mendola, M.
Mesay, Y.
Mignouna, H.
Mincer, J.
Mishra, S.

Mitchell, D. J.
Mittone, I.
Moccero, D.
Monyo, E.
Moore, M.
Moreno, F.
Morrissey, O.
Moser, G. G.
Mridusmita, B.
Muehlbache, S.
Mugisha, J.
Muhammed, A.
Muricho, G.
Murray, M.
Musaba, E. C.
Muturi, W.
Muturi, W. M.
Mwabu, G.
Naimul, S.
Naimul, S.
Narayan, K. P.
Narayan, S.
Nasiru, I.
Ndudu, B. J.
Negassa, A.
Nel, E.
Nell, K. S.
Nelson, F. D.
Neumann, R.
Nguimkeu, P.
Nguyen, A. D.
Nguyen, H. M.
Nguyen, V. B.
Niedermeier, E. W.
Nightingale, P.
Noble, M.
Nurudeen, A.
Nziguheba, G.
O'connell, S. A.
Ochieng, J.
Ocran, M. K.
Odhiamb, G.
Olabisi, A. S.
Omanya, G.
Pahlavani, M.

Palangkaraya, A.
Pandey, S.
Parend, M.
Park, D.
Parsons, W.
Patrinos, H. A.
Pattanaik, P.
Persson, A.
Persson, T.
Pesaran, M. H.
Petersen, D. R.
Pfau, W. D.
Philip, N.
Pinzon, R.
Premand, P.
Preston, I.
Prinz, A.
Puente, S.
Rahmto, N.
Raknerud, A.
Ramakrishna, G.
Ramakrishna, J.
Ramirez-Pacillias, M.
Rao, R.
Rashidghalam, M.
Ravallion, M.
Rawlings, L. B.
Raynor, M.
Renshaw, E. F.
Reobelo, S.
Riely, F.
Rijkers, B.
Robson, P.
Roche, J. M.
Romer, D.
Rosenbaum, P. R.
Roy, A.
Rubin, D. B.
Sahu, S. K.
Saith, R.
Sajaia, Z. Z.
Sala-I-Martin, X.
Salazar, R.
Sanchez, I.
Sanchez, P. A.

Sandmo, A.
Sangraula, P.
Santos, J. M.
Santos, M. E.
Sasmal, J.
Schorfheid, F.
Schreyer, P.
Schulze, W. D.
Schüssler, R.
Segarra, A.
Sek, S. K.
Selassie, T.
Sen, A. K.
Seth, S.
Setotaw, F.
Setotaw, S.
Sharma, B.
Shiferaw, B.
Shihab, R. A.
Shin, Y.
Siambi, M.
Siebrits, F. K.
Siebrits, M. E.
Siegfried, B.
Silber, J.
Simtowe, F.
Simtowe, F. P.
Singhal, M.
Siphambe, H. K.
Sjö, B.
Sjursen, I.
Sleuwaegen, L.
Smith, J.
Smith, R. J.
Soderbom, M.
Solomon, A.
Solon, G.
Soludo, C. C.
Song, B.
Soom, A.
Squire, I.
Srinivasan. T. N.
Ssozi, J.
Stewait, F.
Stierwald, A.

Stiglitz, J. E.
Stinchcombe, A. L.
Storey, J.
Strom, S.
Sturdivant, R. X.
Su, B.
Sudarsono, H
Sultana, A.
Sutton, J
Svensson, J.
Takeuchi, L. R.
Tao, D.
Tareq, S.
Tassew, W.
Tausch, A.
Teklewold, H.
Temu, A.
Teo, X. Q.
Teruel, M.
Tesfaye, A.
Tesfaye, S.
Thorbecke, E.
Tigre, G.
Tilksew, G. B.
Todd, P.
Tracy, S.
Tran, V.
Trost, R. P.
Trostel, P. A.
Tsadiku, W.
Tsegaw, E.
Tsui, K. Y.
Tyler, T. R.
Uddin, M. T.
Uddin, S.
Udry, C.
Unsal, F. D.
Usman, A.
Valenzuela, E.
Vance, C.
Varga, J.
Verdire-Chouchane, A.
Vermeersch, C. M. J.
Veronesi, M.
Verspoor, A.

Verwimp, P.
Voracek, M.
Vytlacil, E. J.
Waelchli
Wallenius, H.
Wan, G.
Wartic, M.
Weir, S.
Welday, A.
West, E.
Whitworth, A.
Wilkinson, K.
Williams, O. H.
Wilson, E.
Wilson, J. K.
Wolday, A.
Woldehanna, T.
Wong, Y. N.
Workneh Wu, H.
Workneh, S.
Worthington, A. C.
Xu, T.
Xu, y.
Yalonetzky, G.
Yarnold, P. R.
Yesuf, M.
Yilma, M.
Yirga, C.
Yoon, H.
Yotopoulos, P.
Younger, S.
Zaghini, A.
Zagler, M.
Zakari, S.
Zilberman, D.
Zumbo, B. D.
Zurab-Sajaia, Z.

List of Figures

List of Tables

List of Subjects

Chi-square
Climatic Hazards
Cluster Analysis
Cobb–Douglas production function
Conditional growth
Conditional probability
Consumer Price Index
Core module
Cost-effective manner
Counterfactual
Crowding-out effect
Demand-side factor
Demographic and Health Survey
Density curve
Density distributions
Density function
Dergue regime
Det correlation matrix
Developing Countries
Diagnostic tests
Dichotomous
Direct Tax Revenue
Discount rate
Discrete variable
Disequilibrium
Displacement effects
Disseminating market information
Dissemination of knowledge
Distributional pattern
Domestic prices
Domestic product
Domestic production
Domestic supply
Domestic traders
Domestic workers
Dummy variable
East and North Africa
ECM approach
ECM coefficient measures
Econometric analysis
Econometric estimation
Econometric strategy
Economic activity
Economic behavior
Economic crisis

Social network
Social sanctions
Social service expenditure
Social variables
Social welfare
Socioeconomic characteristics
Socioeconomic analysis
Socioeconomic determinants
Socioeconomic factors
Spearman's rank correlation coefficient
Spurious regression
Standardized Bias
Standardized mean difference
STATA
Static model
Stationarity test
Stationary data
Stationary time series
Stationary trend
Statistical method
Statistical significance
Statistical test
Statistical significance
Standard error t-statistic
Stepwise logistic regression
Stepwise method
Stepwise regression
Stepwise selection procedure
Stochastic dominance analysis
Stochastic methods
Straightforward standard Mincerian regression
Structural equation model
Structural econometric analysis
Structural Equation Model
Sub-Saharan African
Supply-side determinants
Sustainable development
Sustainable economic growth
Swedish international development cooperation agency
Tax compliant attitude
Time-series data
Time-series variable
Tobin's q ratios
Trade-off
Transaction costs

Chapter 1
Introduction and Summary

Almas Heshmati and Haeyeon Yoon

Abstract Sustained and inclusive economic growth has gained much attention in recent years (Acemoglu in Introduction to modern economic growth. Princeton University Press, New Jersey, 2009; Barro in Determinants of growth: a cross country empirical study. MIT Press, Cambridge MA, 1997; Barro and Sala-i-Martin in Economic growth. MIT Press, Cambridge MA, 2004; Griffin in World hunger and the world economy. Springer, Singapore, 1987; Heshmati et al. in Poverty reduction policies and practices in developing Asia. Springer, Singapore, 2015; Kim and Heshmati in Economic growth: the new perspectives for theory and policy. Springer, Singapore, 2014; Tausch and Heshmati in Globalization, the human condition and sustainable development in the 21st century: cross-national perspectives and European implications. Anthem Press, London, 2012; and others).

Keywords Economic growth · Economic development · Agriculture
Food security · Inflation dynamics · Taxes · Government expenditure
Multidimensional poverty · Human capital · Ethiopia

1.1 Background and Motivation

Sustained and inclusive economic growth has gained much attention in recent years (Acemoglu 2009; Barro 1997; Barro and Sala-i-Martin 2004; Griffin 1987; Heshmati et al. 2015; Kim and Heshmati 2014; Tausch and Heshmati 2012; and others). Several studies also focus on growth and development in Africa

A. Heshmati (✉) · H. Yoon
Department of Economics, Sogang University, Seoul, Korea
e-mail: almas.heshmati@gmail.com

H. Yoon
e-mail: hyyoon100@naver.com

A. Heshmati
Jönköping International Business School, Jönköping University,
Jönköping, Sweden

1

(AfDB 2016, 2017; Belshaw and Livingstone 2002; Binns et al. 2012; Chitonge 2014; Johnson 2016; Ndudu et al. 2008; Robson and Lury 2011; Tesfaye 2017). Their focus is on diverse aspects of growth such as its political economy, characterizing the African economies, state of economic development, structural transformation, entrepreneurship and industrialization, determinants of growth, renewal of development, sustainable development, economic diversification and new perspectives on theory and policy. Research on the economic growth of the Ethiopian economy is also growing. For example, Balema (2014) focuses on democracy and economic development in Ethiopia.

For several decades the Swedish International Development Cooperation Agency (SIDA) has financed collaborative higher educational programs and research capacity building in a number of African countries. This development aid has resulted in the publication of a number of academic books which deal with poverty and well-being in Africa (Heshmati 2016a), entrepreneurship and SME management across Africa (Achtenhagen and Brundin 2016), economic integration, currency union and sustainable and inclusive growth in East Africa (Heshmati 2016b), economic growth and development (Heshmati 2017a), economic transformation and poverty reduction (Heshmati 2017b), management challenges in different types of African firms (Achtenhagen and Brundin 2017), contextualizing entrepreneurship in emerging economies and developing countries (Ramirez-Pacillias et al. 2017). Together, these works have improved our understanding of the process of economic development and growth and the challenges facing African countries.

This volume is a collection of empirical studies on the determinants of economic growth and development in Ethiopia. Eleven researchers have contributed their research to this volume. The papers were partially selected from a large set of papers presented at an annual international conference on *Recent Trends in Economic Development, Finance and Management Research in Eastern Africa*, Kigali, Rwanda, 14–16 June 2017; the rest were obtained from researchers by invitation. The studies are grouped into four domains covering: agriculture, food security and inflation; taxes, government expenditure and economic growth; multidimensional poverty; and human capital and firm growth in Ethiopia.

This edited volume provides an up-to-date picture of the state and pattern of growth and development in Ethiopia, a country which has been the focus of attention for researchers, NGOs and social planners because of droughts, war, famines, development changes and the effects of the global economic crisis on the country. A main contribution of this volume is that it helps identify some important determinants of growth and development in Ethiopia and provides an estimation of their effects using a combination of up-to-date primary and secondary datasets, modelling and estimation methods. Since the studies are inter-related and complementary they provide a comprehensive picture of the state of growth and development and measurement issues and causal relationships; they also provide an evaluation of the policies and practices needed for achieving developmental progress in Ethiopia. The development and growth issues covered in this volume represent major challenges for the government and development organizations who are aiming at achieving higher growth and alleviating poverty in Ethiopia. The studies cover aspects of the gradual process of transition from an economy characterized by the dominance of a rural agricultural society to an urban industry and the development of services.

1.2 A Summary of the Studies on Economic Growth and Development in Ethiopia

This volume is a collection of empirical studies on the determinants of economic growth and development in Ethiopia. It contains one introduction and 10 contributory chapters grouped into four domains: agriculture, food security and inflation dynamics; taxes, government expenditure and economic growth; multidimensional poverty; and human capital and firm growth in Ethiopia. This introductory chapter briefly describes the individual studies. The studies jointly provide an up-to-date picture of the state and pattern of growth and development in Ethiopia in recent decades.

Part A. Agriculture, food security and inflation dynamics
This part of the edited volume has 3 chapters estimating the impact of adopting improved agricultural technologies on rural poverty, the determinants of food security and the dynamics of inflation in Ethiopia.

As the title indicates the first study (Chap. 2) by Tsegaye Mulugeta, *Impacts of improved agricultural technology adoption on rural poverty*, evaluates the impact of adopting improved agricultural technologies on rural household welfare. Welfare is measured by consumption expenditure and poverty indices in two regions covering 51 villages in rural Ethiopia. The study which is based on World Bank data, applies two potential program evaluation techniques propensity score matching and endogenous switching regression in concurrence. The analysis shows that adoption of improved agricultural technologies had a robust and positive impact on per capita consumption expenditure and a negative impact on the poverty status of households. This result suggests that there is a need for continued and broad public and private investments in agricultural research to address different development challenges facing Ethiopia. It also suggests that there is a need for policy support aimed at improving efforts at providing agricultural extension services and access to seeds and outlets that encourage adoption of improved agricultural technologies.

The second study (Chap. 3) by Tsegaye Mulugeta, *Determinants of food security in Oromiya region of Ethiopia*, investigates the relative importance of household food security's supply- and demand-side factors through a logistic regression analysis. The model is applied to data collected through a stratified survey of 240 sampled households. The study uses consumption expenditure per adult equivalent income to measure household food security levels. It finds that 54% of the rural households in the sample were food secure while the remaining 46% were food insecure. The empirical results show that out of the five supply-side factors expected to impact the status of household food security, four had a significant relationship with household food security while from the eight demand-side factors five were associated with food security levels. Based on the estimated partial effects on the probability of food security, the study finds that supply-side factors were more influential as compared to demand-side factors in determining household food security. This implies that public food security related interventions focused on supply-side factors need to get policymakers and practitioners' priority attention.

The third study (Chap. 4) by Jonse Bane, *Dynamics and determinants of inflation in Ethiopia*, investigates the dynamics and determinants of inflation in Ethiopia over the period 1975–2015 using annual data from various national sources. The study uses the autoregressive distributed lag (ARDL) inflation model by synthesizing monetarist and structuralist views of the determinants of inflation. The findings show that the major determinants of dynamics of inflation in Ethiopia are both monetary sector and structural factors. The monetary determinants of inflation are money supply and the real interest rate. Inflation both in the short and long run is not only a monetary phenomenon (such as money expansion, government spending and the real interest rate) but also the result of structural factors like shocks to the real sector (consisting mainly of agricultural GDP). The policy implications of the result are that to control the inflation rate, the Government of Ethiopia needs to follow conservative or contractionary fiscal and monetary policies. It is also important to enhance economic growth that reduces inflationary pressures on the economy.

Part B. Taxes, government expenditure and economic growth

Part B contains 3 chapters which analyze the effects of taxes and government expenditure on economic growth; the impact of government sectoral expenditure on economic growth; and the tax compliance attitude of rural farmers in Ethiopia.

The first study in this part (Chap. 5) by Selamawit Gebreegziabher, *Effects of tax and government expenditure on economic growth in Ethiopia*, examines the effects of fiscal policy, government expenditure and taxation on economic growth in Ethiopia. The empirical part uses time series data covering the period 1975–2014. A major finding of this study is that tax revenue and productive government expenditure did not have a significant effect on economic growth in the long run. This may be attributed to weak public institutional quality but the study finds that better human capital formation and good performance in the collection of non-tax revenues had a significant and positive effect on economic growth in the long run. In addition, it finds that unproductive government consumption was a significant factor that negatively affected growth in the long run. The study also finds that in the short run the effects of government public investments, human capital investments and government consumption expenditure on economic growth were positive.

The second study (Chap. 6) by Tufa Garoma and Mekonnen Bersisa, *Impact of government sectoral expenditure on economic growth in Ethiopia*, examines government expenditure which is one of the important tools that contributes to economic growth. Government expenditure continues to be the main source of investment expenditure and its trends show great increment with rising annual budget allocations. In an analysis of economic growth in Ethiopia covering the period 1975–2015 this study focuses on the effects of sectoral expenditure on economic, social and services sectors. The study uses both methods of descriptive and econometrics data analyses and conducts tests for stationarity and cointegration to analyze the long and short run dynamics of the models. Its empirical results suggest that general service expenditure had a negative and significant effect on economic growth in Ethiopia.

The third study (Chap. 7) by Hassen Azime and Gollagari Ramakrishna, *Tax compliance attitude of the rural farmers*, applies logit regression models to identify the factors that determine the tax compliance attitude of individual smallholder farmers in Ethiopia. Using the 2014 Afrobarometer survey this study finds both similarities and differences in factors that are correlated with smallholder farmers' tax compliance attitudes. It argues that outcomes of tax compliance are a function of farmers' characteristics and related variables. It also confirms that people who are happier with open administrative arrangements probably have a tax compliant attitude. However, those farmers who perceive that their ethnic groups are being treated unfairly are less likely to have a positive tax compliant attitude. Smallholder farmers' tax knowledge is also significantly correlated with their tax compliant attitude. The study identifies taxpayers' satisfaction with local government officials as an important promoter and tax compliance factor.

Part C. Multidimensional poverty
Part C has one chapter that analyzes multidimensional poverty and its dynamics in Ethiopia. This study (Chap. 8) by Getu Tigre, *Multidimensional poverty and its dynamics in Ethiopia*, studies poverty which is pervasive and deeply rooted in Ethiopia. The study is in line with recent research trends that are shifting from unidimensional to multidimensional poverty analyses. It conducts a multidimensional poverty analysis using four rounds of the Ethiopian demographic and health survey data. It concludes that poverty is generally high in Ethiopia but that it is specifically higher in rural areas. Poverty has decreased moderately over time but still a large proportion of the population lives below the multidimensional poverty line. Among the poverty dimensions, living standard contributes the most to poverty followed by education with the least contribution being of the health dimension. The study estimates and analyzes the different indicators and their contributions to each poverty dimension.

Part D. Human capital and firm growth
This part includes 3 studies on returns to education and an analysis of education's effects on the growth of firms, a firm's ageing and experience related to its performance and high growth firms in Ethiopia. These indicators are considered important determinants of sound economic development and growth.

The first study (Chap. 9) by Yonatan Desalegn, *Returns to education in Ethiopia*, measures marginal private returns to education using the data from the latest national labor force survey. It measures the average marginal returns to education by examining the presence of the non-linearity effect in the returns to different levels of education. It also explores determinants of education other than schooling and experience by using a sample selection model when adopting an earnings function. The results suggest that the average marginal returns to a year of schooling was 14.43% and that the effect of a year of experience is only 0.5%. Schooling increased marginal returns whereas experience decreased marginal returns. The non-linear effect of the returns at different levels of education imply that the government should focus on basic primary education and create increased access to higher education to promote economic growth and development.

The second study in this part (Chap. 10) by Guta Legesse, *Analysis of Firm Growth in Ethiopia: An Exploration of the High-growth Firms* discusses the incidence of high growth firms in Ethiopia by studying business obstacles and the determinants of growth. The study is based on data from the World Bank's Enterprise Survey dataset of 2015. The survey covered firms distributed over six major regions in Ethiopia. The study does an analysis using ordinary least squares (OLS) and quantile regression methods. Its results show that high growth firms were concentrated in small and medium enterprises (SMEs) in capital Addis Ababa. Lack of access to finance was the biggest perceived obstacle to high growth firms, while high tax rates were the next obstacle for non-high growth firms in the informal sector. Access to finance across the regions differed and firm growth was negatively related to firm size and export engagement while it was positively associated with a firm's product and process innovations, resources and ownership. The heterogeneity in business obstacles across regions and firms' growth performance can be taken as important lessons for public policy interventions to achieve desired outcomes.

The last study (Chap. 11) by Guta Legesse, *An Analysis of effects of ageing and experience on firms' performance*, identifies the effects of a firm's age on its performance measured by labor productivity and the total value of sales. It uses survey based panel data of large and medium scale manufacturing firms in Ethiopia during 2010–15. It finds no evidence of a significant relationship between a firm's age and its performance. The average marginal effect of age is negative but insignificant for both labor productivity and sales measures of performance. The study shows that the effect of a firm's size on its performance depends on the choice of the dependent variable. Firm size is predominantly associated with lower labor productivity but higher sales value. Capital intensity and wage expenditure have a positive and significant effect on a firm's performance. Lack of a firm's age has an effect on its performance and shows that the effect of 'learning by doing' is weak. A focus on this issue could be one of the many possible policy options for reducing the high exit rates of low performing firms.

1.3 Final Words and Policy Recommendations

This volume is a valuable contribution to the growing but limited literature on economic growth and development in Ethiopia. The primary readership market for this volume includes undergraduate and graduate students, lecturers, researchers, public and private institutions, non-governmental organizations (NGOs), international aid agencies and national development planning decision makers. This volume can also serve as supplement reading to texts on economic growth, development, investment, welfare and poverty in Ethiopia and other sub-Saharan African (SSA) countries. The organizers of the annual conference on economic development in East Africa will market the book at its annual conferences.

There are several books on development and growth in Ethiopia published in earlier years and written by or in cooperation with non-locals. The novelty of this volume is that it is an up-to-date study about the Ethiopian economy and has been written by Ethiopian researchers with deep knowledge about the economy. The authors use diverse up-to-date data and methods to provide robust empirical results based on representative firms, household surveys and secondary national level datasets. It contains a wealth of empirical evidence, deep analyses and recommendations for policymakers and researchers for designing and implementing effective social and economic policies and strategies to cope with poverty and its negative effects on the poor. The volume is a useful resource for policymakers and researchers promoting economic growth and fighting poverty in Ethiopia. It will also appeal to a broader audience interested in economic development, growth and policies, especially in sub-Saharan Africa.

Based on the studies presented as part of this edited volume and information and insights from literature, the Editors recommend policy measures to promote growth and development in Ethiopia. These include:

In the case of the agricultural sector, estimating the impact of adopting improved agricultural technology on rural poverty and the determinants of food security in Ethiopia show that there is a need for continued and broad public and private investments in agricultural research to address different development challenges facing food security and the rural economy in Ethiopia. There is also a need for policy support aimed at improving agricultural extension services and access to seeds, fertilizers, machineries and irrigation that encourage adoption of improved agricultural technologies. Public food security related interventions focused on demand and supply related factors need to be policymakers and practitioners' focus in determining household food security. To control the inflation rate, the Government of Ethiopia needs to follow mixed conservative fiscal and monetary policies for reducing inflationary pressures while promoting economic growth.

An analysis of the effects of taxes and government expenditure on economic growth, the impact of government sectoral expenditure on economic growth and the tax compliance attitude of rural farmers in Ethiopia shows the importance of short run positive effects of government public investments, human capital investments and consumption and service expenditure on economic growth. Using the taxpayers' satisfaction with local government officials as an important promoter and tax compliance are also growth promotors.

Based on studies of returns to education and an analysis of education's effects on firm growth, this volume considers a firm's ageing and experience in relation to its performance and incidence of high growth firms as important determinants of sound economic development and growth. The non-linear effect of the returns at different levels of education implies that the government should focus on basic primary education and try and create increased access to higher education for promoting sustained economic growth and development. Lack of the effect of a firm's age on its performance shows that the 'learning by doing' effect is relatively weak in Ethiopia. Hence, focusing on this issue could be one of the many possible policy options for reducing low performing firms' high exit rates.

Among the growth and development obstacles across the region are regional heterogeneity in the level of development and inclusiveness in public policy, participation in decision making and resource allocations. Heterogeneity in firms' growth and performance can be taken as important lessons for public policy interventions to achieve desired equality and growth outcomes. The quality of governance, participation in the process and effectiveness of its institutions and investments in education, health and productive infrastructure combined with continued inflows of development assistance, foreign direct investments and public policies towards interest rates, savings, capital accumulation and technology are crucial determinants of sustained and inclusive economic growth in Ethiopia.

The Editors are grateful to the dedicated authors, reviewers and conference participants who helped in assessing the submitted papers. Many were presenters at the 2017 conference at the University of Rwanda. Special thanks go to Bideri Ishuheri Nyamulinda, Rama Rao and Lars Hartvigson for their efforts in organizing the conference. The Editors would also like to thank William Achauer at Springer Nature for guidance and assessing this manuscript for publication by Springer. Generous financial support by the Swedish International Development Cooperation Agency (SIDA) for the collaborative Ph.D. program between Addis Ababa University and Jönköping University and for organizing the conference is gratefully acknowledged.

References

Acemoglu, D. 2009. *Introduction to modern economic growth*. New Jersey: Princeton University Press.

Achtenhagen, L., and E. Brundin (eds.). 2016. *Entrepreneurship and SME management across Africa: Context, challenges, cases*. Singapore: Springer.

Achtenhagen, L., and E. Brundin (eds.). 2017. *Management challenges in different types of African firms: Processes, practices and performance*. Singapore: Springer.

AfDB. 2016. *Africa economic outlook 2016: Sustainable cities and structural transformation*. Abidjan: African Development Bank Group.

AfDB. 2017. *Africa economic outlook 2017: Entrepreneurship and industrialization*. Abidjan: African Development Bank Group.

Balema, A.A. 2014. *Democracy and economic development in Ethiopia*. Trenton: The Red Sea Press.

Barro, R.J. 1997. *Determinants of growth: A cross country empirical study*. Cambridge MA: MIT Press.

Barro, R.J., and X. Sala-i-Martin. 2004. *Economic growth*, 2nd ed. Cambridge MA: MIT Press.

Belshaw, D., and I. Livingstone. 2002. *Renewing development in sub-saharan Africa: Policy, performance, and prospects*. London: Routledge.

Binns, T., A. Dixon, and E. Nel. 2012. *Africa: Diversity and development*. London: Routledge.

Chitonge, H. 2014. *Economic growth and development in Africa: Understanding trends and prospects*. London: Routledge.

Griffin, K. (ed.). 1987. *World hunger and the world economy*. Singapore: Springer.

Heshmati, A. (ed.). 2016a. *Poverty and well-being in east Africa: A multi-faceted economic approach*. Singapore: Springer.

Heshmati, A. (ed.). 2016b. *Economic integration, currency union, and sustainable and inclusive growth in east Africa*. Singapore: Springer.

Heshmati, A. (ed.). 2017a. *Studies on economic development and growth in selected African countries*. Singapore: Springer.

Heshmati, A. (ed.). 2017b. *Economic transformation for poverty reduction in Africa: A multidimensional approach*. London: Routledge.

Heshmati, A., E. Maasoumi, and G. Wan (eds.). 2015. *Poverty reduction policies and practices in developing Asia*. Singapore: Springer.

Johnson, O.E.G. 2016. *Economic diversification and growth in Africa: Critical policy making issues*. London: Palgrave Macmillan.

Kim, T.Y., and A. Heshmati. 2014. *Economic growth: The new perspectives for theory and policy*. Singapore: Springer.

Ndudu, B.J., S.A. O'Connell, R.H. Bates, P. Collier, and C.C. Soludo (eds.). 2008. *Political economy of growth in Africa, 1960–2000*. Cambridge: Cambridge University Press.

Ramirez-Pacillias, M., E. Brundin, and M. Markowska. 2017. *Contextualizing entrepreneurship in emerging economies and developing countries*. London: Edward Elgar.

Robson, P., and D.A. Lury. 2011. *The economies of Africa*. London: Routledge.

Tausch, A., and A. Heshmati. 2012. *Globalization, the human condition and sustainable development in the 21st century: Cross-national perspectives and European implications*. London: Anthem Press.

Tesfaye, A. 2017. *State and economic development in Africa: The case of Ethiopia*. Singapore: Springer.

Part I
Agriculture and Food Security

Chapter 2
Adoption and Impact of Improved Agricultural Technologies on Rural Poverty

Tsegaye Mulugeta Habtewold

Abstract This paper evaluates the impact of adopting improved agricultural technologies (high yielding varieties, HYVs) on rural household welfare measured by consumption expenditure and poverty indices in two regions of rural Ethiopia (Amhara and Tigray) and 51 rural villages based on data drawn from the World Bank (2010). It applies two potential program evaluation techniques (propensity score matching, PSM, and endogenous switching regression, ESR). The analysis reveals that adoption of improved agricultural technologies has a robust, significant and positive impact on per capita consumption expenditure and a negative impact on the poverty status of households. The overall average gain in per capita consumption expenditure ranges from Birr 582.67 to Birr 606.69 annually. The estimated impact on poverty reduction as measured by the headcount index ranges from 6.7 to 8.3% points. The findings also indicate that this reduces the depth and severity of poverty. The estimated effect on reducing the depth of poverty is in the range of 0.5–0.6% points and it decreases inequality (severity) of poverty by about 0.1% points. This suggests the need for continued and broad public and private investments in agriculture research to address vital development challenges and the need for policy support for improving extension efforts and access to seeds and market outlets that encourage adoption of improved agricultural technologies.

Keywords Rural poverty · Technology adoption · PSM · ESR
Ethiopia

2.1 Introduction

Agricultural production can be increased through extensification (that is, through expansion of farmland) or intensification (that is, by using more inputs and technologies per unit of land). Extensification is not a viable strategy for increasing

T. M. Habtewold (✉)
Department of Economics, Addis Ababa University, Addis Ababa, Ethiopia
e-mail: abtse2002@gmail.com

© Springer Nature Singapore Pte Ltd. 2018
A. Heshmati and H. Yoon (eds.), *Economic Growth and Development in Ethiopia*, Perspectives on Development in the Middle East and North Africa (MENA) Region, https://doi.org/10.1007/978-981-10-8126-2_2

agricultural production in most of the food insecure countries where high population pressure is a critical bottleneck. Where land is scarce, intensification which entails investments in modern inputs and technologies, is a better option for increasing agricultural production and reducing food insecurities. This option was effectively implemented by several Asian countries in the 1970s and was dubbed the 'green revolution.'

Agricultural growth is essential for fostering economic development and feeding growing populations in most of the less-developed countries (Datt and Ravallion 1996). Yet, since area expansion and irrigation have already become a minimal source of output growth on a world scale, agricultural growth depends more on yield-increasing technological changes (Hossain 1989).

New agricultural technologies and improved practices play a key role in increasing agricultural production (and hence improving national food security) in developing countries. Where successful, adoption of improved agricultural technologies can stimulate overall economic growth through inter-sectoral linkages while conserving natural resources (Faltermeier and Abdulai 2006; Sanchez et al. 2009). Given the close link between food insecurity, poverty, farming and environmental degradation the impact of cultivation practices has received significant attention in the last few decades. New cultivation techniques have been introduced in many countries to enhance productivity in the agriculture sector.

In much of sub-Saharan Africa (SSA), the agricultural sector is a key fundamental for spurring growth, overcoming poverty and enhancing food security. However, agriculture is often characterized by low use of modern technology and low productivity (Solomon et al. 2012). Improving the productivity, profitability and sustainability of smallholder farming is therefore the main pathway out of poverty for this region (The World Bank 2008).

Similarly, in a region where agriculture is the predominant sector that underpins the livelihoods of a majority of the poor, increasing adoption of technologies such as new agricultural practices, high-yielding varieties and associated products such as crop insurance have the potential to contribute to economic growth and poverty reduction among the poor (Kelsey 2011). According to Ravallion et al. (2007) 'many of the poor in SSA and South Asia are living in rural areas and they are farmers. Nearly 75% of those living in less than one dollar a day will remain rural until 2040.' Similarly Mendola (2007) states that, 'of the poor people worldwide (those who consume less than a "standard" dollar-a-day), 75% work and live in rural areas. Projections suggest that over 60% will continue to do so in 2025.' Thus, there is a direct link between poverty reduction and increasing agriculture productivity. This can also create employment opportunities for landless wage laborers. As most of the world's poor work in agricultural occupations and agriculture is an important industry in most poor countries, our study focuses on the role that new and improved agricultural technologies can play in addressing the issues of impact evaluation that most other research puts less weight on (for example, issues like endogeneity which our study considers).

Our study's objective is to assess the role of adopting improved agricultural technologies on consumption expenditure and poverty status measured by the headcount index, the poverty gap index and the poverty severity index. The empirical question that we address is: Do improved agricultural technologies (hereafter, HYVs) have the potential to reduce poverty? If yes, under which circumstances?

2.2 Literature Review

An innovation within a social system takes place when it is adopted by individuals or groups. Feder et al. (1985) define adoption as the integration of an innovation into farmers' normal farming activities over an extended period of time. They also note that adoption is not permanent behavior. This implies that an individual may decide to discontinue the use of an innovation for a variety of personal, institutional or social reasons one of which might be the availability of another practice that is better in satisfying his or her needs. Adoption is a mental process through which an individual moves from hearing about an innovation to adopting it. This follows awareness, interest, evaluation, trial and adoption stages (Bahadur and Siegfried 2004). Adoption can be considered a variable representing behavioral changes that farmers undergo in accepting new ideas and innovations in agriculture anticipating some positive impacts of these ideas and innovations.

A large body of empirical literature has documented that adopting agricultural technologies reduces poverty, increases household incomes, raises productivity, tends to open more access to market participation, reduces food insecurity and increases overall social welfare.

Hundie and Admassie (2016) state that technologies are important sources of productivity growth in agriculture leading to better incomes and lower poverty. This was observed in particular in Asia and parts of South and Central America during the green revolution in the 1960s and 1970s.

Setotaw et al. (2003) found that adoption of improved agricultural technologies (improved varieties and agronomic practices) positively and significantly affected households' food security in Ethiopia. Solomon et al. (2010) examined the impacts of adopting chickpea varieties on the level of commercialization of smallholder farmers in Ethiopia. They found that adoption of improved chickpea varieties had a positive and robust effect on the marketed surplus which reduced food insecurity in adopter households. A study by Adekambi et al. (2009) on the impact of agricultural technology adoption on poverty in Benin, indicates an increase in rice farmers' productivity after they adopted NERICA varieties. These results suggest that promotion of NERICA cultivation can help in improving farmers' expenditure/income and consequently lead to poverty reduction. Similarly, Kassie et al. (2010) found that improved groundnut technologies had a significant positive impact on crop incomes and poverty reduction in Uganda. Using a propensity score matching method, Tsegaye and Bekele (2012) examined the impact of adopting improved wheat technologies on households' food security levels. Their results show that this adoption had a robust and positive effect on farmers' food consumption per adult equivalent per day. Based on three estimation algorithms, the average treatment effect on the treated (ATT) ranged from 377.37 calories per day to 603.16 calories per day which indicates that efforts to disseminate existing wheat technologies will contribute to food security among farm households.

Mendola (2007) studied the impact of agricultural technology adoption on poverty reduction in rural Bangladesh and found a robust and positive effect on farm households' wellbeing. Using the nearest-neighbor matching method he evaluated the causal effects of technology adoption on household wellbeing and his results show a significant and positive impact. The results show that on average the incomes of adopters were almost 30% higher than the incomes of non-adopters, which is the average difference between incomes of similar pairs of households belonging to different technological status.[1] The results of technology adoption were statistically significant in reducing the probability of being poor for small and medium farmers by more than 20% points and this was interpreted as evidence that achieving production enhancements in small and medium farms based on three estimation algorithms, through better targeting of technological programs, for example, may have an important causal impact in terms of household wellbeing.

Wu et al. (2010) conducted an impact study in rural China and found that adoption of agricultural technologies had a positive impact on farmers' wellbeing thereby improving household incomes.

Simtowe et al. (2012) evaluated the welfare effects of adopting agricultural technologies of improved groundnut varieties in rural Malawi and their results show robust, positive and significant impacts of this adoption on per capita consumption expenditure and on poverty reduction. Tesfaye et al. (2016) examined the impact of improved wheat technology adoption on productivity and income in Ethiopia and their results show that on average this adoption increased wheat productivity of adopters than of non-adopters. Similarly, their results of propensity score matching estimates showed that the average incomes of adopters was 35–50% more than that of non-adopters.

Shiferaw et al. (2014), study on adoption of improved wheat varieties and impacts on household food security in Ethiopia shows that adoption increased average per capita consumption expenditure in the range of Birr 209–260.[2] It also increased the probability of food security in the range of 2.5–8.6% and significantly reduced the probability of chronic food insecurity from 1.3 to 3.0% and transitory food insecurity in the range of 1.3–5.9%.

In a micro-level analysis, Mendola (2003) evaluated the causal effects of agri-cultural technology and poverty reduction and his findings show a robust and positive effect of adopting agricultural technology on farm households' wellbeing suggesting that there is scope for enhancing the role of agricultural technology indirectly contributing to poverty alleviation. Sahu and Das (2015) studied the impact of agricultural related technology adoption on poverty in rural India and

---

[1]The outcome variable here is log of households' income.

[2]Birr is the official currency of Ethiopia.

found robust, positive and significant impacts of adopting agriculture related technologies on per capita consumption expenditure and on poverty reduction in sample households. Becerril and Abdulai (2010) also used PSM to analyze the impact of adopting improved maize varieties on household incomes and poverty reduction using cross-sectional data for 325 farmers in Mexico. Their findings show a robust, positive and significant impact of improved maize variety adoption on farm household welfare measured by per capita expenditure and poverty reduction. The adoption of improved maize varieties helped in raising household per capita expenditure by an average of 136–173 Mexican pesos thereby reducing their probability of falling below the poverty line by roughly 19–31%. Given these conditions and variations in the methodologies used we add some more scope in impact evaluation by using both propensity score matching and endogenous switching regression methods.

2.3 Empirical Impact Evaluation Challenges and Estimation Strategies

As Gertler et al. (2011) state the basic impact evaluation question essentially constitutes a causal inference problem. Assessing the impact of a program on a series of outcomes is equivalent to assessing the causal effect of the program on those outcomes. Most policy questions involve cause-and-effect relationships.

Another way of explaining this is that one of according to Simtowe et al. (2012) the standard problems in impact evaluation involves the inference of causal relationships between the treatment and the outcome. There are two problems specifically related to evaluating the impact of an intervention on targeted individuals: (1) selection bias and (2) missing data in case of the counterfactual (Sahu and Das 2015).

There are many important theoretical reasons (and huge empirical literature supporting the theories) why agricultural technologies might improve farm households' wellbeing, but how can we be sure that the better wellbeing of adopters compared to non-adopters is because of technology adoption (or not)? In other words, the differences between the treated and control groups could be because of pre-treatment differences.

Ideally, experimental data will provide us with the information on the counterfactual[3] situation that will solve the problem of causal inference. According to Becker (2009) the fundamental problem of impact evaluation is causal inference and he shows that it is impossible to observe for the same unit i the values $D_i = 1$ and $D_i = 0$ as well as the values $Y_i (1)$ and $Y_i (0)$ and, therefore, it is impossible to observe the effect of D on Y for unit i.[4] Another way of expressing this problem is by saying that we cannot infer the effect of a treatment because we do not have the

---

[3]What would have happened to participating units if they had not participated?

[4]D is the treatment variable and Y for the outcome variable.

counterfactual evidence, that is, what would have happened in the absence of the treatment.

Experimental data should provide information on the counterfactual situation that will solve the problem of causal inference. As this is not the case (in the presence of a problem of 'missing data') the direct 'welfare effects' of technology are estimated from the variations in welfare across households. However, to do this some statistical pitfalls of cross-sectional inferences need to be avoided while seeking to isolate the technology effect from other socioeconomic determinants of household income.

As Doagostino (1998) argues, in a randomized experiment the randomization of units (that is, subjects) to different treatments guarantees that on average there will be no systematic differences in observed or unobserved covariates (that is, bias) between units assigned to the different treatments. However, in a non-randomized observational study, investigators have no control over the treatment assignment and therefore direct comparisons of outcomes from the treatment groups may be misleading. This difficulty may be partially avoided if information on measured covariates is incorporated into the study design (for example, through matched sampling) or into the estimation of the treatment effect (for example, through stratification or covariance adjustment). Traditional methods of adjustment (matching, stratification and covariance adjustment) are often limited since they can only use a limited number of covariates for adjustment.

Solomon and Bekele (2010) argue that analyzing the welfare implications of agricultural technology poses at least two challenges: unobserved heterogeneity and possible endogeneity. There seems to be a two-way link between technology adoption and household wellbeing. Technology adoption may result in productivity enhancements for small producers and also in greater incomes but it may also be that greater incomes lead to more technology adoption. Thus, the differences in welfare outcome variables between those farm households that did and those that did not adopt improved technology could be due to unobserved heterogeneity. Not distinguishing between the casual effects of technology adoption and the effects of unobserved heterogeneity could lead to misleading policy implications.

Solomon et al. (2012) state that households are not randomly distributed into two groups (adopters and non-adopters), but rather they make their own adoption choices, or are systematically selected by development agencies and/or by project administrators based on their propensity to participate in technology adoption. Therefore, adopters and non-adopters may be systematically different. Thus, possible self-selection due to observed and unobserved plots and household characteristics makes it difficult to perform ex-post assessment of gains from technology adoption using observational data. Failure to account for this potential selection bias could lead to inconsistent estimates of the impact of technology adoption.

According to Hausman (1978), the simplest approach for examining the impact of adoption of improved technologies on welfare outcomes is to include a dummy variable equal to one if a farm-household adopted new technology in the welfare equation and then apply ordinary least squares. However, this approach might lead to biased estimates because it assumes that adoption of improved technologies is exogenously determined while it is potentially endogenous. The decision to adopt or not is voluntary and may be based on individual self-selection. Farmers who adopt new technologies may have systematically different characteristics from farmers who do not adopt and they may have decided to adopt based on expected benefits. Unobservable characteristics of farmers and their farms may affect both adoption decisions and welfare outcomes resulting in inconsistent estimates of the effect of adoption of agricultural technologies on household welfare. For instance, if only the most skilled or motivated farmers choose to adopt and we fail to control for skills, then we will have an upward bias. The solution to this is to explicitly account for such endogeneity using simultaneous equation models.

There is extensive literature that describes developments in addressing this problem. Broadly, empirical literature categorizes evaluation methods under five categories: (1) pure randomized experiments; (2) natural experiments; (3) the matching method/and endogenous switching regression method; (4) the selection or instrumental variable model which relies on the exclusion restriction; and (5) the structural simulation model.[5] The choice of method is largely driven by the assumptions made and the availability of data. Empirical studies have used different econometric techniques to correct for selection bias and missing data problems. The commonly used analytical approaches in literature include the sample selection model (Alene et al. 2008; Balagtas et al. 2007; Winter-Nelson and Temu 2005), the propensity score matching method (Esquivel and Huerta-Pineda 2006; Mendola 2003, 2007; Simtowe et al. 2012; Solomon et al. 2010; Tsegaye and Bekele 2012; Wu et al. 2010) and the switching regression model (Bwalya et al. 2013). Solomon and Bekele (2010), Solomon et al. (2012) and Vance and Geoghegan (2004) have used both the propensity score matching method (PSM) and the endogenous switching regression (ESR) model.

The endogeneity of the adoption decision, that is, for the heterogeneity in the decision to adopt or not to adopt new agricultural technologies and for unobservable characteristics of farmers and their farms is accounted by estimating a simultaneous equations model with endogenous switching by using the full information maximum likelihood estimation (FIML). The non-parametric regression method, the propensity score matching (PSM), is also employed to assess the robustness of the results.

Matching is one of the widely-used non-parametric estimation techniques of impact evaluation. It is based on the intuitively attractive idea of contrasting the outcomes of program participants (denoted by Y_1) with the outcomes of 'comparable' non-participants (denoted by Y_0). Differences in the outcomes between the two groups are attributed to the program (Heckman et al. 1998).

Propensity score matching is a two-step procedure. First, a probability model for adoption of HYVs is estimated to calculate the probability (or propensity scores) of adoption for each observation. In the second step, each adopter is matched to a non-adopter with similar propensity score values to estimate the average ATT.

---

[5]For a detailed description of the methods see Blundell and Dias (2000).

Several matching methods have been developed to match adopters with non-adopters of similar propensity scores. Asymptotically, all matching methods should yield the same results, even though in practice there are trade-offs in terms of bias and efficiency with each method.[6]

2.4 Data Description

Our analysis is based on household level data collected by the Farmer Innovation Fund (FIF) impact evaluation survey conducted in Ethiopia by the World Bank in 2010–13. The survey covered 2675 households drawn from two regions (Amhara and Tigray) and 51 rural villages. The survey is a rich dataset which contains information on several factors determining technology adoption including household specific characteristic, asset holding (farm and non-farm assets), institutional factors, indicators of infrastructure facilities, the rural social network system, membership of households in several rural associations and households' participation in the output market. The dataset contains information on the adoption status of households and food and non-food consumption expenditure levels of each group (adopters and non-adopters). The food consumption expenditure includes food grains, livestock products (such as meat and milk), vegetables and other food items (such as sugar and salt) and beverages (such as coffee and tea leaves) while non-food expenditure includes clothing and energy (such as shoes and kerosene), education and medical expenditure and expenditure on both durable and non-durable services.

The three rounds of the survey collected baseline data in 2010, mid-line survey in 2012 and the end-line survey in 2013. A total of 2675 households were originally interviewed but information on agricultural technology adoption, consumption expenditure and production was completed only for 1900 households during the baseline. Our study relies on this data. Relevant data is not available in mid-line and end-line surveys.

2.5 Analytical Framework

2.5.1 Propensity Score Matching Procedures

PSM does not require an exclusion restriction or a particular specification of the selection equation to construct the counterfactual and reduce selection problems. The main purpose of using matching is to find a group of treated individuals

---

[6]See Caliendo and Kopeinig (2008) for some practical guidance in the implementation of propensity score matching.

(adopters) which is similar to the control group (non-adopters) in all relevant pre-treatment characteristics, where the only difference is that one group adopted improved agricultural technologies and the other group did not.

Let Di denotes a dummy variable such that $Di = 1$ if the ith individual adopts improved agricultural technologies and $Di = 0$ otherwise. Similarly, let Y_{1i} and Y_{2i} denote potential observed welfare outcomes for adopter and non-adopter units respectively. The observed welfare is $Yi = Di\,Y_{1i} + (1 - Di)\,Y_{2i}$ rather than Y_{1i} and Y_{2i} for the same individual and we are unable to compute the treatment effect for every unit.

Rosenbaum and Rubin (1983) show that if the exposure to treatment is random within cells defined by X, it is also random within cells defined by the values of the mono-dimensional variable p(X). As a result, given a population of units denoted by i, if the propensity score $P(X_i)$ is known, ATT can be estimated as:

$$
\begin{aligned}
\text{ATT} &= E\{Y_{1i} - Y_{2i} | D_i = 1\} \\
&= E\{E\{Y_{1i} - Y_{2i} | D_i = 1, P(X_i)\}\} \\
&= E\{E\{Y_{1i} | D_i = 1, P(X_i)\} - E\{Y_{2i} | D_i = 0, P(X_i)\} | D_i = 1\}
\end{aligned}
\tag{2.1}
$$

The propensity score is defined as the conditional probability of receiving a treatment given pre-treatment characteristics:

$$
P(X) \equiv \Pr\{D_i = 1 | X\} = E\{D_i | X\}
\tag{2.2}
$$

where, $Di = \{0, 1\}$ is the indicator of exposure to treatment and X is the multidimensional vector of pre-treatment characteristics. The average treatment effect (ATE) is defined as the expectation of the treatment effect across all farmers:

$$
\text{ATE} = E(Y_1 - Y_2)
\tag{2.3}
$$

Finally, the average treatment effect on the untreated (ATU) measures the impact that the program will have had on those who did not participate:

$$
\text{ATU} = E(Y_1 - Y_2 | D = 0)
\tag{2.4}
$$

Formally, two hypotheses/basic assumptions need to be satisfied when using the PSM method (Becker and Ichino 2002):

(a) Conditional Independence or the Unconfoundedness Assumption (CIA): the potential outcomes are independent of technology adoption given X. This implies:

$$
Y_{1i}, Y_{2i} \perp D/X, \quad \forall X \quad \text{or} \quad E(Y_{2i}/D = 1, P(X)) = E(Y_{2i}/D = 0,\ P(X))
\tag{2.5a}
$$

(b) Common Support Condition: for all X there is a positive probability of either adopting ($D = 1$) or not adopting ($D = 0$), this guarantees every adopter a counterpart in the non-adopter population:

$$0 < P(D = 1 | X) < 1 \qquad (2.5b)$$

Several matching algorithms such as nearest neighbor matching (NNM), radius matching (RM) and kernel matching (KM) (Heckman et al. 1998; Smith and Todd 2005), have been suggested in published literature and thus we applied all three matching algorithms in our study.

Because the matching procedure conditions on the propensity score but does not condition on individual covariates, one must check that the distribution of variables is 'balanced' across the adopter and non-adopter groups. Rosenbaum and Rubin (1985) recommend that a standardized bias (SB) and a t-test for differences be used to check matching quality. If the covariates Xs are randomly distributed across adopter and non-adopter groups, the value of the associated pseudo-R^2 should be fairly low and the likelihood ratio should also be insignificant. We used the bootstrapping methodology to calculate the standard error for an estimate of technology impact. Normally there are two types of standard errors in such a case: analytical and bootstrapped standard errors.

Rosenbaum (2002) argues that even though propensity score matching tries to compare the differences between the outcome variables of adopters and non-adopters with similar inherent characteristics, it cannot correct unobservable bias because propensity score matching only controls for observed variables (to the extent that they are perfectly measured). If there are unobserved variables that simultaneously affect the adoption decision and the outcome variables, a selection or hidden bias problem might arise to which matching estimators are not robust. Thus, our study uses the endogenous switching regression (ESR) model to account for hidden bias that affects technology adoption and consumption expenditure and then the poverty status.

2.5.2 Endogenous Switching Regression Models

We also used the endogenous switching regression (ESR) techniques to support the PSM techniques and to assess consistency of the results with different assumptions. Let household welfare be indicated by 'consumption expenditure and poverty status,' Y_{1i} for adopters and Y_{2i} for not-adopters. The endogeneity of the adoption decision is accounted for by estimating a simultaneous equations model with endogenous switching by the full information maximum likelihood (FIML). The selection equation for technology adoption is specified as:

$$D_i^* = \beta X_i + U_i \quad \text{with} \quad D_i = \begin{cases} 1 & \text{if } D_i^* > 0 \\ 0 & \text{otherwise} \end{cases} \tag{2.6}$$

where, D_i^* is the unobservable or latent variable for technology adoption, D_i is its observable counterpart (the dependent variable adoption of improved HYVs equals 1 if a farmer has adopted the technology and 0 otherwise), X_i are non-stochastic vectors of observed farm and non-farm characteristics determining adoption and U_i is random disturbances associated with the adoption of improved agricultural technologies.

To account for selection bias we adopted an endogenous switching regression model of welfare outcomes (that is, consumption expenditure per capita and poverty status) where farmers faced two regimes: (1) to adopt, and (2) not to adopt defined as:

$$\text{Regime 1}: Y_{1i} = \alpha_1 J_{1i} + e_{1i} \quad \text{if } D_i = 1 \tag{2.7a}$$

$$\text{Regime 2}: Y_{2i} = \alpha_2 J_{2i} + e_{2i} \quad \text{if } D_i = 0 \tag{2.7b}$$

where, Y_i, outcome variables is household consumption expenditure per adult equivalent and poverty status of households in regimes 1 and 2, J_i represents a vector of exogenous variables thought to influence consumption expenditure and poverty levels. Thus Eqs. 2.7a and 2.7b describe the relationship between the variables of interest in both the regimes. Finally, the error terms are assumed to have a trivariate normal distribution with zero mean and non-singular covariance matrix expressed as:

$$Cov(e_{1i}, e_{2i}, u_i) = \begin{pmatrix} \sigma_{e1}^2 & . & \sigma_{e1u} \\ . & \sigma_{e2}^2 & \sigma_{e2u} \\ . & . & \sigma_u^2 \end{pmatrix} \tag{2.8}$$

where, σ_u^2 is the variance of the error term in the selection Eq. 2.6 (which can be assumed to be equal to 1 since the coefficients are estimable only up to a scale factor), σ_{e1}^2 and σ_{e2}^2 are the variances of the error terms in the welfare outcome functions (2.7a) and (2.7b), and σ_{e1u} and σ_{e2u} represent the covariance of u_i, e_{1i} and e_{2i},. Since Y_{1i} and Y_{2i} are not observed simultaneously the covariance between e_{1i} and e_{2i} is not defined (Maddala 1983: 224; Lokshin and Sajaia 2004). An important implication of the error structure is that because the error term of the selection Eq. 2.6 u_i is correlated with the error terms of the welfare outcome functions (2.7a) and (2.7b) (e_{1i} and e_{2i}), the expected values of e_{1i} and e_{2i} conditional on the sample selection are non-zero:

$$E[e_{1i}/D_i = 1] = \sigma_{e1u} \frac{\phi(\beta X_i)}{\Phi(\beta X_i)} = \sigma_{e1u} \lambda_{1i} \text{ and } E[e_{2i}/D_i = 0] = -\sigma_{e2u} \frac{\phi(\beta X_i)}{1 - \Phi(\beta X_i)}$$
$$= \sigma_{e2u} \lambda_{2i}$$

where, $\Phi(\cdot)$ is the standard normal probability density function, $\Phi(\cdot)$ the standard normal cumulative density function and $\lambda_{1i} = \frac{\phi\beta X_i}{\Phi\beta X_i}$ and $\lambda_{2i} = \frac{\phi\beta X_i}{1-\Phi\beta X_i}$. If the estimated covariances $\hat{\sigma}_{e1u}$ and $\hat{\sigma}_{e2u}$ are statistically significant, then the decision to adopt and the welfare outcome variables are correlated, that is, there is evidence of endogenous switching and thus a rejection of the null hypothesis of absence of sample selectivity bias. This model is defined as a 'switching regression model with endogenous switching' (Maddala and Nelson 1975).

An efficient method of estimating endogenous switching regression models is by the full information maximum likelihood (FIML) estimation (Di Falco et al. 2011; Lee and Trost 1978; Lokshin and Sajaia 2004; Solomon and Bekele 2010; Solomon et al. 2012).[7] The FIML method simultaneously estimates the probit criterion or selection equation and the regression equations to yield consistent standard errors. Given the assumption of trivariate normal distribution for the error terms, the logarithmic likelihood function for the system of Eqs. 2.6, 2.7a and 2.7b can be given as:

$$LNL_i = \sum_{i=1}^{N} D_i \left[\ln \phi \left(\frac{e_{1i}}{\sigma_{e1}} \right) - \ln \sigma_{e1} + \ln \Phi(\varphi_{1i}) \right]$$
$$+ (1 - D_i) \left[\ln \phi \left(\frac{e_{2i}}{\sigma_{e2}} \right) - \ln \sigma_{e2} \langle 1 - \Phi(\varphi_{21}) \rangle \right]$$

(2.9)

where, $\varphi_{ji} = \frac{(\beta X_i + \gamma_j e_{ji}/\sigma_j)}{\sqrt{1-\gamma_j^2}}$, $j_i = 1, 2$, with σ_j denoting the correlation coefficient between the error term U_i of the selection Eq. 2.6 and the error term e_{ij} of Eqs. 2.7a and 2.7b respectively. The FIML estimates of the parameters of the endogenous switching regression model can be obtained using the *movestay* command in Stata (see Lokshin and Sajaia 2004).

2.5.3   Poverty Measurement Approaches

Income versus Expenditure Approach: Most rich countries measure poverty using income, while most poor countries use expenditure. The reason is that in rich countries income is comparatively easy to measure (much of it comes from wages and salaries), while expenditure is complex and hard to quantify. On the other hand, in less-developed countries income is hard to measure (much of it comes from self-employment) while expenditure is more straightforward and hence easier to estimate. The arguments for and against income and consumption as appropriate

---

[7]An alternative estimation method is the two-step procedure (see Maddala 1983: 224, for details). However, this method is less efficient than FIML, it requires some adjustments to derive consistent standard errors (Maddala 1983: 225), and it shows poor performance in case of high multicollinearity between the covariates of the selection Eq. 2.6 and the covariates of the regression Eqs. 2.7a and 2.7b.

welfare measures for poverty analyses are summarized in Haughton and Khandker (2009: 30).[8]

Duclos and Araar (2010) state, 'it is frequently argued that consumption is better suited than income as an indicator of living standards, at least in many developing countries. One reason is that consumption is believed to vary more smoothly than income, both within a given year and across the life cycle. Income is notoriously subject to seasonal variability, particularly in developing countries, whereas consumption tends to be less variable. Life-cycle theories also predict that individuals will try to smooth their consumption across their low- and high-income years (in order to equalize their "marginal utility of consumption" across time), through appropriate borrowing and saving behavior.'

In practice, however, consumption smoothing is far from perfect in part due to imperfect access to commodity and credit markets and also because of the difficulties in estimating one's 'permanent' or lifecycle income precisely. Using short-term versus longer-term consumption or income indicators can therefore change the assessment of wellbeing.

Unlike other studies (for example, Wu et al. 2010; Mendola 2007; Kassie et al. 2011), who used per capita income to examine the impacts of improved agricultural technologies on income and poverty status, our study relied on per adult equivalent (AEU) consumption expenditure as a measure of household welfare which is a more reliable welfare indicator and is less prone to measurement errors than total household income in the two regions. Besides, household income indicates a household's ability to purchase its basic needs while AEU expenditure reflects the effective consumption of households and therefore provides information on the food security status of households and their poverty conditions.

The consumption expenditure components include both food and non-food expenditures. Food consumption expenditure includes that on food grains, livestock products (such as meat), vegetables and other food items (such as sugar and salt) and beverages (such as coffee and tea leaves). Non-food expenditure includes clothing and energy (such as shoes and kerosene), education and medical expenditure and expenditure on both durable and non-durable services.

"The threshold level of welfare that distinguishes poor households from non-poor households is a poverty line. A number of aggregate measures of poverty can be computed using a poverty line," Simtowe et al. (2012). We used a more general class of poverty measures proposed by Foster-Greer-Thorbecke (FGT) (1984) since it is decomposable across sub-groups such as adopters and non-adopters; by region; education levels; and income sources given by:

$$P_\alpha = \frac{1}{n} \sum_{i=1}^{q} \left[\frac{Z - y_i}{Z} \right]^\alpha 1(y_i - Z) \qquad (2.10)$$

---

[8]A further discussion on this can be found in Hentschel and Lanjouw (1996), Blundell and Preston (1998) and Donaldson (1992).

where, the poverty line is z, y_i is expenditure per capita of the ith household measured in the same unit as z, n is the total number of individuals in the population, q is the total number of poor individuals whose consumption expenditure is less than the poverty line, $1(y_i - z)$ is an indicator variable that takes a value of 1 if the consumption expenditure is below the poverty line and 0 otherwise and α is the poverty aversion parameter. When $\alpha = 0$, P_0 is simply the headcount ratio, the proportion of people at and below the poverty line. When $\alpha = 1$, P_1 is the poverty gap index (or depth of poverty), defined by the mean distance to the poverty line where the mean is formed over the entire population with the non-poor counted as having a zero-poverty gap. When $\alpha = 2$, P_2 (the squared poverty gap) is called the severity of poverty index because it is sensitive to inequalities among the poor.

We used the national food and non-food poverty line in Birr per adult equivalent of 2012–13 to calculate FGT values. According to the Ministry of Finance and Economic Development's (MOFED 2012) Interim Report on Poverty Analysis, the food and non-food poverty lines in Birr per adult equivalent were 1985 and 3781 respectively.

2.6 The Causal Effect of Technology Adoption on Poverty

The relationship between technology adoption and rural poverty is theoretically complex and there are further empirical pitfalls regarding the problem of impact evaluation. We performed our data analysis in two steps. In the first step, we give a description of the socioeconomic characteristics of the sample households comparing adopters and non-adopters and in the second we give the econometric results of the role of improved agricultural technology adoption on household welfare outcomes (consumption expenditure and poverty status).

2.6.1 Results of Descriptive Analyses

We classified adopters as households who planted any of the improved HYVs and non-adopters as those who did not use any of the improved varieties.

Table 2.1 gives the summary statistics and tests of statistical significance on equality of means for continuous variables and equality of proportions for binary variables for adopters and non-adopters. The dataset contains 1900 farm households of which about 24% adopted improved HYVs (planted at least one of the improved seeds) and there were some significant differences in household characteristics. Non-adopters, for example, were more likely to be constrained by lack of access to credit services and they had less contact with extension agents and were less likely to participate in group discussions. Though it is early to conclude at this point (we need a multivariate analysis) this could explain why non-adopters did not adopt improved agricultural technologies.

Table 2.1 Descriptive summary of selected variables used in estimations

Variables	Non-adopters (N = 1453)	Adopters (N = 447)	t-stat/ Chi-square
Age of HH head(years)	42.78	42.16	0.96
Region (Amhara = 1)	0.56	0.55	0.41
Sex (male = 1)	0.75	0.73	0.72
Walking time (minute)	75.52	69.26	0.45
Fertilizer use (yes = 1)	0.49	0.53	−2.46**
HH size (hh members)	4.17	4.14	0.29
Livestock holdings	0.56	0.70	−1.19
Credit access (yes = 1)	0.24	0.29	−3.19**
Other income sources (yes = 1)	0.221	0.217	0.031
Know FTC location (yes = 1)	0.959	0.971	−1.65*
Group participation (yes = 1)	0.908	0.942	−4.96***
Educational level of head (year of schooling)	3.97	3.41	1.82**

Note Statistical significance at the 1% (***), 5% (**) and 10% (*) probability levels
Source Author's computation

The adopter group was also significantly distinguishable in terms of welfare which is measured by consumption expenditure per adult equivalent. The average consumption expenditure per capita for adopters was Birr 4372.61 per year while non-adopters had Birr 3782.14 as annual expenditure per capita. After transforming the consumption variable into a logarithm form, the test shows a significant difference between adopters and non-adopters. On average, a higher proportion of adopters had better knowledge and they were from farmer training centers (FTCs) in the kebeles but they had less years of schooling as compared to non-adopters. The average years of schooling was about 3.41 for adopters and 3.97 for non-adopters. This suggests that more educated households were more reluctant to adopt new agricultural technologies. There were also significant differences between adopters and non-adopters in fertilizer use.

Average age of the sample household heads was about 43 years and about 25% were female-headed households. No significant differences were observable in the age, gender and marital status of the sample households between adopters and non-adopters.

There were no significant differences between the two groups in areas like average walking time to the farmland. On average, it took about 70 min to the farm for adopters while it took an average of about 76 min for non-adopters to reach their farmland. The results also show that the adopter category was non-distinguishable in terms of its average family size (household members) and livestock holdings. This simple comparison of the two groups of households suggests that adopters and non-adopters differed (though not strongly) in some characteristics.

We used the national poverty lines constructed by MOFED (2012) to estimate the poverty index disaggregated by the adoption status of the households. Table 2.2

Table 2.2 Poverty measures by adoption status (pooled sample)

Poverty measures	Adopters (N = 447)	Non-adopters (N = 1453)	Difference
Per capita expenditure (Birr)	4372.61	3782.14	6.14***
Ln (Per capita expenditure)	8.30	8.22	7.01***
Poverty Headcount (%)	0.5302	0.5946	−0.064***
Poverty gap index	0.04042	0.04536	−0.0049**
Severity gap index	0.00484	0.00551	−0.00068

Note Statistical significance at the 1% (***) and 5% (**) probability levels
Source Author's computation using the FGT poverty formula, 2017

presents the incidence of poverty, poverty gap and poverty severity of adopters and non-adopters based on the results of the Foster-Greer-Thorbecke (FGT) poverty measure. The results indicate that there is a significant difference between the adopter and non-adopter categories in terms of welfare indicators.

Around 58% of the households lived below the poverty line. These poverty levels were much higher than the national poverty rate. Adopters of improved HYVs were better off than non-adopters. The incidence of poverty was higher among non-adopters (59.46%) than it was among adopters (53.02%) indicating an unconditional headcount ratio of poverty for the adopters that was about 6.4% points lower compared to non-adopters. Similarly, both poverty gap and poverty severity were also higher among non-adopters than among adopters suggesting that improved agricultural technology adoption was positively correlated to wellbeing.

In general, the unconditional summary statistics and tests in Tables 2.1 and 2.2 suggest that agricultural technology may have a role in improving household wellbeing but because adoption is endogenous a simple comparison of the welfare indicators of adopters and non-adopters has no causal interpretation. That is, these differences may not (only) be the result of new agricultural technology adoption, but instead may also be due to other factors such as differences in household characteristics and endowments (for example, Hailemariam et al. 2016; Simtowe et al. 2012; Solomon et al. 2012). To measure the impact of adoption, it is necessary to take into account the fact that individuals who adopt improved varieties might have had a higher level of welfare even if they had not adopted these technologies. Therefore, a multivariate analysis is needed to test the impact of improved agricultural technology adoption on household welfare.

2.6.2 Econometric Results

2.6.2.1 Estimation of Propensity Score

As literature on household welfare points out, besides technology, specific household characteristics also have a role in determining the status of wellbeing of household members. To measure the impact of adoption, it is necessary to take into account the fact that individuals who adopt improved varieties might have achieved a higher level of welfare even if they had not adopted. As a consequence, we applied the propensity score matching method to control for these observable characteristics and isolated the intrinsic impact of technology adoption on household welfare.

Before estimating the causal effects of improved agricultural technology adoption, we tested the quality of the matching process. After estimating the propensity scores for the adopter and non-adopter groups we checked the common support condition. A visual inspection of the density distributions of the estimated propensity scores for the two groups (Fig. 2.1) indicated that the common support condition was satisfied: there was substantial overlap in the distribution of the propensity scores of both adopter and non-adopter groups. The bottom half of the graph in Fig. 2.1 shows the propensity score distribution for non-adopters and the upper half shows it for the adopters; the densities of the scores are on the y-axis.

Table 2.3 gives the results of the covariate balancing tests before and after matching. The standardized mean difference for overall covariates used in the propensity score (around 7.4% before matching) reduced to less than 2% after matching. The p-values of the likelihood ratio tests indicate that the joint significance of covariates was always rejected after matching, whereas it was never rejected before matching. The pseudo R^2 also dropped significantly from around 4% before matching to about 0.3–1.7% after matching under the three matching algorithms. The low pseudo R^2, high total bias reduction and the insignificant p-values of the likelihood ratio test after matching (see Table 2.3) suggest that the proposed specification of the propensity score was fairly successful in terms of balancing the distribution of covariates between the two groups.

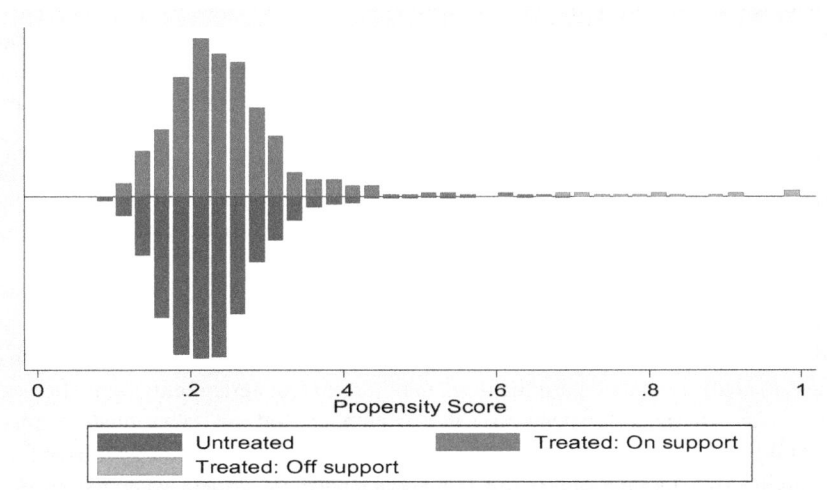

Fig. 2.1 Propensity score distribution and common support for propensity score estimation. *Source* Author's calculation using WB data (2010)

Table 2.3 Covariate balance indicators before and after matching

Before matching	Values	After matching	Values
Pseudo R^2	0.036	Nearest neighbor matching (NNM)	
LR χ^2 (p-value)	74.57 (0.000) ***	Pseudo R^2	0.004
Mean standardized bias	7.44	LR χ^2 (p-value)	4.57 (1.00)
		Mean standardized bias	2.6
		Kernel-based matching (KM)	
		Pseudo R^2	0.003
		LR χ^2 (p-value)	3.65 (1.00)
		Mean standardized bias	1.6
		Radius matching(RM)	
		Pseudo R^2	0.017
		LR χ^2 (p-value)	18.80 (0.801)
		Mean standardized bias	1.08

***is statistically
Note Statistical significance at 1% probability level
Source Author's computation using pstest and psmatch2 Stata commands

The logit[9] estimates of the adoption propensity equation are presented in Table 2.4. The table provides information about some of the driving forces behind farmers' decision to adopt improved agricultural technologies where the dependent variable takes the value of 1 if a farmer adopts at least one improved agricultural technology and 0 otherwise. The results show that the coefficients of some of the variables expected/hypothesized to influence adoption had the expected signs (but not household head's education level) and include factors such as group participation of households, fertilizer use, education level of the household head and the household's access to credit.

The coefficient for group participation (whether the household participated in meetings, discussions etc.) was positive and significant at 5% suggesting that the probability of adopting at least one of the improved high yielding varieties increased as a household participated in more group discussions.

Access to credit had a positive and significant coefficient, suggesting that agricultural credit in the two regions can have a significant impact in facilitating the adoption of improved seed varieties. One possible reason for this could be that access to credit is a key determinant of adoption of most agricultural innovations as this increases farmers' financial capacity to purchase seeds and other related inputs.

Unlike other studies, years of schooling negatively and significantly affected the probability of adopting suggesting that more educated farmers were risk-averse.

[9]The default is logit, but probit could also be used by specification.

Table 2.4 Determinants of improved HYVs-estimated coefficients: adoption (1/0)

Variables	Estimates	Variables	Estimates
Age (years)	0.004	Livestock (TLU)	0.003
Sex (male = 1)	−0.099	Credit access (yes = 1)	0.169**
Walking time to farm (minutes)	−0.001	Group participation (yes = 1)	0.434**
Fertilizer use (yes = 1)	0.129*	Head's education(years)	−0.055*
HH size (hh members)	−0.035	Model farmer (yes = 1)	0.149
HH has bank account (yes = 1)	0.152	$Educ^2$ (Head's education square)	0.002
HH has other income source (yes = 1)	−0.164	Constant	−2.979***
No of observations	1900	Model chi^2	74.57***
Pseudo R^2	0.036	Log likelihood	−999.27

Note Statistical significance at the 1% (***), 5% (**) and at 10% (*) probability levels
Source Author's calculations using World Bank data (2010)

Therefore, the negative effect of education on adoption can be interpreted in terms of the risk-aversion paradigm assuming that farmers consider the new technologies to be riskier than the existing and older ones which they know more about and that they have been growing for a long period of time. This finding is in line with Jung (2014) where he investigated the issue of 'does education affect risk aversion?' His findings indicate that increasing the number of years of schooling increased the level of risk aversion. Thus, this finding implies that more educated individuals were more risk averse. This is consistent with previous studies of adoption models in which fertilizer usage had a positive and significant coefficient.

After estimating the propensity scores and checking their matching quality, we estimated ATT. The estimated results based on the three matching algorithms—the nearest neighborhood (NNM), radius matching (RM) and kernel method (KM)— are given in Table 2.5. It reports bootstrap standard errors based on 100 replications. Four outcome variables were used in the analysis: per capita consumption expenditure (and natural logarithm of per capita consumption expenditure), head-count index, poverty gap index and severity index. The results indicate that adoption of HYVs had a positive and significant effect on consumption expenditure and a negative impact on poverty.

The overall average gains of adopting improved agricultural technologies in per capita consumption expenditure ranged from Birr 582.67 to Birr 606.69 under the three algorithms. The estimated gain was statistically significant at the 99% confidence level for all matching methods. This measures the average difference in consumption expenditure of similar pairs of households that have different technological status (that is, adopters and non-adopters). This indicates that (assuming there is no selection bias due to unobservable factors, but to be checked later under the endogenous switching regression, ESR, method) per capita consumption expenditure for farmers who adopted improved HYVs was significantly higher than that for non-adopters.

Table 2.5 Impact of HYVs adoption on per capita expenditure and poverty status

	Outcome variables	Outcome mean		ATT
		Adopters	Non-adopters	
NNM	Cons. expenditure	4372.61	3787.72	606.69(3.91)***
	Ln (Cons. expenditure)	8.261	8.215	0.046(4.09)***
	Headcount ratio	0.5302	0.6129	−0.08(−2.61)***
	Depth of poverty	0.04042	0.04595	−0.006(−1.5)*
	Severity of poverty	0.004835	0.005496	−0.001(−0.98)
KM[1]	Cons. expenditure	4372.61	3787.72	58489(4.06)***
	Ln (Cons. expenditure)	8.2609	8.2132	0.048(4.60)***
	Headcount ratio	0.5302	0.5983	−0.068(−2.84)***
	Depth of poverty	0.04042	0.04565	−0.005(−1.82)*
	Severity of poverty	0.00484	0.00552	−0.001(−1.40)
KM[2]	Cons. expenditure	4372.16	3789.95	582.67(4.63)***
	Ln (cons. expenditure)	8.2609	8.2131	0.0478(4.86)***
	Headcount ratio	0.53020	0.59715	−0.06695(−2.85)***
	Depth of poverty	0.04042	0.04571	−0.0053(−1.83)*
	Severity of poverty	0.004836	0.005540	−0.001(−1.40)
RM	Cons. expenditure	4372.16	3782.72	586.98(3.84)***
	Ln (Cons. expenditure)	8.261	8.213	0.048(4.85)***
	Headcount ratio	0.5302	0.6129	−0.068(−2.95)***
	Depth of poverty	0.04042	0.04565	−0.005(−1.90)*
	Severity of poverty	0.00484	0.00550	−0.001(−1.40)

Note Statistical significance at the 1% (***), 5% (**) and 10% (*) probability levels. T-statistics in parenthesis
KM^1 kernel based matching with a band width of 0.06
KM^2 kernel based matching with a band width of 0.03
Source Author's calculations using WB data (2010)

An increase in consumption expenditure can help adopters reduce their poverty levels. Depending on the specific matching algorithm used the estimated impact of technology adoption on poverty reduction as measured by the headcount index ranged between 6.7 and 8.3% points and they were all statistically significant at less than 1% probability (see Table 2.5).

Our findings also indicate that adoption had an impact on reducing the depth and severity of poverty. The estimated effect of adoption on reducing the depth of poverty was in the range of 0.5–0.6% points using all matching estimators. Further, technology significantly decreased the inequality (severity) of poverty by about 0.1% points using all matching estimators but the estimated reduction was not statistically significant at the 90% confidence level under all the three algorithms

Table 2.6 Full information maximum likelihood estimates of the switching regression model. Dependent variables: HYVs adoption (1/0) and per capita consumption expenditure (consexpr)

Variables	FIML Endogenous Switching Regression		
	Adoption (1/0)	Adoption = 1 (adopters)	Adoption = 0 (non-adopters)
Region	0.0815776	223.862**	−1.618544
Bank acct.	0.0239505	205.1287	34.86514
Model farmer	−0.0792594	−120.5136	23.85026
Group participate	0.2881624**	451.9954**	−67.86693*
Credit	0.1863914***	406.9296***	−8.465735
hhsize	−0.0571203**	−13.63829	10.41632*
Fertilizer	0.1561852***	273.7268***	−36.14034*
Age^2	−0.0000243**		
Hhsize^2	0.0035646		
Educ^2	−0.0000964		
Know FTC	−0.0047636		
Constant	−0.9443379***	1127.59***	3600.03***
(ϕ_j)		−0.817***	−0.997***
LR test of indep. eqns: 513.80***			

Note Statistical significance at the 1% (***), 5% (**) and 10% (*) probability levels
Source Author's calculations using WB data (2010), by movestay command in Stata

indicating that unlike the earlier two poverty conditions (P_0 and P_1)[10] adoption did not affect inequality (severity) much more. These findings are consistent with recent studies on the impact of modern and improved agricultural technologies on household welfare (for example, Kassie et al. 2011 in Uganda; Mendola 2007 in Bangladesh; Simtowe et al. 2012 in Malawi; Solomon et al. 2012 in Ethiopia and Tanzania; Solomon and Bekele 2010 in Ethiopia and Tanzania; Tsegaye and Bekele 2012 in Ethiopia; Wu et al. 2010 in China) which show that the adoption of improved agricultural technologies had a significant impact on variables of household welfare indicators in general.

One of the drawbacks of the PSM estimation is that it cannot provide consistent estimations of causal effects in the presence of a hidden bias. Thus, to check for the robustness of our PSM findings and to control for unobservable selection bias we estimated the endogenous switching regression (ESR). The full information maximum likelihood (FIML) estimates of the endogenous switching regression model are reported in Table 2.6. The first column gives the estimated coefficients of selection Eq. 2.6 on adopting improved HYVs whereas the second and third

---

[10]P_0 P_1, P_2 stands for headcount index, poverty gap index and severity index respectively of the FGT values.

columns give the consumption expenditure functions (2.7a) and (2.7b) for farm households that did and did not adopt improved agricultural technologies.[11]

The results of the endogenous switching regression model estimated by full information maximum likelihood show that the estimated coefficient of correlation between the HYVs adoption equation and the consumption expenditure function (Φ_j) was negative and significantly different from zero. The results suggest that both observed and unobserved factors influenced the decision to adopt modern agricultural technologies and welfare outcomes given the adoption decision. The significance of the coefficient of correlation between the adoption equation and the welfare of adopters indicates that self-selection occurred in the adoption of improved agricultural technologies.

The differences in the consumption expenditure equation coefficient between farm households that adopted improved agricultural technologies and those that did not indicates the presence of heterogeneity in the sample households (see Table 2.6, columns 2 and 3). For example, the two groups (adopters and non-adopters) differ in factors like region dummy, group participation, fertilizer use, access to credit services and family size as the consumption expenditure equation of ESR shows. The consumption expenditure function of farm households that adopted improved agricultural technologies is significantly different (at the 1% level) from the consumption function of farm households that did not adopt and the likelihood-ratio test for joint independence of the three equations is reported in the last line of the output and is statistically significant at a less than 1% probability level.

2.7   Conclusion

This study evaluated the potential impact of adoption of improved agricultural technologies (HYVs) on rural household welfare measured by consumption expenditure and poverty. The relationship between agricultural technology and poverty is complex. The dataset contained 1900 farm households of which about 24% had adopted improved HYVs (planted at least one of the improved seeds) and there were some significant differences in household characteristics. Non-adopters, for example, were more likely to be constrained by lack of access to credit services, had less contact with extension agents and were less likely to participate in group discussions. The adopter group was significantly distinguishable in terms of welfare measured by consumption expenditure per adult equivalent. The average consumption expenditure per capita for adopters was Birr 4372.61 per year while for non-adopters it was Birr 3782.14 annual expenditure per capita.

Around 58% of the households lived below the poverty line. These poverty levels are much higher than the national poverty rate. Adopters of improved HYVs were

---

[11]The 'movestay' command of Stata was used to estimate the endogenous switching regression model by FIML (Lokshin and Sajaia 2004).

better-off than non-adopters. The incidence of poverty was higher among non-adopters (59.46%) than it was among adopters (53.02%) indicating an unconditional headcount ratio of poverty for the adopters that was about 6.4% points lower compared to non-adopters. Similarly, both poverty gap and poverty severity were also higher among non-adopters as compared to adopters suggesting that improved agricultural technology adoption was positively correlated with wellbeing.

Estimation of a logit model showed that the coefficients of some of the variables hypothesized to influence adoption had the expected signs (but not household head's education level) including factors such as group participation of households, fertilizer use, educational level of household head and household's access to credit.

The causal impact estimation of both the propensity score matching and switching regression showed that adoption of improved agricultural technologies had a robust, significant and positive impact on per capita consumption expenditure and a negative impact on the poverty status of households. The overall average gain of adopting improved agricultural technologies in per capita consumption expenditure ranged from Birr 582.67 to Birr 606.69 under the three algorithms. The estimated impact of technology adoption on poverty reduction as measured by the headcount index ranged between 6.7 and 8.3% points. The findings also indicate that adoption had an impact on reducing the depth and severity of poverty. The estimated effect of adoption on reducing the depth of poverty was in the range of 0.5–0.6% points using all matching estimators and it decreased inequality (severity) of poverty by about 0.1% points using all matching estimators.

This suggests the need for continued and broad public and private investments in agricultural research to address vital development challenges and the need of policy support for improving extension efforts and access to seeds and market outlets that simulate adoption of improved agricultural technologies.

References

Adekambi, S.A., A. Diagne, F.P. Simtowe, and G. Biaou. 2009. The impact of agricultural technology adoption on poverty: The case of, NERICA rice varieties in Benin. Paper prepared for presentation at the International Association of Agricultural Economists' conference, Aug 16–22, Beijing, China.

Alene, A.D., V. Manyong, G. Omanya, H. Mignouna, M. Bokanga, and G. Odhiambo. 2008. Smallholder market participation under transactions costs: Maize supply and fertilizer demand in Kenya. *Food Policy* 33 (4): 318–328.

Bahadur, K.L., and B. Siegfried. 2004. Technology adoption and household food security. Analyzing factors determining technology adoption and impact of project intervention: A case of smallholder peasants in Nepal. Paper prepared for presentation at the Deutscher Tropentag, 5–7 Oct, Humboldt University, Berlin.

Balagtas, V., J.Y. Coulibaly, M. Jabbar, and A. Negassa. 2007. Dairy market participation with endogenous livestock ownership: Evidence from cˆote d'ivoire. AAEC annual meeting, Portland, Oregon TN.

Becerril, J., and A. Abdulai. 2010. The impact of improved maize varieties on poverty in Mexico: A propensity score-matching approach. *World Development* 38 (7): 1024–1035.

Becker, S.O. 2009. *Methods to estimate causal effects theory and applications*. U Stirling, Ifo, CESifo and IZA last update: 21 Aug 2009. Stirling Management School, UK.

Becker, S.O., and A. Ichino. 2002. Estimation of average treatment effects based on propensity scores. *The Stata Journal* 2 (4): 358–377.

Blundell, R., and I. Preston. 1998. Consumption inequality and income uncertainty. *Quarterly Journal of Economics* 113: 603–640.

Blundell, R., and M. Costa-Dias. 2000. Evaluation methods for non-experimental Data. *Fiscal Studies* 21 (4): 427–468.

Bwalya, R., J. Mugisha, and T. Hyuha. 2013. Transaction costs and smallholder household access to maize markets in Zambia. *Journal of Development and Agricultural Economics* 5 (9): 328–336.

Caliendo, M., and S. Kopeinig. 2008. Some practical guidance for the implementation of propensity score matching. *Journal of Economic Surveys* 22 (1): 31–72.

Datt, G., and M. Ravallion. 1996. How important to India's poor is the sectoral composition of growth? *World Bank Economic Review* 10 (1): 1–26.

Di Falco, S., M. Veronesi, and M. Yesuf. 2011. Does adaptation to climate change provide food security? A micro-perspective from Ethiopia. *American Journal of Agricultural Economics* 93 (3): 829–846.

Doagostino, R.B. 1998. Tutorial in biostatistics propensity score methods for bias reduction in the comparison of a treatment to a non-randomized control group. Department of Public Health Sciences, Winston-Salem, USA.

Donaldson, D. 1992. On the aggregation of money measures of well-being in applied welfare economics. *Journal of Agricultural and Resource Economics* 17: 88–102.

Duclos, J.-Y., and A. Araar. 2010. *Poverty and equity: Measurement, policy and estimation with DAD. Economic studies in inequality, social exclusion and well-being*. Berlin: Springer.

Esquivel, G., and A. Huerta-Pineda. 2006. *Remittances and poverty in Mexico: A propensity score matching approach*. Unpublished.

Faltermeier, L., and A. Abdulai. 2006. *The adoption of water conservation and intensification technologies and farm income: A propensity score analysis for rice farmers in Northern Ghana*. Unpublished.

Feder, G., R.E. Just, and D. Zilberman. 1985. Adoption of agricultural innovations in developing countries. *Chicago Journal, Economic Development and Cultural Change* 33 (2): 255–298.

Foster, J., J. Greer, and E. Thorbecke. 1984. A class of decomposable poverty measures. *Econometrica* 52 (3): 761–766.

Gertler, P.J., S. Martinez, P. Premand, L.B. Rawlings, and C.M.J. Vermeersch. 2011. *Impact evaluation in practice*. Available at: http://www.worldbank.org/.

Hailemariam, T., M. Alemu, G. Köhlin, and S. Di Falco. 2016. Does adoption of multiple climate-smart practices improve farmers' climate resilience? Empirical evidence from the Nile Basin of Ethiopia. Discussion Paper Series, August.

Haughton, J., and S.R. Khandker. 2009. *Handbook on poverty and inequality*. Washington DC: The World Bank.

Hausman, J.A. 1978. Specification tests in econometrics. *Econometrica* 46: 1251–1272.

Heckman, J., H. Ichimura, J. Smith, and P. Todd. 1998. Characterizing selection bias using experimental data. *Econometrica* 66 (5): 1017–1098.

Hentschel, J. and P. Lanjouw. 1996. Constructing an indicator of consumption for the analysis of poverty: Principles and illustrations with reference to Ecuador. Working Paper No. 124, Living Standards Measurement Study. Washington, DC: The World Bank.

Hossain, M. 1989. *Green revolution in Bangladesh: Impact on growth and distribution of income*. Dhaka: University Press Ltd.

Hundie, B., and A. Admassie. 2016. *Potential impacts of yield-increasing crop technologies on productivity and poverty in two districts of Ethiopia*. Unpublished.

Jung, S. 2014. Does education affect risk aversion?: Evidence from the British education reform. Thema Working Paper, Université de Cergy Pontoise, France.

Kassie, M., B. Shiferaw, and G. Muricho. 2011. Agricultural technology, crop income, and poverty alleviation in Uganda. *World Development* 39 (10): 1784–1795.

Kassie, M., B. Shiferaw, and G. Muricho. 2010. Adoption and impact of improved groundnut varieties on rural poverty. Evidence from rural Uganda. Discussion Paper Series, May.

Kelsey, J. 2011. *Market inefficiencies and the adoption of agricultural technologies in developing countries*. Unpublished.

Lee, L.F., and R.P. Trost. 1978. Estimation of some limited dependent variable models with application to housing demand. *Journal of Econometrics* 8: 357–382.

Lokshin, M., and Z. Zurab-Sajaia. 2004. Maximum likelihood estimation of endogenous switching regression models. *The Stata Journal* 4 (3): 282–289.

Maddala, G.S. 1983. *Limited dependent and qualitative variables in econometrics*. Cambridge: Cambridge University Press.

Maddala, G.S., and F.D. Nelson. 1975. Switching regression models with exogenous and endogenous switching. In *Proceeding of the American statistical association* (*Business and Economics Section*), 423–426.

Mendola, M. 2003. Agricultural technology and poverty reduction: A micro-level analysis of causal effects. Development Studies Working Papers No. 179 November, University of Milan-Bicocca, Italy.

Mendola, M. 2007. Agricultural technology adoption and poverty reduction: A propensity score matching analysis for rural Bangladesh. *Food Policy* 32 (3): 372–393.

MOFED (Ministry of Finance and Economic Development). 2012. *Ethiopia's progress towards eradicating poverty: An interim report on poverty analysis study (2012/13)*. Addis Ababa: The Federal Democratic Republic of Ethiopia.

Ravallion, M., S. Chen, and P. Sangraula. 2007. New evidence on the urbanization of global poverty. *Population and Development Review* 33 (4): 667–701.

Rosenbaum, P.R. 2002. *Observational Studies*. New York: Springer.

Rosenbaum, P.R., and D.B. Rubin. 1985. Constructing a control group using multivariate matched sampling methods that incorporate the propensity score. *American Statistician* 39 (1): 33–38.

Rosenbaum, P.R., and D.B. Rubin. 1983. The central role of the propensity score in observational studies for causal effects. *Biometrika* 70 (1): 41–55.

Sahu, S.K., and S. Das. 2015. Impact of agricultural related technology adoption on poverty: A study of select households in Rural India. Madras School of Economics Working Paper 131.

Sanchez, P.A., G.L. Denning, and G. Nziguheba. 2009. The African green revolution moves forward. *Food Security* 1: 37–44.

Setotaw, F., G. Ayele, and H. Teklewold. 2003. Impact of technology on households food security in tef and wheat farming systems of Moretna Jiru woreda. Ethiopian Agricultural Research Organization (EARO), Research Report No. 48.

Shiferaw, B., M. Kassie, M. Jaleta, and C. Yirga. 2014. Adoption of improved wheat varieties and impacts on household food security in Ethiopia. *Food Policy* 44: 272–284.

Simtowe, F., A. Solomon, B. Shiferaw, and L. Lipper. 2012a. Impact of modern agricultural technologies on smallholder welfare: Evidence from Tanzania and Ethiopia. *Food Policy* 37: 283–295.

Simtowe, F., M. Kassie, S. Asfaw, B. Shiferaw, E. Monyo, and M. Siambi. 2012. Welfare effects of agricultural technology adoption: The case of improved groundnut varieties in rural Malawi. Paper prepared for presentation at the international association of agricultural economists (IAAE) Triennial Conference, 18–24 Aug, Foz do Iguaçu, Brazil.

Smith, J., and P. Todd. 2005. Does matching overcome LaLonde's critique non-experimental estimators? *Journal of Econometrics* 125 (1–2): 305–353.

Solomon, A., and S. Bekele. 2010. Agricultural technology adoption and rural poverty: Application of an endogenous switching regression for selected East African Countries. Cape Town, South Africa, September 19–23, 2010.

Solomon, A., B. Shiferaw, and F. Simtowe. 2010. *Does technology adoption promote commercialization? Evidence from Chickpea Technologies in Ethiopia*. Unpublished.

Solomon, A., M. Kassie, F. Simtowe, and Leslie Lipper. 2012. *Poverty reduction effects of agricultural technology: A Micro-evidence from Tanzania.* Unpublished.

Tesfaye, S., B. Bedada, and Y. Mesay. 2016. Impact of improved wheat technology adoption on productivity and income in Ethiopia. Wheat regional centre of excellence, Kulumsa Agricultural Research Centre, Ethiopia Department of Agricultural Economics, Pretoria University, South Africa. *African Crop Science Journal* 24: 127–135.

Tsegaye, M., and H. Bekele. 2012. Impacts of adoption of improved wheat technologies on households' food consumption in Southeastern Ethiopia. Selected poster prepared for presentation at the International Association of Agricultural Economists (IAAE) Triennial Conference, 18–24 Aug, Foz do Iguaçu, Brazil.

The World Bank. 2008. *World development report 2008: Agriculture for development.* Washington, DC: The World Bank.

Vance, C., and J. Geoghegan. 2004. Modeling the determinants of semi-subsistent and commercial land uses in an agricultural frontier of Southern Mexico: A switching regression approach. *International Regional Science Review* 27 (3): 326–347.

Winter-Nelson, A., and A. Temu. 2005. Impacts of prices and transactions costs on input usage in a liberalizing economy: Evidence from Tanzanian coffee growers. *Agricultural Economics* 33 (3): 243–253.

Wu, H., S. Ding, S. Pandey, and D. Tao. 2010. Assessing the impact of agricultural technology adoption on farmers' well-being in Rural China. *Asian Economic Journal* 24 (2): 141–160.

Chapter 3
Determinants of Food Security in the Oromiya Region of Ethiopia

Tsegaye Mulugeta Habtewold

Abstract The present study identifies and investigates the importance of supply- and demand-side factors of household food security by doing a logistic regression analysis of data collected through a survey of 240 sample households in Arsi zone, Lode Hetosa district. Rather than using per capita income we use consumption expenditure per adult equivalent (AEU) to measure household food security levels. Out of the 240 sample rural households, 53.75 and 46.25% were found to be food secure and food insecure respectively. The empirical results show that out of the five supply-side factors hypothesized to have an impact on household food security status, four—education level, landholding, technology adoption and access to credit service—had a significant relationship with household food security while from the eight demand-side factors, five—farm experience, participation in off-farm activities, annual farm income, market distance and livestock holdings—were associated with food security levels. Depending on the relative effects of the two sides on the probability of food security, supply-side factors are more important and powerful than demand-side factors in affecting and determining household food security. This implies that policy interventions focused on supply side factors need to get priority attention.

Keywords Food security · Household · Binary logit · Arsi zone
Ethiopia

3.1 Introduction

Despite the fact that it is one of the most consistently enshrined rights in international human rights laws which is constantly reaffirmed by governments, no human right has been so frequently violated in recent times as the right to food (Clover

T. M. Habtewold (✉)
Department of Economics, College of Business and Economic,
Addis Ababa University, Addis Ababa, Ethiopia
e-mail: abtse2002@gmail.com

© Springer Nature Singapore Pte Ltd. 2018   39
A. Heshmati and H. Yoon (eds.), *Economic Growth and Development in Ethiopia*, Perspectives on Development in the Middle East and North Africa (MENA) Region, https://doi.org/10.1007/978-981-10-8126-2_3

2003). Concerns generated by the food crisis in the mid-1970s led world leaders to accept for the first time the common responsibility of the international community to abolish hunger and malnutrition. Nevertheless, between 1980 and 1998 per capita food consumption in the 48 least developed countries declined, while for developing countries as a whole it improved.

Worldwide the trends are alarming as progress in reducing hunger in the developing world has slowed to a crawl and in most regions the number of under-nourished people is actually growing despite the fact that world food production has grown faster than world population in the last three decades. Latest estimates indicate that 840 million people were under-nourished in 1998–2000 (11 million in the industrialized countries, 30 million in countries in transition and 799 million in the developing world).

There are numerous, varied and complex reasons for the food crises in Africa. The principal factors attributed to the continent's failure to adequately feed its population include: (i) climatic hazards; (ii) severe environmental degradation; (iii) rapid population growth outstripping agricultural growth; (iv) unstable macroeconomic environments and inappropriate government policies in some nations; (v) low purchasing power of the people (poverty); (vi) the absence of food security policies at national or regional levels; (vii) lack of storage facilities; (viii) limited access to infrastructure and basic services; (ix) civil war; (x) inappropriate incentives; and (xi) low productivity of agriculture as a result of insufficient fertilizer use and poor control of weeds (ECA 1992; FAO 1994).

About 52% of the population in Ethiopia is food insecure with average consumption of approximately 1770 kcal per capita which is considerably lower as compared to the FAO/WHO recommended 2100 kcal per person per day (FAO 1998a, b). Despite improvements in main macroeconomic indicators in recent years food security remains one of the most important issues in Ethiopia's development agenda.

Agriculture is the main source of income for society in the study area and food security related problems of the district are similar to those in the rest of the country. To the best of our knowledge there is no official study determining the food security status of people in the study area and demand and supply side factors too have not been considered by studies. However, there is a large body of empirical literature on the country level that documents the determinants of household food security, but none of them identify the supply versus demand side factors except a study by Feleke et al. (2003). Our study determines the status of households' food security and identifies its factors using both demand and supply related issues.

The study area, Arsi zone, is one of the surplus producing areas in the country in general and in Oromia region in particular. Lode Hetosa woreda [1] (the area where our study was conducted) is part of the zone where agriculture is practiced (Arsi Zone Finance and Economic Development Office 2016). Crop production is the

---

[1]Woreda is the second lowest administrative unit in the country above the kebele.

major agricultural activity in the woreda. Crops such as cereals, pulses and oil seeds and vegetable are grown in the area. The weather conditions in the woreda are suitable for crop production. The temperature varies between 10 and 25 °C. The annual rainfall ranges from 800 to 1400 mm and on average there are round 120 rainy days in the year. The rainfall pattern is bi-modal: a short rainy season (Belg) from February to March and a long rainy season (Meher) from June to September.

According to Feleke et al. (2003), "food self-sufficiency is neither a necessary nor a sufficient condition for food security. It is not a necessary condition because food imports can be used to fill the gap. It is not a sufficient condition because a country is sufficient in food production, but people may face food insecurity". So irrespective of the fact that this is a surplus producing district, households face food security problems caused by one or a combination of factors. Our study aims to find the factors affecting households' food security status by reviewing both the demand and supply side factors. Specifically, our study assesses the relative importance of supply-side versus demand-side factors in influencing food security levels.

3.2 Literature Review

A large body of empirical literature is available on factors affecting food security/insecurity, or determinant of household consumption, nutrition and so forth. But only Feleke et al.'s study (2003) clearly identifies the supply and demand side factors separately.[2]

Their study identifies determinants of food security in southern Ethiopia considering the supply and demand side factors independently. Their supply side findings indicate that adoption of agricultural technology increased the probability of food security from 0.11 to 0.98 using a base group. It also found that the probability of food security increased from 0.11 to 0.20 with a change in the average farm size by 10%. With everything held constant, if land quality improved, the probability of household food security increased from 0.11 to 0.40. On the demand side, an increase in household size by a unit reduced the probability of food security from 0.11 to 0.07.

In Feleke et al.'s (2003) study a one-unit increase in the average level of livestock size raised the probability of food security to 0.13. Similarly, access to off-farm jobs increased the probability of food security from 0.11 to 0.23.

Faridi and Naimul (2010) assess household food security in Bangladesh and state that relating house quality and food security, houses made with brick walls and mud walls were 3 and 4.7% more likely to be food secure respectively than houses made of hey/straw. Their research also found that a one-unit increase in

---

[2]See Maxwell (1996a, b) and FAO's World Food Summit of (FAO 1996) for a discussion on food security concepts and definitions.

landholdings led to around 5.1 more likelihood of a household being food secure. In relation to electricity and food security, households with electricity connections were around 4% more likely to be food secure than those which did not have an electricity connection.

Zakari et al. (2014) evaluated the factors influencing household food security in Niger and found that male-headed households were more food secure compared to female headed households. The odds ratio of gender was equal to 2.64 which indicates that male-headed households had a 2.64 times chance to be food secure as compared to female-headed households. Their results also show a negative and significant association between disease and insect attacks on the one hand and food security on the other. This indicates that the probability of household food security decreased by 0.56 due to an increase in disease and insect attacks. A unit kilometer away from a market center led to a 0.34 decrease in the likelihood of a household being food secure.

Haile et al. (2005) identified the major food security determinants for Korodegaga peasants in Ethiopia. An increase in the availability of fertilizers for food insecure households increased the probability of food security by 10%. Similarly, improvements in the education levels of food insecure household heads and reduction of family size of food insecure households increased the probability of food security by 5 and 6% respectively.

Mannaf and Uddin (2014) identified socioeconomic factors influencing the food security status of maize growing households in selected areas of Bogra district in Bangladesh. Their results show that household food security decreased with an increase in the age of the household head and increased with an increase in household monthly income. A one-year increase in the age of the household head reduced the probability of the household being food secure by 0.73. A unit increase in the level of income increased the probability of a household being food secure by 0.99. Their food security analysis showed that a unit increase in food expenditure increased the probability of a household being food secure by 1.002; and household food security decreased with an increase in household size. A unit increase in household size (member) reduced the probability of the household being food secure by 1.6.

Abu and Soom (2016) examined the factors affecting household food security status among rural and urban farming households in Benue state, Nigeria. Their results show that the income of the household head, farm size and rural household size had a positive impact on household food security while age of the household head and urban household size had a negative relationship with household food security.

Sultana and Kiani (2011) examined the determinants of a household's food security in Pakistan using a logistic regression procedure and found that controlling other factors if the household head's education level was above primary level, on average the probability of food security increased by a factor of 0.25. If the education attainment was beyond the intermediate level, then probability of food security increased by 0.35. Their study also examined the relationship between unemployment status and food security and they found that unemployment reduced food security status by about 1.4 units.

Abafita and Kim (2014) examined the determinants of food security among rural households in Ethiopia using both OLS and IV methods. Their results show that participation in off-farm activities, age of the household head, education of the household head, livestock possession, rainfall index, soil conservation practices and per capita consumption expenditure enhanced household food security while remittances, being a male-headed household, household size, fertilizer use and access to credit reduced household food security.

Getahun and Beyene (2014) examined the status and factors affecting food insecurity in rural households in Babile district, Ethiopia. Their result show that the educational status of the household head, annual farm income, use of irrigation schemes, and size of cultivated land were associated negatively with household food insecurity levels while insect and pest infestation demonstrated a positive and significant association with household food insecurity.

3.2.1 Food Insecurity in Ethiopia

Worldwide 800 million people are chronically malnourished and 2 billion lack access to sufficient, safe and nutritious food needed for a healthy life. More than half the world's population lives in low-income, food-deficit countries that are unable to produce or import enough food to feed the people. In 64 of the 105 developing countries, food productivity increased at a slower rate than population growth during 1985–95 (UNPF 2001, as cited in Yilma 2005).

At the UN Millennium Summit in 2000 world leaders agreed to halve the proportion of people suffering from hunger by 2015. This required unprecedented cooperation within and among countries. The transfer of modern agricultural technologies and knowledge can help protect soil. Research and development on new high-yield crops will have to continue and distribution of existing food supplies will have to be improved. Women, responsible in most countries for family health and for raising children, must be empowered to better manage food resources.

New agricultural technologies and improved practices play a key role in increasing agricultural production (and hence improving national food security) in developing countries. Where successful, adoption of improved agricultural technologies stimulates overall economic growth through inter-sectoral linkages while conserving natural resources (Faltermeier and Abdulai 2006; Sanchez et al. 2009). Given the close link between food insecurity, farming and environmental degradation the impact of cultivation practices has received significant attention in the last two decades.

In Ethiopia improved cultivation techniques are not new but their rate of adoption is much lower than the required level. The history of agricultural sciences in Ethiopia coincides with the establishment of the Ambo Junior Colleges of Agriculture (AJCA) and the Jima Junior Colleges of Agriculture (JJCA) in 1947 and of the Imperial College of Agriculture and Mechanical Arts in 1953 (later called the Alemaya College and now the University of Alemaya) (The National Agricultural Research System of Ethiopia 1999).

According to FAO (2001, as cited in Feleke et al. 2003), "over the last three decades, Ethiopia has been challenged by lack of food security. The growth trend in domestic food production matched population growth only in the 1960s".

Ethiopia is among the poorest and most food insecure countries in the world. On the United Nations Development Program's (UNDP) Human Development Index (HDI) it ranked 173rd out of 186 countries in the world (with a HDI value of 0.396) and about 60% of its population lived below the poverty line (UNDP 2013; FAO 2001). In terms of food security, it is one of the seven African countries that constitute half of the food insecure population in sub-Saharan Africa. Average calorie intake in rural areas was 1750 calories/person/day (FAO 1998a, b) which is far below the medically recommended minimum daily intake of 2100 calories/person/day. As a result, about 51% of the population was under-nourished (FAO 2001).

In Ethiopia, the trends of both per capita real consumption expenditure and the level of poverty are the two important indicators of food security. According to the results of the Household Income Consumption Expenditure (HHICE) survey, in 1999–2000 the per capita consumption expenditure in Ethiopia was estimated at Birr 1057 at constant 1995–96 prices. The real per capita consumption expenditure of the rural people was Birr 995 and that of urban people was Birr 1453. These levels of real per capita consumption expenditure were equivalent to US$ 139, 131 and 191 at the national, rural and urban levels respectively in 1999–2000 (MoFED 2002).

According to the Ministry of Finance and Economic Development's (MoFED 2012) Interim Report on Poverty Analysis the national food and non-food poverty line in Birr per adult equivalent of 2012–13 were estimated at 1985 and 3781 respectively (Table 3.1).

Ethiopia has been facing massive drought and food insecurity crises over the last decades. Droughts, recurring food shortages and famines are challenges faced by the Ethiopian people. Different studies on the current food security situation in the

Table 3.1 Total and food poverty line (average price) (in Birr)

	1995–96	2010–11
Kcal per adult per day	2200	2200
Food poverty line in Birr per adult per year	647.81	1985
Total poverty line in Birr per adult per year	1075.03	3781

Source MoFED (2012)

country show that there is growing consensus that food insecurity, famine and poverty problems are closely related in the Ethiopian context for which drought and weather-related shocks are the main driving forces (Abduselam 2017).

A number of factors can explain the trend towards increasing food insecurity in Ethiopia. The interaction between environmental degradation, high population growth, diminishing landholdings, outbreak of plant and livestock diseases, chronic shortage of cash incomes, poor social and infrastructural facilities, instability and armed conflicts, pre- and post-harvest crop losses and lack of on-farm technological innovations have led to a significant decline in productivity per household and led to food insecurity and starvation. These trends have combined with the effects of repeated droughts to substantially erode the productive assets of rural households (Ministry of Agriculture and Rural Development, MoARD 2007).

Wolday (1995, as cited in Feleke et al. 2003) explain that food insecurity and poverty in Ethiopia can be attributed to the poor performance of the agricultural sector; the poor performance of the agricultural sector in turn is attributed to both policy and non-policy factors. Among the non-policy factors, recurrent droughts is the most important reason for food shortages in Ethiopia. Among the policy factors are some ill-conceived development policies that were implemented before 1991.

A large portion of the country's population is affected by chronic and transitory food insecurity. More than 41% of the Ethiopian population lived below the poverty line and above 31 million people were under-nourished (World Food Program, WFP 2014). The situation of chronically food insecure people is becoming severe. Similarly, the number of food insecure people in the country has also increased—it was estimated at 2.9 million in 2014 and 4.5 million in August 2015 which more than doubled to 10.2 million at the end of the year; 27 million Ethiopians became food insecure as a result of the 2015 El Niño drought and 18.1 million were dependent on food relief assistance in 2016 out of which 7.9 million were supported by the Ethiopian government's productive safety net program (SNP).

3.3 Models

3.3.1 Measuring Household Food Security

Assessing food security is difficult as there are no universally established indicators that serve as measuring tools. Food security requires multi-dimensional considerations since it is influenced by different inter-related socioeconomic, environmental and political factors. Because of this problem, assessing, analyzing and monitoring food security follows different approaches.

Maxwell (1996a, b) states that a complete analysis of food security is challenged by situations in which there are variable household compositions, the harvest of subsistence production is piecemeal and this is neither measured nor recorded and there are also differing income sources which household members do not want to disclose. Hence, measuring food security in a valid, reliable and cost-effective manner is a problem for researchers. Besides, the question of access to food is addressed through households, as a household is a sound logical social unit. This requires details about a household's consumption and needs and the dynamics of intra-household resource allocations that affect distribution and procurement of food.

As Feleke et al. (2003) state, "two objective methods of food security measurement have been widely used in most food security studies: Consumption level of a given household during a given period (disappearance) and the calorie content of a 24-hour diet recall".

Along with the development of the concept of food security, a number of food security indicators have also been identified to make it possible to monitor the food situation. These include food supply indicators (meteorological data, information on natural resources, agricultural production data, market information, information on pest damage and regional conflict); food access indicators (diversification of income sources, change of food source, access to credit, sale of production assets and migration) and outcome indicators (household budget and expenditure, food consumption frequency, nutritional status and storage estimates). These indicators are important for taking decisions on possible interventions and timely responses (Debebe 1995).

Chung et al. (1997) identify and propose two types of indicators at individual and household levels. First, generic indicators which can be collected in a number of different settings and are derived from a well-defined conceptual framework of food security. Second, location specific indicators which are typically carried out only within a particular study area because of unique agro-climatic, cultural or socioeconomic factors. Location-specific indicators can be identified only from a detailed understanding of local conditions by using qualitative data collection methods while the generic indicators are drawn from food security literature and tested using statistical methods.

Haile et al. (2005) used the disappearance method in the Koro Degaga district of Ethiopia to determine calorie consumption at the household level. Accordingly, they calculated calorie availability from cereals for a given household by accounting for own production and net transaction in a given period. What came into and out of the household door was accounted to arrive at the disappearance. Then what had disappeared was converted to total calorie consumption by a conversion unit.

We employ the disappearance method and compute it in stages. The first stage is conversion of different sources of grains into equivalent calories by a given conversion rate so that the different types of grains are standardized in similar units of kcal enabling additions and subtractions. Second, as Haile et al. (2005) state, "the medically recommended levels of calories per adult equivalent are used to determine calorie demand for each household. Third, the differences between calorie availability and calorie demand for households is used to determine a household's food security status." They add, "households whose per capita available calories were found to be greater than their calorie demand were regarded as food secure (1), while households experiencing a calorie deficit were regarded as food insecure and they were assigned a value of 0".

3.3.2 Modeling Types

3.3.2.1 Theoretical Model

Following the modeling of production and consumption behaviors of a rural household by Strauss (1983), Barnum and Squire (1979) and Yotopoulos (1983), we model the extent of household food security within the framework of consumer demand and production theories. Households derive utility from the consumption of food through the satisfaction found in a set of taste characteristics and the health effects of the nutrients consumed. Among the various nutrients derived from the consumption of food, only calories are considered in our study.

Following Strauss (1983) we specify the household utility function as:

$$U = U(F_i, F_j, F_m, l) \qquad (3.1)$$

where, F_i and F_j are home produced goods consumed by the household; F_m is a market-purchased good consumed by the household; and l is leisure. For the sake of a simplistic exposition, only three goods and leisure are considered in the model. The results can be generalized to more goods (Faridi and Naimul 2010; Feleke et al. 2003). The household, as both a producer (firm) and a consumer, is assumed to maximize its utility from the consumption of these goods subject to farm production, income and time constraints specified as:

$$G(Q_i, Q_j, L, R, A^0, K^0) = 0 \qquad (3.2)$$

$$P_i(Q_i - F_i) + P_j(Q_j - F_j) - P_m F_m - w(L - L_f) + N = 0 \qquad (3.3)$$

$$T = L_f + l \qquad (3.4)$$

Adopting the definition given by Feleke et al. (2003) we have the following specifications: $G(.)$ is an implicit production function that is assumed to be well-behaved (twice differentiable, increasing in output, decreasing in inputs and strictly convex); Q_i and Q_j are the vectors of the quantities of the goods produced on farm; L is total labor input on the farm; R is farm technology; A^0 is the household's fixed quantity of land; K^0 is the fixed stock of capital; P_i is price of good i; P_j is the price of good j; P_m is the price of a market-purchased good; (Q_i-F_i) and (Q_j-F_j) are marketed surpluses of goods i and j respectively; w is the wage rate; L_f is the household labor supply for on-farm use; N is non-farm income which adjusts to ensure that Equation 3 equals 0 and T is total time available to the household to allocate between work and leisure.

Income and time constraints can be combined into one by incorporating the time constraint (Eq. 3.4) into the income constraint (Eq. 3.3) as:

$$P_i(Q_i - F_i) + P_j(Q_j - F_j) - P_m F_m - w(L - T + l) + N = 0 \tag{3.5}$$

Rearranging Eq. 3.5 gives the following expression:

$$P_i F_i + P_j F_j + P_m F_m + wl = P_i Q_i + P_j Q_j + wT - wL + N \tag{3.6}$$

The left-hand side of Eq. 3.6 is household expenditure on food and leisure and the right-hand side is the 'full' income equation. The expenditure side includes purchases of its own farm-produced good i ($P_i F_i$), the household's purchase of its own farm-produced good j ($P_j F_j$), the household's purchase of the market good ($P_m F_m$) and the household's purchase of its own leisure time (wl). The full income side consists of the value of total agricultural production $P_i Q_i$ and $P_j Q_j$, the value of the household's entitlement of time wT, the value of labor on the farm including hired labor wL and non-farm income N.

The lagrangian is:

$$Max\ \psi = U\left(F_i, F_j, F_m, l\ \right) + \lambda[(P_i Q_i + P_j Q_j + wT - wL + N) - (P_i F_i + P_j F_j$$
$$+ P_m F_m + wl)] + \mu\left[G\left(Q_i, Q_j, L, R, A^0, K^0\right)\right]$$
$$\tag{3.7}$$

Following Strauss (1983), from the first order conditions the relationship between production and consumption can be established as:

$$\left(\frac{\partial U}{\partial l} \middle/ \frac{\partial U}{\partial F_i}\right) = \frac{w}{P_i} = \left(\frac{-\partial G}{\partial L} \middle/ \frac{\partial G}{\partial Q_i}\right) = \frac{\partial Q_i}{\partial L} \tag{3.8}$$

$$\left(\frac{\partial U}{\partial F_i} \middle/ \frac{\partial U}{\partial F_j}\right) = \frac{P_i}{P_j} = \left(\frac{\partial G}{\partial Q_i} \middle/ \frac{\partial G}{\partial Q_j}\right) = \frac{-\partial Q_i}{\partial Q_j} \tag{3.9}$$

An important property of this model is its recursiveness in the sense that production decisions are made first and subsequently used in allocating the full income between consumption of goods and leisure (Strauss 1983). A decision about the consumption of the bundle (F_i, F_j) is influenced by the decision to produce the quantities (Q_i, Q_j).

As a consumer, the household maximizes its utility by equating (Eq. 3.8) the marginal rate of substitution between leisure and consumption of good i to w/P_i. In Eq. 3.9, the household maximizes its utility by equating the marginal rate of substitution between the two goods (F_i and F_j) to the price ratio.

Given the assumption of 'separability' mathematically the production and consumption-side equations can be derived separately. Starting with the production side, the first order conditions can be solved for the input demand (L*) and output supply (Q*) in terms of all prices, the wage rate, technology, fixed land and capital as:

$$L^* \left(P_i P_j w, R, A^0 K^0 \right) \tag{3.10}$$

and

$$Q^* = Q^* \left(P_i P_j w, R, A^0 K^0 \right) \tag{3.11}$$

The solutions in Eqs. 3.10 and 3.11 involve the decision that will rule for the quantities of labor input used and the output produced (production-side). After the optimum level of labor is chosen, the value of full income when profits have been maximized (under the assumption of maximized profit π^*) can be obtained by substituting L* and Q* into the right-hand side of the income constraint in Eq. 3.6 as:

$$Y^* = P_i Q_i^* + P_j Q_j^* + wT - wL^* + N \tag{3.12}$$

and

$$Y^* = wT + \pi^* \left(P_i P_j w, R, A^0 K^0 \right) + N \tag{3.13}$$

where, Y* is the 'full' income under the assumption of maximized profit, π^*.

The first order conditions can be solved for consumption demand in terms of prices, the wage rate and income as:

$$F_k = F_k \left(P_i, P_j, P_m, w, Y^* \right) \tag{3.14}$$

where, k = I, j, m.

These solutions involve decisions about the quantities of goods and leisure consumed (consumption demand-side). The three equations (Eqs. 3.10, 3.11 and 3.14) give a complete picture of the economic behavior of the farm household. They are combined through the profit effect. This occurs in semi-subsistence households in the study area where income is determined by the households' production activities, implying that changes in factors influencing production also change income which in turn affects consumption behavior. Incorporating demographic factors (D), the household utility function of Eq. 3.1 can be rewritten as:

$$U = U(F_i, F_j, F_m, 1, D) \tag{3.15}$$

and the demand for food indicated in Eq. 3.14 becomes:

$$F_k = F_k[P_i, P_j, P_m, w, Y^*(w, R, A^0, K^0, N), D] \tag{3.16}$$

where, k = i, j, m.

3.3.2.2   Empirical Model

Having determined the demand for both home-produced and market-purchased goods, now it is possible to calculate the amount of calories (C_i) available in the respective food items. Given that the indicator of food security is defined by calorie availability (C_i) and consumption needs of calories γ, household food security is determined by the differences between calorie availability and needs. Calorie availability is calculated from Eq. 3.16 using calorie conversion factors. The needs are computed based on the requirement of the family members depending on age, sex, etc.

Defining $C_I^* = C_i - \gamma_i$, where C_i is the calorie availability determined from Eq. 3.16 and γ is the consumption needs for the ith household, $C_i^* > 0$ corresponds to the consumption demand exceeding the household calorie needs and thus the household is 'food secure' while $C_i^* < 0$ corresponds to the consumption demand failing to meet the household's calorie needs indicates that the household is 'food insecure.' Hence, assuming a linear function we can write the unobserved calorie availability/consumption demand as:

$$C_i* = \sum_{j=1}^{n=k} \beta_i X_{ij} + \varepsilon_i \tag{3.17}$$

where, X_{ij} are explanatory variables indicated in Eq. 3.16 and ε_i is the error term.

The household observed to be food secure ($Z_i = 1$) is assumed to have $C_i^* \geq 0$; (the ith household has a consumption demand or calorie availability greater than or equal to its needs) while the household observed to be food insecure ($Z_i = 0$) is assumed to have $C_i^* < 0$, has a consumption demand/calorie availability less than its needs.

Now, since the observed dependent variable Z_i is a discrete variable, the food security model can be cast as a qualitative response model. When the dependant variable is dichotomous the logit and probit models will guarantee that the estimated probabilities will lie between the logical limits 0 and 1. Because of this and other facilities, the logit and probit models are the most frequently used models when the dependent variable is dichotomous (Gujarati 1995; Maddala 1989).

Therefore, our study applied the binary logit model to identify the determinants of food secure and insecure groups. Following Gujarati (1995) the functional form of the logit model is specified as:

$$\pi(X) = \frac{1}{1 + e^{-(\beta_0 + \beta_i X_i)}} \tag{3.18}$$

We can write Eq. 3.18 as:

$$\pi(X) = \frac{1}{1 + e^{-Zi}} \tag{3.19}$$

where, $\pi(x) =$ is the probability of being food secure.

$$Z_i = \beta_0 + \beta_1 X_1 + \beta_2 X_2 + \cdots + \beta_n X_n$$

β_0 is an intercept
$\beta_1, \beta_2, \cdots, \beta_n$ are slopes of the equation
X_i n explanatory variables in our study.

The probability that a given household is food secure is expressed by Eq. 3.19. Similarly, the probability for being food insecure is gives as:

$$1 - \pi(X) = \frac{1}{1 + e^{Zi}} \tag{3.20}$$

Therefore, the two equations can be written together as:

$$\frac{\pi(X)}{1 - \pi(X)} = \frac{\frac{1}{1+e^{-Zi}}}{\frac{1}{1+e^{Zi}}} = e^{Zi} \tag{3.21}$$

Then $\frac{\pi(X)}{1-\pi(X)}$ is simply the odds ratio in favor of food security.

Again, taking the natural log of Eq. 3.21 yields the following expression:

$$L_i = \ln\left\langle \frac{\pi(X)}{1 - \pi(X)} \right\rangle = Z_i \tag{3.22}$$

where, as expressed above, Z_I is

$$Z_i = \beta_0 + \beta_1 X_1 + \beta_2 X_2 + \cdots + \beta_n X_n$$

And if the disturbance term (ε_i) is introduced, the logit model becomes:

$$Z_i = \beta_0 + \beta_1 X_1 + \beta_2 X_2 + \cdots + \beta_n X_n + \varepsilon_i \tag{3.23}$$

L_I is log of the odds ratio which is not only linear in X_i but also linear in the parameters.
X_i Vector of relevant explanatory variables.

Finally, if the conditional probabilities are calculated for each sample household, the 'partial' effects of the continuous individual variables on household food security can be calculated using:

$$\frac{\partial \pi(X_i)}{\partial X_{ij}} = \pi(X_i)\langle(1 - \pi(X_i))\rangle\beta_j \tag{3.24}$$

Note also that the 'partial' effects of the discrete variables will be calculated by taking the difference of the mean probabilities estimated for the respective discrete variable, $X_i = 0$ and $X_i = 1$.

3.4 Data and Variable Measurement

The primary data used in our study is adapted from a survey carried out by the district for a socioeconomic analysis of the woreda in 2016 (Socio-Economic profile of Lode Hetosa 2016). Our analysis is based on data from a sample of 240 households selected using a two- stage sampling technique. The first stage is the selection of kebeles[3] which is followed by the selection of representative sample households from the selected kebeles.

Food security: The dependent variable is household food security (HFS) status. We use the consumption based (disappearance method) rather than the income-based measure of HFS. This is because consumption captures long-run welfare better and it better reflects a household's ability to meet its basic needs. Consumption is preferred for measuring HFS than income as it is less vulnerable to seasonality and life-cycle, less vulnerable to measurement errors because respondents have less reasons to lie, it is closer to the utility that people effectively extract from income and for the poor most of the income is consumed (CSA 2005; FAO 2002). In addition, the arguments for and against income and consumption as an appropriate welfare measure are summarized in Haughton and Khandker (2009: 30).[4]

Following this approach, household food security status was set on the basis of the calorie content of consumed food items. For this, first the bundle of food items consumed by households (for 7 days) was listed and measured in terms of 100-g solid food using conversion factors and liters for the liquid and semi-liquid food items. Second, for each food item the calorie content value was assigned based on the Ethiopian Nutrition and Health Research Institute's (ENHRI) 1968–97 (Part III) food composition table. Total net calories (TNC) was estimated based on the total edible portions of weights of consumed food items for each household. Third, due to differences in household composition in terms of age and sex, there was a need to

---

[3]Kebele is the lowest administrative unit in the country.

[4]Further discussion may be found in Hentschel and Lanjouw (1996), Blundell and Preston (1998) and Donaldson (1992).

adjust the household size to adult equivalent household size. Following MoFED (2013) and other literature in the area, 2200 kcal per day was assumed to be the minimum energy demand enabling an adult to lead a healthy and moderately active life.

Explanatory Variables: The following explanatory variables were considered as affecting the status of household food security status. The '+' and '−' signs are positive and negative expected effect on food security levels respectively.

Adoption Status (AS, +): Adoption refers to using improved wheat varieties in recommended spacing; it adopts code 1 otherwise 0 as many studies indicate that adoption influences household's well-being positively and significantly (Wu et al. 2010). The sex of the household head (SEX, +) variable is a nominal variable as used as the dummy (1 if male, 0 otherwise). Due to the lack of labor in female headed households, they are forced to rent their land as a share crop and plots controlled by women are farmed much less intensively than similar plots in households controlled by men.[5] The household head's education (EDUHH, +) variable is measured in terms of years of schooling and is assumed to increase farmers' ability to obtain, process and use relevant information. Family size (FAMSIZE, −) is measured by the number of members in a household. Food requirements increase with the number of persons in a household. The farming experience (FAREXP, ±) variable is measured in the number of years since a respondent started farming on his own. Farmers with more experience appear to often have full information and better knowledge and are able to evaluate the advantages of technology. It may also be the case that older farmers are reluctant to adopt new technologies. Participation in off-farm activities (PAOFA, +) off-farm work was measured based on whether or not the household had an off-farm job. A household with no off-farm job took the value 0 and a household with an off-farm job took the value 1. Annual farm income (FAI, +) refers to the total annual earnings of the family from sale of agricultural produce such as sale of crops, livestock and livestock products after meeting family requirements. The access to market (DISMACE, −) variable was measured in kilometers. The longer the time taken to get to the market, the less frequently will a farmer visit the market and hence he is less likely to get market information.

The farm size (FARSIZE, +) variable is the total farmland owned by a household as measured in hectares. It is expected that households with larger farmlands are more likely to be food secure as opposed to those with small farmlands. The number of livestock (LIVST, +) variable is the total number of livestock owned and was measured in terms of the tropical livestock unit (TLU). Access to credit (ACCTC, +) is measured in terms of whether respondents had access to credit sources and the possibility of getting credit. In other words, households which had access to credit are given value 1 and 0 otherwise. The participation in field days (FIELD, +) variable is measured by the number of times the farmer has participated

---

[5]For more discussion on gender and agricultural production see Udry (1996).

in field days in the last five years. Number of oxen owned (NUMOX, +) is mea-sured in terms of the number of oxen that a farmer owns.

3.5 Results and Discussions

3.5.1 Descriptive Results

Our study examined supply and demand side factors affecting food security in the study area and found out the effects of hypothesized independent variables on the dependent variables. Based on a calorie requirement of 2200 kcal per day per person, out of the 240 (55 females and 185 males) sample rural households in the study area 129 (53.75%) and 111 (46.25%) were found to be food secure and food insecure respectively.

3.5.1.1 Supply-Side Determinants

The first supply side variable is the education level of the household. Education normally increases the probability of being food secure. The survey results approved this hypothesis and indicated that education was statistically significant at less than a 5% level of probability. Average years of schooling was found to be 4.5 years with a standard deviation of 3.35. Food secure households had five years of schooling on average while food insecure households had four years of schooling on average.

In rural areas landholding matters for production and consumption. Land is perhaps the single most important resource, as it is a base for any economic activity especially in the rural and agricultural sectors. Farm size influenced a household's decision to adopt new technologies. The average total landholding of the sample households was almost 2.31 ha. The average total landholding of the food secure households was 2.51 ha whereas for the food insecure group it was 2.07 ha. The independent sample t-test revealed that the mean difference between the two groups was statistically significant (Table 3.2).

Table 3.2 Summary statistics (continuous variables) of supply-side factors of sample respondents (N = 240)

Variable	Food secure		Food insecure		Total		t-value
	Mean	SD	Mean	SD	Mean	SD	
Education (year)	5	3.23	4	3.42	4.5	3.35	2.31*
Land holding (ha)	2.51	1.33	2.07	1.00	2.31	1.17	2.76**
field days (no. of visits)	1.52	0.94	1.41	0.77	1.47	0.86	1.02

Source Author's computation
* and ** Indicate statistically significant at the 5 and 1% probability levels

Access to credit is one way of improving farmers' access to new production systems in which agricultural output increases. Farmers' ability to purchase inputs such as improved seeds and fertilizers is particularly important. The formal sources of credit in Ethiopia are the Office of Agriculture, service cooperatives and the Ethiopian Development Bank (Rahmeto 2007). Farmers who have access to credit can minimize their financial constraints and buy inputs more readily. The results of credit accessibility indicate that out of the farmers surveyed 74.6% had access to credit. An analysis of the results shows that 45% of the food secure and 29.6% of the food insecure households had access to credit. The Chi-square test showed a significant association between access to credit and food security.

Adopters of improved seeds along with improved agronomic practices were more likely to be food secure than non-adopters. Supporting this hypothesis the Chi-square test showed a significant association between technology adoption and the food security status of the respondents. This finding is in line Tsegaye and Bekele (2012).

3.5.1.2 Demand-Side Determinants

Out of the 240 respondents 77.1% were male-headed and 22.9% were female-headed households. Among male-headed households 53.52% were food secure and 46.48 were food insecure. In female-headed households 54.55 and 45.45% were food secure and food insecure respectively. The Chi-square test indicates that the relationship between food security and sex of the household head was insignificant (Table 3.3).

Households in the sample had an average family size of 5.43 persons per household. Food secure households had an average family size of 5.5 while food insecure farmers had 5.36 members. The mean difference between food secure and food insecure households in relation to family size was found to be statistically insignificant (Table 3.4).

Another important variable in this category is farming experience of the sample households. Farmers with more experience often had full information and better knowledge and were able to evaluate the advantages of the technology considered. However, farmers with more experience may also be reluctant to new farming systems. But as shown in Table 3.4 the results of this statistical test show that there was no relationship between farm experience and food security.

Total farm income was the main and dominant source of earnings for the sample households. Household farm income in 2016 was estimated based on the sale of crops produced, livestock and livestock products. The major cash income for sample households in the study area was from sale of crops like wheat, barley, teff and vegetables including onions and tomatoes (Tsegaye 2011). As Table 3.4 shows the average farm income of the sample households was Etb 42,823[6] for the survey

---

[6]Etb is the official (national) currency of Ethiopia, Birr.

Table 3.3 Summary statistics (dummy variables) of supply-side factors of sample respondents (N = 240)

Variable	Food secure		Food insecure		Total		χ2-value
	No	%	No	%	No	%	
Adoption							13.12***
Adopter	104	43.3	65	27.1	169	70.4	
Non-adopter	25	10.4	46	19.2	71	29.6	
Credit service							12.28***
User	108	45	71	29.6	179	74.6	
Non-user	21	8.8	40	16.7	61	25.4	

Source Author's computation
***Significant at the 1% probability level, total % is calculated from the total sample

Table 3.4 Summary statistics (continuous variables) of demand-side factors of sample respondents (N = 240)

Variable	Food secure		Food insecure		Total		t-value
	Mean	SD	Mean	SD	Mean	SD	
FAMSIZE	5.5	2.59	5.36	2.35	5.43	2.47	0.59
FAREXP	25.1	11.94	25.88	11.35	25.49	11.65	0.53
FAI	45,970	43,165	39,675	33,416	42,823	38,291	1.24
DISMACE	4.74	2.46	4.30	2.18	4.52	2.32	1.44
LIVST	6.84	3.39	5.69	3.17	6.26	3.28	2.69*
NUMOX	2.7	0.97	2.14	0.99	2.16	0.98	0.21

Source Author's computation
*Indicates statistically significant at the 1% probability level

year. The mean annual farm income of food secure households (Etb 45,970) was more than that of food insecure households (Etb 39,675) and the mean difference was Etb 6295. But the descriptive statistical test revealed that this difference in farm income was not statistically significant.

Another basic income source of the sample households in the study area was participation in off-farm activities. Out of the total households interviewed 57.5% had participated in off-farm activities. Among the households which had participated in off-farm activities, 70.3% were food secure households. Supporting the priori expectation, participation in off-farm activities had a significant relationship with food security (Table 3.5).

Regarding the distance from home to the nearest marketplace, sample farmers reported that on average they had to travel 4.52 km with standard deviation of 2.32 km. Mean distance traveled to the nearest market center by food secure and food insecure respondents was 4.74 and 4.3 km respectively. The results of the independent sample T-test revealed that there was no statistically mean difference among food secure and food insecure households.

Table 3.5 Summary statistics (dummy variables) of demand-side factors of sample respondents (N = 240)

Variable	Food secure		Food insecure		Total		χ2-value
	No	%	No	%	No	%	
Sex							0.018
Male	99	41.2	86	35.8	185	77.1	
Female	30	12.5	25	10.4	55	22.9	
Off-farm							35.7***
Yes	97	40.4	41	17.1	138	57.5	
No	32	13.3	70	29.2	102	42.5	

Source Author's computation
***Significant at the 1% probability level. Total % is calculated from the total sample

In rural areas livestock holdings play a big role in determining household status. In the study area mixed farming was practiced with crop and livestock production (Tsegaye 2011). Each household owned at least one or more types of livestock and different sizes of land for crop and livestock production. Livestock is an important source for farmers' food, traction power and manure and serves as a source of income through sale of animals and their products. The survey results on livestock holdings of sampled households are given in Table 3.4. The independent sample test results support the hypothesis that a person who owned more TLU was more likely to be food secure than the one who owned less TLU.

In rural areas, oxen is an important indicator of a household's wealth position. Oxen are an important source of traction power and they also serve as a source of income. The respondents on average owned 2.16 oxen. Food secure and insecure households owned 2.17 and 2.14 oxen respectively. The independent sample T-test revealed that there was no significant difference between the two groups with regard to oxen ownership.

3.5.2 Model Characteristics

We used the likelihood ratio Chi-square statistic to test the dependence of food security on the selected variables in the model. Under the null hypothesis (H_0) where there was only one parameter, the intercept (β_0), the value of the restricted log likelihood function was -152.76 while under the alternative hypothesis (H_1) with all the parameters, the value of the unrestricted log likelihood function was -67.13. The model Chi-square statistic, which is the difference in the values of the two log likelihood functions was 85.63. It was highly significant ($P < 0.00$) indicating that at least one of the parameters in the equation was non-zero. Thus, the log odds of household food security are related to the independent variables.

Concerning the predictive efficacy of the model, out of the 240 sample households included in the model, 213 were correctly predicted or there was a 88.75%

Table 3.6 ML estimates and ME of the binary logit model

Variables	Coefficients	Odds ratio	Z-values	ME
CONSTANT	−3.8976***		2.91	
SEX	0.4262	1.5244	0.84	0.0467
EDUHH	0.1823***	1.999	3.05	0.0202
FAMSIZE	0.0875	1.0915	0.59	0.0097
FAREXP	−0.0484*	0.9527	1.70	−0.0054
PAOFA	2.5023***	12.2111	5.01	0.3804
FAI	−0.0003***	0.9999	2.62	−3.36E − 06
DISMACE	−0.8659***	0.4207	4.25	−0.0961
FARSIZE	0.3355*	1.3987	1.83	0.0373
LIVST	0.3365***	1.4000	3.49	0.0374
ACCTC	1.0845**	2.9578	1.99	0.1001
FIELD	−0.1397	0.8696	0.61	−0.0155
AS	2.7330***	15.3786	3.97	0.2257
NUMOX	0.2916	1.3386	1.09	0.0324

Chi-squared = 74.82***
Prediction success = 88.75%
Pseudo R^2 = 0.5606

ML Maximum Likelihood, *ME* Marginal Effect. *Source* Author's computation
***, **and * are significant at less than the 1, 5 and 10% probability levels respectively

prediction. The Chi-square showed a significant association between observed food security/insecurity and model prediction of food security/insecurity (χ^2 = 74.82; $P < 0.00$) (Table 3.6).

3.5.2.1 Parameter Estimates of Determinants of Food Security

Among the 13 factors considered in the model, nine were found to have a significant impact in determining household food security—education level, farm experience, participation in off-farm activities, annual farm income, market distance, landholding, livestock holding, access to credit service and technology adoption. Among the significant factors, education levels, landholding, technology adoption and access to credit service were supply-side determinants while farm experience, participation in off-farm activities, annual farm income, market distance and livestock holding were demand-side determinants.

Supply-Side Determinants

Out of the five supply-side factors included in the model four were found to have a significant relationship with household food security—technology adoption, education levels, landholding and access to credit services.

Keeping the other variables in the model constant, technology adoption was positively and significantly related to the probability of food security, implying that the likelihood of food security increased with farmers' use of agricultural technologies. The odds ratio of 15.37 implies that other things being constant the odds ratio in favor of being food secure was 15.37 times higher for adopters as compared to non-adopters of technology. According to Feleke et al. (2003), "Such a significant effect of technology adoption on probability of food security can be explained in two ways. One is that the adoption of a package of high yielding varieties along with improved agronomic practices directly increased food availability at the household level" and "the second reason is related to the cash income effect. An adopter was better off than a non-adopter as an adopter earned more income than a non-adopter because of market surplus" (Also see Tsegaye and Bekele 2012). The marginal effect of adoption was 0.23 which indicates that the probability of being food secure increased by approximately 23% as a household adopted the package.

Education was positively and significantly related to the probability of food security in the study area. The possible reasons for this include literate farm household heads were more willing to adopt better production technologies, accepted technical advice from extension workers and diversified their sources of income than illiterate ones. As a result, literacy reduced the risk of food insecurity among the sample households. Keeping other factors constant, the odds ratio in favor of food security increased by a factor equal to 1.9 as the household head became literate. The marginal effect of education of 0.02 indicates that the probability of being food secure increased by about 2% as the household's grade increased by one.

Another supply-side factor found to have a significant impact on household food security was landholding (farm size). A positive and significant relationship was found between farm size and the probability of food security, implying that the probability of food security increased with farm size. The odds ratio of landholding was 1.39, indicating that the probability of being food secure was 1.39 times higher for a one hectare increase in farm size.

The final supply-side factor found to have a significant impact on household food security was access to credit service. A positive and significant relationship was found between access to credit services and the probability of food security, implying that the probability of food security increased with credit services. The odds ratio of credit services was 2.96, indicating that the probability of being food secure was 2.96 times higher for credit users as compared to households who did not have access to credit services.

Demand-Side Determinants

Among the eight demand-side factors included in the model, farm experience, participation in off-farm activities, annual farm income, market distance and live-stock holding were found to have a significant relationship with household food security.

Farm experience was found to have a negative and significant relationship with households' status of food security. This means that an increase in the farm experience of the household head decreased the likelihood of the household becoming food secure. The odds ratio of farm experience of 0.95 implies that keeping other factor unchanged the likelihood of the household in favor of food security decreased by a factor of 0.95 as the farming experience of the household increased by one year. This is possible because as farmers get more experience in farming operations, they continue using old and traditional technologies which result in low production.

As anticipated participation in off-farm work also had a significant impact on the probability of household food security. The odds ratio of off-farm activities of 12.21 implies that other things remaining constant households who participated in off-farm activities were about 12.21 times food secure as compared to those who did not have this access.

Annual farm income was negatively and significantly related to the probability of household food security. The odds ratio of this variable was 0.99. This means that each unit increase in annual farm income (1 Birr) decreased the probability of food security by a factor of 0.99. Such a negative relationship is explained through the income effect of a price change from the producers' standpoint. Given that the sample farm households are producers, an increase in annual farm income this year will increase aggregate production in the next year and increase market supply and depress prices given that the price elasticity of demand for most products in developing countries is inelastic (Foster 1992, cited in Feleke et al. 2003). A decline in price reduces producers' income the next time and reduces food security.

The other possible reason for a negative relationship between annual farm income and food security is that most high-income farmers engaged in commercial and cash crop farming, especially onion production. But the prices of such products are highly unstable. There is evidence that the prices of onions are high during cultivation and low during harvest time. These low prices reduce household incomes the next time which reduces food security.

Physical access to the market, the distance between the household's location and the nearest market center were also found to have a negative and significant relationship with food security. The odds ratio of market distance was 0.42 implying, ceteris paribus, in favor of food security decreasing 0.42 times if market distance increased by one kilometer. As the marginal effect shows, the probability of being food secure decreased by 9.61% with a one kilometer increase in market distance.

The final demand-side factor found to have a significant impact on household food security was livestock ownership (TLU). A positive and significant relationship was found between livestock holding and the probability of food security. The odds ratio of livestock holding was 1.4, indicating that the probability of food security increased by 1.4 for a one-unit increase in livestock holding measured in TLU. With a one-unit increase in livestock holding in TLU terms, the probability of being food secure increased about 3.74% other things remaining constant. In the rural context, livestock holding is an important indicator of a household's wealth position.

3.6 Summary and Policy Implications

3.6.1 Summary

Our study analyzed supply and demand-side determinants of household food security status in Lode Hetosa district in Arsi zone. It described socioeconomic characteristics of the food security levels of sample household groups by using descriptive statistics. Based on the calorie requirements of 2200 kcal per day per person, out of the 240 sample rural households in the study area, Lode Hetosa woreda, 129 (53.75%) and 111 (46.25%) households were found to be food secure and food insecure respectively. Out of the five supply-side factors hypothesized to have an impact on household food security, four (technology adoption, education level, landholding and access to credit services) were found to have a significant relationship with household food security. Two of the eight demand-side factors (livestock holding and participation in off-farm activities) were positively associated with food security levels of the sample households.

We identified supply and demand-side factors that affect household food security using the binary logit model of regression. The results of the logistic regression model indicated that nine of the thirteen variables (education level, farm experience, participation in off-farm activities, annual farm income, market distance, landholding, livestock holding, access to credit services and technology adoption) were statistically significant as determinants of household food security in the study area.

Education level, participation in off-farm activities, landholding, livestock holding, access to credit services and technology adoption were found to be positively related to the probability of being food secure while farm experience, annual farm income and market distance were negatively related with the probability of being food secure. Based on the magnitude of their partial effects on the probability of food security, supply-side factors were more powerful than demand-side factors in determining household food security implying that interventions focused on these factors need to get priority attention of policymakers, researchers and extension programs.

3.6.2 Policy Implications

The possible areas of intervention from the results of our study are:

Farm experience and food security were negatively related. This means that the longer a farmer has stayed in farming the more likely he is to be food insecure. Therefore, capacity building of old household heads should be done. The effect of education on household food security confirmed the significant role of this variable in the betterment of living conditions. The more the household head is educated, the higher is the probability of family members getting education and being familiar with modern technology. This increases the probability of being food secure. So, strengthening both formal and informal education and vocational or skill training should be promoted to reduce food insecurity in the study area.

Access to credit positively affected the probability of food security. It can create an opportunity to be involved in economic activities that generate revenue for households. Development partners operating in the study area should implement provisions of credit to eligible households using targeting criteria that reflect the characteristics of food insecure households. The other pressing issue related to provision of credit is the requirement of collateral and group lending procedures which discourage many households.

Adoption was found to have a robust and positive impact on food security. For agricultural technologies to be successful, farmers' attributes should be considered. Clearly understanding farmers' adoption preferences is necessary for this. A one time trial or use of an agricultural technology cannot change livelihoods thus reinforcing the need that technologies should be used on a continuous basis. Given that farmers' variety-attribute preferences determine both their propensity to use improved varieties and the chances of using them successfully adoption should satisfy the demands of different farm household types classified according to resource endowments, preferences and constraints. For this analyzing farmers' variety-attribute preferences will help target farmers' demands in developing technologies. Simply providing the technologies may create doubts in the minds of the farmers. When a new technology is introduced the options are whether extension workers want to convince farmers who what to use it (persuasive methods) or whether they seek to inform and educate farmers about different market opportunities, technical options and/or management strategies and then let them decide which option would work best for them. The latter case should be followed with some guiding principles from experts and government bodies.

Annual farm incomes and market distance were negatively related to food security. This means that the longer the distance to the nearest market center and the higher the annual farm income, the more the farmer is likely to be food insecure. Therefore, infrastructural development should be expanded and market centers established near the farm households. Further, there should be a way of disseminating market information to farmers on prices of agricultural products. Most high-income farmers engaged in commercial and cash crop farming, especially onion production. But the prices of such products are highly unstable. Hence, awareness should be created among farmers on diversifying their crops and they should be told that stable crops need to be produced to increase the food security status of rural households.

As participation in off-farm activities affected food security positively attention should be paid to facilitating ways in which rural households engage in these jobs. Landholding and livestock holding are positively related to the probability of being food secure. This implies that the more farmland and livestock that a farmer has the less he/she is food insecure. This calls for fair land distribution and good livestock health and nutrition concerns.

Our study also concluded that the supply-side determinants were more powerful than demand-side factors affecting food security. This implies that interventions focused on supply-side factors need to get priority attention by policymakers, researchers and extension programs. Hence, the government and other concerned bodies should primarily work on expansion of both formal and informal education, adoption and diffusion of modern and improved agricultural technologies, provision of credit services and farmland distribution and certification (property right).

Our study also discussed the results of an analysis with a defined scope. However, a lot of questions remained unanswered. To provide basic information on the determinants of food security, the social, political, natural and environmental dimensions in food insecurity, descriptive data on purchasing patterns of food insecure households and specific characteristics that make the poor more vulnerable to food insecurity need future researchers' attention.

References

Abafita, J., and K.R. Kim. 2014. Determinants of food security among rural households in Ethiopia: An empirical analysis. *Journal of Rural Development* 37 (2): 129–157.

Abduselam, A.M. 2017. Food security situation in Ethiopia: a review study. *International Journal of Health Economics and Policy* 2 (3): 86–96.

Abu, G.A., and A. Soom. 2016. Analysis of factors affecting food security in rural and urban farming households of Benue State, Nigeria. *International Journal of Food and Agricultural Economics* 4 (1): 55–68.

Arsi Zone Finance and Economic Development Office. 2016. *Socio-economic Profile of Arsi Zone, annual publication, 2016.*

Barnum, H., and L. Squire. 1979. A model of an agricultural household: Theory and evidence. *World Bank Occasional Papers* 27. Baltimore and London: The Johns Hopkins University Press.

Blundell, R., and I. Preston. 1998. Consumption inequality and income uncertainty. *Quarterly Journal of Economics* 113: 603–640.

CSA (Central Statistical Agency). 2005. *The 2005 national statistics.* Addis Ababa, Ethiopia.

Chung, K., L. Haddad, J. Ramakrishna, F. Riely, and F. Eiely. 1997. *Identifying the food insecure: The application of mixed-method approaches in India.* Washington, DC: International Food Policy Research Institute.

Clover, J. 2003. Food security in Sub-Saharan Africa. *African Security Review* 12 (1): 1–7.

Debebe, H. 1995. Food security: A brief review of concepts and indicators *Proceedings on the inaugural and first annual conference of the Agricultural Economics Society of Ethiopia,* Addis Ababa, Ethiopia, 8–9 June.

Donaldson, D. 1992. On the aggregation of money measures of well-being in applied welfare economics. *Journal of Agricultural and Resource Economics,* 17: 88–102.

ECA. 1992. *Food security in Africa. In The challenges of agricultural production and food security in Africa.* Addis Ababa: ECA.

Faltermeier, L., and A. Abdulai. 2006. The adoption of water conservation and intensification technologies and farm income: A propensity score analysis for rice farmers in Northern Ghana.

Faridi, R., and S. Naimul. 2010. An econometric assessment of household food security in Bangladesh. *The Bangladesh Development Studies* 33 (3): 97–111.

FAO. 1994. *The state of food and agriculture 1994.* Rome: FAO.

FAO. 1996. *World food summit: Rome declaration on world food security and world food.* Rome, Italy: FAO.

FAO. 1998. *Agriculture, food and nutrition for Africa. A resource book for teachers of agriculture.* Rome, Italy: FAO.

FAO. 1998. Crop and food supply assessment mission to Ethiopia. FAO global information and early warning system on food and agriculture. *World Food Program.*

FAO. 2001. Crop and food supply assessment mission to Ethiopia. FAO Global Information and Early Warning System on Food and Agriculture. *World Food Program.*

FAO. 2002. *The state of food insecurity: Report 2002.* Rome, Italy: Food and Agricultural Organization.

Feleke, S., R.L. Kilmer, and C. Gladwin. 2003. *Determinants of food security in southern Ethiopia.*http://ageconsearch.umn.edu/bitstream/22010/1/sp03fe02.pdf.

Getahun, B., and F. Beyene. 2014. Factors influencing rural household food insecurity: The case of Babile district, East Hararghe Zone, Ethiopia. *Journal of Development and Agricultural Economics* 6 (4): 149–158.

Gujarati, D.N. 1995. *Basic econometrics,* 3rd ed. New York: McGraw Hill Inc.

Haughton, J., and S.R. Khandker. 2009. *Handbook on poverty and inequality.* Washington, DC: The World Bank.

Hentschel, J., and P. Lanjouw. 1996. Constructing an indicator of consumption for the analysis of poverty: Principles and illustrations with reference to ecuador. *Working paper No. 124, Living standards measurement study.* Washington, DC: The World Bank.

Kidane, H., Z.G. Alemu, and G. Kundhlande. 2005. Causes of household food insecurity in Koredegaga Peasant Association, Oromiya Zone, Ethiopia. *Agrekon* 44: 543–560. https://doi.org/10.1080/03031853.2005.9523727.

Maddala, G.S. 1989. *Limited dependent and qualitative variable in econometrics.* New York: Cambridge University Press.

Mannaf, M., and Md Taj Uddin. 2014. Socioeconomic factors influencing food security status of maize growing households in selected areas of Bogra District. *The Bangladesh Journal of Agricultural Economics* 35 (1–2): 177–187.

Maxwell, S. 1996a. Food security: A post-modern perspective. *Food Policy* 21 (2): 155–170.

Maxwell, D. 1996b. Measuring food insecurity: The frequency and severity of 'coping strategies'. *Food Policy* 21: 291–303.

MoFED (Ministry of Finance and Economic Development). 2002. *Development and poverty profile of Ethiopia (analysis based on the 1999/00 HH income, consumption and expenditure and welfare monitoring unit).* Addis Ababa: Federal Democratic Republic of Ethiopia.

MoARD. 2007. *Horn of Africa consultations of food security, country report.* Addis Ababa, Ethiopia: Ministry of Agriculture and Rural Development, Government of Ethiopia.

MoFED (Ministry of Finance and Economic Development). 2012. *Ethiopia's Progress towards eradicating poverty: An interim report on poverty analysis study (2012/13).* Addis Ababa: The Federal Democratic Republic of Ethiopia.

MoFED (Ministry of Finance and Economic Development). 2013. *Development and poverty in Ethiopia*. Addis Ababa, Ethiopia: Ministry of Finance and Economic Development, Federal Democratic Republic of Ethiopia.

Rahmeto, Negash. 2007. Determinants of adoption of improved haricot bean production package in Alaba Special Woreda, Southern Ethiopia. M.Sc. thesis, Haramaya University.

Sanchez, P.A., G.L. Denning, and G. Nziguheba. 2009. The African green revolution moves forward. *Food Security* 1: 37–44.

Strauss, J. 1983. Socioeconomic determinants of food consumption and production in rural Sierra Leone: Application of an agricultural household model with several commodities. MSU International Development Papers. Department of Agricultural Economics, Michigan State University, East Lansing, Michigan.

Sultana, Anila, and Adiqa Kiani. 2011. Determinants of food security at household level in Pakistan. *African Journal of Business Management* 5 (34): 12972–12979.

The National Agricultural Research System. 1999. *NARS study of Ethiopia*. Addis Ababa.

Tsegaye, Mulugeta. 2011. Impacts of improved wheat technology adoption on households' food security in Lode Hetosa Woreda, Oromia Region. M.Sc. thesis submitted to the Department of Development Economics, Institute of Public Management and Development Studies (IPMDS). Ethiopian Civil Service University.

Tsegaye, Mulugeta, and Hundie Bekele. 2012. Impacts of adoption of improved wheat technologies on households' food consumption in Southeastern Ethiopia. Selected Poster prepared for presentation at the International Association of Agricultural Economists (IAAE) Triennial Conference, Foz do Iguaçu, Brazil, 18–24 August.

Udry, Christopher. 1996. Gender, agricultural production, and the theory of the household. *Journal of Political Economy* 104 (5): 1010–1046.

UNDP. 2013. *Human development report 2013. The Rise of the South: Human Progress in a Diverse World*. UNDP.

WFP. 2014. Global food security update: Tracking food security trends in vulnerable countries. *World Food Program*, 13.

Wu, H., S. Ding, S. Pandey, and D. Tao 2010. Assessing the impact of agricultural technology adoption on farmers' well-being in rural China. *Asian Economic Journal* 24 (2): 141–160.

Yilma, M. 2005. Measuring rural household food security status and its determinants in the Benishangul Gumuz Region, Ethiopia: The Case of Assosa Woreda. M.Sc. thesis submitted To the Department of Agricultural Economics, School Of Graduate Studies, Alemaya University.

Yotopoulos, P. 1983. *A micro economic-demographic model of the agricultural household in the Philippines*. Rome, Italy: FAO Economic and Social Development Paper.

Zakari, S., L. Ying, and B. Song. 2014. Factors influencing household food security in West Africa: The case of Southern Niger. *Sustainability* 6 (3): 1191–1202.

Chapter 4
Dynamics and Determinants of Inflation in Ethiopia

Jonse Bane

Abstract This study investigates the dynamics and determinants of inflation in Ethiopia over the period 1975–2015 using annual data from the National Bank of Ethiopia (NBE), the Central Statistical Agency (CSA) and the Ministry of Finance and Economic Cooperation (MOFED). The study uses the ARDL inflation model by synthesizing monetarist and structuralist views of the determinants of inflation in the country. The findings show that the major determinants of dynamics of inflation in Ethiopia are both monetary sector and structural factors. Specifically, the ARDL model shows that monetary determinants of inflation are money supply and the real interest rate. Inflation in Ethiopia both in the short and long run is not only a monetary phenomenon (such as money expansion via credit and money printing; government spending and the real interest rate) but also the result of structural factors like shocks to the real sector (mainly agricultural GDP as the agriculture sector dominates the country's GDP). This study's policy implications are that the Government of Ethiopia needs to follow conservative fiscal and monetary policies. It is also important to enhance economic growth as higher economic growth reduces inflationary pressures.

Keywords Inflation · Dynamics · Determinants · ARDL · Ethiopia

4.1 Introduction

As in other countries, the central objective of macroeconomic policies in Ethiopia is macroeconomic stability (that is, better and stable economic growth and lower inflation and unemployment). Price stability is one of the factors for determining the growth rate of an economy; hence, the National Bank of Ethiopia (NBE) implements monetary policies to maintain inflation at a desirable rate. As economic and institutional determinants (central bank's independence) of inflation

J. Bane (✉)
Department of Economics, Addis Ababa University, Addis Ababa, Ethiopia
e-mail: jonseboka@yahoo.com

© Springer Nature Singapore Pte Ltd. 2018   67
A. Heshmati and H. Yoon (eds.), *Economic Growth and Development in Ethiopia*, Perspectives on Development in the Middle East and North Africa (MENA) Region, https://doi.org/10.1007/978-981-10-8126-2_4

have implications for monetary policy, there is a large and growing literature on the determinants of inflation (Catao and Terrones 2005).

The classical school of thought considers inflation as an outcome of monetary expansion and the quantity theory of money as an explanation. Monetarists hold money supply as the sole cause of inflation. Friedman is the biggest proponent of this school of thought who regarded inflation everywhere as a monetary phenomenon. The post-Keynesian structuralists, however, emphasize various factors for explaining changes in the price level. Thus, for post-Keynesian structuralists some of the drivers of soaring global prices (mainly commodity prices) are long term factors like economic growth and demographic changes in association with short term constraints such as climate change, price speculation, increasing oil prices and export restrictions in several countries.

4.2 The Macroeconomic Environment and Inflation Trends in Ethiopia

Ethiopia has experienced remarkable growth over the last decade registering an average GDP growth rate of about 11% over 2005–15 with the highest growth rate (13.6%) in 2005 and the lowest (8.8%) in 2010 (Fig. 4.1). Agriculture, which accounts for over 40% of the country's GDP and nearly 85% of its employment, grew by 8.4%. However, despite this growth about 30% of Ethiopia's 84.7 million people lived below the official poverty line in 2011 (Government of Ethiopia 2012), but it is likely that an even larger proportion experienced extended periods of poverty due to shocks. The rise in food inflation, for instance, is likely to have increased urban poverty.

Even if Ethiopia has had a historically low inflation rate (compared to other developing countries), its recent impressive growth has been accompanied by high inflation. That is, regardless of remarkable GDP growth in general and agricultural

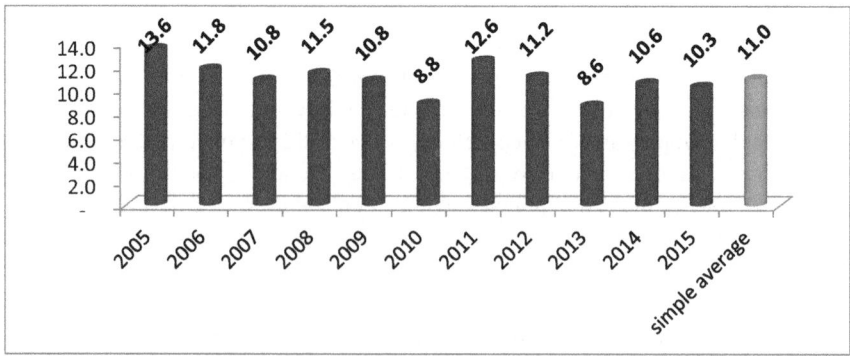

Fig. 4.1 Trends in real GDP growth rate (2005–15)

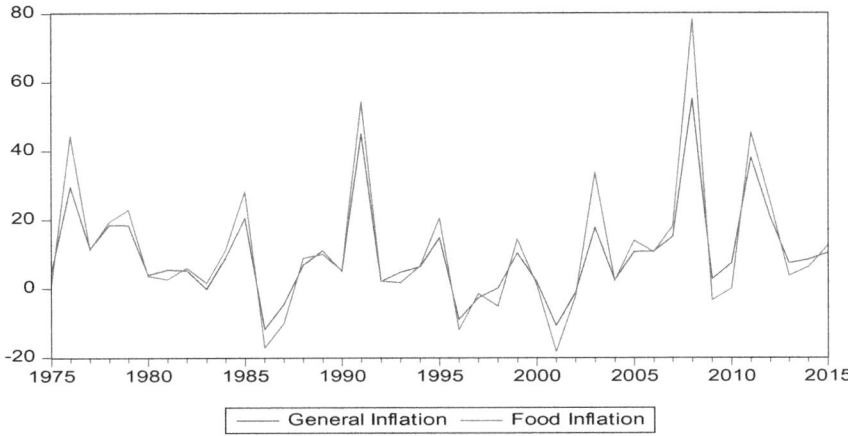

Fig. 4.2 Trends in general and food inflation rates (1975–2015)

GDP in particular, inflation has been rising in recent years. For instance, despite a reported significant increase in output (especially in agriculture) the prices continued to increase. Food inflation increased from 21.5% in 2003 to 35% in 2008 and reached its climax of 44.2% in 2009. During this period, food inflation was abnormally high and much above non-food inflation mainly due to global food and oil price shocks. On the other hand, the non-food inflation rate before 2008 was recorded below 20%. In 2009, it reached a peak of 24.6%. Generally, non-food inflation appeared relatively stable and increased at a slower pace than food inflation.

Since the economy is predominantly rural-agrarian, general inflation closely follows the trends in food inflation (Fig. 4.2) indicating that what happens to food inflation determines the trends of general inflation in the country. Trends in general inflation are also highly correlated with the growth rate of money supply. Thus, inflation in Ethiopia is a result of both monetary phenomena and structural problems like supply side shocks (for example, a drought). Trends in non-food inflation, however, are closely related to the growth rate of money supply and less related to trends in food inflation indicating that Ethiopian non-food inflation mainly occurs due to monetary expansion (Fig. 4.3).

4.3 Theoretical and Empirical Literature Review

4.3.1 Theoretical Review: Monetarist Versus Structuralist Views of Inflation

The first major definition of inflation is a decline in the purchasing power of the currency held and inflation is usually referred to as a process of a sustained increase

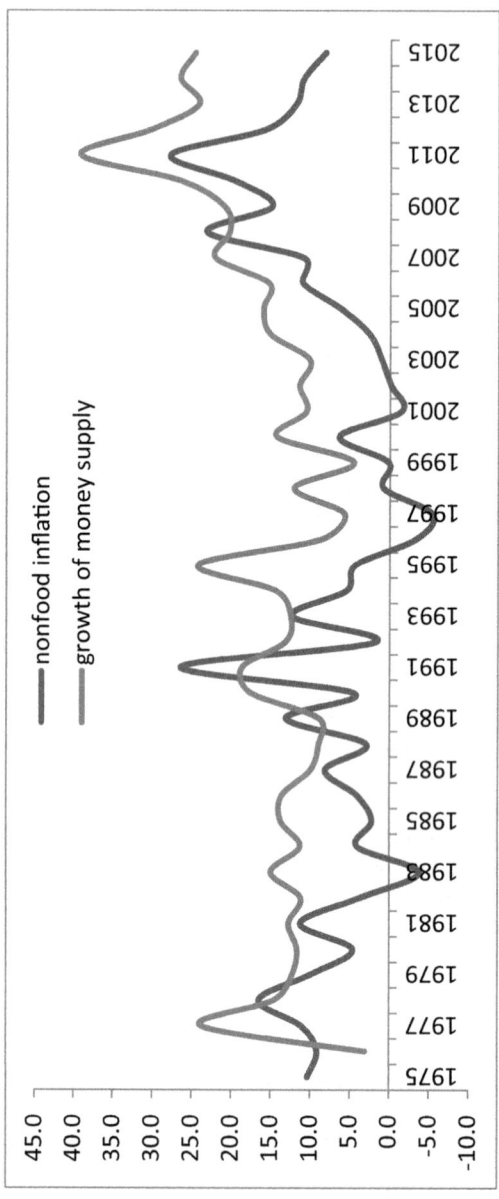

Fig. 4.3 Trends of non-food inflation versus growth in money supply

in the general price levels. CPI is usually used as the best indicator of the performance of retail prices or the purchasing power of money due to the relevance that this kind of an index gives to the total traded goods and services in the market within an economy. However, CPI is not always deemed the most relevant indicator for monetary policy purposes.

The second definition of inflation is expansion of money and credit which results in rising prices (the quantity theory of money). This is the basic tenet of the monetarist view which states that inflation mainly arises from monetary expansion. However, the key challenge here is that neither the meaning of sustained nor the general level of prices on which inflation should be measured are usually explained. The second key challenge is the definition of money supply: when individuals talk about 'money supply', which one are they referring to? M1, M2, money zero maturity or the amount of money in their accounts in banks or in their wallets?

According to the monetarist viewpoint which has its roots in neoclassical economic theories inflation is exclusively a monetary phenomenon arising from excessive demand, in particular, when there is 'too much money for few goods.' Two facts can be stressed in a monetarist analysis: higher inflation erodes real income and inflation depends on the difference between the rate of growth in money supply and the demand for money. The monetarist conclusion is that inflation in an economy is purely a monetary phenomenon; hence the only way to stop it quickly is to curb excess demand via a reasonable combination of monetary and fiscal policies. Monetarists have used the quantity theory of money to model the relationship between inflation and money supply.

The post-Keynesian structuralist approach emphasizes on the need to construct models appropriate to specific institutional and geographical constraints (Taylor 1988). Thus, from a post-Keynesian structuralist perspective, there is no single model which is appropriate for all developing countries due to their differences in economic, social, physical, cultural and social settings. Prominent post-Keynesian structuralist theoretical and empirical literature on inflation exists (see, for example, Nell 2004). For structuralists, inflation arises mainly from structural maladjustments, bottlenecks and rigidities in the economic system all of which are related to some kind of inelasticity especially in the supply side of the market.

When it comes to causes of inflation in developing countries, structuralists and monetarists have some basic differences. Structuralists consider several factors that monetarists see as the main drivers of inflation as transmission mechanisms of inflation. For structuralists it is impossible to control inflationary pressures via monetary and fiscal policies alone without addressing structural problems in developing countries like unemployment and stagnation in economic growth (Kay 2010).

4.3.2 Empirical Review

4.3.2.1 Other Developing Countries

There have been a number of cross-country and country-specific studies in developing countries in general and in African countries in particular, that examine the dynamics and determinants of inflation. Several of these studies have mixed results. Specifically, most cross-country studies found that inflation was mainly driven by monetary growth (see, Mello and Moccero 2009; Nguyen 2015; Ojede 2015) implying that the monetary sector is a critical determinant of inflation in developing countries, which is in line with the monetarist view. Other studies have found that internal aspects like supply side shocks, fiscal deficit, government expenditure and interest rate are statistically significant determinants of inflation in developing countries (Catao and Terrones 2005; Lin and Chu 2013; Narayan et al. 2011). The external sector like openness to the rest of the world, exchange rate liberalization, depreciation and world inflation have significant effects on inflation (see Ojede 2015). Oil prices also have a considerable effect on domestic prices in developing countries which are highly oil dependent (Sek et al. 2015).

Similarly, country-specific evidence shows mixed results on the determinants of inflation in developing countries. For instance, Jiang et al. (2015) found that in China money growth and inflation were positively related in a one-to-one fashion in the medium or long run whereas they deviated from such a positive relation in the short run due to temporary shocks and significant lag effects. The authors also claim that the long-run relationship between M0 growth and inflation supported the modern quantity theory of money. However, Sasmal (2015) found no long run relationship between money supply and agricultural prices in India. Instead, he found that an increase in per capita income and shortages in supply were responsible for an increase in agricultural food prices. Increasing public expenditure and an unfavorable foreign exchange rate had some effects on price although the results are not robust. Thus, the claim that money supply is the sole cause of inflation is not fully supported by empirical evidence in transitional and developing countries.

Uddin et al. (2014) report that in Bangladesh gross domestic product, money supply and interest rate in the current year as well as previous year's real exchange rate and interest rate contributed to an increase in the inflation rate. Similarly, Nguyen et al. (2012) found that in Vietnam inflation was persistent and that money supply, oil prices and rice prices presented the strongest influences on CPI inflation. However, Hung and Pfau's (2008) study failed to confirm a significant connection between money and inflation.

Cross-country evidence from African countries shows that the monetary sector, the internal sector and the external sector are major determinants of inflation. Neumann and Ssozi (2016) found money growth and budget deficits being directly inflationary in SSA countries. Similar results were also reported by Nguyen et al. (2015) who analyzed inflation dynamics in SSA using a global VAR model to capture trade and financial linkages among countries and included the role of regional and global demand and inflationary spillovers. They found that domestic supply shocks and shocks to the exchange rate and monetary variables were major drivers of inflation in SSA countries over the past 25 years. However, in recent years the contribution of monetary and exchange rate shocks to inflation fell while shocks to output and global shocks played a larger role in driving inflation over the last decade.

Some studies have strengthened the assertion that country characteristics matter —the extent of oil and food imports, vulnerability to weather shocks, economic importance of agriculture, trade openness and policy regime help in explaining the role of shocks (Nguyen et al. 2015). Durevall and Sjo (2012) found in the East and Horn of Africa (Ethiopia and Kenya) that inflation rates in both countries were driven by similar factors—world food prices and exchange rates had a long run impact, whereas money growth and agricultural supply shocks had short-to-medium run effects. There is also evidence of substantial inflation inertia in both the countries.

Country-specific evidence shows that inflation in African countries is determined by monetary, structural and external factors. In Nigeria, for instance, monetary expansion, fiscal deficits, interest rate, devaluation of the Nigerian currency and agro-climatic conditions affect the inflationary process (Bayo 2006; Moser 1995). Thus, monetary expansion, currency devaluation and shocks to the agricultural sector are major drivers of dynamics of inflation in Nigeria. Ocran (2007) used an error correction model to model inflation in Ghana and identified inflation inertia, changes in money, changes in the government's Treasury bill rates and changes in the exchange rate as determinants of inflation. Durevall and Sjo (2012) found that the monetary sector (money supply and exchange rate), agricultural supply shocks and the external sector (like world food prices) in Kenya were the major drivers of dynamics of inflation. In South Africa, inflation was mainly driven by structural factors rather than monetary factors (Akinboade et al. 2004; Nell 2004). Thus, in most African countries inflation is a structural phenomenon as opposed to the monetary phenomenon of the monetarist view.

4.3.2.2 The Ethiopian Experience

In Ethiopia, the recent soaring and dynamics of inflation are attributed to the monetary sector (money supply, exchange rate, real interest rate); the internal sector (supply shocks to the agricultural sector and the resulting higher price expectations and speculative prices, budget deficit) and the external sector (mainly import prices).

Alemayehu and Kibrom (2011) report that food inflation in the long run is determined by a rise in money supply/credit expansion, inflation expectation and international food price hikes. However, in the long run non-food inflation is mainly affected by money supply, the interest rate and inflation expectations. In the short run, salaries/wages, changes in global prices, supply and movement of exchange rates and limited food supply due to bad weather conditions are major drivers of inflation (Geda and Tafere 2008). Assefa (2013) concludes that a combination of supply and demand-side factors leads to high price increases. However, food inflation is primarily caused by domestic factors including the speculative behavior of the market's participants, while developments in the international market have little impact. However, Durevall et al. (2013) found that the long-run trend of domestic prices is determined by changes in global food and non-food prices which are expressed in the domestic currency. The short-run movement in food inflation is affected by shocks to agricultural output while growth in money supply influences dynamics of non-food inflation. Thus, monetary policy mainly helps in controlling an increase in non-food inflation.

4.4 Data Sources and the ARDL Inflation Model

4.4.1 Data Sources

We got data from the National Bank of Ethiopia (NBE), Ministry of Finance and Economic Cooperation, Central Statistical Agency (CSA) and other relevant sources for our study. The data is yearly covering the period 1975–2015. Specifically, real GDP and government spending were obtained from MOFED; the consumer price index (CPI), which is the proxy measure for inflation, was obtained from CSA. Finally, data on money supply and the real interest rate was collected from NBE.

4.4.2 The ARDL Model of Inflation

The autoregressive distributed lag (ARDL) model deals with a single cointegration and was introduced by Pesaran and Shin (1999) and further extended by Pesaran et al. (2001). The ARDL approach has the advantage that it does not require all variables to be I(1) as the Johansen framework does and it is still applicable if we have I(0) and I(1) variables in our set. That is, the variables included in the ARDL model are combinations of stationary and non-stationary time-series for ARDL bounds testing approach proposed by Pesaran et al. (2001).

Following Catao and Terrones (2005), the ARDL model for inflation rate where dependent and independent variables enter the right-hand side with lags of order p and q respectively can be specified as:

$$p_t = \alpha + \sum_{j=1}^{p} \lambda_j \pi_{t-j} + \sum_{l=0}^{q} \delta_i{}' x_{t-l} + \varepsilon_t \qquad (4.1)$$

where, P_t is the observed inflation rate at time t; α is the intercept term; and X_{t-1} is a $(k-1, 1)$ is the vector of explanatory variables including money supply, real GDP, government expenditure and real interest rate; λ_j are scalars; and δ_l are (k by 1) coefficient vectors. One well-known advantage of working with this ARDL specification, where all right-hand side variables enter the equation with a lag, is that it mitigates any contemporaneous causation from the dependent to the independent variable(s) which might bias the estimates.

Equation 4.1 can be re-parameterized and written in terms of a linear combination of variables in levels and first-differences as:

$$\Delta p_t = \alpha + \phi \pi_{t-1} + \varphi' x_t + \sum_{j=1}^{p-1} \lambda_j^* \Delta \pi_{t-j} + \sum_{l=0}^{q-1} \delta_l^{*\prime} \Delta x_{t-l} + \varepsilon_t \qquad (4.2)$$

where, $\phi = -\left(1 - \sum_{j=1}^{p} \lambda_j\right)$; $\varphi = \sum_{j=0}^{q} \delta_j$; $\lambda_j^* = -\sum_{m=j+1}^{p} \lambda_m$, and $\delta_l^* = -\sum_{m=l+1}^{q} \delta_m'$ with j = 1, 2, ..., p − 1; and l = 1, 2, ..., q − 1.

By grouping the variables in levels, Eq. 4.2 can be re-written as:

$$\Delta p_t = \alpha + \phi(\pi_{t-1} - \theta' x_t) + \sum_{j=1}^{p-1} \lambda_j^* \Delta \pi_{t-j} + \sum_{l=0}^{q-1} \delta_l^{*\prime} \Delta x_{t-l} + \varepsilon_t \qquad (4.3)$$

where, $\theta = \varphi^{-1} \phi$ defines the long-run equilibrium relationship between the variables involved and ϕ is the speed with which inflation adjusts toward its long-run equilibrium following a given change in X_t.

4.5 Tests, Estimation Results and Discussion

4.5.1 Unit Root Tests

We used the ADF unit root test to evaluate the order of integration of variables to verify the applicability of the ARDL bounds method (Table 4.1). According to the ADF test results, all variables are integrated of order one (that is, $I(1)$). Since none of the variables is integrated of a higher order, it is possible to apply the ARDL estimation technique to capture the dynamic effects of inflation in Ethiopia. That is, based on these results we can apply the ARDL technique.

4.5.2 Optimal Lag Length

In estimating the ARDL model, determining the optimal lag length of each variable in the model (both dependent and independent variables) is crucial. The best model fitted by Eviews-9 has different lag lengths for each variable in the model.

Table 4.1 Unit root tests

Variables	ADF-test	Probability	Order
Log consumer price index	−5.176*	0.0002	I(1)
Log narrow money supply	−3.291**	0.0153	I(1)
Log real GDP	−4.291*	0.0018	I(1)
Log government expenditure	−4.259**	0.0020	I(1)
Log real interest rate	−5.481*	0.0000	I(1)

Note * and ** represent level of significance at 1 and 5% respectively

Table 4.2 Optimal lag length selected by AIC

Variables	Optimal lag length
Log of general CPI	1
Log of government expenditure	1
Log of money supply	2
Log of real GDP	2
Log of real interest rate	0

According to Lutkepohl (2006) the dynamic link among the series can be captured if proper lags are identified and used. In our study, the optimal lag length for each variable is determined using the Akaike information criterion (AIC) so that the selected model is ARDL (1, 1, 2, 2, 0). The summary of the optimal lag length for each variable is given in Table 4.2.

4.5.3 Long Run Analysis

4.5.3.1 Cointegration Tests

Since the pre-condition for applying the ARDL model is the existence of a long run relationship between the dependent variable (inflation rate) and the vectors of independent variables, it is only possible to proceed to the ARDL model when the cointegration test reveals the existence of such long run relationships. We applied the bounds test based on the F-test statistic to detect the existence of a long run relationship.

The ARDL approach to cointegration has three advantages with respect to the two most popular approaches—the Engle–Granger two-step method and Johansen's system-based reduced rank regression method. First, cointegration can be carried out even if the variables are $I(0)$, $I(1)$, or mutually cointegrated (Pesaran and Shin 1999). Thus, the ARDL approach is suitable for econometric models that combine level and growth variables (for instance, inflation with GDP, government consumption, real money balance and an effective interest rate). Second, cointegration is possible even when the independent variables are endogenous. The method computes accurate long-run parameters and valid *t*-values; moreover, the endogeneity bias tends to be irrelevant and very small. Third, in small sample sizes (more than 30 observations) the estimates of the short-run model are highly consistent with their respective long-run parameters and therefore inferences are based on the standard normal asymptotic theory.

In the bounds test approach, the null hypothesis of no cointegration among the variables is tested against the alternative hypothesis that there is cointegration among the variables under study. Two sets of critical values are reported by Pesaran et al. (2001) for any given significance level. While one set of critical values assumes that all variables included in the ARDL model are I(0), the other set assumes that the variables are I(1). When the computed test statistic exceeds the upper critical bounds value, then the Ho hypothesis is rejected. When the F-statistic is lower than the lower bounds value, then the null hypothesis of no cointegration cannot be rejected. However, when the F-statistic falls into the bounds the cointegration test becomes inconclusive. Using both methods, the result of the test indicates the existence of a long-run relationship as the calculated F-statistic (5.81) exceeds the upper bounds for both I(0) and I(1) which is 3.74 and 5.06 respectively at the 1% level of significance (Table 4.3).

4.5.3.2 Estimation Results of the ARDL Model

The estimation results of the ARDL model reveal that inflation in the country is positively affected by money supply; lagged value of government expenditure; real interest rate; and the lagged value of real GDP. Specifically, a 1% increase in money supply results in a 0.84% increase in the inflation rate, which is statistically significant at the 1% level of significance. This implies that in Ethiopia inflationary pressure is a monetary phenomenon with nearly one-on-one effects (consistent with the quantity theory of money). This finding is in accordance with Alemayehu and Kibrom (2011), Neumann and Ssozi (2016) and Nguyen et al. (2015). The same result is reported for food inflation (see Table 4.8).

However, it is not consistent with Durevall et al.'s (2013) results who found that a growth in money supply affected short-run non-food price inflation. A 1% increase in the real interest rate led to about a 0.17% increase in the inflation rate in

Table 4.3 ARDL bounds test for cointegration

Test statistic	Value	I(0) bound	Critical value bounds	
			I(1) bound	Significance (%)
F-statistic	5.809	2.45	3.52	10
		2.86	4.01	5
		3.25	4.49	2.5
		3.74	5.06	1

Note H0: No long run relationships exist

the country, which is again consistent with previous results (for example, Alemayehu and Kibrom 2011). When lagged values of real GDP and government expenditure increase by 1%, general CPI of the country moves up by about 0.56–0.25% respectively. This result is consistent with previous studies (for example, Neumann and Ssozi 2016). However, the current value of real GDP is negatively related to movements in inflation rate indicating that higher real GDP (or more real goods) results in a reduction in the inflation rate. The lagged value of inflation has the expected sign (positive) but the effect is statistically insignificant implying that the role of expected inflation is less important in developing economies like Ethiopia (Table 4.4). Similar results are indicated for food inflation (see Tables 4.8, 4.9 and 4.10 and 4.11).

In general, inflation in Ethiopia is a result of both monetary phenomena and structural factors like shocks to the real sectors. As a result, inflation in the country is not explained by a single factor like money growth, real interest rate, exchange rate, government spending and real GDP. Instead, the dynamics of inflation are justified by a combination of factors. Similarly, food inflation is affected by both monetary and real sectors.

Table 4.5 gives the diagnostic tests of the ARDL inflation model. According to the test statistics, the model has no specification problem, the residuals are normally

Table 4.4 Estimation results of ARDL inflation model (Dependent variable-log of CPI)

Variable	Coefficient	t-Statistic	Prob.	
Log of lagged general CPI	0.068439	0.461664	0.6487	
Log of government expenditure	0.052813	0.495186	0.6252	
Log of government expenditure(−1)	0.251412	2.628945	0.0150	
Log of money supply	0.843635	4.734235	0.0001	
Log of money supply (−1)	0.311845	1.031130	0.3132	
Log of money supply (−2)	−0.618641	−3.155826	0.0044	
Log of real GDP	−0.751098	−3.692926	0.0012	
Log of real GDP (−1)	0.562735	2.002606	0.0571	
Log of real GDP (−2)	0.739672	2.883002	0.0084	
Log of real interest rate	0.172229	3.150111	0.0045	
Constant term	−7.268649	−3.992074	0.0006	
R-squared	0.996264	Mean dependent var		3.330882
Adjusted R-squared	0.994640	S.D. dependent var		0.780906
SE of regression	0.057172	Akaike info criterion		−2.629303
Sum squared resid	0.075179	Schwarz criterion		−2.135480
Log likelihood	55.69815	Hannan-Quinn criter.		−2.460895
F-statistic	613.3595	Durbin-Watson stat		2.336098
Prob (F-statistic)	0.000000			

Table 4.5 Diagnostic tests of the ARDL inflation model

Tests	Statistics	df	p-value
Ramsey RESET test (F-statistic)	0.411664	(1, 22)	0.5278
Normality test of the residual-Jarque-Bera test	2.842850		0.2414
Breusch-Godfrey LM serial correlation test	1.187508	(2, 21)	0.3246
Breusch-Pagan-Godfrey Heteroskedasticity test	0.506652	(10, 23)	0.8679

distributed with constant variance and there is no serial correlation. Thus, the classical assumptions are satisfied indicating that the estimates of the efficiency and policy implications of the model are reliable.

4.5.3.3 Long Run Estimation Results

General inflation in Ethiopia in the long run is negatively affected by government expenditure as more government investments result in more production of goods and services and hence a lower inflation rate. However, in the long run, real GDP growth, money supply and real interest rate have positive effects on the dynamics of inflation. Thus, in the long run inflation is a monetary phenomenon caused by structural factors. The long run positive relationship between inflation and real GDP is witnessed by the Phillips curve and Okun's law. There is also empirical evidence supporting this claim in developing countries. Comparing the coefficient of money supply in the ARDL and long run models, the effect of money supply on inflation is larger in the ARDL model than in the long run model (Table 4.6).

4.5.4 Results of the Dynamic Short Run Model

In the short run, the inflation rate is also affected by money supply, real GDP, government spending and the real interest rate. Thus, both in the long and short run,

Table 4.6 Estimation results of the long run inflation model

Variable	Coefficient	t-Statistic	Prob.
Log of government expenditure	−0.213189	−2.520447	0.0191
Log of money supply	0.576280	9.588656	0.0000
Log of real GDP	0.591811	3.736322	0.0011
Log of real interest rate	0.184882	4.527764	0.0002
Constant term	−7.802652	−6.012594	0.0000

Table 4.7 Estimation results of the error correction model

Variable	Coefficient	t-Statistic	Prob.
D(Log of government expenditure)	0.052813	0.495186	0.6252
D(Log of money supply)	0.843635	4.734235	0.0001
D(Log of money supply (−1))	0.618641	3.155826	0.0044
D(Log of real GDP)	−0.751098	−3.692926	0.0012
D(Log of real GDP (−1))	−0.739672	−2.883002	0.0084
D(Log of real interest rate)	0.172229	3.150111	0.0045

Ethiopian inflation is not only a monetary phenomenon but it is also a result of structural factors like shocks to real sectors and real GDP. The error correction term is interpreted as the speed of adjustment towards long run equilibrium or the measure of removing the disequilibrium of inflation due to various shocks to its long run equilibrium. Thus, the ECM coefficient measures how quickly/slowly the relationship returns to its equilibrium path and it must have a statistically significant coefficient with a negative sign.

In our short run model, the coefficient of the error correction term of the ARDL inflation model is negative and less than one. It is also statistically significant at less than a 1% level of significance. This result ensures that inflation converges to its long run equilibrium. Its magnitude indicates that about 93% of the disequilibrium in the inflation is corrected per year implying that the disequilibrium due to various shocks is nearly corrected within one year. This shows that it takes about one year to return to the long-run equilibrium level after the shocks which is a reasonably short period (Table 4.7).

4.6 Concluding Remarks and Policy Implications

This study investigated the dynamics and determinants of inflation in Ethiopia over the period 1975–2015 using annual data from NBE, CSA and MOFED. The study applied the ARDL inflation model by synthesizing monetarist and structuralist views of determinants of inflation in Ethiopia.

The estimation results of the ARDL model show that inflation in the country was positively and statistically significantly affected by money supply; the lagged value of government expenditure; the real interest rate and the lagged value of real GDP. When money supply increased by 1%, the resulting inflation increased by 0.84% implying that in Ethiopia inflationary pressure is a monetary phenomenon with nearly one-on-one effects (consistent with the quantity theory of money). However, the current value of real GDP had negative and statistically significant effects on the inflation level in the country.

In the long run, real GDP growth, money supply and real interest rate had positive effects on the dynamics of inflation in Ethiopia. This claim is in line with Alemayehu and Kibrom (2011) who concluded that inflation was mainly due to domestic monetary developments and was influenced mostly by income growth as income growth through increased demand for food more than offset the negative effect through growth in money demand and a significant proportion of household incomes being spent on food items. Thus, in the long run, inflation is both a monetary phenomenon and is also caused by structural factors. The central claim of our study is that inflation dynamics in Ethiopia are not only a monetary phenomenon like higher money supply due to credit expansion and government expenditure on construction and pro-poor sectors but it is also due to real factors like change in real GDP. In the short run, the inflation rate is also affected by money supply, real GDP, government spending and the real interest rate. The magnitude error correction coefficient indicates that about 93% of the disequilibrium in inflation is corrected per year implying that the disequilibrium due to various shocks is nearly corrected within one year. This shows that it takes about one year to return to the long-run equilibrium level after the shocks which is a reasonably short period.

The study has two relevant policy implications. First, there is an output-inflation trade-off in Ethiopia both in the long and short run as excess government spending and monetization fuel inflation levels. Thus, the Government of Ethiopia needs to follow conservative fiscal and monetary policies. It is also important to enhance economic growth as higher economic growth reduces inflationary pressures. Second, in recent years food inflation has fueled general inflation in the country as food inflation constitutes the lion's share of the general inflation level as there is high demand for food due to remarkable levels of urbanization and income growth. Thus, the government and its development partners need to focus on an adequate food supply in their development plans in addition to promoting exports.

Annexures

Results of ARDL Food Inflation Model.
See Tables 4.8, 4.9, 4.10 and 4.11.

Table 4.8 Estimation result of ARDL food inflation model

Variable	Coefficient	Std. error	t-Statistic	Prob.*
LOGFCPI(−1)	0.046793	0.166432	0.281152	0.7816
LOGFCPI(−2)	−0.200258	0.169929	−1.178478	0.2532
LOGFCPI(−3)	−0.193251	0.147948	−1.306215	0.2071
LOGGE	0.151411	0.187303	0.808375	0.4289
LOGGE(−1)	−0.531798	0.158317	−3.359065	0.0033
LOGM1	0.877645	0.280228	3.131901	0.0055
LOGM1(−1)	0.410235	0.449678	0.912287	0.3730
LOGM1(−2)	−0.568063	0.314460	−1.806471	0.0867
LOGRGDP	−0.975465	0.355658	−2.742702	0.0129
LOGRGDP(−1)	1.168398	0.467896	2.497133	0.0219
LOGRGDP(−2)	0.445244	0.464956	0.957605	0.3503
LOGRGDP(−3)	0.599749	0.405469	1.479148	0.1555
LOGRIR	0.282033	0.087018	3.241091	0.0043
C	−14.70439	3.669497	−4.007194	0.0008
R-squared	0.993912	Mean dependent var		3.267879
Adjusted R-squared	0.989747	S.D. dependent var		0.834733
SE of regression	0.084521	Akaike info criterion		−1.807208
Sum squared resid	0.135733	Schwarz criterion		−1.172326
Log likelihood	43.81893	Hannan-Quinn criter.		−1.593589
F-statistic	238.6255	Durbin-Watson stat		2.458192
Prob(F-statistic)	0.000000			

*Note p-values and any subsequent tests do not account for model selection

Table 4.9 Estimation result of long run food inflation model

Long run coefficients				
Variable	Coefficient	Std. error	t-Statistic	Prob.
LOGGE	−0.282455	0.102622	−2.752376	0.0127
LOGM1	0.534499	0.067068	7.969445	0.0000
LOGRGDP	0.919218	0.210525	4.366319	0.0003
LOGRIR	0.209422	0.043221	4.845372	0.0001
C	−10.918696	1.745693	−6.254648	0.0000

Table 4.10 Estimation result of short run and ECM food inflation model

Cointegrating form				
Variable	Coefficient	Std. error	t-Statistic	Prob.
D(LOGFCPI(−1))	0.393509	0.164389	2.393766	0.0272
D(LOGFCPI(−2))	0.193251	0.147948	1.306215	0.2071
D(LOGGE)	0.151411	0.187303	0.808375	0.4289
D(LOGM1)	0.877645	0.280228	3.131901	0.0055
D(LOGM1(−1))	0.568063	0.314460	1.806471	0.0867
D(LOGRGDP)	−0.975465	0.355658	−2.742702	0.0129
D(LOGRGDP(−1))	−0.445244	0.464956	−0.957605	0.3503
D(LOGRGDP(−2))	−0.599749	0.405469	−1.479148	0.1555
D(LOGRIR)	0.282033	0.087018	3.241091	0.0043
CointEq(−1)	−1.000000	0.227185	−4.401699	0.0000

Table 4.11 ARDL bounds test: food inflation

Null hypothesis: no long-run relationships exist		
Test statistic	Value	k
F-statistic	5.236396	4
Critical value bounds		
Significance	I(0) Bound	I(1) Bound
10%	2.45	3.52
5%	2.86	4.01
2.5%	3.25	4.49
1%	3.74	5.06

References

Akinboade, O.A., F.K. Siebrits, and E.W. Niedermeier. 2004. The determinants of inflation in South Africa: An econometric analysis. AERC Research Paper 143.

Alemayehu, G., and T. Kibrom. 2011. The galloping inflation in Ethiopia: A cautionary tale for aspiring 'developmental states' in Africa. IAES Working Paper No. WP-A01-2011.

Assefa, A. 2013. The political economy of food prices: The case of Ethiopia. WIDER Working Paper 2013/001, United Nations University.

Bayo, F. 2006. Determinants of inflation in Nigeria: An empirical analysis. *International Journal of Humanities and Social Science* 5 (1): 1–8.

Catão, L. and L. Terrones. 2005. Fiscal deficits and inflation. *Journal of Monetary Economics* 52: 529–554.

Durevall, D., and B. Sjö. 2012. The dynamics of inflation in Ethiopia and Kenya. Working Paper Series No. 151, African Development Bank, Tunis, Tunisia.

Durevall, D., L.J. Loening, and Y. Ayalew Birru. 2013. Inflation dynamics and food prices in Ethiopia. *Journal of Development Economics* 104: 89–106. https://doi.org/10.1016/j.jdeveco.2013.05.002.

Geda, A., and K. Tafere. 2008. *The galloping inflation in Ethiopia: A cautionary tale for aspiring 'developmental states' in Africa*. Department of Economics, AAU.

Government of Ethiopia (2012). *Ethiopia's Progress Towards Eradicating Poverty: An Interim Report on Poverty Analysis Study (2010/11)*. Development Planning and Research Directorate. Ministry of Finance and Economic Development, Addis Ababa.

Jiang, C., T. Chang, and L.X. Li. 2015. Money growth and inflation in China: New evidence from a wavelet analysis. *International Review of Economics and Finance* 35: 249–261.

Hung, Le Viet, and W.D. Pfau. 2008. VAR analysis of the monetary transmission mechanism in Vietnam. VDF Working Paper Series. Working Paper 081, Vietnam Development Forum, Hanoi.

Kay, C. 2010. *Latin American theories of development and underdevelopment*, 54–55. Routledge.

Lin, Hsin-Yi, and Hao-Pang Chu. 2013. Are fiscal deficits inflationary? *Journal of International Money and Finance* 32: 214–233.

Lutkepol, H. 2006. Structural vector autoregressive analysis for cointegrated variables. *Algemines Statistisches Archive* 90 (1): 75–88.

Mello, L.D., and D. Moccero. 2009. Monetary policy and inflation expectations in Latin America: Long-run effects and volatility spillovers. *Journal of Money, Credit and Banking* 41 (8): 1671–1690.

Moser, G.G. 1995. The main determinants of inflation in Nigeria. *Staff Papers (International Monetary Fund)* 42 (2): 270–289.

Narayan, K.P., S. Narayan, and S. Mishra. 2011. Do remittances induce inflation? Fresh evidence from developing countries. *Southern Economic Journal* 77 (4): 914–933.

Nell, K.S. 2004. The structuralist theory of imported inflation: An application to South Africa. *Applied Economics* 36: 1431–1444.

Neumann, R., and J. Ssozi. 2016. Political influence on fiscal and monetary policy in Sub-Saharan Africa. *Journal of African Economies* 25 (1): 55–109.

Nguyen, Van Bon. 2015. Effects of fiscal deficit and money M2 supply on inflation: Evidence from selected economies of Asia. *Journal of Economics, Finance and Administrative Science* 20: 49–53.

Nguyen, H.M., T. Cavoli, and J.K. Wilson. 2012. The determinants of inflation in Vietnam, 2001–09. *ASEAN Economic Bulletin* 29 (1): 1–14.

Nguyen, A.D.M., J. Dridi, F.D. Unsal, and O.H. Williams. 2015. On the drivers of inflation in Sub-Saharan Africa. IMF Working Paper, WP/15/189.

Ocran, M.K. 2007. A Modelling of Ghana's Inflation Experience: 1960–2003. Research Paper 169, African Economic Research Consortium (AERC), Nairobi.

Ojede, Andrew. 2015. Is inflation in developing countries driven by low productivity or monetary growth? *Economics Letters* 133: 96–99.

Pesaran, M.H., and Y. Shin. 1999. An autoregressive distributed lag modelling approach to cointegration analysis. In *Centennial volume of Rangar Frisch*, ed. S. Strom, A. Holly, and P. Diamond. Cambridge: Cambridge University Press.

Pesaran, M.H., Y. Shin, and R.J. Smith. 2001. Bounds testing approaches to the analysis of level relationships. *Journal of Applied Econometrics* 16: 289–326.

Sasmal, J. 2015. Food price inflation in India: The growing economy with sluggish agriculture. *Journal of Economics, Finance and Administrative Science* 20: 30–40.

Sek, S.K., X.Q. Teo, and Y.N. Wong. 2015. A comparative study on the effects of oil price changes on inflation. *Procedia Economics and Finance* 26: 630–636.

Taylor, L. 1988. *Varieties of stabilization experience: Towards sensible macroeconomics in the third world*. Oxford and New York: Clarendon Press.

Uddin, S., N.M. Chowdhury, and M.A. Hossain. 2014. Determinants of inflation in Bangladesh: An econometric investigation. *Journal of World Economic Research* 3 (6): 83–94.

Part II
Taxes and Government Expenditure

Chapter 5
Effects of Tax and Government Expenditure on Economic Growth in Ethiopia

Selamawit Gebreegziabher

Abstract This study examines the effects of fiscal policy—particularly government expenditure and taxation—on economic growth in Ethiopia using the ARDL modeling approach. It finds that both in the short and long run, the effect of better human capital formation, increased availability of the economy's capital stock and labor force had a significant positive effect on the growth of the economy. On the fiscal side, a good performance in the collection of indirect tax revenue and increased productive government consumption had a significant positive effect on the growth of the economy both in the short and long run.

Keywords Fiscal policy · Growth · Taxation · Government expenditure
Ethiopia · ARDL

JEL Classification E62 · H20 · H27 · H30 · H50

5.1 Introduction

Conventionally, fiscal policy has been associated with the use of taxation and public spending to influence the level of economic activity (Zagler and Durnecker 2003). Fiscal policy deals with a government's deliberate actions in spending money and levying taxes with a view to influencing macroeconomic variables in a desired direction including sustainable economic growth, high employment creation and low inflation (Easterly and Levine 1997; Shihab 2014).

Economic growth is presumed to be the most important determinant of economic welfare and over the last two decades economic growth and its determinants have been of great importance in both theoretical and applied studies (Acemoglu 2009; Romer 2011). In the neoclassical growth model, steady state growth is driven by

S. Gebreegziabher (✉)
Department of Economics, Addis Ababa University, Addis Ababa, Ethiopia
e-mail: selam3MG@yahoo.com

© Springer Nature Singapore Pte Ltd. 2018
A. Heshmati and H. Yoon (eds.), *Economic Growth and Development in Ethiopia*, Perspectives on Development in the Middle East and North Africa (MENA) Region, https://doi.org/10.1007/978-981-10-8126-2_5

exogenous factors such as the dynamics of population and technological progress so much so that fiscal policy can only affect the rate of growth during a transition to the steady state (Barro and Sala-i-Martin 1997). Based on the neoclassical model, conventional wisdom says that differences in tax systems and in debt and expenditure policies can be important determinants of the level of output but they are unlikely to have an important effect on the rate of growth. On the other hand, endogenous growth models tend to transform fiscal policy's temporary growth effects implied by the neoclassical model into permanent growth effects (Easterly and Reobelo 1993). That is, fiscal policy in endogenous growth theories is assumed to affect both the level and growth rate of per capita output and has been recognized as one of the determinants of economic growth (Barro and Sala-i-Martin 1992, 1995; Easterly and Reobelo 1993).

A theoretical and empirical debate on whether fiscal policy stimulates growth has been going on for a while (M'Amanja and Morrissey 2005; Ocran 2009). On the theoretical front, there are two main strands of literature regarding fiscal policy's role in fostering economic growth. One view is that a government's support to knowledge accumulation, research and development, productive investments, maintenance of law and order and the provision of other public goods and services can stimulate growth in both the short and long run. In addition, fiscal policy can also foster growth and human development through a number of different channels provided that they are supported by complementary political and economic institutions (Goldsmith 1998). On the other hand, there is also the view that governments are inherently bureaucratic and less efficient and as a result they tend to hinder rather than facilitate growth if they get involved in the productive sectors of the economy. Thus, government fiscal policy is thought to stifle economic growth by distorting the effects of taxes and inefficient government expenditure (Ocran 2009).

The results are equally mixed on the empirical front and include the effect of fiscal policy on a country's economy being positive, negative or indeterminate depending on several factors (Ali and Ahmad 2010). Not surprisingly, the empirical findings have been diverse and there are many empirical problems contributing to the mixed results in empirical literature including the use of different model specifications and estimation techniques, sample sizes, quality of data and limited availability of data on relevant variables (M'Amanja and Morrissey 2005).

While a large body of empirical literature on the fiscal effects of economic growth in both the developed and developing worlds exists, little has been done to investigate the fiscal policy-economic growth relationship in Ethiopia. The few available Ethiopian studies are in general unpublished graduate theses. In addition, these Ethiopian studies report different effects of fiscal policy on economic growth depending on the empirical methodology used, the type of data and period covered and the variables used to represent fiscal policy. For instance, Adnan (2014) examined the impact of public final consumption and investment spending on economic growth in Ethiopia using a vector error correction model. The study

concluded that long run government investments and final consumption had positive and negative effects on economic growth respectively. Private investments,
private final consumption and primary education enrolment rates had positive
effects on economic growth. However, all the variables included in the model
except government consumption did not have an impact on economic growth in the
short run. Ketema (2006) examined the impact of government spending on
Ethiopian economic growth using the VAR model and found that only expenditure
on human capital had a long-run significant positive impact. Demssie (2011)
assessed the relationship between fiscal policy and economic growth in Ethiopia
using the ECM approach and his main findings include that tax had a significant
growth effect and the government's recurrent expenditure had a significant
expansionary effect in the long run but were contradictory in the short run. The
impact of capital expenditure on growth was positive but insignificant in the long
run and a budget deficit had a significant negative effect in the long run but a
positive effect in the short run.

Therefore, one can observe that there are mixed empirical results depending on
the approaches used, the type of data used, the variables taken to represent fiscal
policy and the period covered. In addition, some of the studies date back to more
than a decade stressing that the issue needs to be revisited using recent data.
Another limitation of existing studies is that they estimate the effects of fiscal policy
without decomposing the effects into a short run and long run analyses. Further,
most of the existing studies suffer from the problem of short series data, omission of
relevant macroeconomic variables in the models and lack of appropriate econometric techniques in modeling both the short run and long run dynamics simultaneously. They do not use a theoretical framework either. Thus, our study addresses
these gaps and analyzes the long run as well as short run effects of fiscal policy
variables on economic growth in Ethiopia.

5.2 Overview of Fiscal Performance in Ethiopia

This section gives a summary of Ethiopia's fiscal performance over the period
1966–2014. Specifically, it reviews developments in the general government
domestic revenue, expenditure and budget balance.

5.2.1 Revenue

Domestic government revenue from tax and non-tax items registered a steady
increase over the period of our study (Figs. 5.1 and 5.2). In general there was a
steady increase till 1999 after which, in particular in the last decade, it registered a

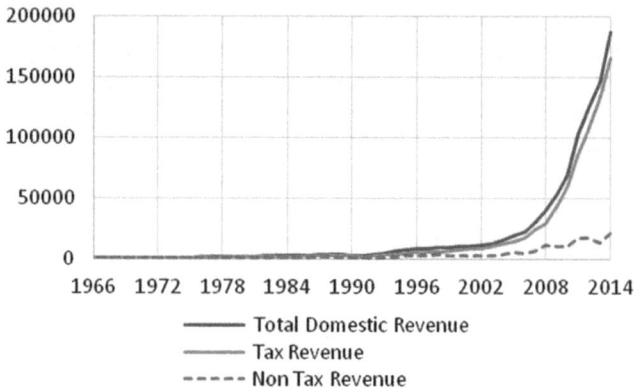

Fig. 5.1 Total tax and non-tax revenue of the government (in birr million)

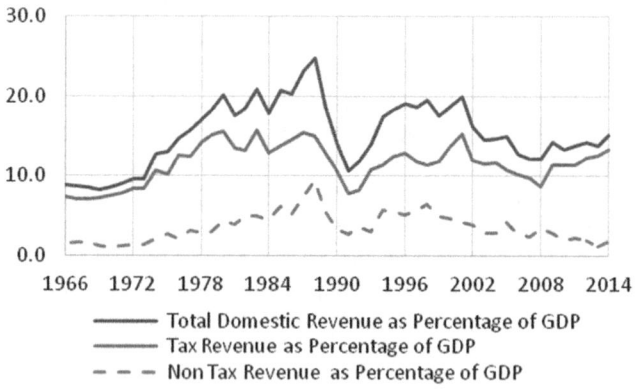

Fig. 5.2 Total tax and non-tax revenue of the government (as percentage of GDP)

steeper increase in absolute terms (Fig. 5.1). The large increase in the government's total revenue was mainly attributed to the increased revenue flows from taxes. Non-tax revenue increased steadily over the years, although at a much slower rate than tax revenue. In 2014, government revenue as a percentage of GDP reached a little over 115%, albeit with ups and downs over the years.

5.2.2 Expenditure

Figures 5.3 and 5.4 present trends of total government expenditure in absolute terms and as percentage of GDP for 1966–2014. Total government expenditure was more or less stable for the first two decades (Fig. 5.3) but it started increasing steadily in subsequent years, particularly in the post-1991 period. In particular

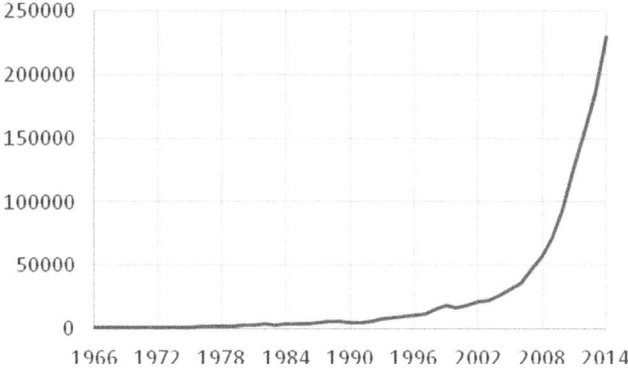

Fig. 5.3 Total government expenditure (in birr million)

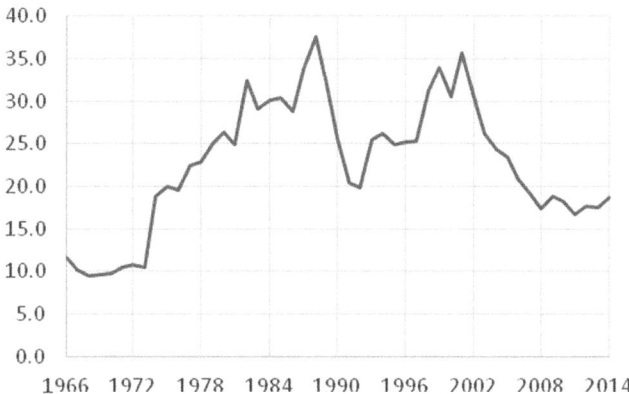

Fig. 5.4 Total government expenditures (as percentage of GDP)

government expenditure in the last decade registered a steeper increase following the implementation of ambitious mega projects. However, government expenditure as a percentage of GDP had a different feature where it showed a relatively fluctuating pattern implying that even if total government expenditure registered a steady increase in general over the years, and a steeper increase in the last decade in absolute terms, its share as a percentage of GDP was somewhat modest around 19% in 2014 (Fig. 5.4).

5.2.3 Fiscal Balance

Figures 5.5 and 5.6 show the fiscal balance of the government in terms of total government revenue and total expenditure and deficit for 1966–2014. In the earlier

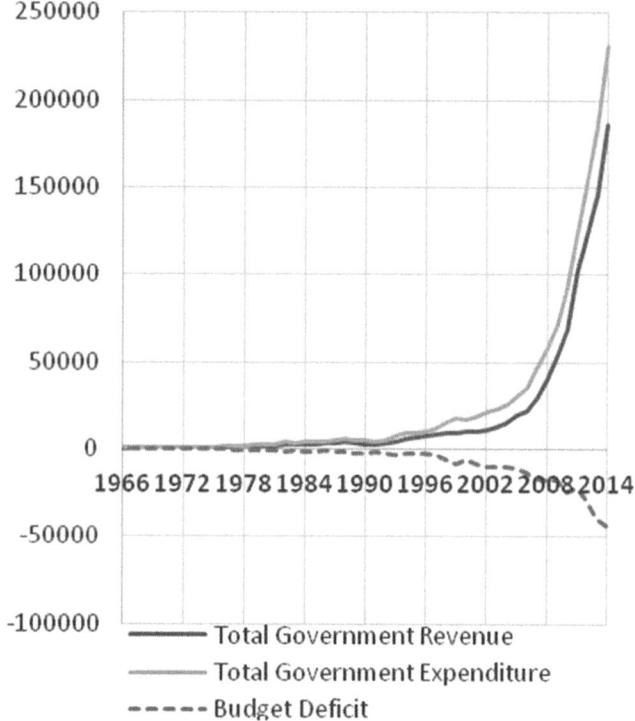

Fig. 5.5 Fiscal balance (in birr million). *Source* Own computation using MOFED (2017) data

decades, the government's budget deficit was very small both in absolute terms and as percentage of GDP. However, since 1999, though fluctuating the fiscal balance has shown a sharp increase in absolute terms (Fig. 5.5). In the post-2002 period, the government's budget deficit increased steeply both in absolute terms and as percentage of GDP. This was mainly due to the fast increase in the expenditure side of the government compared to the growth in its revenue.

5.3 Review of Empirical Literature

There are several empirical studies which assess the effects of fiscal policy on economic growth in different countries. In our study we pay attention to the empirical work done on the effect of fiscal policy in developing countries in general and in African countries in particular.

M'Amanja and Morrissey (2005) analyzed the effect of fiscal policy on economic growth in Kenya. Using an autoregressive distributed lag (ARDL) model and M'Amanja and Morrissey (2005) categorized government expenditure into

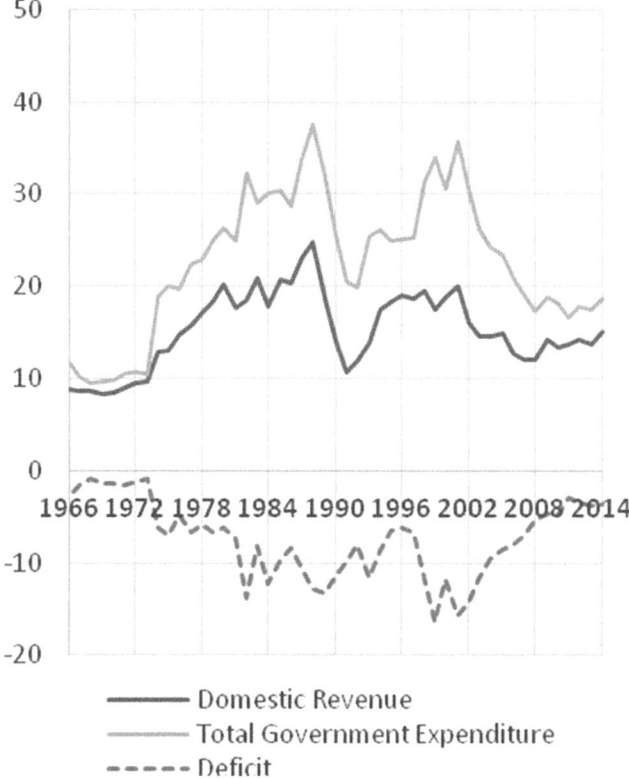

Fig. 5.6 Fiscal balance (as percentage of GDP). *Source* Own computation using MOFED (2017) data

productive and unproductive expenditure and classified tax revenue as distortionary and non-distortionary. They found that non-distortionary taxes and unproductive expenditure had a neutral effect on economic growth in Kenya. According to M'Amanja and Morrissey (2005, page 7), productive expenditure had a strong adverse effect on growth. They also found that government investments were a significant factor affecting growth in the long-run.

Focusing on fiscal policy Mansouri (2008) analyzed the impact of the public spending structure on short and long-run economic growth in Egypt, Morocco and Tunisia. He reported that government investments positively affected economic growth both in the short run and long run in Morocco, and only in the long run in Tunisia and Egypt. On the other hand, the government's recurrent expenditure affected economic growth negatively both in the short and long run in Morocco and Tunisia and only in the short run in Egypt.

Ocran (2009) examined the relationship between fiscal policy and economic growth in South Africa. Using quarterly data for the period 1990–2004 and the vector autoregressive modeling approach this study reported that government consumption expenditure, gross fixed capital formation and tax receipts had a significant positive effect on economic growth in South Africa. However, the size of the deficit had no significant effect on the growth outcomes of the South African economy.

Ali and Ahmad (2010) did an empirical study on the effects of fiscal policy on economic growth in Pakistan. Using the ARDL approach they found that rising fiscal deficit created excess demand which encouraged firms to use more of their existing capacity and people to spend more, and hence the economic situation improved in the short run. In the long run the rising fiscal deficit had a negative effect on economic growth.

Shihab (2014) did an empirical study on the causal relationship between economic growth and fiscal policy in Jordan. Using Granger causality to determine the direction of the relationship between the two variables during the period 2000–12, the study found that there was a causal relationship going from economic growth to budget deficit but not vice versa. Abdon et al. (2014) studied the relationship between fiscal policy and growth in developing Asian countries and concluded that the composition of taxes and government spending mattered for economic growth. Moreover, property taxes were more conducive for growth than personal and corporate income taxes. In addition, the study found that the composition of government spending also mattered for growth. Specifically, shifting public spending to education yielded a sizable growth dividend.

Ahmad and Loganathan (2016) investigated the causal nexus between government expenditure and economic growth in Nigeria based on the bootstrap Granger non-causality test with fixed size rolling windows approach for the period 1961–2014. Based on the full sample Granger causality test, they found that none of the series Granger caused the other. On the other hand, the bootstrap rolling windows estimation proved the existence of bidirectional and unidirectional causal relationships between the variables in the sub-samples. The bidirectional relationship occurred in the sub-sample period 2011–14, while the unidirectional causality running from GDP per capita to total government expenditure occurred in the sub-sample periods 1989–95 and 2000–09. This implies that government expenditure had no predictive power during most of the sub-sample periods.

There are very few empirical studies on the effects of fiscal policy on economic growth in Ethiopia. In his unpublished study Demssie (2011) assessed the relationship between fiscal policy and economic growth in the country by decomposing government revenue and government expenditure into various broad categories for the period 1960/61–1999/2000 using a cointegration analysis. He found that direct taxes depressed growth significantly and indirect domestic taxes had a significant growth enhancing effect. In addition, government recurrent expenditure had a significant expansionary effect in the long run but was contractionary in the short run. The effect of capital expenditure on growth was insignificant the long run and budget deficit had a significant negative effect in the long run and a positive effect in the short run. Adnan (2014) examined the impact of public final consumption and investment expenditure on economic growth in Ethiopia using the vector error correction modeling approach for the period 1960–2014 and reported that in the long run government consumption and investment expenditure had a negative and positive effect respectively on Ethiopia's economic growth. In addition, private investments, consumption expenditure and primary education enrolment rates had positive effects on the economic growth of the country in the long run. However, except government consumption all variables included in the model had no effect on economic growth in the short run.

These empirical studies have some limitations. Among other things, they suffer from a problem of aggregation of the government spending variable (see, for example, Ahmad and Loganathan 2016). Given the evidence from other studies even a broad categorization of the government expenditure variable into government consumption and investment expenditure has a different effect on economic growth. Some of the studies also suffer from lack of a clear and coherent theoretical framework for the empirical analysis (see, for example, Adnan 2014; Mansouri 2008). Lack of a sound theoretical framework may lead to the problem of model misspecification. In Ethiopian studies, problems related to the econometric techniques adopted can also be mentioned as one of the limitations (see, for example, Adnan 2014; Demssie 2011). The Johansson VAR based cointegration analysis used in these studies is quite demanding of a long series of data for the results to be reliable. Given the problem of finding reliable long span data for most macro-variables in Ethiopia, the results from these studies should be interpreted carefully.

5.4   Methodology

5.4.1   Data and Variable Definition

Our study is based on annual data covering the period from 1974–75 to 2014–15 taken from the Ministry of Finance and Development (MOFED). To identify the effects of fiscal policy on the Ethiopian economy we used both fiscal and non-fiscal variables where the non-fiscal variables include PY real per capita GDP at factor cost at which it is used as a dependent variable to proxy for real output growth. Private investment (PI)[1] which was obtained by deducting government investment (GIV) from gross fixed capital investment (GFCF) and is expected to impact economic growth positively. Real capital stock (RCS) is also expected to affect growth positively. Log of primary school enrolment, proxy for human capital development with a positive impact on growth, labor force growth (LF) is again expected to have a positive correlation with economic growth, AID[2] here is also included as a control variable and expected to impact growth negatively. The fiscal

---

[1]There is no data for private investments from 25 years ago or before the current regime. Hence, private investments are excluded and only government investments are included in our model.

[2]Aid has been included as a control variable but was found to be statically insignificant and is not revealed in the estimated output.

variables include unproductive government consumption (UGC) which is recurrent expenditure (GC) less recurrent expenditure on health, education and economic services and theoretically it is expected to have a negative but insignificant impact on growth. Productive consumption expenditure (PGC) which includes expenditure on health, education and economic services and have a positive relationship with economic growth is hypothesized but may be negative depending on its actual composition. Direct tax revenue (DTR) (distortionary revenue) has a mostly negative association with growth and distorts incentives of private agents. Indirect tax revenue (ITR) or non-distortionary revenue is hypothesized to have a positive but insignificant effect on growth (does not distort incentives). Non-tax revenue (NTR) includes capital revenue, fines, forfeitures and dividends which are expected to have a positive effect on growth since it is a non-distortionary way of financing government expenditure. All variables except school enrolment are expressed as ratios of PY and their natural logs are taken in the analysis.

5.4.2 Analytical Framework for the Study

Several studies have used the Kneller et al. (1999) and the Bleaney et al. (2000) presentation of the Barro and Sala-i-Martin (1992, 1995) model of endogenous growth as an analytical framework for their analysis. Fiscal policy analyses in developing countries including in Africa rely on this theoretical framework of which Amanja and Morrissey (2005), Ocran (2009), Ali and Ahmad, (2010) can be cited as some examples. Accordingly, our study used this analytical framework to analyze the fiscal policy and economic growth relationship in Ethiopia.

In the neoclassical growth model, fiscal variables do not affect economic growth in the long run whereas the endogenous growth model permits fiscal effects to change the slope of the long run output path (Amanja and Morrissey 2005; Barro 1990; Ocran 2009). We used the Bleaney et al. (2000) presentation of the Barro and Sala–i–Martin (1992, 1995) model of endogenous growth as a theoretical framework. Accordingly, the Cobb Douglas production function was considered that there are n producers, each producing output:

$$Y = Ak^{(1-\alpha)}g^{\alpha} \tag{5.1}$$

where, A is a positive constant, k is private capital, g is a publicly provided inputs and α is a parameter between zero and one. The government funds its budget with a proportional tax on output at the rate r. Therefore, the government budget constraint is:

$$ng + Crny \tag{5.2}$$

where, C is government–provided consumption (or 'non–productive') goods. Subject to a specified utility function, Barro (1990) and Barro and Sala-i-Martin (1992) derive the long run growth rate (g) in this model as:

$$g = 1(1 - t)(1 - \alpha)A^{\frac{1}{1-\alpha}}\left(\frac{g}{y}\right)^{\alpha/(1-\alpha)} - m \qquad (5.3)$$

where, l and m stand for parameters in the assumed utility function. In Eq. 5.3, distortionary tax rate (t) and productive government expenditure (g) are negative and positive functions of the growth rate respectively. Here, unproductive government expenditure (C) and non-distortionary taxes (L) do not affect the growth rate (Bleaney et al. 2000; M'Amanja and Morrissey 2005).

$$ng + C + b = L + tny \qquad (5.4)$$

where, b is the budget deficit/surplus in a given period. Since g is productive, its predicted sign is positive, but t is negative as it distorts incentives of private agents. Both C and L are hypothesized to have zero effects on growth. Similarly, the effect of b is expected to be zero so long as the Ricardian equivalence holds, but may be non-zero otherwise (Bleaney et al. 2000; M'Amanja and Morrissey 2005).

The growth equation here is specified in the spirit of Kneller et al. (1999) and Amanja and Morrissey (2005) by considering both fiscal (x_t) and non-fiscal (z_t) variables so that the growth equation becomes:

$$y_t = \alpha + \sum_{i=1}^{k} \beta_i z_t + \sum_{j=1}^{m} G_j x_t + e_t$$

where, y_t is the growth rate of output, x_t is the vector of fiscal variables, z_t is the vector of non-fiscal variables and e_t are white noise error terms.

Accordingly, this model is estimated to determine the fiscal policy effects on Ethiopian economic growth. While estimating this, a dummy variable was included to incorporate a political system change across different regimes.

5.4.3   Method of Data Analysis

To determine the long run and short run relationship among fiscal variables and economic growth the appropriate method to be used is the error correction model and a cointegration analysis. In applying any cointegration technique the first exercise is to determine the degree of integration of each variable in the model. However, Pesaran and Shin (1999) and Pesaran et al. (2001) introduced a relative cointegration test known as the autoregressive distributed lag (ARDL) approach (Pahlavani et al. 2005).

The autoregressive distributed lag (ARDL) model deals with a single cointegration and it has the advantage that it does not require all variables to be I(1) as the Johansen framework does and it is still applicable if we have variables with different orders of integration. We chose the ARDL model as it can be applied to a small sample size and this approach also enables us to estimate the short run and long run dynamic relationships simultaneously. Further, it can distinguish dependent and independent or explanatory variables and allows testing for the existence of relationships between variables of interest. Besides, with ARDL it is possible that different variables have different optimal number of lags (Green 2007).

5.5   Results and Discussion

5.5.1   Unit Root Test Results

The first step before estimation is doing a unit root test (Table 5.1). The Dickey-Fuller test shows that all variables are non-stationary at level. However, at first difference all variables become stationary. This implies that the variables have an integrated order of one I(1). Therefore, this allows us to apply the ARDL approach as it can even be used for a case where different orders of integration exist.

5.5.2   ARDL Bounds Test Results

To test for cointegration using the bounds test approach, we have to first estimate the ARDL model using the appropriate lag-length. The Schwarz Bayesian Criterion (SBC) is used to select the appropriate lag length following Pesaran et al. (2001) which shows that SBC is preferable to other model specification criteria in small sample sizes (which is 40 annual observations in our study). The maximum lag

Table 5.1 Unit root test results

Variables	At level	At first difference	Conclusion
	Intercept and trend	Intercept and trend	
lnPY	1.00	0.00	I(1)
lnDTR	0.62	0.02	I(1)
lnITR	0.97	0.00	I(1)
lnNTR	0.15	0.00	I(1)
lnPGC	0.24	0.00	I(1)
lnUGC	0.23	0.00	I(1)
lnRCS	1.00	0.09	I(1)
lnLF	0.89	0.00	I(1)
lnHC	0.42	0.03	I(1)

Note p-values reported

Table 5.2 Bounds test for cointegration	F-test statistic	Critical value at 5 and 10% bound level of significance			
		5%		1%	
		I0 bound	I1 bound	I0 bound	I1 bound
	6.78	1.91	3.11	2.45	3.79

length in the ARDL model is chosen at 2 following the small sample of the data in our study.

In the bounds test for cointegration, the null hypothesis of no long run relationship among the variables is rejected as the computed F-statistic is greater than the upper bound critical value at the 1% level of significance. Thus, we conclude that there is a long run relationship among the variables in the estimated model (Table 5.2).

5.5.3 ARDL Error Correction Model: Long Run and Short Run Coefficients

We used the ADRL approach to analyze the long run and short run effects of fiscal policy in Ethiopia. In the long run, productive government consumption, indirect tax revenue, human capital, labor force and capital stock were statistically significant and had a long run effect on Ethiopian economic growth. For instance, indirect tax revenue and human capital affected growth positively (Table 5.3). According to Barro and Sala-i-Martin (1997) indirect tax revenue and unproductive government consumption are presumed to have a neutral effect on economic growth. In Ethiopia UGC was statistically insignificant implying that higher government expenditure on unproductive sectors will impact the economy neutrally which coincides with the neutral effect hypothesis of economic theories. The positive effect of indirect tax revenue might be attributed to the fact that it does not discourage incentives for investments. The positive effect of human capital is obvious and can be attributed to total factor productivity. Again, capital stock and labor force in Ethiopia were statistically significant factors that affected growth positively. In our model, direct tax revenue, unproductive government consumption and non-tax revenue were statically insignificant in the long run. In the short run, indirect tax revenue, human capital, productive government consumption, labor force and capital stock were statistically significant with a positive effect on Ethiopian economic growth. However, direct tax revenue, non-tax revenue and unproductive government consumption were statistically insignificant in the short run and had no effect on growth. In our model, the adjustment coefficient was statistically significant and the model adjusted from short run deviation to long run equilibrium by 30% annually.

Variable	Coefficient	t-statistic	Prob.
Short run coefficients			
Δ(lnUGC)	0.05	0.69	0.50
Δ(lnPGC)	0.38*	4.21	0.00
Δ(lnNTR)	−0.02	−1.20	0.25
Δ(lnITR)	0.06***	1.80	0.09
Δ(lnDTR)	0.02	0.40	0.70
Δ(lnHC)	0.22**	2.66	0.02
Δ(lnLF)	5.56**	2.33	0.04
Δ(lnRCS)	0.01**	2.84	0.01
ECM(−1)	−0.29*	−3.75	0.00
Long run coefficients			
lnUGC	−0.23	−1.21	0.25
lnPGC	0.36**	2.12	0.05
lnNTR	0.15	1.17	0.26
lnITR	0.22**	2.65	0.02
lnDTR	0.06	0.43	0.67
lnHC	0.75***	2.04	0.06
lnLF	0.47*	18.75	0.00
lnRCS	0.15*	4.22	0.00
Constant	6.56*	20.56	0.00

Table 5.3 Estimation results of the ARDL cointegrating and long run form ARDL cointegrating and long run form, selected models: ARDL (1, 1, 1, 1, 0, 0, 0, 1, 1), Sample: 1975 2015

NB *, **, *** significant at 1, 5 and 10% respectively

5.5.4 Model Diagnostic Tests

To check the robustness of the estimated model, it is checked for a number of post-estimation model diagnostic tests. Such tests include tests for normality, heteroskedasticity, serial correlation, model specification and parameter stability. The model passed all the diagnostic tests applied (see Table 5.4). As can be seen from a very high value of adjusted R-square of 98% the model had a good fit. In addition, the model passed such tests as those for normality, heteroskedasticity, serial correlation, model specification and parameter stability. The high value of the Jarque–Bera test statistic P-value failed to reject the null of errors which were normally distributed and thus confirm the normality of the residual. The tests for autocorrelation and heteroskedasticity also failed to reject the null-hypotheses of no serial correlation and no heteroscedasticity of the residuals in the estimated model. In addition, the correct functional form specification of the model is confirmed by the Ramsey regression equation specification error test (RESET) as the test failed to reject the null of correct functional form of the model estimated.

To test the stability of the short run and long run coefficients estimated by the ARDL model, we did a test for parameter stability using the cumulative sum (CUSUM) and cumulative sum of squares (CUSUMSQ) tests (Figs. 5.7 and 5.8).

Table 5.4 Model diagnostic tests

R-squared	0.99
Adjusted R-squared	0.98
F-statistic	102.75
Prob (F-statistic)	0.00
Jarque—Berra	0.65
Prob (Jarque—Berra)	0.72
Breusch-godfrey serial correlation LM test*	0.58
Heteroskedasticity test: ARCH*	0.48
Heteroskedasticity test: Breusch-Pagan-Godfrey*	0.26
Ramsey RESET test*	0.44

Note *p-values reported

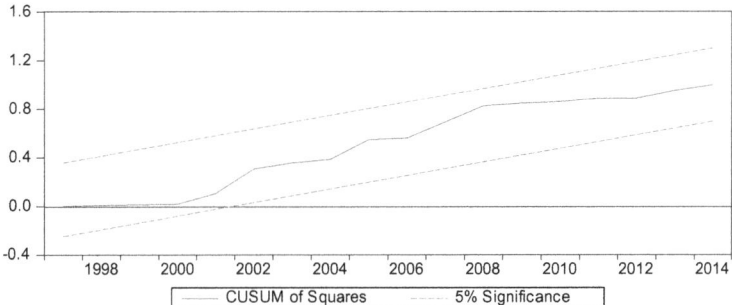

Fig. 5.7 Parameter stability tests CUSM squares

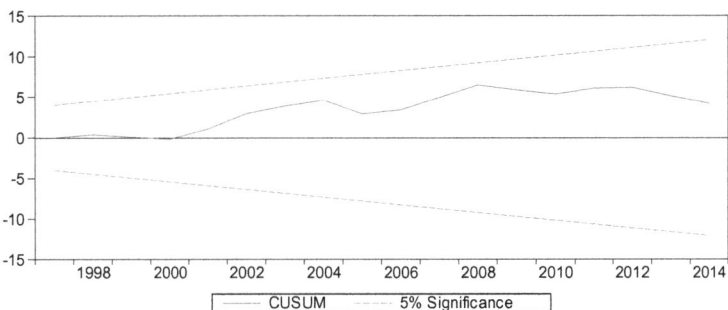

Fig. 5.8 Parameter stability tests CUSM

The plots of both CUSUM and CUSUMSQ statistics lie between the critical bounds at the 5% significance level and did not cross the lower and upper critical limits in both the tests. Thus, the estimated coefficients were parametrically stable over the sample period.

5.6   Conclusion and Policy Implications

This study analyzed the effects of fiscal policy on the Ethiopian economy. It used the ARDL approach and 40-year time-series data. It used different variables such as direct tax revenue, non-direct tax revenue, non-tax revenue, productive government consumption and unproductive government consumption to represent the fiscal effects. Besides, capital stock, labor, human capital and per capita GDP were also included in the model.

A major finding of our study is the existence of a long run relationship between fiscal policy and economic growth in Ethiopia. The prominent factors that affected growth in the long run were human capital, indirect tax revenue, productive government expenditure and capital stock. As predicted in different theories these variables positively affected growth. But unproductive government consumption, tax revenue and non-tax revenue had a statistically insignificant effect on growth.

In the short run, capital stock and productive government consumption had a statically significant effect on per capita GDP of the Ethiopian economy. Productive consumption expenditure had a positive effect on growth suggesting that the composition of this expenditure was good enough to positively contribute to economic growth. However, we have to be cautious of this finding because previous studies show that the results vary depending on the methods used or the variables adopted. Further, indirect tax revenue, human capital and labor were statistically significant in the short run and affected growth positively. Another major finding is that there is an adjustment from short run deviation to long run equilibrium at 30% annually.

A key policy implication of this study is for the government to invest in human capital development both in the short run and long run because among the variables in the model this variable was statistically significant and contributed the lion's share of per capita growth. How to capacitate human capital can be taken as an empirical research question for further studies. Further, the government should decrease unproductive government consumption and enhance its productive consumption to enhance economic performance. Another implication of the study is that labor should be considered a prominent factor in the short run that contributes to economic growth relative to capital stock as our study found that indirect tax revenue had a positive effect on economic growth. This can be attributed to reinvestment of this particular revenue stream in productive government consumption. Ultimately, the government should create awareness and work on how to manage direct tax revenue and its ultimate destination as well as making direct taxes a policy instrument.

References

Abdon, A., G.B. Estrada, M. Lee, and D. Park. 2014. Fiscal policy and growth in developing Asia. ADB Economics Working Paper. No. 412, Asian Development Bank.

Acemoglu, D. 2009. *Introduction to modern economic growth*. USA: Princeton University Press.

Adnan, A.S. 2014. *The impact of public final consumption and investment spending on economic growth in Ethiopia: An application of vector error correction model*. Project submitted to the school of graduate studies of Addis Ababa University, Addis Ababa, Ethiopia.

Ahmad, U.G, and N. Loganathan. 2016. The causal nexus between government expenditure and economic growth in Nigeria: Evidence from a bootstrap rolling window approach. *The American Journal of Innovative Research and Applied Sciences*. Available at www.american-jiras.com.

Ali, S., and N. Ahmad. 2010. The effects of fiscal policy on economic growth: Empirical evidences based on time series data from Pakistan. *The Pakistan Development Review* 449: 497–512.

Barro, R.J. 1990. Government spending in a simple model of endogenous growth. *Journal of Political Economy* 98 (2): 103–125.

Barro, R.J., and X. Sala-I-Martin. 1992. Public finance in models of economic growth. *Review of Economic Studies* 59: 645–661.

Barro, R.J., and X. Sala-I-Martin. 1995. *Economic growth*. McGraw-Hill.

Barro, R.J., and X. Sala-I-Martin. 1997. Technological diffusion, convergence, and growth. *Journal of Economic Growth* 2: 1–27.

Bleaney, M., N. Gemmel, and R. Kneller. 2000. Testing the endogenous growth model: Public expenditure, taxation and growth over the long-run. Discussion paper no. 00/25, University of Nottingham.

Demssie, M.W. 2011. Fiscal policy and economic growth, in Ethiopia: An empirical investigation. Thesis submitted to the School of Graduate Studies of Addis Ababa University, Addis Ababa, Ethiopia.

Easterly, W., and S. Reobelo. 1993. Fiscal policy and economic growth: An empirical investigation. *Journal of Monetary Economics* 32: 417–458.

Easterly, W., and R. Levine. 1997. Africa's growth tragedy: Policies and ethnic divisions. *The Quarterly Journal of Economics* 112 (4): 1203–1250.

Goldsmith, A. 1998. *Institutions and economic growth in Africa*. African Economic Policy Paper, Harvard Institute for International Development, Discussion Paper No.7.

Green, W.H. 2007. *Econometric analysis*, 6th ed. Pearson Education, Inc.: Upper Saddle River, New York University.

Ketema, T. 2006. The impact of government spending on economic growth: The case of Ethiopia. Thesis submitted to the School of Graduate Studies of Addis Ababa University, Addis Ababa Ethiopia.

Kneller, R., M.F. Bleaney, and N. Gemmell. 1999. Fiscal policy and growth: Evidence from OECD countries. *Journal of Public Economics* 74: 171–190.

M'Amanja, D., and O. Morrissey. 2005. Fiscal policy and economic growth in Kenya. CREDIT Research Paper. https://www.nottingham.ac.uk/credit/documents/papers/05-06.pdfhttps://www.nottingham.ac.uk/credit/documents/papers/05-06.pdf

Mansouri, B. 2008. *Fiscal policy and economic growth: Egypt*. Morocco and Tunisia Compared: Unpublished.

MoFED. 2017. *Data from ministry of finance and economic development*. Addis Ababa, Ethiopia

Ocran, M.K. 2009. Fiscal policy and economic growth in South Africa. A paper presented at the centre for the study of african economies in a conference on economic development in Africa, March 22–24, in St. Catherine's College, Oxford University, UK.

Pahlavani, M., E. Wilson, and A.C. Worthington. 2005. Trade-GDP nexus in Iran: An application of the autoregressive distributed lag (ARDL) model. *American Journal of Applied Sciences* 2 (7): 1158–1165.

Pesaran, M.H., and Y. Shin. 1999. An autoregressive distributed lag modelling approach to cointegration analysis. In *Centennial volume of rangar frisch*, ed. S. Strom, A. Holly, and P. Diamond. Cambridge: Cambridge University Press.

Pesaran, M.H., Y. Shin, and R.J. Smith. 2001. Bounds testing approaches to the analysis of level relationships. *Journal of Applied Economics* 16: 289–326.

Romer, D. 2011. *Advanced macroeconomics*, 4th ed. Berkeley: University of California.

Shihab, R.A. 2014. The causal relationship between fiscal policy and economic growth in Jordan. *International Journal of Business and Social Science* 5 (3): 203–208.

Zagler, M., and G. Durnecker. 2003. Fiscal policy and economic growth. *Journal of Economic Surveys* 17 (3): 397–418.

Chapter 6
Impact of Government Sectoral Expenditure on Economic Growth in Ethiopia

Tufa Garoma and Mekonnen Bersisa

Abstract The main objective of this study is examining the impact of government sectoral expenditure on economic growth in Ethiopia over the period 1975–2015. It focuses on sectoral expenditures on economic, social, general services and other services sectors. The major contributions of this study are studying expenditure components in line with the current categorization using up-to-date data. The study uses secondary data collected from the Ministry of Finance and Economic Cooperation of Ethiopia and the National Bank of Ethiopia. It uses both descriptive and econometrics data analysis methods as also the Augmented Dickey Fuller, the Johansen cointegration test and the vector error correction model to test for stationarity and cointegration and to analyze the long run and the short run dynamics of the model. The empirical results show that general services expenditure had a negative and significant effect on economic growth.

Keywords Economic growth · Ethiopia · Sectoral government expenditure
Vector autoregressive

JEL Classification Codes E62 · H50

6.1 Introduction

Government spending can be defined as any expenditure made by local, regional and national governments. It makes up a considerable portion of the gross national product (GNP). This spending is in the form of future investments, transfer

T. Garoma (✉)
Department of Development Economics, Rift Valley University,
Addis Ababa, Ethiopia
e-mail: garomatufa@gmail.com

M. Bersisa
Economics at Department of Economics, Ambo University
Woliso Campus, Woliso 217, Ethiopia
e-mail: mbersisa@gmail.com

© Springer Nature Singapore Pte Ltd. 2018
A. Heshmati and H. Yoon (eds.), *Economic Growth and Development in Ethiopia*, Perspectives on Development in the Middle East and North Africa (MENA) Region, https://doi.org/10.1007/978-981-10-8126-2_6

payments and acquisitions. The concept of government expenditure has a wider meaning as it is associated with the functioning of the government and is not a subject of public finance. It includes all government consumption, investments and transfer payments. In a broader sense, public expenditure means the government's functions in various sectors. In its narrower sense, however, it implies the government's identified and prioritized areas of spending and the implementation of identified projects in a particular fiscal year (Tsegaw 2009).

The relationship between economic growth and government spending has been a topic for researchers in public finance and in macroeconomic modeling. In public finance, studies have mainly focused on understanding the reasons for the growth of the public sector. Hence, they stress on the effects of government spending on economic growth. A fundamental question in growth theory asks whether increasing government expenditure encourages or discourages economic growth. Theoretical as well as empirical research so far gives contradictory answers providing inconclusive evidence. While the Keynesian theory and Wagner's theory support a positive public expenditure and economic growth nexus, supporters of a laisser-faire policy consider it as a detriment through its crowding-out effect. Opponents of the role of public expenditure contend that an increase in government expenditure may slow down the overall performance of the economy. For instance, in an attempt to finance rising expenditures, the government may increase taxes and/or borrowings. A higher income tax discourages individuals from working for long hours or even searching for jobs. This in turn reduces incomes and aggregate demand. In the same way, a higher profit tax tends to increase production costs and reduce investment expenditure as well as firms' profitability. Moreover, if the government increases borrowings (especially from banks) to finance its expenditure it will crowd-out the private sector thus reducing private investments. Thus, government activities sometimes produce a misallocation of resources and slow down the growth of national output (Nurudeen and Usman 2010; Sudarsono 2010).

However, government spending cannot be zero as it has to at least enforce contracts, protect property rights and develop economic and social infrastructure. Some government spending is necessary for the successful operation of the rule of law (Mitchell 2005). Some studies find a significant positive relationship between public sector growth and economic growth only for developing nations and not for developed countries. This is due partly to the variations in the composition of government expenditure in different parts of the world. Asian countries have witnessed a steady increase in education spending and social security, but the region's spending on agriculture has decreased by roughly half. Asian governments have also reduced their spending on health as a share of total government spending which indicates that the economies are recovering from the 1990s Asian financial crisis (Fan 2008). The role of the government in less developed countries (LDCs) like Ethiopia is quite significant for at least short-run growth. The government's fiscal policies which include taxation, expenditure, correcting market failures and providing public goods and services have become crucial instruments of economic growth in these countries, including in Ethiopia (Berihun 2014).

Through its various developmental programs the Government of Ethiopia has been actively engaged in the economy to reduce poverty and achieve sustained and broad-based economic growth. In its recent development plan, the Growth and Transformation Plan (GTP), the Government of Ethiopia envisaged achieving macroeconomic stability, rapid and sustainable economic growth and increased public spending in the pro-poor sectors. Over GTP I (2010–15), on average, the government spent about Birr 125.5 billion per annum. Out of this, more than 69% was spent on pro-poor sectors of education, health, water and sanitation, agriculture and road infrastructure (MOFED 2014). The country registered one of the fastest economic growths over the last decade. One of the major drivers of this was large scale public sector investments. From 2010 to 2013, total spending on growth-oriented pro-poor sectors of education, agriculture and food security, water and sanitation, health and roads amounted to $12.7 billion. In 2012–13 alone, the spending on these sectors accounted for over 70% of the government's general spending (AfDB 2015).

The Government of Ethiopia has been committing considerably huge resources to attain GTP with the aim of achieving middle income status by 2025. The outcome of this huge expenditure needs to be evaluated over time to ensure efficiency and make clear the real effects of this expenditure on economic growth. However, there is deviation between the performance of the Ethiopian economy and the huge increase in government expenditure over the years posing a critical question about its role in promoting economic growth. As a result, one can ask questions like: What is the reason behind this divergence? Which part of the government expenditure plays a vital role in this development objective?

Despite the overall progress, Ethiopia still faces challenges which will reverse the recent progress and result in lower consumption growth among the bottom percentiles of its population. There is also the worrying trend of negative consumption growth for the very poorest households. There are huge unmet needs and very limited reach on the part of public services in targeting youth and the extremely poor. A number of empirical papers are available for Ethiopia on the effects of public expenditure on economic growth (Bargicho 2016; Berihun 2014; Kebede 2015; Ketema 2006; Muhammed 2015; Tsadiku 2012). Our study is different in the way in which it considers the components of public expenditure. It analyzes the impact of sectoral expenditure on economic growth in line with the government categorization (economic, social, general and other expenditures) rather than components (sub-sectors). This approach will help the government to evaluate the effectiveness of each public expenditure component. Moreover, our study period is more recent and up-to-date. We systematically assess and draw some conclusions about the questions raised and indicate which sectors are more efficient in enhancing economic growth in the country.

The primary objective of our study is examining the impact of government sectoral expenditure on economic growth in Ethiopia. Specifically, it addresses the following objectives:

- Analyzing the effects of disaggregated sectoral government expenditure on Ethiopia's economic growth.
- Identifying the long-run and short-run linkages between these sectors and economic growth.

6.2 Literature Review

Various theories explain the relationship between public expenditure and economic growth. The most frequently cited ones are: Wagner's law 'of increasing government activities'; Peacock Wiseman's hypothesis of 'displacement effects' as a reason for the shift of demand for public goods and services; the Musgrave theory of public expenditure and growth; and the Keynesian theory of public expenditure (Guandong and Muturi 2016; Mahmoodi and Mahmoodi 2014; Sharma 2012; Tsadiku 2012).

Wagner's theory relates to the 'law of increasing expansion of public and particularly state activities'. It analyzes trends in the growth of public expenditure and in the size of the public sector. Wagner's law postulates that an extension of the functions of the state leads to an increase in public expenditure on the administration and regulation of the economy. The law also states that the development of a modern industrial society will give rise to increasing political pressure for social progress and call for increased allowances for social considerations in the conduct of industry. In this case, an increase in public expenditure will be more than proportional to an increase in national income and will thus result in a relative expansion of the public sector.

Wagner's law focuses on the nexus between the size of the economy and the size of the public sector and postulates that the latter grows at a faster pace than the former during the process of industrialization and urbanization. This reflects an expansion of government activities that complement or substitute private activities. The law attributes the growth of the public sector to higher expenditures in areas such as enforcing contracts and regulatory activities which are driven by a higher demand for government intervention in an economy with new layers of externalities and interdependencies. An implication of Wagner's law is that increased division of labor will be accompanied by the development of new technological processes which will lead to the growth of monopolies in the private sector. In his view, private sector monopolies will not adequately take into account the social needs of society as a whole and therefore need to be replaced by public corporations. Further, if private sector companies became too large, the economy will become unstable because problems of individual companies will become problems for society as a whole (Tsadiku 2012).

Peacock and Wiseman tested Wagner's law and found that 'displacement effects' were responsible for a shift in demand for public goods and services. A government faces difficulties when it tries to re-establish the structure of public expenditure which was customary before these unusual moments. As a result, there is a tendency to increase the amount of public outlays after such a period. Peacock and Wiseman formulated the 'displacement effect' hypothesis. Their hypothesis rests on three basic propositions: (i) governments can always find profitable ways to expend available funds, (ii) citizens, in general, are unwilling to accept higher taxes, and (iii) governments must be responsive to the wishes of their citizens. Peacock and Wiseman derive the key concept of a 'tolerable burden of taxation' which has an important implication for economic growth (Mahmoodi and Mahmoodi 2014).

On the other hand, Musgrave's theory of public expenditure growth found changes in the income elasticity of demand for public services in three ranges of per capita incomes. He posits that at low levels of per capita income, demand for public services tends to be very low because according to him such income is devoted to satisfying primary needs and that when per capita income starts rising above these low-income levels, the demand for services supplied by the public sector such as health, education and transport starts increasing thereby forcing the government to increase expenditure on them. He observes that at high levels of per capita income, which are typical of developed economics, the rate of public sector growth tends to fall as the more basic wants are satisfied. His theory states that there is a functional relationship between the growth of an economy and the growth of government activities so that the government sector grows faster than the economy (Tsadiku 2012).

Finally, failures of 18th century economists of lassie-faire policies and in the post WW I scenario, the government's role was revitalized by the influential work of Johan Maynard Keynes. He argued that the government still had many things to do that were not being done (Fan 2008). Keynes regarded public expenditure as an endogenous factor which can be utilized as a policy instrument to promote economic growth. In the Keynesian view, public expenditure can contribute positively to economic growth. Hence, an increase in government consumption is likely to lead to an increase in employment, profitability and investments through multiplier effects on aggregate demand. As a result, government expenditure increases aggregate demand, which leads to an increased output depending on expenditure multipliers. Here increased government spending is thought to raise aggregate demand and increase consumption, which in turn leads to increased production. According to the Keynesian view, a severe recession or depression may never end if the government does not intervene.

In line with this school of thought, some scholars argue that an increase in government expenditure on socioeconomic and physical infrastructure encourages economic growth. For example, government expenditure on education and health raises the productivity of labor and increases the growth of national output. Similarly, expenditure on infrastructure such as roads, communication and power reduces production costs and increases private sector investments and the profitability of firms thus fostering economic growth (Guandong and Muturi 2016).

Even though Wagner's law supports an increase in government activities, his hypothesis states that as an economy grows so does the size of the public sector. This is in contrast to the Keynesian view that the growth of government expenditure results in GDP growth. Hence, the existing theories on the relationship between public expenditure and economic growth show conflicting results especially on the causality issue. This means that there is no clear explanation about this relationship as the explanations are inconclusive.

6.2.1 Empirical Literature Review

Numerous studies have been conducted to analyze the role of government spending in the long-term growth of national economies. However, there is no consistent evidence providing unequivocal causality of public spending on economic growth. At worst it is hard to find consistent empirical papers supporting the theoretical wisdom established to justify the role of public expenditure in economic growth. Therefore, our empirical review provides some evidence on the effect of government spending on economic growth in different parts of the world.

Sudarsono (2010) tested the causal relationship between economic growth and government spending for OIC countries during 1970–2006. He found that government spending led to economic growth in Iran, Nigeria and Tunisia, which is compatible with Keynesian theory. However, economic growth did lead to an increase in government spending in Algeria, Burkina Faso, Benin, Indonesia, Libya, Malaysia, Morocco and Saudi, which are well-suited to Wagner's law.

Using a panel cointegration analysis of the joint development of government expenditures and economic growth in 23 OECD countries, Lamartina and Zaghini (2010) provide empirical results which indicate the existence of a structural positive correlation between public spending and per capita GDP which is again consistent with Wagner's law. Afzal and Abbas (2010) tested the applicability of Wagner's law in Pakistan. Their results do not support the hypothesis for aggregate public spending and income. It found no evidence of a long-run relationship between aggregate expenditure and income or between disaggregated expenditure and income.

Ghosh Roy (2012) explored the association between government size and economic growth in the United States using time-series data over the period 1950–2007. The results suggest that an increase in government consumption slowed economic growth, while an increase in government investments enhanced economic growth; this supports the Keynesian view. On the other hand, Alshahrani and Alsadiq (2014) investigated the relationship between government expenditure and economic growth in Saudi Arabia using VECM. Their results show that economic growth was positively related to private domestic and public investments and healthcare expenditure in the long run but spending on education, defense and housing had a negative long run relationship with GDP growth.

Al-Fawwaz (2016) measured the impact of government expenditure on economic growth in Jordan in 1980–2013 and the results indicate that there was a positive impact of both total government expenditure and current government expenditure on economic growth. This result supports the Keynesian model.

Hua (2016) studied the relationship between public expenditure on education and economic growth in China. His empirical findings show that there was a positive and significant relationship between public expenditure, education and economic growth.

In another related study in developing countries, Bose et al. (2007) examined the growth effects of government expenditure for a panel of 30 developing countries over the 1970s and 1980s, with a particular focus on disaggregated government expenditure. They found that government investments and total expenditure in education were the only outlays that were significantly associated with growth.

Nasiru (2012) investigated the relationship between government expenditure (disaggregated into capital and recurrent) and economic growth in Nigeria over the period 1961–2010 by employing the bounds test approach to cointegration based on the unrestricted error correction model and the pair-wise Granger causality tests. The results of the bounds test showed that there was no long-run relationship between government expenditure and economic growth in Nigeria. Another study by Olabisi and Elizabeth (2012) using the vector autoregressive approach found that expenditure on education had failed to enhance economic growth in Nigeria. On the other hand, Ditimi et al. (2011) using a multivariate cointegration approach concluded that expenditure on agriculture had a significant influence on economic growth while expenditure on education, health, transport and communication had an insignificant influence on economic growth in Nigeria.

Mahjoub (2013) determined the nature and direction of causality between government expenditure and national income in Sudan using the Granger causality test and the error correction model (ECM) for 1970–2008. The results of the cointegration test showed a long-run relationship between government expenditure and national income in Sudan. The results also indicated the direction of causality running from government expenditure to national income both in the short and long-run. Musaba et al. (2013) studied the impact of government sectoral expenditure on Malawi's economic growth. The study employed time series data for 1980–2007. Methodologically, it applied a cointegration analysis and error correction methods to examine the relationship between economic growth and government sectoral expenditure. The results showed no significant short-run relationship between government sectoral expenditure and economic growth. The results, however, revealed the existence of a long-run relationship between the two. While expenditure on agriculture and defence had a positive and significant relationship with economic growth, expenditure on education, health, social protection, transportation and communication had a negative and significant effect on the country's economic growth.

Gisore et al. (2014) studied the effects of government spending on economic growth in East Africa and their findings show that expenditure on health and defense had a positive and statistically significant effect on growth. In contrast, expenditure on education and agriculture had an insignificant effect on economic growth.

Adamu and Hajara (2015) examined the impact of public expenditure on economic growth in Nigeria using time-series data for 1970–2012 and his empirical findings show that there was a positive and insignificant relationship between capital expenditure and economic growth while recurrent expenditure had a significant positive impact on economic growth. Guandong and Muturi (2016) analyzed the relationship between public expenditure and economic growth in South Sudan and concluded that public expenditure on infrastructure, the productive sector and security was a positive determinant of economic growth. But government expenditure on the social services sector had a negative impact on economic growth.

Bahaddi and Karim (2017) evaluated the effect of public expenditure on economic growth in Morocco and assessed the quality of governance impact on public spending by using ECM following Johansen's approach. In the light of the results of the econometric regression, good governance remained the best option that allowed the Moroccan government to achieve considerable macroeconomic performance; this has similarities with the Keynesian theory.

Like in other developing countries, issues of government expenditure have been under scrutiny in Ethiopia for a long time. However, there are mixed results on the impact of government expenditure on economic growth. For instance, Ketema (2006) studied the impact of various components of government spending (investments, consumption and human capital) on economic growth and found that only human capital (education and health) had a long run impact on economic growth. Endale (2007) assessed the effects of defense expenditure on economic growth based on the Hauseman test of random effects estimator and his empirical results showed that the defense burden was negative to real GDP growth.

Using the vector error correction mechanism Tsadiku (2012) found that expenditure on education and road construction had a positive short-run impact on economic growth while expenditure on health, agriculture and non-poverty sectors had a negative and insignificant effect on GDP growth.

Berihun (2014) investigated the impact of government expenditure on economic growth in Ethiopia over the period 1975–2013, with a particular focus on sectoral expenditure on agriculture, defense, health and education sectors and his empirical results showed that expenditure on agriculture and defense negatively affected economic growth but that on the health and education sectors positively affected economic growth.

Kebede (2015) analyzed the impact of government spending on economic growth in Ethiopia and shows that expenditure on the electric power sector had a significant positive effect and expenditure on the road sector's development had an insignificant effect on the growth of real per capita income growth. Muhammed (2015) investigated the composition of government expenditure and economic growth in Ethiopia using data for 1975–2011. His study considered the composition of public expenditure on agriculture, health, trade and industry and found that these were statistically significant in explaining changes in economic growth. However, expenditure on road transport and communication was statically insignificant in explaining economic growth in Ethiopia.

Bargicho (2016) analyzed the effect of government expenditure and tax on economic growth in Ethiopia for the sample period 1980–81 to 2013–14 and he found that long run current expenditure and direct taxes had a negative and significant effect on real GDP but capital expenditure and indirect taxes had a positive and significant effect on real GDP; he thus finally proved the Keynesian theory.

6.3   Data and Methodology

6.3.1   Types and Sources of Data, Theoretical Framework and Model Specification

We used secondary data to analyze the impact of sectoral government expenditure on economic growth in Ethiopia. Time-series data of the total federal government's budget expenditure on economic services, social services, general services and other services expenditure was collected from 1975 to 2015. The data was obtained from the Ministry of Finance and Economic Cooperation (MOFEC) and the National Bank of Ethiopia (NBE).

Our study used a theoretical framework like Nurudeen and Usman's (2010) study our study is also grounded in the Keynesian and endogenous growth models. While the Keynesian model emphasizes the importance of government expenditure in accelerating economic growth, the endogenous growth models give no distinguishable role to the government in the growth process. However, our study found components of government expenditure to be important in accelerating economic growth. In the Keynesian model economic growth is a function of public expenditure. It defines total public expenditure as a function of summation of all individual government expenditure in all components:

$$\text{TGE} = f \left(\sum Gi \right) \tag{6.1}$$

where, TGE is total government expenditure and Gi are components of individual government expenditure. The modification of the model helps investigate the relationship between government expenditure and economic growth. Thus, the model expresses economic growth (GDP) as a function of various components of government expenditure including economic services, social services, general services and other expenditure. The model is represented in functional form as:

$$\text{RGDPt} = f(\text{ESexp} + \text{SSexp} + \text{GSexp} + \text{Osexp}) \tag{6.2}$$

where, RGDPt is real gross domestic product at time t, Esexp is economic services expenditure, Ssexp is social services expenditure, Gsexp is general services expenditure and Osexp is other services expenditure.

Based on this function we can establish the VAR model with maximum lag of n equal to 3. Each variable in the model has one equation and the current time t observation of each variable depends on its own lagged values as well as on the lagged values of each other's variables. Thus, the vector autoregressive (VAR) model is summarized as:

$$Esexpt = B1 + B21 \sum_{n=1}^{3} B2nRGDPt - n + \sum_{n=1}^{3} B2nESexpt - n + \sum_{n=1}^{3} B3nSSexpt - n$$

$$+ \sum_{n=1}^{3} B4nGSexpt - n + \sum_{n=1}^{3} B5nOSexpt - n + et$$

$$SSexpt = B2 + B31 \sum_{n=1}^{3} B1nRGDPt - n + \sum_{n=1}^{3} B2nESexpt - n + \sum_{n=1}^{3} B3nSSexpt - n$$

$$+ \sum_{n=1}^{3} B4nGSexpt - n + \sum_{n=1}^{3} B5nOSexpt - n + et$$

$$GSexpt = B3 + B41 + \sum_{n=1}^{3} B1nRGDPt - n + \sum_{n=1}^{3} B2nESexpt - n + \sum_{n=1}^{3} B3nSSexpt - n$$

$$+ \sum_{n=1}^{3} B4nGSexpt - n + \sum_{n=1}^{3} B5nOSexpt - n + et$$

$$OSexpt = B4 + B51 \sum_{n=1}^{3} B1nRGDPt - n + \sum_{n=1}^{3} B2nESexpt - n + \sum_{n=1}^{3} B3nSSexpt - n$$

$$+ \sum_{n=1}^{3} B4nGSexpt - n + \sum_{n=1}^{3} B5nOSexpt - n + et$$

$$(6.3)$$

6.3.2 Diagnostic Tests

A majority of the macroeconomic time-series variables are non-stationary at a level, which means their mean and variance are a function of time or are not constant. If we regress non-stationary time-series data the result will be a spurious regression, which will not produce the right results. Hence, the issue of stationary is the main part in the time-series variable and for this we did a unit root test. A commonly applied formal test for the existence of a unit root in the data is the Dickey-Fuller (DF) test and its simple extension the Augmented Dickey Fuller (ADF) test. We applied the Augmented Dickey-Fuller test which involves estimating the following regression equations:

$$\Delta y_t = \delta_1 y_{t-1} + \sum \beta_1 \Delta y_{t-i} + e_t \qquad (6.4)$$

$$\Delta y_t = \delta_0 + \delta_1 y_{t-1} + \sum \beta_1 \Delta y_{t-i} + e_t \qquad (6.5)$$

$$\Delta y_t = \delta_0 + \delta_1 y_{t-1} + \sum \beta_1 \Delta y_{t-i} + \alpha T + e_t \qquad (6.6)$$

where, δ_0 is constant (drift), T is a trend, i is the lag length and e_t is the error term which is normally distributed with zero mean and constant variance. Testing for unit roots using Eq. 6.4 assumes that the underlying data generating process has no intercept term and time trend. Equation 6.5 is used to account for the existence of an intercept term or trend only and Eq. 6.6 suggests using intercept and a deterministic term to test for the unit root. In these equations, if $\delta_1 = 0$, then Y_t series contains a unit root.

After testing the stationary of the data, we also examined the optimum number of lags to be used for the nest jobs because the lag length is very sensitive and changes the results as the number of lags increase. We used the Hannan-Quinn information criteria (HQIC), the Akaike information criteria (AIC) and the Schwarz-Bayesian information criteria (SBIC) to determine the optimum lag length among the selection criteria tests. Thus, the lag with the smallest result is the lag order selected for the model.

After tests for stationary and determining the lag order, the next task is testing for cointegration, which enables checking whether the linear combination of variables is also stationary or not. One possible means of avoiding a spurious regression is by using cointegration techniques which allow the estimation of non-spurious regressions with non-stationary data. Variables are said to be cointegrated if a long-run equilibrium relationship exists among them; we applied the Johansen cointegration test.

We also conducted other diagnostic tests such as normality and serial correlation, autocorrelation or serial correlation test, Portmanteau test for white noise, line plots test of stationarity, Bartlett's period gram-based white noise test and the Breusch-Godfrey LM test for autocorrelation.

6.3.3 VEC Model Estimation, VEC Stability Test and Impulse Response Function

VEC was estimated to test long-run cointegrating relationships while allowing for short-run adjustment dynamics. Further, stability of the model and post-estimation diagnostics could affect the validity of the estimated model; thus, checking whether the model was correctly specified with the number of cointegrating equations was important. If the process is stable, the moduli of the remaining n Eigen values are strictly less than one. The necessary and sufficient condition for stability is that all characteristic roots lie inside the unit circle with full rank and that all variables are stationary.

Further, we examined the impulse response function to analyze the long-run effects of a unit shock of a given variable. This shows the effect of a one-time shock to one of the innovations on current and future values of the variable itself and also compares this response to shocks from other variables. We applied the impulse response function to examine the impulse response of endogenous variables to a one-time shock in other variables in the model.

6.3.4 Definition of the Variables

Regarding the functional expenditure of the government, we considered four major categories of sectoral spending:

- Economic Services Expenditure (ESexp) consists of expenditure on agriculture and natural resources, trade and industry, mines and energy, tourism, transport and communication, urban development and construction.
- Social Services Expenditure (SSexp) consists of expenditure on education, culture and sports, public health, labor and social welfare and rehabilitation.
- General Services Expenditure (GSexp) consists of organs of the state, defense, justice, public order and security and other general services expenditure.
- Other Services Expenditure (OSexp) consists of expenditure on pension payments, interest and charges, internal and external debt, regional subsidy (transfer), miscellaneous and external assistance.

6.4   Results and Discussion

6.4.1 Descriptive Statistics of the Variables Used for the Analysis

Government spending in Ethiopia has changed completely with time. Thus, it is important to examine trends in the level and composition of government expenditure and also to assess the causes of the change over time. It is even more important to analyze the relative contribution of sector expenditure to economic growth. According to an EEA (2017) report, Ethiopia's total federal government budget expenditure is divided into four expenditure categories: economic services, social services, general services and other services.

6.4.1.1 Trends in Economic Growth and Economic Services Expenditure

Economic services expenditure consists of expenditure on agriculture and natural resources, trade and industry, mines and energy, tourism, transport and communication, urban development and construction.

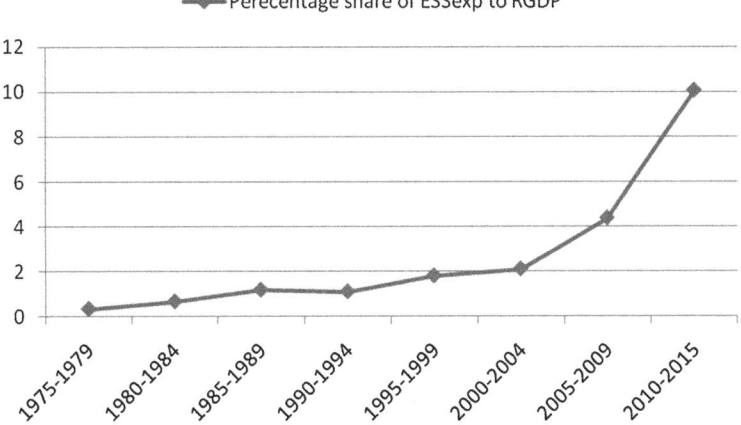

Fig. 6.1 Percentage share of economic service expenditure to economic growth. *Source* Authors'
computation based on NBE data

According to Fig. 6.1, there was an increasing trend in economic services
expenditure during the study period (1975–79) when the average percentage share
of economic services expenditure in economic growth was around 0.33% which
increased to 1.09% during 1990–94. This figure reached nearly 10.06% of RGDP in
2010–15. Thus, economic services expenditure showed an increasing trend during
the study period.

6.4.1.2 Trends in Economic Growth and Social Services Expenditure

Social services expenditure consists of expenditure on education, culture and sports,
public health, labor and social welfare and rehabilitation.

Figure 6.2 shows that there was an increasing trend in social services expenditure during the study period. In 1975–79, the average percentage share of social
services expenditure to economic growth was around 0.24% which increased to
0.76% in 1990–94 and reached nearly 7.58% of RGDP in 2010–15. Thus, social
services expenditure showed an increasing trend during the study period.

6.4.1.3 Trends in Economic Growth and General Services
         Expenditure

General services expenditure consists of expenditure on the organs of the state,
defense, justice, public order and security and other general services expenditure.

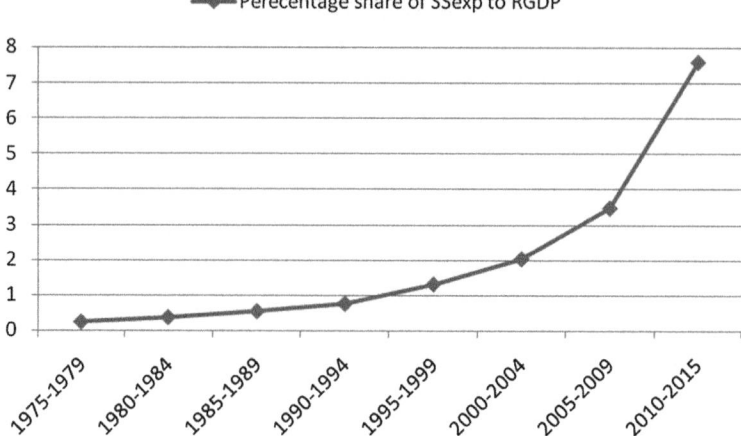

Fig. 6.2 Percentage share of social service expenditure to economic growth. *Source* Authors' computation based on NBE data

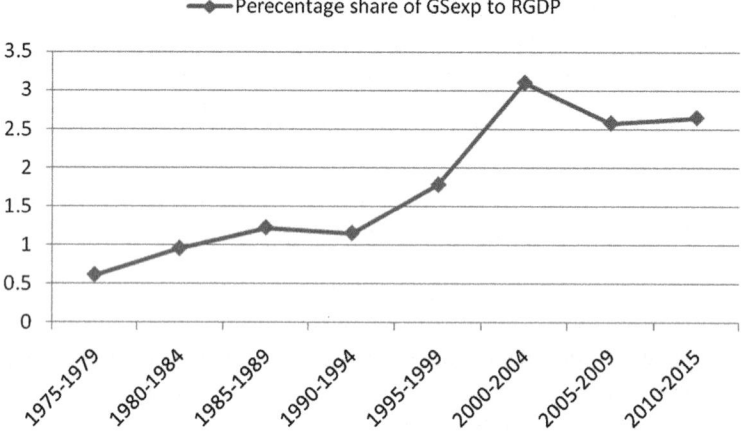

Fig. 6.3 Percentage share of general service expenditure to economic growth. *Source* Authors' computation based on NBE data

According to Fig. 6.3, there was increasing trend in general services expenditure during the study period. In 1975–79, the average percentage share of general services expenditure to economic growth was around 0.61% which increased to 3.1% in 2000–04. However, this declined to 2.65% of RGDP in 2010–15. Thus, general services expenditure showed a decreasing trend during the study period.

6.4.1.4 Trends in Economic Growth and Other Services Expenditure

Other services expenditure consists of expenditure on pension payments, interest and charges, internal and external debt, regional subsidy (transfers), pension payments, miscellaneous and external assistance.

Figure 6.4 shows an increasing trend in general services expenditure during the study period. In 1975–79, average percentage share of general services expenditure to economic growth was around 0.19% which increased to 1.8% in 2000–04. However, this declined to 1.2% of RGDP in 2010–2015 showing a decreasing trend during the study period.

Table 6.1 shows that during the Dergue regime (1975–91), the general services budget allocation on average was around 41% of the total government expenditure which was the highest share of government expenditure. Economic services expenditure had a 28% share next to general services expenditure and other sectors

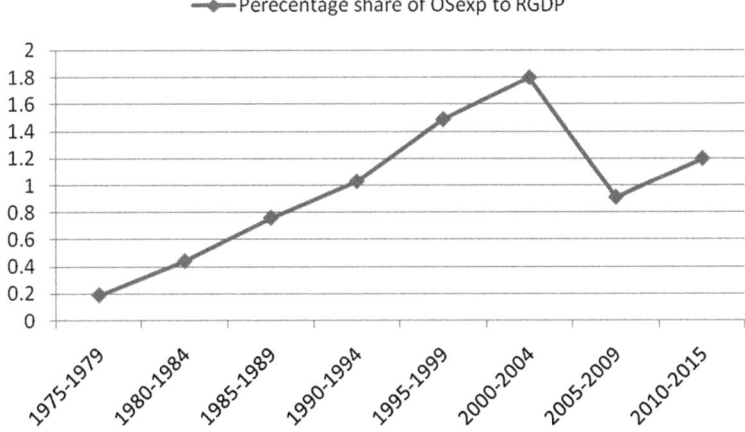

Fig. 6.4 Percentage share of other service expenditure to economic growth. *Source* Authors' computation based on NBE data

Table 6.1 Average percentage share of sectoral expenditure from total government expenditure in both regimes

Regime	Period	Percentage share of economic service from total expenditure	Percentage share of social service from total expenditure	Percentage share of general service from total expenditure	Percentage share of other service from total expenditure
Dergue	1975–1991	28.27	16.54	40.51	18.36
EPRDF	1992–2015	34.10	26.97	26.35	16.86

Source Authors' computation based on NBE data

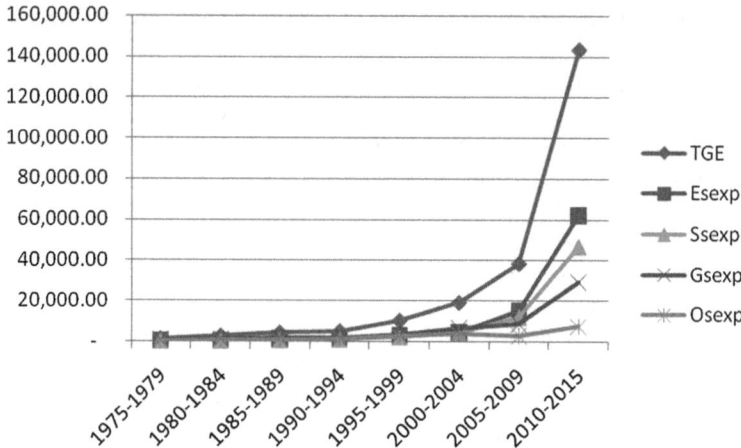

Fig. 6.5 Trends in sectoral services expenditure and total government expenditure. *Source* Authors' computation based on NBE data

accounted for an 18% share and the social services sector for around 17% of TGE. From this we can infer the Dergue regime give priority to general services expenditure especially to defense expenditure which is categorized as an unproductive sector. In contrast, during EPRDF the economic services budget allocation on average was around 34% of the total government expenditure which was the highest share and indicates that EPDRF may shift attention to the productive sector. Further, the share of general services and social services was nearly the same (about 26% each), on average and other sectors accounted for around 17% of the total expenditure during the EPDRF regime.

Although economic services expenditure had the highest share, general services expenditure was very close to this sector in 1998–2000 and the budget allocation for this sector was about 42% of the total government expenditure due to the Ethio-Eritrea war. Defense and security services had a bigger share (50% up to the end of 2001).

From 2004 to 05 onwards the government has redirected its focus and most of the budget allocations are in favor of pro-poor sectors (education, health, agriculture and natural resources, roads and urban development) which is defined as economic and social services expenditure in the study period (Fig. 6.5).

6.4.2 Descriptive Statistics of the Major Variables

We used annual time-series data covering the period 1975–2015. The variables under consideration are real gross domestic product and sectoral government expenditure on economic services, social services, general services and other

Table 6.2 Descriptive statistics of the economic variables (1975–2015), (in million Birr)

Measurements	RGDP	ESexp	SSexp	GSexp	Osexp
Mean	236.06	12.40	9.50	7.20	2.63
Std. dev.	172.66	23.12	17.80	108.00	2.77
Max.	753.23	230.23	240.90	363.16	15.72
Min.	102.41	91.24	80.33	51.02	13.30

Source Authors' computation using Stata 13 software

services. Real gross domestic product (RGDP) is a dependent variable, whereas the other variables are determinant factors of RGDP.

Table 6.2 gives a description of the variables used in the estimation and they are all expressed in millions of the local currency (Ethiopian Birr). RGDP averaged Birr 236 million and varied from Birr 102 to 753 million with a standard deviation of Birr 172 million. Economic services expenditure averaged Birr 12 million and went from Birr 230 to Birr 91 million with a standard deviation of Birr 23 million. Similarly, social services expenditure averaged Birr 9 million and ranged from Birr 240 million with a standard deviation of Birr 17 million. General services expenditure, with a mean of Birr 7 million also varied from a minimum of Birr 51 million to a maximum of Birr 363 million with a standard deviation of Birr 108 million and finally other services expenditure averaged Birr 2 million and went from Birr 13 to Birr 15 million with a standard deviation of Birr 2 million during the study period.

6.4.3 Results of Diagnostic Tests

The time-series under consideration should be checked for stationary before one can attempt to fit a suitable model. That is, the variables have to be tested for the presence of unit root(s) thereby determining the order of integration of each series. The non-stationary of the series can be tested by using an Augmented Dickey-Fuller test. The hypotheses to be tested are: H0: the series is non-stationary or has a unit root against the alternative hypothesis H1: the series is stationary or has no unit root. The results of the ADF unit root test with intercept only and with intercept and trend at a level and first and second difference for each series are presented in Table 6.2; the critical values used for the tests are the McKinnon (1991) critical values.

The test results in Table 6.3 show that the series at level and first difference contained unit root. Even though some values were more than critical, their coefficient of L1 contained positive (divergent from regression line) values which made no sense for the model so we passed to the second difference and here all their respective ADF test statistics were less than their respective *p*-values and their respective L1 coefficients contained negative (the long-run adjustment towards the regression line) values which fit the model.

Table 6.3 Augmented Dickey-Fuller unit root test results at level, first and second difference

Series	At a level		First difference		Second difference		Oder
	With intercept no trend	With intercept and trend	With intercept no trend	With intercept and trend	With intercept no trend	With intercept and trend	
RGDP	14.257	7.027	−0.742	−2.604	−7.822	−7.978	I(2)
ESexp	8.108	4.845	−1.651	−2.572	−6.910	−6.832	I(2)
SSexp	16.327	11.706	1.977	0.690	−5.936	−6.827	I(2)
GSexp	11.039	8.492	1.000	−0.125	−5.863	−6.410	I(2)
OSexp	3.765	2.506	−3.339	−4.001	−11.009	−11.221	I(2)
1% Critical values	−3.648	−4.242	−3.655	−4.251	−3.662	−4.260	
5% Critical values	−2.958	−3.540	−2.961	−3.540	−2.964	−3.548	
10% Critical values	−2.612	−3.204	−2.613	−3.204	−2.614	−3.209	

Source Authors' computation using Stata 13 software

Table 6.4 VAR lag order selection criteria

Lag	LL	LR	df	P	FPE	AIC	HQIC	SBIC
0	−4154.54	–	–	–	1.6e+94	231.085	231.162	231.305
1	−4111.88	85.316	25	0.000	6.0e+93	230.104	230.565	231.424
2	−4065.47	92.806	25	0.000	2.0e+93	228.915	229.76	231.335
3	−3990.91	149.13[a]	25	0.000	1.6e+92[a]	226.162[a]	227.39[a]	229.681[a]

Note [a]Indicates lag order selected by the criterion: each test at the 5% level
Source Authors' computation using Stata 13 software

Estimating the VAR/VEC order

Before estimating the VAR/VEC model, it is critical to choose the order of the model that yields a good model and hence a precise forecast. The VAR order refers to the optimal number of lags that should be included in the model since choosing too few lags could lead to systematic variations in the residuals whereas if too many lags are chosen there are fewer degrees of freedom. Thus, we applied the Akaike information criterion (AIC), the Schwarzbirth information criterion (SBC) and the Hannan-Quinn (HQ) information criteria to determine the lag order.

As shown in Table 6.4, the lag length selection criterion was tabulated and the AIC, SCB and HQI tests suggest that the appropriate lag length for the VAR model was three (3). That is, the best fitting model was three that minimized AIC, SCB and HQ where the optimal lag length for the VAR model was selected by criteria.

Lag Exclusion Test

Given that VAR modeling requires a uniform lag length for each variable we used the Wald lag exclusion test to check whether the chosen lag was optimal.

According to Table 6.5, almost all the variables were significant at lag three with a 5% level of significance expect RGDP. But these lag variables combined were significant, that is the value in the square brackets indicates probability value for the corresponding Chi-square statistics. Therefore, lag three was found to be suitable for the dataset and could be applied.

Residual Normality Test

We applied the Jarque-Bera, Skewness and Kurtosis test to check whether the residuals were normally distributed or not. We directly applied this test at the 5% level and applied the guidance: if all p-values were more than 5%, the residuals were normally distributed.

As shown in Table 6.6, the Jarque-Bera, Skewness and Kurtosis test contained more than 5%, as a result we can accept this model and can say that the residuals were normally distributed.

Autocorrelation/serial correlation test

A test for autocorrelation or serial correlation is done to check whether the residuals are serial correlated or not and for this we applied the Lagrange-multiplier (LM) test.

As shown in Table 6.7, the corresponding probable values were more than 5% at lag order three, as a result we can agree with the null hypothesis, which is no autocorrelation at lag order three.

Table 6.5 VAR lag exclusion Wald tests

Lag	RGDP	Esexp	Ssexp	GSexp	OSexp	Joint (all)
Lag3	1.100705	33.67415	284.6125	31.99783	81.14783	564.5657
p-value	0.954	0.000	0.000	0.000	0.000	0.000
df	5	5	5	5	5	25

Source Authors' computation using Stata 13 software

Table 6.6 Residual normality test

Jarque-Bera test				Skewness test			Kurtosis test		
Equation	chi2	df	Prob > chi2	chi2	Df	Prob > chi2	chi2	df	Prob > chi2
D_D2RGDP	0.449	2	0.79884	0.434	1	0.51002	0.015	1	0.90203
D_D2ESesp	1.470	2	0.47945	1.445	1	0.22934	0.025	1	0.87367
D_D2SSesxp	2.122	2	0.34618	1.498	1	0.22100	0.624	1	0.42967
D_D2GSexp	13.146	2	0.14023	2.924	1	0.08727	10.222	1	0.10139
D_D2OSexp	1.216	2	0.54447	0.655	1	0.41850	0.561	1	0.45370
ALL	18.403	10	0.4854	6.955	5	0.22398	11.447	5	0.14320

Source Authors' computation using Stata 13 software

Table 6.7 Autocorrelation test

Lag	chi2	df	Prob > chi2
1	41.7670	25	0.01904
2	38.1163	25	0.04507
3	36.6383	25	0.06246

Source Authors' computation using Stata 13 software

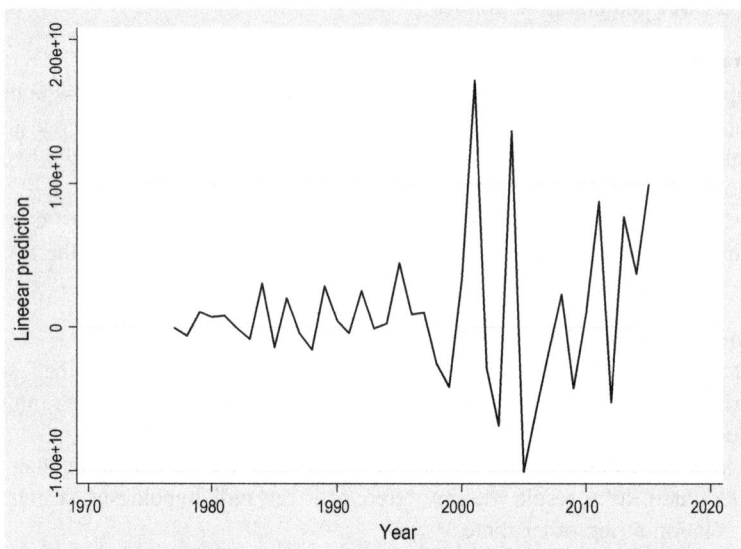

Fig. 6.6 Line plot stationarity test. *Source* Authors' computation using Stata 13 software

Removal of serial correlation

Removal of serial correlation is important for a further check-up and excludes serial correlation of residuals which are included in the model. The residual variable was a white noise meaning that there was no serial correlation, the residual was homoscedastic and mean of the residuals was random or independent and the residuals were stationary. If we fail to reject null hypothesis, meaning that our residuals variable had these three features then it is a good model. This is possible through differencing the residuals at first and second (r1 and r2) levels.

As illustrated in Fig. 6.6, the line trend looked stationary or like white noise because there was only a stationary trend.

Bartlett's period gram-based white noise test

As shown in Fig. 6.7, all points were distributed between the two lines, so we can say that still the residuals were normally distributed.

Portmanteau test for white noise

According to Table 6.8, the portmanteau test for white noise (Q) statistic was at a more than 5% level, so we can accept that there was no serial correlation.

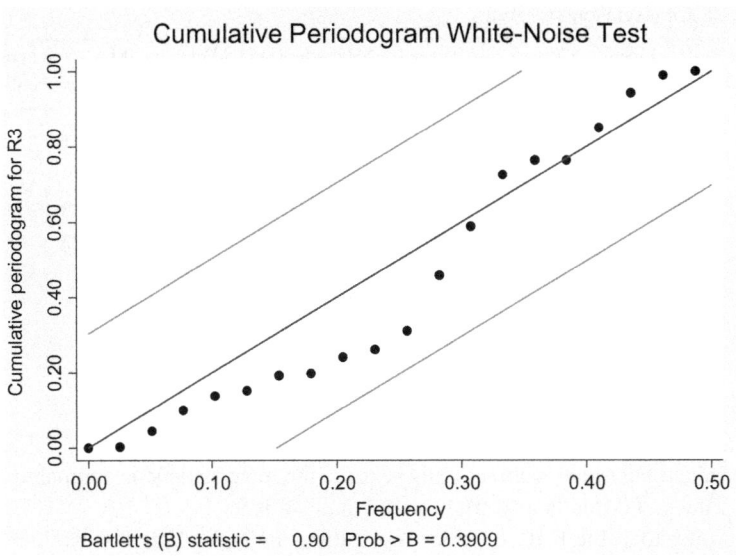

Fig. 6.7 Bartlett's period gram-based white noise test. *Source* Authors' computation using Stata 13 software

Table 6.8 Portmanteau test for white noise

Portmanteau test for white noise	Portmanteau (Q) statistic = 25.9180	Prob > chi2 (17) = 0.0760

Source Authors' computation using Stata 13 software

Table 6.9 Breusch-Godfrey LM test for autocorrelation

Lags (P)	Ch2	df	Prob > chi2
1	0.500	1	0.4796

H0 No serial correlation

Breusch-Godfrey LM test for autocorrelation

As we can observe from Table 6.9, the corresponding probability values were more than the 5% level, thus we can say that there was no autocorrelation between the residuals.

Cointegration Analysis

Since the order of integration of each variable in the model is equal to three and the residuals are stationary, we applied the cointegration tests developed by Johansen (1988) to investigate whether there was more than one cointegration relationship. The cointegration tests include real gross domestic product, economic services, social services, general services and other services expenditure over the period 1975–2015. The Johansen cointegration tests were applied at the

Table 6.10 Cointegration test results

Hypothesized no. of CE(s)	Eigen value	Trace statistic	Percent critical value	Hypothesized no. of CE(s)	Eigen value	Max statistic	Percent critical value
0	–	137.7101	68.52	0	–	55.4381	33.46
1	0.78561	82.2721	47.21	1	0.78561	44.6319	27.07
2	0.71055	37.6402	29.68	2	0.71055	23.7138	20.97
3	0.48249	13.9263*	15.41	3	0.48249	13.8993	14.07
4	0.32029	0.0270	3.76	4	0.32029	0.0270	3.76
5	0.00075	–	–	5	0.00075	–	–

*shows the number of cointegrating vectors. It indicates at least three (3) cointegrating vectors are available using the trace statistics test
Source Authors' computation using Stata 13 software

predetermined lag order of three. In these tests, the trace statistic is compared to 5% critical values and this is also true for the max statistic.

According to Table 6.10, the trace test statistic indicated that at least three cointegrating vectors ($r \geq 3$) existed in the system at the conventional 5% significance level and using *p*-values <5% and the test results showed the existence of long-run equilibrium relationships and three cointegrating equations among the variables.

Granger causality test

We also applied the Granger causality test to know the direction of causality and the behavior of the variables in the current period and also to forecast growth in the long-run.

As shown in Table 6.11, the direction of causality was based on probability values. We made use of the 0.05 level of significance in deciding the direction of causality. So, from the first equation, economic services expenditure, social services expenditure, general services expenditure and other services expenditure did not Granger cause real GDP individually or jointly at lag three.

Similarly, from the second equation, by taking economic services expenditure as the dependent variable, real gross domestic product, social services expenditure, general services expenditure and other services expenditure can cause economic services expenditure either individually or jointly. When we come to the third equation, real gross domestic product, economic services expenditure, general services expenditure and other services expenditure can cause social services expenditure either individually or jointly. Further, when we take general services expenditure as the dependent variable, real gross domestic product, social services expenditure and other services expenditure Granger cause general services expenditure individually and as a whole. Finally, when we take other services expenditure as the dependent variable, real gross domestic product, social services expenditure and general services expenditure can Granger cause other services expenditure individually and jointly.

Table 6.11 Granger causality Wald tests results

	Excluded	chi2	df	Prob > chi2
Equation (A)				
D2RGDP	D2ESesp	0.15882	3	0.984
D2RGDP	D2SSesxp	3.0868	3	0.378
D2RGDP	D2GSexp	3.5119	3	0.319
D2RGDP	D2OSexp	1.9073	3	0.592
D2RGDP	ALL	20.634	12	0.056
Equation (B)				
D2ESesp	D2RGDP	8.0822	3	0.044
D2ESesp	D2SSesxp	9.2262	3	0.026
D2ESesp	D2GSexp	8.0213	3	0.046
D2ESesp	D2OSexp	31.798	3	0.000
D2ESesp	ALL	40.128	12	0.000
Equation (C)				
D2SSesxp	D2RGDP	3.8917	3	0.273
D2SSesxp	D2ESesp	146.43	3	0.000
D2SSesxp	D2GSexp	9.4872	3	0.023
D2SSesxp	D2OSexp	7.1923	3	0.066
D2SSesxp	ALL	749.32	12	0.000
Equation (D)				
D2GSexp	D2RGDP	6.5591	3	0.087
D2GSexp	D2ESesp	24.167	3	0.000
D2GSexp	D2SSesxp	25.841	3	0.000
D2GSexp	D2OSexp	1.4822	3	0.686
D2GSexp	ALL	106.35	12	0.000

(continued)

Table 6.11 (continued)

Excluded	chi2	df	Prob > chi2
Equation (E)			
D2Osexp	D2RGDP	6.6969	3	0.082
D2Osexp	D2ESesp	2.3314	3	0.507
D2Osexp	D2SSesxp	24.446	3	0.000
D2Osexp	D2Gsexp	46.994	3	0.000
D2Osexp	ALL	229.05	12	0.000

Source Authors' computation using Stata 13 software

Table 6.12 VECM result summary for target model only

D_D2RGDP	Equations	Coef.	Std. err.	z	$P > |z|$	95% Conf. interval	
	CE-1 (L1)	−0.923308	0.4480552	−2.06	0.039	−1.80148	−0.045136
	CE-2 (L1)	−3.565935	2.713866	−1.31	0.189	−8.885016	1.753145
	CE-3 (L1)	−0.0856157	5.852434	0.01	0.988	−11.55618	11.38494
	RGDP (LD)	0.3284321	0.3284321	−0.15	0.885	−0.6913394	0.5960909
	RGDP (L2D)	−0.3546365	0.2134437	−1.66	0.097	−0.7729784	0.0637055
	ESexp (LD)	2.090782	2.330836	0.90	0.370	−2.477572	6.659136
	ESexp (L2D)	0.7010454	1.531519	0.46	0.647	−2.300676	3.702767
	ESSexp (LD)	−1.165203	4.043108	−0.29	0.773	−9.0896	6.759143
	ESSexp (L2D)	−0.4394409	1.958166	−0.22	0.822	−4.277375	3.398494
	GSexp (LD)	−4.761519	3.627218	−1.31	0.189	−11.87074	2.347697
	GSexp (L2D)	−1.184561	2.881663	−0.41	0.681	−6.832517	4.463395

Note L-Stands for lag
Source Authors' computation using Stata 13 software

6.4.4 Vector Error Correction Model Estimation

Since the model passed all the diagnostic tests, we applied the vector error correction model to examine the cointegrating relationship. This approach controls for the long-run behavior of our endogenous variables and shows their cointegrating relationship. Moreover, it also allows for short-run dynamics. Here, the error correction term indicates a cointegrating relationship in the long-run which leads to long-run equilibrium which is restored gradually through a series of partial short-run adjustments. When the variables are cointegrated, the corresponding error correction representations must be included in the system. By doing so, one can avoid misspecification and omission of important constraints. The vector error correction model (VECM) is summarized in Table 6.12.

Long Run Vector error correction Model
The long run relationship between variables can be analyzed by looking at the cointegration equations and as a result we have long run causality running from economic services expenditure, social services expenditure, general services expenditure and other services expenditure to real gross domestic product and this value was statistically significant and also tended to 1, indicating that the speed of adjustment to equilibrium was high. Therefore, there was a long run association between the dependent variable and the explanatory variables.

Short Run Vector error correction Model
To explore the short run effects of sectoral expenditures on economic growth during the study period it is necessary to find out whether the short-term dynamics were influenced by the estimated long-term equilibrium conditions or not.

Table 6.13 Johansen restriction on coefficients

Equations	Variables	Coef.	Std. error	Z	$p > |z|$
CE-1	RGDP	1	–	–	
	GSexp.	−9.50	2.00	−4.72	0.000
	OSexp.	−9.57	5.53	1.73	0.084
	Cons.	−1320			
CE-2	ESesp.	1			
	GSexp	−0.06	0.24	−0.28	0.779
	OSexp	−2.84	0.66	−4.29	0.000
	Cons.	−222			
CE-3	SSesxp	1			
	GSexp	−0.33	0.16	−2.01	0.004
	OSexp	−2.64	0.45	−5.90	0.000
	Cons.	−145			

Source Authors' computation using Stata 13 software

If we look at the causal relationship from the short run results of the VECM model's estimation, the relationship between current RGDP and lagged values of economic services expenditure, social services expenditure, general services expenditure and other expenditures were not statistically significant. That means there was no short run association running from the independent variables to the dependent variables individually. However, there was a short run association running from the explanatory variables to RGDP jointly.

As shown in Table 6.13, the coefficients of other expenditures in the first equation and general services expenditure in the second equation, all the coefficients of the cointegrated equation were significant at the 5% level. All coefficients in the three equations are negative, implying the negative relationship between the right hand and left-hand side variables. Hence, the cointegrating equations can be derived as:

$$RGDP = -1320 - 9.50GSexp + 9.57Osexp \tag{6.7}$$

$$ESexpt = -222 - 0.06Gsexp - 2.84Osexp \tag{6.8}$$

$$SSespt = -145 - 0.33GSexp - 2.64Osexp \tag{6.9}$$

Equation 6.7 shows that a 1% increase in general services expenditure will decrease economic growth by about 9.50% in the long run whereas a 1% increase in other services expenditure could increase economic growth by about 9.57% in real terms but this is an insignificant shock. The negative relationship between general services expenditure and real gross domestic product is consistent with our hypothesis which states that an increase in general services expenditure decreases real gross domestic product.

While the positive relationship between other services expenditure and RGDP supports economic growth it has an insignificant impact. Equation 6.8 shows that a

1% increase in general services expenditure significantly decreased economic services expenditure by 0.06% and other services expenditure decreased economic services expenditure by 2.84% but it was insignificant. Similarly, from Eq. 6.9, a 1% increase in general services expenditure and other services expenditure declined social services expenditure by 0.33 and 2.64% respectively.

Social services expenditure is expected to have a significant effect on economic growth with a positive sign. However, our results indicate a negative relation though its impact on economic growth is insignificant. This may in turn show that utilization of social services expenditure is inefficient and the nature of public investments is poor. Further, our study is partially similar to Tsadiku (2012) who found that economic services expenditure had a positive but insignificant effect on economic growth in Ethiopia. It is also similar to Muhammed's (2015) study which showed that expenditure on agriculture, transport and communication, urban development and housing (part of economic services expenditure) had a positive impact but this was statistically insignificant.

Unproductive sectors (general services expenditure) have a significant impact on economic growth with a negative relation. This parallels Endale's (2007) work that assessed the effect of defense expenditure on economic growth and his empirical results showed that the defense burden was negative to real economic growth. Berihun (2014) investigated the impact of government expenditure on economic growth in Ethiopia over the period 1975–2013, with a particular focus on sectoral expenditure on agriculture, defense, health and education sectors and his empirical results showed that expenditure on defense negatively affected economic growth.

VEC stability

We conducted the VEC stability test to check the stability of the VEC model. VEC stability exists if the Eigen value and the modulus values are both less than 1.

As shown in Table 6.14, the process is stable and the moduli of the remaining Eigen values are strictly less than one.

As shown in Fig. 6.8, all roots of the companion matrix revealed a sufficient condition for stability as all characteristic roots were inside the unit circle with full

Table 6.14 VEC stability

Eigen value	Modulus
1	1
1	1
−0.2143124	0.894604
−0.2143124	0.894604
−0.8101469	0.81143
−0.8101469	0.81143
−0.3640227	0.730514
−0.3640227	0.730514
−0.1668788	0.226296
−0.1668788	0.226296

Source Authors' computation using Stata 13 software

Fig. 6.8 The VEC stability roots of the companion matrix. *Source* Authors' computation using Stata 13 software

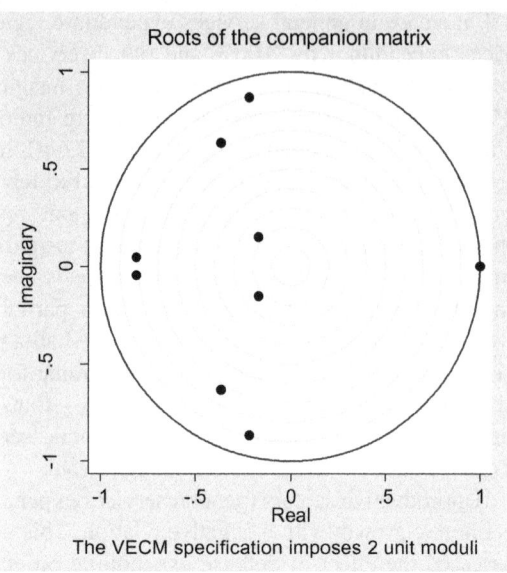

rank and all variables were stationary. The graph of the Eigen values shows that none of the remaining Eigen values appear close to the unit circle. The stability check does not indicate a misspecified model.

6.4.5 Impulse Response Analysis

An impulse response analysis helps examine the impulse reply of endogenous variables to a one-time shock to the other variables in the model. In our case it tells us how economic growth (RGDP) may respond to any shock at any point in time or a one-standard deviation impulse generated from any of the variables in earlier times and how that effect may be multiplied, that is, whether it will last for a long period or die out in the short run.

The results in Table 6.15 for the impulse response function indicate that if real RGDP's response to a positive impulse of RGDP showed fluctuations throughout the period then there was a permanent positive effect. Real RGDP had no response in the first period as the shock came from economic services expenditure (Esexp); however its positive response starting from the second period rose continuously. Likewise, real RGDP's response resulting from a one-standard deviation impulse generated from social services expenditure was nil; starting from the second period it was a positive response which increased permanently.

Real RGDP had no response in the first and second periods as the shock acme from general services expenditure (Gsexp); however its negative response starting from the third period and decreased continuously. Similarly, RGDP had no any

Table 6.15 Impulse response analysis of real GDP

Response of RGDP					
Period	RGDP	ESexp	SSexp	GSexp	OSexp
1	1.000	0.000	0.000	0.000	0.000
2	0.947	0.004	0.041	0.000	0.006
3	0.923	0.011	0.297	−0.012	0.002
4	0.905	0.018	0.038	−0.017	0.018
5	0.912	0.023	0.032	−0.015	0.015
6	0.907	0.286	0.035	−0.013	0.014
7	0.915	0.258	0.033	−0.012	0.013
8	0.921	0.022	0.033	−0.010	0.012
9	0.925	0.021	0.031	0.010	0.011
10	0.927	0.208	0.0318	0.009	0.010

Source Authors' computation using Stata 13 software

response in the first period as the shock came from the other services expenditure (Osexp); however, its negative response starting from the second period decreased continuously with insignificant values. In short, RGDP's response to any shock was zero in the first period, except for the shocks that came from real GDP itself. Hence, RGDP's response resulting from a shock in economic and social expenditure was positive and increasing in the long run. On the other hand, RGDP responded negatively to a shock that came from general and other services expenditure.

6.5 Conclusion and Policy Implications

6.5.1 Conclusion

Though there is extensive research on government expenditure in Ethiopia, our study contributes to a further understanding of government sectoral expenditure patterns and their effect on economic growth using up-to-date national data. The primary objective of our study was to examine the impact of government sectoral expenditure on economic growth in Ethiopia with a particular focus on sectoral expenditure on economic services, social services, general services and other services.

Our study used both descriptive and econometric analyses and also used Augmented Dickey-Fuller (ADF) for stationary test, which was followed by a cointegration test, a Granger casualty test, VECM and all diagnostic tests. It also used a VEC stability and impulse response analysis. Our empirical results showed that the effects of economic and social services expenditure on economic growth were indeterminate in the long run. However, government expenditure on other services had a negative though insignificant impact on economic growth.

General services expenditure had a negative and significant impact on economic growth. Despite the Government of Ethiopia's commitment to this sector for promoting economic growth, it was unproductive and had a negative impact on economic growth. Therefore, if government expenditure patterns are not well designed to fit the economy's needs, they could significantly influence economic growth in an undesired way. The negative and insignificant effect of other services expenditure on economic growth in turn may signal the inefficiency of this sector in supporting economic growth.

6.5.2 Recommendations

Based on the findings of our study we make the following policy recommendations:

- There has been an increase in general services expenditure in which expenditure on defense and security constitutes the highest share which has diverted scarce public funds from productive sectors to relatively less productive sectors. Thus, the study recommends that the government should reduce spending on this sector to promote economic growth.
- Our study shows that government expenditure on economic services is positively related to economic growth. Based on this, more and better-distributed economic services expenditure will help create conditions that enhance economic growth so the government should give priority to economic services expenditure to sustain economic growth.
- Social services expenditure is expected to have significant effect on economic growth with a positive sign. However, the results of our study indicate a negative impact on economic growth. This shows that utilization of social services expenditure is inefficient and public investments in the country are of poor quality. Thus, the government should pay attention to this sector for achieving sustainable development goals.

References

Adamu, J., and B. Hajara. 2015. Government expenditure and economic growth nexus: Empirical evidence from Nigeria. *IOSR Journal of Economics and Finance* 6 (2): 61–69.

AfDB. 2015. *Ethiopian development effectiveness review*. Abidjan, Côte d'Ivoire: African Development Bank Group.

Afzal, M., and Q. Abbas. 2010. Wagner's law in Pakistan: Another look. *Journal of Economics and International Finance* 2 (1): 12–19.

Al-Fawwaz, T.M. 2016. The impact of government expenditures on economic growth in Jordan (1980–2013). *International Business Research* 9 (1): 99–105.

Alshahrani, S.A., and A.J. Alsadiq. 2014. Economic growth and government spending in Saudi Arabia: An empirical investigation. Saudi Arabia, *IMF Working Paper*, WP/14/3.

Bargicho, S. 2016. *The effects of government expenditure and tax on economic growth in Ethiopia.* Ethiopia: Addis Ababa University.

Bahaddi, T., and M. Karim. 2017. Impact of public expenditure on the growth in Morocco: Role of governance. *International Journal of Economics and Finance* 9 (4): 12–19.

Berihun, B. 2014. *Impact of government sectoral expenditure on economic growth in Ethiopia with a particular focus on agriculture, defense, education and health sectors.* Ethiopia: Addis Ababa University.

Bose, N., M.E. Haque, and D.R. Osborn. 2007. Public expenditure and economic growth: A disaggregated analysis for developing countries. *The Manchester School* 75 (5): 533–556.

Ditimi, A., N. Philip, and A.J. Adebayo. 2011. Components of government spending and economic growth in Nigeria: An error correction modelling. *Journal of Economics and Sustainable Development* 2 (4): 219–237.

EEA. 2017. *Budget braekdown.* The Reporter: Ethipean Economic Association.

Endale, K. 2007. *Effect of defense expenditure on economic growth in the Sub Saharan Africa Countries: Panel data evidence.* Ethiopia: Addis Ababa University.

Fan, S. 2008. Public expenditures, growth and poverty: Lessons from developing countries. *IFPRI Issue Brief 51.*

Ghosh Roy, A. 2012. Revisiting the relationship between economic growth and government size. *Economics Research International,* 1–8.

Gisore, N., S. Kiprop, A. Kalio, J. Ochieng, and L. Kibet. 2014. Effect of government expenditure on economic growth in East Africa: A disaggregated model. *European Journal of Business and Social Sciences* 3 (8): 289–304.

Guandong, B.Y., and W.M. Muturi. 2016. The relationship between public expenditure and economic growth in South Sudan. *International Journal of Economics, Commerce and Management* 4 (6): 235–259.

Hua, Y. 2016. *The relationship between public expenditure on education and economic growth: Evidence from China.* China: Clemson University. Available at: http://tigerprints.clemson.edu/all_theses.

Johansen, S. 1988. Statistical analysis of cointegrating vectors. *Journal of Economic Dynamics and Control* 12: 231–254.

Kebede, B. 2015. *The impact of public sector spending on the economic growth: A particular focus on road and electric power sector, the case of Ethiopia.* Ethiopia: Addis Ababa University.

Ketema, T. 2006. *The impact of government spending on economic growth in Ethiopia.* Ethiopia: Addis Ababa University.

Lamartina, S., and A. Zaghini. 2010. Increasing public expenditures: Wagner's Law in OECD countries. *German Economic Review* 12 (2): 149–164.

Mahjoub, E. 2013. Causality between government expenditure and national income: Evidence from Sudan. *Journal of Economic Cooperation and Development* 34 (4): 61–76.

Mahmoodi, M., and E. Mahmoodi. 2014. Government expenditure-GDP nexus: Panel causality evidence. *International Journal of Economy, Management and Social Sciences* 3 (1): 37–42.

MacKinnon, J. 1991. Critical values for cointegration tests. *Queen's Economics Department Working Paper,* 1227.

Mitchell, D.J. 2005. *The impact of government spending on economic growth. Executive summary background, no. 1831.* Washington, DC: Heritage Foundation.

MOFED. 2014. *Growth and transformation plan annual progress report for F.Y. 2012/13.* Addis Ababa: MOFED.

Muhammed, A. 2015. Composition of government expenditure and economic growth in Ethiopia (1971–2011G.C). *European Journal of Business and Management* 7 (27): 28–37.

Musaba, E.C., P. Chilonda, and G. Matchaya. 2013. Impact of government sectoral expenditure on economic growth in Malawi, 1980–2007. *Journal of Economics and Sustainable Development* 4, 71–78.

Nasiru, I. 2012. Government expenditure and economic growth in Nigeria: Cointegration analysis and causality testing. *Academic Research International* 2 (3): 718–723.

Nurudeen, A., and A. Usman. 2010. Government expenditure and economic growth in Nigeria: A disaggregated analysis. *Business and Economics Journal* 4: 1–11.

Olabisi, A.S., and F. Elizabeth. 2012. Composition of public expenditure and economic growth in Nigeria. *Journal of Emerging Trends in Economics and Management Sciences* 3 (4): 403–407.

Sharma, B. 2012. Government expenditure and economic growth in Nepal a minute analysis. *Basic Research Journal of Business Management and Accounts* 1 (4): 37–40.

Sudarsono, H. 2010. The reletionship between economic growth and government expenditure: A case study in OIC countries. *Jurnal Ekonomi Pembangunan* 11 (2): 149–159.

Tsadiku, W. 2012. *Impact of government sectoral spending on economic growth: A particular focus on human capital and agriculture sector*. Ethiopia: Addis Ababa University.

Tsegaw, E. 2009. *Fiscal federalism, teaching material*. Addis Ababa: Justice and Legal System Research Institute. Available at: https://chilot.files.wordpress.com/2011/06/fiscal-federalism.pdf.

Chapter 7
Tax Compliance Attitude of Rural Farmers: An Analysis Based on Survey Data in Ethiopia

Hassen Azime and Gollagari Ramakrishna

Abstract Applying logit regression models, we present the factors that determine the tax compliance attitude of individual smallholder farmers in Ethiopia. The evidence presented in this article is based on the 5th Afrobarometer Survey (2014). We find some similarities and some differences with earlier studies in factors that are correlated with the tax compliance attitude of smallholder farmers in Ethiopia. We argue that tax compliance is a function of individual smallholder farmers and related variables and confirm that people who are happier with open administration arrangements have a tax compliant attitude. Those farmers who perceive that their ethnic group thinks that they have been treated unfairly are less likely to have a tax compliant attitude. Smallholder farmers' tax knowledge is also significantly correlated with a tax compliant attitude in Ethiopia. We identify a taxpayer's satisfaction with local government officials as another determinant of tax compliance. These findings are robust to different econometric specifications.

Keywords Tax compliance · Smallholder farmers · Ethiopia

JEL Classification Codes C380 · H260 · H730 · K420

H. Azime (✉)
Department of Public Finance, Institute of Tax and Customs Administration,
Ethiopian Civil Service University, Addis Ababa, Ethiopia
e-mail: azimeadem@gmail.com

G. Ramakrishna
School of Graduate Studies, Ethiopian Civil Service University,
Addis Ababa, Ethiopia
e-mail: profgrk@gmail.com

© Springer Nature Singapore Pte Ltd. 2018   137
A. Heshmati and H. Yoon (eds.), *Economic Growth and Development
in Ethiopia*, Perspectives on Development in the Middle East
and North Africa (MENA) Region, https://doi.org/10.1007/978-981-10-8126-2_7

7.1 Introduction

In several sub-Saharan African countries, agriculture is one of the most important economic sectors contributing to economic development. The Ethiopian economy too is largely agrarian and agriculture contributes a major portion of the country's GDP. Agriculture as a predominant sector in the country is dominated by small-holders. In Ethiopia the agricultural sector contributes 43% to GDP, 80% to employment and 85% to foreign exchange earnings (MoFED 2012). The remaining contribution comes mainly from the services sector.

According to conventional wisdom, expansion of the non-agricultural sector is a part of the development process and is based on increases in the marketed supply of food, in the non-agricultural labor force and in capital formation outside agriculture. Agricultural taxation is one of the instruments available to the government to bring in transformations.

In developing countries, economic growth and rural development require substantial financial resources for infrastructure, education, health and other social services. One of the ways in which resources can be collected to meet the developmental needs is in the form of taxation. In this respect, the sub-Saharan African countries face a challenge in improving their tax collections (Gupta and Tareq 2008). Rural development to a great extent relies on the agricultural sector's contribution to the economy even though agricultural tax revenue is not buoyant in the country (Azime et al. 2017).

Agricultural policy practices differ across countries as some countries have subsidized their agricultural sector while many others tax the sector using both direct and indirect methods (Anderson and Hayami 1986; Anderson and Valenzuela 2008). Scholars have various views on agricultural taxes and subsidies. Bird (1983) argues that agriculture is commonly rated as the hardest to tax among all the hard-to-tax sectors. However, according to Skinner (1991) land tax has a significant potential for revenue collection since land is readily observable and is in a fixed supply. Some scholars also argue that agriculture is a primary source of tax in the initial stages of the overall economic development. They argue that any increase in agricultural productivity increases a country's capacity to increase tax revenues which facilitates spending on infrastructure (Chang et al. 2006).

Improving tax revenue collections is essential for developing economies like Ethiopia where the tax revenue as a share of GDP is low. According to Besley and Persson (2014) one of the reasons why developing countries have poor levels of taxation may be because of a weaker attitude towards tax paying as compared to what has evolved in developed countries. Hence, the absence of strong compliance norms may result in less revenue than would otherwise be expected.

Smallholder farmers' compliance with tax payments depends on a variety of variables, both internal and external which relate compliance with willingness to cooperate with the local administration and its institutions. Economists also focus on external variables such as the tax rate, income and fines while psychological research focuses on internal variables such as taxpayers' knowledge about tax, attitude towards the administration, personal norms, perceived social rules and motivational tendencies of fairness (Kirchler and Braithwaite 2007). Hence, there is a need to integrate psychological insights into an economic model of tax compliance.

Fjeldstad and Heggstad (2012) note that measures to enhance tax compliance include building a taxpaying culture and following different structures that suit different segments of taxpayers. They also discuss the constraints faced in this. In our case, smallholder farmers are a different segment of taxpayers. The agricultural sector in Ethiopia is primarily dependent on smallholder farming as smallholders cultivating fragmented micro-holdings produce more than 90% of the annual agricultural output.

The aim of our research is assessing the instruments that influence smallholder farmers' tax compliance in rural Ethiopia and the factors that affect tax compliance of smallholder farmers. It also discusses the extent to which farmers feel a moral obligation to pay taxes; their willingness to pay taxes may be related to economic factors, land security and the services provided by the government. Till now no study has been done to explore how these factors affect farmers' attitude to paying taxes.

7.2   Literature Review

Tax compliance research has largely ignored low-income individual taxpayers such as smallholder farmers. Our study extends and complements existing tax research by examining the compliance intentions of low-income individual taxpayers. Relying on different theories of tax compliance behavior, we examine the extent to which agricultural tax affects tax compliance intentions.

According to Besley and Persson (2014) one reason why low-income countries have lower levels of taxation is because of a weaker ethic of tax compliance as compared to the one that has evolved in high-income countries. The absence of strong compliance norms results in less revenue than would otherwise be expected. Fjeldstad and Heggstad (2012) note that measures to enhance tax compliance and building a taxpaying culture need to be customised for different groups of taxpayers and the specific constraints that they face. The economics of tax compliance can be investigated from different perspectives. It can be viewed at equity, incidence, efficiency, law enforcement, organizational design and ethics or a combination of these (Andreoni et al. 1998). Scholars have identified different economic, social and psychological factors that influence tax compliance (Alm et al. 1990, 1995; Bobek et al. 2013; Erard 2009; Heinemann and Kocher 2013; Kastlunger et al. 2010). According to Luttmer and Singhal (2014) the tax schedule structure could influence compliance through a tax morale. Fischer et al. (1992) integrate economic, social and psychological factors into a framework for understanding tax compliance behavior.

Compliance with tax laws means strict adherence to the legal provisions of tax codes. Therefore, tax compliance is based on data of official estimations (Bergman 1998). Tax compliance is what the state assumes that the taxpayers legally owe it, but the state and taxpayers do not necessarily share the same thinking. Smallholder farmers in Ethiopia are a major engine of employment creation and growth, but they are also a major challenge regarding compliance with agricultural taxation. Analyzing the tax policy of revenue enhancement and tax compliance requires an understanding of the factors that influence smallholder farmers on paying taxes. However, smallholder taxpayers' views have to a large extent been ignored in policy debates.

Designing effective agricultural tax policies for increasing tax compliance requires understanding the overall *behavioral* aspects of the taxpayers' compliance decisions. Individual taxpayer's attitudes toward tax compliance depend on social values and cultural norms (Fig. 7.1).

The relationship between a smallholder taxpayer and the local government includes at least five factors—tax enforcement; fiscal exchange; social influences; comparative treatment; and political accountability (Ali et al. 2013; Fjeldstad and Semboja 2001).

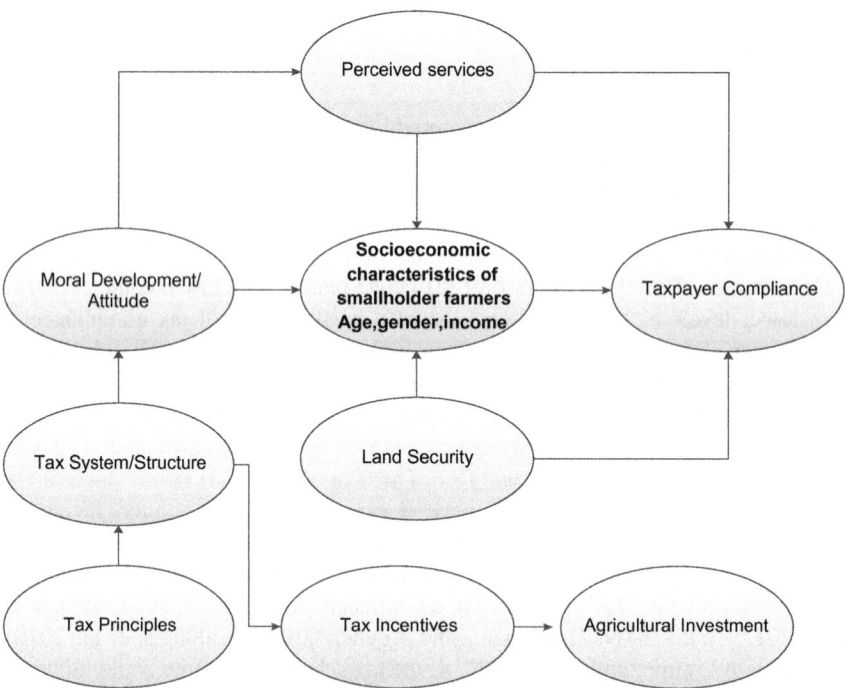

Fig. 7.1 Tax compliance model. *Source* Adapted from Fischer et al. (1992) tax compliance model

7.2.1   Tax Enforcement or Economic Deterrence

Allingham and Sandmo (1972) have developed a methodology for the economic deterrence theory which states that taxpayers' behavior is affected by factors including the tax rate and the probability of detection and penalties. This shows that if detection is more likely and the penalties are strict only a few taxpayers will not pay taxes.

The hypothetical standards of financial prevention have been broadly accepted by assessment organizations when creating implementation methodologies that depend primarily on punishments and the dread of getting caught (Andreoni et al. 1998).

7.2.2   Fiscal Exchange

There is strong agreement among social scientists that the existence of government expenditure may increase tax compliance by providing public goods that citizen need efficiently (Cowell and Gordon 1988). This view is supported by Alm et al. (1992) who maintain that tax compliance increases with the availability of public goods and services. Moore (2004) adopts a wider perspective when he argues that there should be a contractual relationship between taxpayers and the government due to the provision of public goods financed by taxation. Similarly, Fjeldstad and Semboja (2001) assert that the reason why individuals pay taxes is because they recognize that their contribution is essential for financing goods and services. There will be a high probability that taxpayers will comply more voluntarily when there is an expectation of positive benefits. Therefore, it is rational to assume that taxpayers' behavior can be affected by the level of satisfaction with the government.

7.2.3   Social Influences

A taxpayer's compliant behavior and attitude towards the the tax system is affected by the behaviour of the individual's reference group such as family, neighbors and friends. Social norms consist of a pattern of behavior which must be shared by other people as it is dependent on their approval and disapproval.

Many social factors also influence taxpayers' decision making including what others around them are doing. This social influence may discourage individuals from paying taxes due to fear of social sanctions imposed by the group (Banerjee 1992). One of the most consistent findings suggests that perceptions about the honesty of others may affect compliance behavior.

7.2.4 Comparative Treatment

Research has shown that the comparative treatment factor also affects taxpayers' compliance. The comparative treatment factor is based on the equity theory. According to Prinz et al. (2014) citizens may consider how the state behaves towards them relative to another member of another group. If the state treats certain groups favorably and something which they are given is better than what other people receive, this may color a citizen's connections with the state and the group or individual receiving favors.

7.2.5 Political Legitimacy

Citizens' trust in the government is another factor which influences tax compliance (Tyler 2006). Trust is required for fair and just activities of government institutions and authorities. For studies on the empirical literature on the determinants of tax morale based on international surveys see Table 7.1.

7.3 Methodology

7.3.1 Data Collection

We used the survey data from Afrobarometer 5th round (2014) to study tax compliance among rural farmers. The Afrobarometer[1] survey is an international research project which collects public opinion data from African countries on the quality of governance, democracy, markets, taxation and civil society (Afrobarometer, International Research Project). A total of 2400 individuals with 16 data variables were extracted from the survey which provides all factors of tax compliance. All this data was categorical data or ordinal data and was assigned with integer values for easy treatment by the Stata software.

The Afrobarometer data survey collects information on public attitudes to democracy, governance, markets, taxation and civil society in more than 30 African countries. The survey questionnaire also includes a series of questions of which those on tax are important for our study.

---

[1]For details, see www.afrobarometer.org.

Table 7.1 Empirical literature on the determinants of tax morale based on international surveys

Reference	Sample and econometrics	Tested variables	Findings
Torgler (2005)	Switzerland (Data from ISSP). Year: 1998. Weighted ordered probit estimation	Gender, age, marital status, education, employment status, personal income, church attendance, direct democracy, trust in the court and legal system, tax rate, fine rate and audit probability and culture variables (language as the dummy variable)	Education and trust in the legal system had a positive effect on tax morale. In addition, being religious and democratic increased tax morale
Martinez-Vazquez and Torgler (2009)	Spain (Data from WVS and EVS). Years 1981, 1990, 1995 and 1999–2000. Weighted ordered probit estimation	Gender, age, marital status, employment status, religiosity, trust in the parliament, national pride and time as dummy variables	Tax morale was higher with increase in age, trust in the parliament and national pride. Also, religiosity increased tax morale but it was lower in upper-class individuals
Cummings et al. (2009)	Botswana (1999) and South Africa (2000) (Data from Afrobarometer). Common cross-country slopes imposed. Ordered probit estimation	Gender, age, education, employment status and country as dummy variables	Tax morale increased with age in Botswana
Ali et al. (2013)	Kenya, Tanzania, Uganda and South Africa (Data from the new round 5 of Afrobarometer surveys). Year: 2013. Binary logit model estimation	Gender, age, education, employment status, public service and country as dummy variables	Individuals who are more satisfied with public service provisions are more likely to have a tax compliant attitude in all the four countries. Those who perceived that their ethnic groups were treated unfairly were less likely to have a tax compliant attitude in Tanzania and South Africa

Source Lago-Peñas and Lago-Peñas (2010) modified by the authors

7.3.2   Analysis

We applied a two-stage analysis procedure. In the first stage, we used a descriptive statistical method to examine the distribution of compliance factors over the various variables. The influential factors for each variable, defined as the factors which are responsible for a high proportion, were determined.

In the second stage, the analysis emphasized on what factors influenced the likelihood of tax compliance. For this we developed predictive models to describe the relationship between the probability of the occurrence of tax compliance and explanatory variables. Since the likelihood of tax compliance by smallholder farmers is a binary value (1 if an individual considers not paying taxes as *wrong and punishable* and 0 if he considers that it is not wrong), we adopted the binary logistic regression to develop the models which predict the probability of the occurrence of tax compliance.

For the logistic regression analysis model, parameter estimates for (α, $\beta 1$, $\beta 2$, …, βp) should be estimated; the model fitness also needs to be determined. Then, the potential dependent variables need to be checked to determine whether they are significant enough to be used in our models. To select our significant variables of compliance we used the regression analysis with selection steps.

7.3.3   Model Assumptions

The logistic regression does not assume a linear relationship between the dependent and independent variables. The dependent variables do not need to be normally distributed, there is no homogeneity of variance assumption (in other words variances do not have to be the same within categories) and normally distributed error terms are not assumed and the independent variables do not have to be interval or unbounded (Grimm and Yarnold 1995). The model should also be based on the absence of multicollinearity; no outliers; and independence from errors.

Binary logistic regression is used to predict a dichotomous variable from a set of explanatory variables. For a binary logistic regression, the predicted dependent variable is a function of the probability that a particular subject will occur and the explanatory variables could be nominal data or continuous data or a mix of them.

The dependent variable, tax compliance, were regressed on 16 independent variables as outlined in Table 7.2. The factors influencing tax compliance of smallholder farmers were classified into five main categories.

The general logit model is written as:

$Y_i = f$(Individual characterstics, econmic deterence, fiscal exchange, social influence, comaprative treatment, political legtimacy, knowlege abot tax)

Table 7.2 A description of the variables chosen from the Afrobarometer survey

Variable	Obs	Mean	Std. dev.	Min	Max
Tax compliance	1799	0.876042	0.329625	0	1
Age	1799	36.24958	14.29097	18	86
Sex	1799	0.49861	0.500137	0	1
Education level	1799	1.413007	1.693759	0	9
Ease of evasion	1799	3.472485	1.031319	1	5
Health	1799	3.406893	0.833848	1	5
Education	1799	3.117843	0.953017	1	5
Crime and conflict	1799	1.926626	1.106738	1	4
Satisfaction with electricity, water cell phone service	1799	3.128961	1.509717	1	5
Social influence	1799	0.235687	0.736038	0	3
Unfair treatment	1799	1.153974	1.038831	0	3
Trust	1799	2.875486	1.189991	0	4
Corruption among tax officials	1799	2.561979	1.603118	0	4
Satisfaction with the local council	1799	2.559755	1.041232	0	4
Democracy	1799	3.605336	0.810042	1	5
Knowledge about tax	1799	2.770984	1.211652	1	5

Source Authors' calculations using data from the Afrobarometer 5th round survey

A significant advantage of binary logistic regression is that there is no assumption about the distribution of explanatory variables.

Let Y denote an event (Y = 1 and Y = 0 denote the if an individual thinks that it is wrong and punishable not to pay taxes Y = 1 and otherwise Y = 0) and let a vector X be a set of predictors $\{X_1, X_2, …, X_k\}$, then the probability (P) of the occurrence of Y given X could be expressed as:

$$P(Y = 1|X) = \frac{e^{x\beta}}{1 + e^{x\beta}} \tag{7.1}$$

where, β is the regression parameter vector and $X\beta = \beta_0 + \beta_1 X_1 + \cdots + \beta_k X_k$ This equation can be expressed in a logit form as:

$$\log it(Y = 1|X) = \log(odds) = \log\frac{P}{1 - P} = \beta_0 + \beta_1 X_1 + \cdots + \beta_k X_k \tag{7.2}$$

where, the odds ratio means the ratio of the probability of compliance over the likelihood of non-compliance. It's log value has a linear relationship with the predictors. For Eq. 7.2, the maximum likelihood estimate (MLE) can be used for assessing the parameters' combination that maximizes the likelihood of the observed outcomes. Finally, we have a set of estimated parameters $\widehat{\beta}_1, \widehat{\beta}_2, \ldots, \widehat{\beta}_k$ and then the estimated value P^ of the probability that the event that occurs can be computed based on Eq. 7.2.

After obtaining the estimated values of coefficients it is necessary to examine how well the model fits the observations (goodness-of-fit). The Pearson Chi-square, likelihood-ratio (deviance) and the Hosmer-Lemeshow tests are three widely used statistical indices for measuring the goodness-of-fit of logistic regression models. Since some restrictions for Pearson Chi-square and deviance exist when the model has many variables and variable levels, we adopted the Hosmer-Lemeshow test to check the goodness-of-fit (Allison 2014).

This test divides subjects into several groups (no more than 10) based on the predicted probabilities of the groups. Then we computed a Chi-square from the observed and expected frequencies. This tested the null hypothesis that there was no difference between the observed and predicted values of the response variables. Therefore, when the test was not significant at a significance level (0.05), the null hypothesis cannot be rejected; this means that the model fits the data well. The values of Pearson Chi-square and deviance are also provided as a reference in the results of the model estimation.

7.4 Results and Discussion

Fisman and Svensson (2007) used indirectly framed questions on corruption. Similarly, they also used an indirectly phrased question in investigating tax compliance.

Among our sample responses, 12.4% perceived that citizens must not comply with paying taxes. However, the remaining 87.6% said that citizens must pay taxes. This shows that the respondents have a more tax compliant attitude.

The variables that characterized compliance are age and the level of schooling; wealth gender and employment status were measured in rates while age was measured in mean years. Educational background was measured by a range of variables where $0 =$ no formal tutoring and $9 =$ postgraduate capabilities. Moreover, the level of wealth was measured by a composite variable comprising of a television, auto, water, restroom and rooftop material ($0 =$ respondent has none of these things, $1 =$ respondent has all the things). There was a tendency towards a higher mean level of schooling among respondents with a compliant tax attitude. We also found that respondents with a consistent tax compliance nature were younger taxpayers in relative terms.

In the poll questionnaire, respondents were also asked what they believed was the fundamental reason for a few people evading taxes. As can be seen in Table 7.3, 38.85% people did not avoid paying taxes was the most frequently stated reason. Another frequently mentioned reasons were 'the taxes are too high,' and

Table 7.3 To pay or not to pay tax

	Freq.	Percent	Cum.
No need to tax the people	223	12.4	12.4
Citizens must pay taxes	1576	87.6	100
Total	1799	100	

Source Authors' calculations using data from the Afrobarometer 5th round survey

'people cannot afford to pay' (13.45 and 16.29% respectively) while 1.17% of the respondents considered poor public services to be the main reason why some people evaded taxes.

An 'unfair tax system' and 'they know they will not be caught' were also given as reasons why people avoided paying taxes by more than 3 and 2.22% of the respondents respectively in all the areas. Very few respondents (less than 1%) stated 'government does not listen to them, and government wastes tax money,' as the reason for not paying taxes. See Table 7.4.

Smallholder farmers' tax compliance is affected by various factors. Thus binary logistic models were developed to address the related variables and to explain the impact of predictor variables on agricultural tax compliance.

Figure 7.2 shows box plots of the distribution of age, comparative treatment, knowledge about taxes and trust in tax collectors for tax compliant and non-tax compliant people. The non-tax compliant tended to have lower tax knowledge scores, to be slightly younger and to have higher trust scores than non-compliant taxpayers. The importance of these effects in predicting tax compliance is directly related to the separation between tax compliant and non-compliant scores.

Table 7.4 Reasons for avoiding paying taxes

	Freq.	Percent	Cum.
Missing	6	0.33	0.33
People do not avoid paying taxes	699	38.85	39.19
The tax system is unfair	67	3.72	42.91
The taxes are too high	242	13.45	56.36
People cannot afford to pay taxes	293	16.29	72.65
They receive poor services from the government	21	1.17	73.82
The government does not listen to them	5	0.28	74.1
The government wastes tax money	6	0.33	74.43
Government officials steal tax money	13	0.72	75.15
They know they will not be caught	40	2.22	77.38
Greed/selfishness	4	0.22	77.6
Ignorance, DK how to pay or don't understand	44	2.45	80.04
Opposition against or lack of trust in G	6	0.33	80.38
Others	4	0.22	80.6
Don't know	349	19.4	100
Total	1799	100	

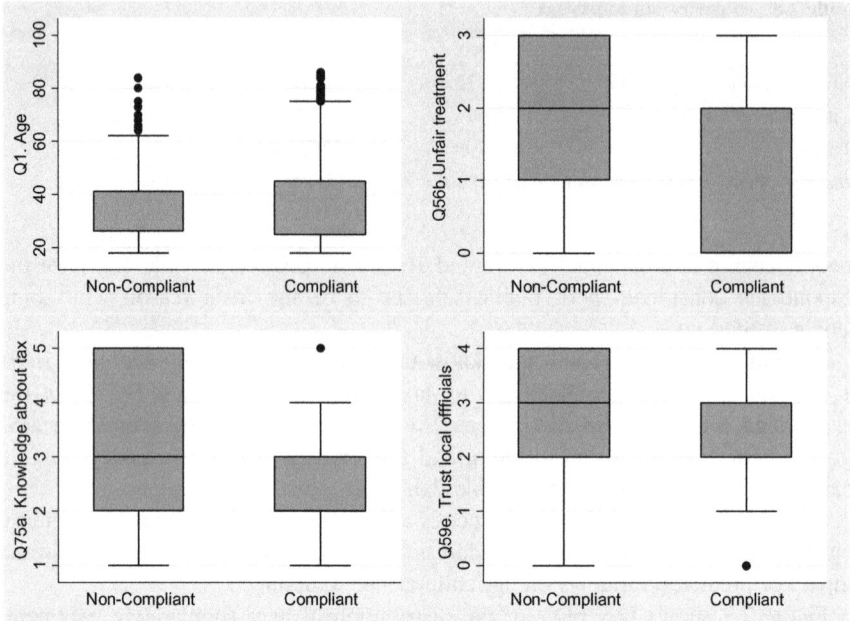

Fig. 7.2 Relationship of some predictor variables with tax compliance

7.4.1 Fitting the Logistic Regression Model

Model specification is an important step before drawing a conclusion or estimating future outcomes. We consider that the data may not be in conflict with the basic assumption that a possible relationship exists. For categorical outcome variables, we used the logistic regression to examine this possible relationship (Hosmer et al. 2013).

A stepwise selection can help identify theoretically plausible alternative models that a researcher may wish to consider and can also be used as a diagnostic device even when a researcher does not want to ultimately present a heterogeneous choice model (Williams 2010). Stepwise selection of covariates has a long history in linear regression. The Stata software package has a program or an option for performing this type of an analysis. It has packages that offer the option of a stepwise logistic regression. At one time, stepwise regression was a very popular method for model building. However, we feel that stepwise methods may be used as effective data analysis tools. Using these methods most studies collect many covariates and screen them for significant associations. A stepwise selection procedure can be more advantageous because it provides an effective means of screening a relatively small number of variables and fit some logistic regression equations simultaneously.

Any stepwise method for choice or cancellation of variables from a model depends on a measurable calculation that checks for the 'significance' of the variables and either includes or excludes them by a fixed decision rule. "The importance of a variable is defined regarding a measure of the statistical significance of the coefficient or coefficients when multiple design variables are used for the variable. The statistics used depend on the assumptions of the model," (Hosmer et al. 2013, p. 137). In logistic regression, the errors are expected to follow a binomial distribution and their significance can be assessed using likelihood ratio and the Wald test.

The rationale for minimizing the number of variables in the model is that the resultant model will probably be numerically steady and be more easily generalized. The more variables included in a model, the greater the assessed standard errors. We selected the following variables: Knowledge about tax, unfair treatment, level of education, satisfaction with the local government, social influence of others, age, satisfaction with democracy, sex and crime and conflict (Table 7.5). Hence, we included intuitively relevant variables in the model regardless of their 'statistical' significance.

The program evaluates the log-likelihood for each model, computes the likelihood ratio test versus the model containing only xe1 and xe2 and determines the corresponding p-value. Following the fit of the multivariable model, the importance of each variable included in the model should be verified. This should examine the extent to which the selected variables should classify correctly.

The results given in Table 7.6 show that the model yields predicted $p > 0.5$ for 1779 people; 1570 of them had a tax compliant attitude. Overall, this model offered accurate predictions as 88.05% of the individuals were correctly classified.

Table 7.5 The selection of variables for a logistic regression model

Logistic regression	Number of obs = 1799					
	LR chi2(9) = 154.89					
	Prob > chi2 = 0.0000					
Log likelihood = −596.70848	Pseudo R2 = 0.1149					
Tax compliance	Coef. interval	Std. err.	z	P > | z|	95% conf.	
Tax knowledge	−0.2920775	0.0600825	−4.86	0.000	−0.409837	−0.1743179
Unfair Treatm	−0.266715	0.0693183	−3.85	0.000	−0.4025763	−0.1308537
Education	0.2327804	0.0622285	3.74	0.000	0.1108148	0.3547459
Satisfa govt	−0.1951407	0.0799281	−2.44	0.015	−0.351797	−0.0384845
Social Influe	−0.1834453	0.083502	−2.20	0.028	−0.3471062	−0.0197845
Age	0.0101095	0.0058527	1.73	0.084	−0.0013615	0.0215805
Democracy	−0.1456815	0.0975768	−1.49	0.135	−0.3369285	0.0455654
Sex	−0.2358769	0.1687316	−1.40	0.162	−0.5665848	0.0948309
Crime and co	−0.0869606	0.0673812	−1.29	0.197	−0.2190253	0.0451041
_cons	4.009649	0.5112529	7.84	0.000	3.007612	5.011686

Source Authors' computation using data from the Afrobarometer 5th round Survey

Table 7.6 Classification statistics

Logistic model for tax compliance			
True			
Classified	D	~D	Total
+	1570	209	1779
−	6	14	20
Total	1576	223	1799
Classified + if predicted Pr(D) >= 0.5			
True D defined as tax compliance != 0			
Sensitivity	Pr(+|D)		99.62%
Specificity	Pr(−|~D)		6.28%
Positive predictive value	Pr(D|+)		88.25%
Negative predictive value	Pr(~D|−)		70.00%
False + rate for true ~ D	Pr(+|~D)		93.72%
False − rate for true D	Pr(−|D)		0.38%
False + rate for classified +	Pr(~D|+)		11.75%
False − rate for classified −	Pr(D|−)		30.00%
Correctly classified			88.05%

Source Authors' computation using data from the Afrobarometer 5th round Survey

Another commonly used test of model fit is the Hosmer and Lemeshow's goodness-of-fit test. The Hosmer-Lemeshow integrity of fit measurement is figured as the Pearson Chi-square from the possibility table of watched frequencies and expected frequencies. A solid match as measured by Hosmer and Lemeshow's test will yield an expansive *p*-value. At the point when there are non-stop indicators in the model there will be numerous cells characterized by indicator factors making an expansive possibility table, which yields a huge outcome. So a typical practice is joining the examples framed by the indicator factors into 10 gatherings and shaping a possible table of 2 × 10.

As per the results in Table 7.7 with a *p*-value of 0.09, we cannot conclude that Hosmer and Lemeshow's goodness-of-fit test shows that our model fit the data well. The sample of 1799 observations had 1743 different covariate patterns so we cannot test goodness-of- fit this way. Instead we used the Homer-Lemeshow test asking for 10 groups. We also specified the options to get more detailed information. Now as per the results in Table 7.7 our model fits well. However, the number of covariate patterns is close to the number of observations, making the applicability of the Pearson χ^2 test questionable but not wrong. Hosmer et al. (2013: 156–160) suggest regrouping the data by ordering the predicted probabilities and then forming, say, 10 nearly equal-sized groups. This result is given in Table 7.7 and has a *p*-value of 0.32; we can state that Hosmer and Lemeshow's goodness-of-fit test shows that our model fit the information well. We can state that Hosmer and Lemeshow's goodness-of-fit test indicates that our model fit the information well.

Table 7.7 Logistic model for tax compliance, goodness-of-fit test

(a)
Number of observations = 1799
Number of covariate patterns = 1743
Pearson chi2(1733) = 1811.90
Prob > chi2 = 0.0915

(b)

(Table collapsed on quantiles of estimated probabilities)

Group	Prob	Obs_1	Exp_1	Obs_0	Exp_0	Total
1	0.7362	105	110.9	75	69.1	180
2	0.8241	146	141.2	34	38.8	180
3	0.8689	157	152.9	23	27.1	180
4	0.8937	155	158.8	25	21.2	180
5	0.9108	165	162.6	15	17.4	180
6	0.9267	171	165.5	9	14.5	180
7	0.9389	169	167.9	11	12.1	180
8	0.9507	166	170.1	14	9.9	180
9	0.9634	169	172.2	11	7.8	180
10	0.9891	173	174.0	6	5.0	179

Number of observations = 1799
Number of groups = 10
Hosmer-Lemeshow chi2(8) = 9.25
Prob > chi2 = 0.3217

Therefore, we cannot reject our model. If we specify the options, the results show the groups along with the expected and observed number of positive responses (Table 7.7). We used the likelihood-ratio test, Wald test and the score test to examine the significance of parameters of the overall model (global test). The null hypothesis is that all coefficients of predictors are equal to zero ($\beta_1 = \beta_2 = \cdots \beta_k = 0$). If these tests are significant at a 0.1 level, the null hypothesis will be rejected as it means that the predictors influenced the prediction result. The Wald test was also applied to test the significance of individual model parameters. We expected the p-value for _hat to be highly significant. Evidence of a good fit is reflected in an non-significant hatsq and the p-value for hatsq is 0.053 which suggests good model adequacy.

7.4.2 Multicollinearity

Multicollinearity happens when at least two independent factors in a model are dictated by a straight blend of other autonomous factors in the model. Direct multicollinearity is genuinely basic since any connection among the free factors

Table 7.8 Result for collinearity diagnostics

Variable	SQRT			R-Squared
	VIF	VIF	Tolerance	
Tax Knowledge	1.11	1.06	0.8983	0.1017
Unfair TREA	1.07	1.03	0.9389	0.0611
Education	1.31	1.15	0.7610	0.2390
Satis Govt	1.16	1.08	0.8599	0.1401
Social INF	1.04	1.02	0.9627	0.0373
Age	1.22	1.10	0.8203	0.1797
Democracy	1.17	1.08	0.8531	0.1469
Sex	1.18	1.09	0.8462	0.1538
Crime and Con	1.02	1.01	0.9838	0.0162
Mean VIF	1.14			
	Eigenval	Cond index		
1	7.0553	1.0000		
2	0.8903	2.8151		
3	0.6865	3.2058		
4	0.4381	4.0129		
5	0.3801	4.3084		
6	0.2250	5.5993		
7	0.1338	7.2629		
8	0.1189	7.7026		
9	0.0559	11.2360		
10	0.0162	20.8842		
Condition Number		20.8842		
Eigenvalues and Cond Index computed from scaled raw sscp (w/intercept)				
Det(correlation matrix)		0.5312		

Source Authors' calculations using data from the Afrobarometer 5th round Survey

means that collinearity exists at the point when extreme multicollinearity happens, the standard blunders for the coefficients have a tendency to be expansive (expanded) and some of the time the evaluated calculated relapse coefficients can be exceedingly questionable (Table 7.8).

Every one of the measures stated earlier yield measures of the quality of the inter-relationships among the factors. Two regularly used measures are resilience (a pointer of how much collinearity a relapse examination can endure) and VIF (a fluctuation swelling component that is a marker of the amount of expansion of the standard mistake that could be brought on by collinearity). Comparing VIF is 1/resilience. On the off chance that the greater part of the factors are orthogonal to each other, as they were totally uncorrelated with each other, both the resistance and VIF are 1. On the off chance that a variable is firmly identified with another variable (s), the resistance goes to 0 and the change swelling gets substantial. Therefore, as per Table 7.8 we have no VIFs greater than 10, the mean VIF is greater than 1. VIFs may fail to discover collinearity involving the constant term.

7.4.3 Testing for the Significance of the Coefficients

Once we had fit a particular multiple (multivariable) logistic regression model, we started the process of model assessment. At the first step, we evaluated the significance of the variables in the model. The likelihood ratio test for the significance of p-coefficients for the independent variables in the model was analyzed. In the hypothesis, each variable's coefficient is zero and the statistical distribution considers normal distribution. The p-values computed under this hypothesis are given in Table 7.9. Based on this if we use a level of significance of 0.10, then we conclude that the variables—sex, the level of education, social influence of others, unfair treatment, satisfaction with the local government and tax knowledge are statistically significant, while the others are not significant.

As our goal is obtaining the best fitting model while minimizing the number of parameters, the next logical step is to fit a reduced model containing only those variables that are thought to be significant and compare this reduced model to the full model which has all the variables. The results are given in Table 7.10.

Maximum likelihood estimation fits the model and as the output indicates this uses an iterative process to estimate the parameters.

Table 7.11 presents the main results of the estimation. In disagreement with past literature, age negatively affected attitudes towards tax compliance. We found a statistically significant impact which is now explored further. Still, young smallholder farmers did not have a significantly higher tax morale as compared to the old farmers. When a respondent's educational levels were low he had a more negative attitude towards tax compliance.

We did find strong evidence of social influence in reducing the likelihood of a tax compliant attitude by 0.8%. The extent to which taxpayers assume that their ethnic and social groups which may be treated poorly as compared to the other groups is fundamentally related with a tax compliant attitude. As the extent to which individuals think that their ethnic group is treated unfairly increases by one point, the probability of a tax compliant attitude declines by 0.6%. According to Persson (2008) this may provide an indication of the comparative treatment model which is based on the equity theory and suggests that addressing inequities in the connection between the government and the citizens matter for tax compliance.

We also found that taxpayers' satisfaction with local government officials and politicians increased the level of satisfaction with local politicians which increased the likelihood of having a tax compliant attitude by 0.7%.

Finally, knowledge about tax was significantly correlated with a tax compliant attitude. An increase in know-how about tax by one point increased the probability of a tax compliant attitude by 0.578%.

Table 7.9 Multinomial logit estimation

Variables	With full model Tax compliance	Tax compliance
Age	0.00962	0.0101*
	−0.00587	−0.00585
Sex	−0.253	−0.236
	−0.17	−0.169
Education	0.237***	0.233***
	−0.0629	−0.0622
Ease of evasion	0.0624	
	−0.0914	
Infrastructure health	0.193	
	−0.125	
Crime and conflict	−0.107	−0.087
	−0.0687	−0.0674
Infrastructure edu	−0.0673	
	−0.0568	
Social influence	−0.192**	−0.183**
	−0.0845	−0.0835
Unfair treatment	−0.273***	−0.267***
	−0.0709	−0.0693
Trust	0.0415	
	−0.0883	
Corruption among tax officials	0.0303	
	−0.0549	
Satisfaction govt	0.212**	0.195**
	−0.0915	−0.0799
Democracy	−0.157	−0.146
	−0.099	−0.0976
Tax knowledge	0.325***	0.292***
	−0.0737	−0.0601
Constant	3.758***	4.010***
	−0.574	−0.511
Observations	1799	1799
Pseudo R-squared	0.115	0.115

Note Standard errors in parentheses
***$p < 0.01$, **$p < 0.05$, *$p < 0.1$

Table 7.10 Fitted multiple logistic regression model

Logistic regression					Number of obs = 1799		
					LR chi2(7) = 149.10		
					Prob > chi2 = 0.0000		
Log likelihood = −595.68139					Pseudo R2 = 0.1112		
Tax compliance	Coef.	Std. err.	z	P > |z|	[95% Conf. interval]		
Age	−0.0013325	0.0006237	−2.14	0.033	−0.002555	−0.0001101	
Sex	−0.3354976	0.1632902	−2.05	0.040	−0.6555405	−0.0154548	
Education	0.1954036	0.0578585	3.38	0.001	0.0820029	0.308804	
Social influe	−0.1921917	0.0832436	−2.31	0.021	−0.3553462	−0.0290373	
Unfair treatm	−0.2828508	0.0694156	−4.07	0.000	−0.4189029	−0.1467987	
Satisfac govt	0.2080978	0.0785154	2.65	0.008	0.3619852	0.0542104	
Tax Knowledge	0.313641	0.060117	5.22	0.000	0.4314681	0.1958139	
_cons	3.960703	0.3028205	13.08	0.000	3.367186	4.55422	

Source Authors' computation using data from the Afrobarometer 5th round Survey

Table 7.11 Results of logit regressions with marginal effects

Variables	Tax compliance	Margins
Q1 Age	0.0101*	0.000984*
	−0.00585	−0.00057
Q101 Sex	−0.264	−0.0258
	−0.166	−0.0162
Q97 Education	0.248***	0.0242***
	−0.062	−0.00606
Q26C Social influence	−0.186**	−0.0182**
	−0.0832	−0.00809
Q56B Unfair treatment	−0.278***	−0.0271***
	−0.0691	−0.0067
Q59E Satisfaction with local Govt	0.220***	0.0215***
	0.0783	0.00764
Q75A knowledge	0.303***	0.0296***
	0.0597	0.00578
Constant	3.414***	
	−0.393	
Observations	1799	1799

Source Authors' calculations using data from the Afrobarometer 5th round Survey
Note Standard errors in parentheses
***p < 0.01, **p < 0.05, *p < 0.1

7.5 Policy Recommendations

Effective tax compliance is central to a government's ability to mobilize resources for funding infrastructure and public service delivery. Smallholder farmer taxpayers are influenced by both economic and other motives and policy recommendations for tax compliance must give due weight to every important factor. The policy lessons that can be drawn from our evidence on tax compliance include the extent of fraud that can be affected by policies beyond the probabilities and magnitude of standard tax enforcement actions. Some specific recommendations are:

- Education is the key to improving tax compliance; hence, tax education should be given priority.
- Good governance is the key to improving tax compliance; hence, it should be based on principles of fairness.
- In addition to persuasive measures, the government can also implement mild coercive measures such as penalties for non-compliance.
- Incentives to improve rural tax administration are vital in addressing challenges to agricultural tax enforcement.

7.6 Conclusion

Motivated by the lack of empirical analyses on the determinants of tax compliance for smallholder farmers in Ethiopia, our study addressed this gap. Generally speaking our results are in line with the findings of modern empirical literature on tax morale in other countries.

A key finding of our study is that criminal gangs reduce a tax compliant attitude. Past research states that the way the state treats individuals or groups vis-à-vis their fellow citizens is one of the factors in determining a taxpayer compliance attitude. We tested this hypothesis by inspecting how rural farmers perceived the government's treatment of their ethnic groups in comparison to other groups. This mattered for a rural tax compliant attitude in Ethiopia. Our study found evidence that political legitimacy, which is trust in government structures and institutions, impacted taxpayers' compliant attitude. Our findings were strong in an alternate econometric estimation where we incorporated all the individual responses with other people's action about tax in an ordered logit regression.

Our study provides directions for further research. For an improved understanding of smallholder farmers' tax compliant attitude and behavior in Ethiopia there is a need for a more intensive examination of the idea of decency in monetary trade, that is, the authoritative connection between citizens and the legislature.

References

Ali, M., O.H. Fjeldstad, and I. Sjursen. 2013. *Factors affecting tax compliant attitude in Africa: Evidence from Kenya, Tanzania, Uganda and South Africa.* Paper presented at the In Centre for the Study of African Economies 2013 Conference Oxford.

Allingham, M.G., and A. Sandmo. 1972. Income tax evasion: a theoretical analysis. *Journal of Public Economics* 1 (3–4): 323–338.

Allison, P. D. 2014. *Measures of fit for logistic regression.* Paper presented at the Proceedings of the SAS Global Forum 2014 Conference.

Alm, J., R. Bahl, and M.N. Murray. 1990. Tax structure and tax compliance. *Review of Economics and Statistics* 72 (4): 603–613.

Alm, J., G.H. McClelland, and W.D. Schulze. 1992. Why do people pay taxes? *Journal of Public Economics* 48 (1): 21–38.

Alm, J., I. Sanchez, and A. Dejuan. 1995. Economic and noneconomic factors in tax compliance. *Kyklos* 48 (1): 3–18.

Anderson, K., and Y. Hayami. 1986. *The political economy of agricultural protection: East Asia in international perspective.* Sydney: Allen & Unwin.

Anderson, K., and E. Valenzuela. 2008. *Estimates of global distortions to agricultural incentives, 1955 to 2007.* Washington, DC: The World Bank.

Andreoni, J., B. Erard, and J. Feinstein. 1998. Tax compliance. *Journal of Economic Literature*: 818–860.

Azime, H., G. Ramakrishna, and M. Asfaw. 2017. Agricultural tax responsiveness and economic growth in Ethiopia. In *Studies on economic development and growth in selected African Countries*, ed. A. Heshmati, 291–309. Singapore: Springer.

Banerjee, A. V. 1992. A simple model of herd behavior. *The Quarterly Journal of Economics*: 797–817.

Bergman, M. 1998. Criminal law and tax compliance in Argentina: Testing the limits of deterrence. *International Journal of the Sociology of Law* 26 (1): 55–74.

Besley, T., and T. Persson. 2014. Why do developing countries tax so little? *Journal of Economic Perspectives* 28 (4): 99–120.

Bird, R.M. 1983. Income-Tax reform in developing-countries—the administrative dimension. *Bulletin for International Fiscal Documentation* 37 (1): 3–14.

Bobek, D.D., A.M. Hageman, and C.F. Kelliher. 2013. Analyzing the role of social norms in tax compliance behavior. *Journal of Business Ethics* 115 (3): 451–468.

Chang, J.J., C. Been-Lon, and M. Hsu. 2006. Agricultural productivity and economic growth: Role of tax revenues and infrastructures. *Southern Economic Journal* 72 (4): 891–914.

Cowell, F.A., and P.F. Gordon. 1988. Unwillingness to pay. *Journal of Public Economics* 36 (3): 305–321.

Cummings, R.G., J. Martinez-Vazquez, M. Mckee, and B. Torgler. 2009. Tax morale affects tax compliance: Evidence from surveys and an artefactual field experiment. *Journal of Economic Behavior & Organization* 70 (3): 447–457.

Erard, B. 2009. Tax compliance and tax morale: A theoretical and empirical analysis. *Journal of Economic Literature* 47 (1): 198–200.

Fischer, C.M., M. Wartick, and M. Mark. 1992. Detection probability and taxpayer compliance: A review of the literature. *Journal of Accounting Literature* 11: 1–46.

Fisman, R., and J. Svensson. 2007. Are corruption and taxation really harmful to growth? Firm level evidence. *Journal of Development Economics* 83 (1): 63–75.

Fjeldstad, O.H., and J. Semboja. 2001. Why people pay taxes: The case of the development Levy in Tanzania. *World Development* 29 (12): 2059–2074.

Fjeldstad, O.H., and K.K. Heggstad. 2012. *Building taxpayer culture in Mozambique, Tanzania and Zambia: Achievements, challenges and policy recommendations.* Bergen: CMI.

Grimm, L.G., and P.R. Yarnold. 1995. *Reading and understanding multivariate statistics: American Psychological Association.* Washington, DC: APA Publications Department.

Gupta, S., and S. Tareq. 2008. Mobilizing revenue: Finance and development. *International Monetary Fund* 43 (3): 44–47.

Heinemann, F., and M.G. Kocher. 2013. Tax compliance under tax regime changes. *International Tax and Public Finance* 20 (2): 225–246.

Hosmer, D.W., S. Lemeshow, and R.X. Sturdivant. 2013. *Applied logistic regression*. New Jersey: Wiley.

Kastlunger, B., S.G. Dressler, E. Kirchler, L. Mittone, and M. Voracek. 2010. Sex differences in tax compliance: Differentiating between demographic sex, gender-role orientation, and prenatal masculinization (2D:4D). *Journal of Economic Psychology* 31 (4): 542–552.

Kirchler, E., and V. Braithwaite. 2007. *The economic psychology of tax behaviour*. Cambridge: Cambridge University Press.

Lago-Peñas, I., and S. Lago-Peñas. 2010. The determinants of tax morale in comparative perspective: Evidence from European countries. *European Journal of Political Economy* 26: 441–453. https://doi.org/10.1016/j.ejpoleco.2010.06.003

Luttmer, E.F.P., and M. Singhal. 2014. Tax morale. *Journal of Economic Perspectives* 28 (4): 149–168.

Martinez-Vazquez, J., and B. Torgler. 2009. The evolution of tax morale in modern Spain. *Journal of Economic Issues* 43 (1): 1–28.

MoFED. 2012. *Survey of the Ethiopian economy*. Addis Ababa: Ministry of Finance and Economic Development.

Moore, M. 2004. Revenues, state formation, and the quality of governance in developing countries. *International Political Science Review* 25 (3): 297–319.

Persson, A. 2008. The institutional sources of statehood. Assimilation, multiculturalism, and taxation in Sub-Saharan Africa. PhD Thesis, Gothenburg University, Gothenburg, Sweden.

Prinz, A., S. Muehlbacher, and E. Kirchler. 2014. The slippery slope framework on tax compliance: An attempt to formalization. *Journal of Economic Psychology* 40: 20–34.

Skinner, J. 1991. If agricultural land taxation is so efficient, why is it so rarely used? *The World Bank Economic Review* 5 (1): 113–133.

Torgler, B. 2005. Tax morale and direct democracy. *European Journal of Political Economy* 21 (2): 525–531.

Tyler, T.R. 2006. Psychological perspectives on legitimacy and legitimation. *Annual Review of Psychology* 57: 375–400.

Williams, R. 2010. Fitting heterogeneous choice models with oglm. *Stata Journal* 10 (4): 540.

Part III
Multidimensional Poverty

Chapter 8
Multidimensional Poverty and Its Dynamics in Ethiopia

Getu Tigre

Abstract Traditional one-dimensional income or consumption expenditure-based poverty measures provide a biased and incomplete guide to addressing poverty. Recent research trends are shifting from one-dimensional to multidimensional poverty analyses. This paper uses Alkire and Foster (Understandings and misunderstandings of multidimensional 793 poverty measurement. Springer Science +Business Media, Berlin, 2011) method of multidimensional poverty analysis using data from four rounds of the Ethiopian Demographic and Health Survey. Our study concludes that multidimensional poverty is high in Ethiopia in general and in rural Ethiopia in particular. In Ethiopia, multidimensional poverty has been decreasing moderately over time but still a large proportion of its population is under the multidimensional poverty line. Living standards contribute the most (more than 85%) to multidimensional poverty while education contributes about 14% and health contributes the least (less than 1%). Among the indicators that this paper uses in multidimensional poverty, there is high deprivation in sanitation, cooking fuel, floor and electricity. Further, sanitation and cooking fuel deprivations are increasing but education deprivation and school attendance deprivation have been decreasing over time. Level of education, having a bank account and the number of working age family members reduce multidimensional poverty but the number of children under 5-years and dependent family members (dependency ratio) increase Ethiopian households' multidimensional poverty.

Keywords Poverty · Ethiopia · Multidimensional poverty · Deprivation

JEL Classification Codes C250 · C430 · I320

G. Tigre (✉)
Department of Economics, Addis Ababa University, Addis Ababa, Ethiopia
e-mail: getutigre2002@yahoo.com

© Springer Nature Singapore Pte Ltd. 2018   161
A. Heshmati and H. Yoon (eds.), *Economic Growth and Development in Ethiopia*, Perspectives on Development in the Middle East and North Africa (MENA) Region, https://doi.org/10.1007/978-981-10-8126-2_8

8.1 Introduction

Ethiopia is the second most populous country (after Nigeria) in Africa with a diverse population mix of ethnicity and religion. Large proportions of its population live in rural areas and are engaged in agriculture which accounts for 43% of its gross domestic product (CSA 2009). Coffee and other agricultural products are the main export commodities and Ethiopia is one of the least urbanized countries in the world (CSA 2009).

Poverty is a development challenge for most developing countries (Dercon et al. 2009) and poverty reduction is an important priority for their governments. Ethiopia adopted the Plan for Accelerated and Sustainable Development to end Poverty (PASDEP) to attain the millennium development goals (MDGs) by 2015. The first Growth and Transformation Plan (GTP-I) was developed to bring about rapid and broad-based growth to eventually end poverty (MOFED 2010). Despite all these steps, according to a government report in 2016 (GTP II 2016) around 25% of the population was still living under the poverty line.

Measuring the poverty level is the first step in poverty reduction strategies. Earlier approaches to the measurement of poverty are one-dimensional. They are based on a single indicator, usually income or consumption expenditure, showing the level of deprivation. These monetary measures separate the population between poor and non-poor through the identification of thresholds or poverty lines. Although income measures of poverty have been used frequently, they have some limitations because human life is affected not only by income but also by other dimensions of life like education and health. Therefore, a poverty analysis should also take into consideration these other dimensions. Literature on multidimensional poverty is growing fast (for example, Adetola 2014; Alkire and Foster 2011; Alkire and Santos 2010; Bourguignon and Chakravarty 2003; Dhongda et al. 2015; Hishe Gebreslassie 2013; Maasoumi and Xu 2015).

In a country like Ethiopia where poverty is deep rooted, a rigorous multidimensional poverty measure, trend development and a dynamic adjustment analysis of poverty are important to understand the poverty history of the country. In addition, this will help shed light on whether poverty reduction strategies implemented by federal and regional governments so far have been effective in reducing multidimensional poverty so that appropriate poverty reduction policies can be designed in the future.

Our study uses the Demographic and Health Survey (DHS) data for 2000–2014 and examines the extent, trends and dynamics of multidimensional poverty in the country across regions and over years in the components most relevant and locally feasible. It uses the Alkire and Foster (2011) method of multidimensional poverty index (MPI) measure, adapting the method on which MPI is based to better address local realities, needs and available data.

8.2 Research Motivation

Earlier approaches to the measurement of poverty have some limitations which are mainly related to the way in which they measure income, market failure and how household incomes are used for household members' (women and children's) wellbeing.

While using income or consumption expenditure as a measure of poverty, parts of a household's income including home production and consumption of goods and services may not be reported correctly. This lack of accuracy is attributed to the absence of records and because of tax reasons leading to unreliable statistics. Even if measured and reported, a household's income as a measure of poverty relates only to the resources required to achieve wellbeing and not necessarily to the outcomes, that is, the final condition of an individual.

Some markets do not exist in developing countries (in particular, those related to provision of public goods) and others operate imperfectly. The use of income as a measure of poverty assumes that markets and prices exist for all goods and services. Hence, income poverty measures at best provide only an incomplete and biased guide to addressing poverty. Accounting for multidimensional poverty reduces biases and provides a good picture of the households' wellbeing.

The logic behind the income approach is that a household above the income poverty line possesses potential purchasing power to acquire a bundle of goods and services yielding a level of wellbeing that is sufficient to function (Thorbecke 2008). The income or consumption measure indicates the means, not the end. It is not the amount of tuition fee that determines the level of education, rather the level of education or knowledge acquired that determines the productive capacity of an individual, a household and society. It is not the amount of money that one spends on medical services but the number of days of illness, maternal deaths and child mortality that we are able to reduce which will determine the level of healthcare. Therefore, emphasis has to be shifted from the means to the end.

Poverty arises because poor people's lives can be affected by multiple deprivations that are all of importance (Sen 1992). Hence, arguing against a single monetary dimension (income or consumption) as a sufficient proxy of human welfare to other non-monetary values such as health, education, contribution of the public sector and political participation will result in shifting focus from the means to the end.

Besides the relevance of the multidimensional poverty measure in indicating human wellbeing, more data (for example, DHS data) on non-income dimensions is available today. Further, methodologies for a multidimensional measurement have advanced considerably in recent years and created new possibilities of measuring multidimensional poverty at the national, regional and sub-regional levels. The poverty measure at one point of time or year does not indicate whether poverty reduction policies implemented by federal and regional governments have been effective in reducing multidimensional poverty. Repeated cross-sections with time invariant common characteristics or panel data are required to investigate the dynamics of poverty. Poverty is a stochastic phenomenon; poverty trends and its dynamic analysis are very essential. Thus, it is important to know the history and the dynamics of poverty based on which appropriate national and regional policies can be designed.

In Ethiopia most pervious researches have been one-dimensional (Berisso 2016; Woldehanna and Hagos 2013). There are some multidimensional poverty researches but they are very general and overlook the differences within the country, regions and ethnic groups. Ambel et al. (2015) consider health, education and standard of living. However, they examine poverty diminution by diminution and thus ignore the interdependence and correlation between dimensions and do not come up with a multidimensional poverty index.

Bruck and Workneh (2013) computed a multidimensional poverty index in Ethiopia but did not include some living standard indicators like electricity, sanitation and cooking fuel in their analysis. Using Ethiopia Demographic and Health Survey data, Alemayehu and Addis (2014) found the multidimensional poverty index; however, his research did not consider variations within regions and the poverty trend and its dynamics over time. Others have focused on some deprivation and under-estimated deprivations in other dimensions. Bersisa and Heshmati (2016) focus on energy poverty and do not show poverty changes over time.

Our study examines multidimensional poverty levels in Ethiopia and changes across regions and over time in the components most relevant and locally feasible. It uses the multidimensional poverty measure (Alkire and Foster 2011) method. Adapting the method on which MPI is based helps us address local realities, needs and the available data better.

Our study is different from the others in three aspects. First, it uses the most recent and the four rounds EDHS cross-section data from 2000 to 2014 for measuring MPI. Second, it estimates MPI in these four round periods and conducts trend and dynamic analyses and makes decompositions along time, regions and dimensions. Third, in earlier multidimensional poverty researches, having any two assets or more regardless of the type of assets made households non-deprived of assets. In our study, the living standard indicator—assets—is divided into three categories: information assets, mobility assets and livelihood assets. A household is non-deprived in assets if it owns at least one of the assets from two or more asset categories. This is a new empirical perspective in an analysis of multidimensional poverty.

8.3 Literature Review

8.3.1 Poverty

Poverty has to be defined appropriately or it should at least be understood conceptually before it can be measured (Thorbecke 2008). Literature defines poverty in different ways and there is no consensus on the definition. According to the basic needs approach, poverty is insufficiency of resources and opportunities to satisfy basic human needs. The World Bank (2014) says that 'poverty is pronounced deprivation in well-being.' Wellbeing in this sense means an individual or household's command over commodities in general. It focuses on whether households or individuals have enough resources to meet their needs. Poverty in this case is measured mainly in monetary terms. This is the starting point for most analyses of poverty. The second view is whether people are able to obtain basic consumption goods such as food, shelter, clothes, healthcare and education. In this approach, the emphasis shifts from resources (money) to outcomes.

Other authors define poverty in different ways. Foster et al. (2013), define poverty as the absence of acceptable choices across a broad range of important life decisions, as well as lack of freedom to be or to do what one wants. The inevitable outcome of poverty is insufficiency and deprivation across many of the facets of a fulfilling life.

The most comprehensive and logical attempt to capture the concept of poverty is Sen (1992) capability and functioning approach where wellbeing comes from the capability to function in society, poverty is seen as lack of pre-requisites of a self-determined life and the 'lack of capabilities' to function or manage one's life. People are considered poor when they lack key capabilities and so have inadequate income, education, poor heath, low self-confidence and powerlessness. The human rights-based approach emphasizes that respect for human rights is a necessary condition for various social and economic outcomes. It challenges, to some extent, the approach that poverty be measured by a one-dimensional criterion based on income and/or consumption expenditure and therefore it addresses the multidimensional nature of poverty beyond the lack of income (UNDP 2013).

Poverty is a challenge for developing countries and requires worldwide efforts and collaborations to reduce it. Extreme poverty is observed in all parts of the world and this is a global challenge including in developed countries. In 2013, 767 million people were estimated to be living below the international poverty line of US $1.90 per person per day (The World Bank 2016). Almost 10.7% of the global population was poor by this standard of which Sub-Saharan Africa's share was about 41% showing that poverty is still widespread in Africa (Chen and Ravallion 2008). In 2013, the World Bank adopted two ambitious goals: end global extreme poverty by reducing the poverty headcount ratio from 10.7% in 2013 to 3% by 2030 and promote shared prosperity in every country in a sustainable way (The World Bank 2016). These two goals are part of a wider international development agenda and are closely related to the United Nation's sustainable development goals (SDGs). According to the World Bank, extreme poverty decreased over time and between 1990 and 2015 the percentage of the world's population living in extreme poverty fell from 37.1 to 9.6%. However, it will take another 100 years to bring the world' poorest up to the previous poverty line of $1.25 a day.

8.3.2 Multidimensional Poverty

There has been shift of focus from the one-dimensional nature of poverty to its multidimensional nature in measuring poverty. Considering the multidimensional nature of poverty has become increasingly important over recent years and different contributions to this have been made. In addition to money income or consumption expenditure, human lives and wellbeing are affected by different dimensions such as health and education. A one-dimensional measure of poverty using income or consumption expenditure presupposes that a market exists for all goods and services; however, often markets do not exist for many goods and services or they function imperfectly (Bourguignon and Chakravarty 2003; Thorbecke 2008; Tsui 2002) and therefore, monetary values cannot be assigned to particular aspects of wellbeing (Hulme and McKay 2008; Thorbecke 2008). Also, having sufficient income for purchasing a basic basket of goods does not directly imply that it is also spent on that basket of goods (Thorbecke 2008). Individual wellbeing is a multidimensional notion (Stiglitz et al. 2009), individuals care about many different aspects of their lives, including their material standard of living, health and schooling. As stated by Alkire and Santos (2011) low income, poor health, inadequate education, job insecurity, disempowerment and precarious housing are clear manifestations of multidimensional poverty. The components of poverty change across people, time and context but multiple domains are involved. Empirical literature documents a mismatch between monetary and non-monetary deprivations (Berenger and Verdire-Chouchane 2007; Hishe Gebreslassie 2013; Tran et al. 2015). This difference is attributed to a possible bias in the single dimensional measure of poverty. A study in India by Stewait et al. (2007) found that 53% of the Indian children living in income-poor households were not malnourished and 53% of the malnourished children were not living in income-poor households.

8.3.3 Measurements of Poverty

It is important to identify who the poor are and where they live for measuring the level of poverty so that resources can be directed at them more effectively for addressing poverty. The measurements paint a picture of the magnitude of the problem and can help identify programs that will work well in addressing poverty (Foster et al. 2013). Governments can be accountable for their policies and researchers can explore the relationships between poverty and other economic variables (Foster et al. 2013).

Poverty has often been measured using income or consumption expenditure and can thus be measured in relative, absolute and subjective terms. Relative poverty measures a household or individual's income relative to a certain average income (for example, mean, median), while absolute poverty measures individuals' or households' incomes relative to a certain income threshold (poverty line). The subjective approach defines poverty as subjective judgments of an individual of what constitutes socially acceptable minimum standards of living in society. People value their poverty status within their society using different dimensions and indicators. Thus, this approach provides more information than relative and absolute measures of poverty and is therefore multidimensional in nature or perspective.

The World Development Reports introduced poverty as a multidimensional phenomenon, and the Millennium Declaration and MDGs have been highlighting multiple dimensions of poverty since 2000. The first wellbeing measure on a worldwide scale was the Human Development Index (HDI). The Human Development Report ranks countries by HDI, which consists of their achievements in economic and social spheres such as life expectancy, educational attainments and income. The Human Poverty Index (HPI) developed by the UN was to complement HDI, however in 2010 HPI was substituted by the UN's multidimensional poverty index (UNDP 2013).

The multidimensional poverty index measures a range of deprivations such as inadequate living standards, lack of income, poor health, lack of education, disempowerment and threat of violence (Alkire and Santos 2010) and is currently used in more than 100 countries. In academic literature, interest in multidimensional poverty measurement is growing (Alkire and Foster 2011). Effective multidimensional poverty measures have practical applications such as they can replace or supplement the income or consumption poverty measure. Dimensional decomposability of the multidimensional poverty measure can help monitor the level and composition of poverty and also help evaluate the impact of programs (for example, health and education programs). The multidimensional poverty measure gives more policy relevant information as it can single out the effect of each dimension on poverty and policies for reducing poverty should rely on a multidimensional analysis of poverty (Adetola 2014).

The dashboard approach is a starting point for measuring the multidimensionality of poverty to assess the level of deprivation in the dimensions separately; it applies a standard uni-dimensional measure to each dimension (Alkire et al. 2011; Ravallion 2011). The dashboard approach tries to find deprivation indices for all indicators considered in a multidimensional poverty analysis. The dashboard approach has the advantage of increasing the set of dimensions considered, offering a rich amount of information and potentially allowing the use of the best data source for each particular indicator and for assessing the impact of specific policies (such as nutritional or educational interventions). However, this approach has some significant disadvantages. First, dashboards do not reflect joint distribution of deprivations across the population precisely and because of this they are marginal methods (Alkire et al. 2015).

In literature, the distinction between being poor in all dimensions and in only one dimension has been referred to as the intersection and union definitions of poverty. This can be illustrated using an example drawn from Duclos and Younger (2006). The authors state that if wellbeing is measured in terms of all dimensions then a person can be considered poor if his achievement in each dimension is less than the poverty threshold set for that particular dimension. This is defined as an intersection definition of poverty and will generally produce untenably low estimates of poverty. In contrast, a union definition considers an individual to be poor only if her achievement in one of the dimensions were to fall below its respective threshold. This is very commonly used and may lead to exaggerated estimates of poverty. In between these two extremes the most widely used measure of multidimensional poverty currently is the multidimensional poverty index (MPI).

MPI uses different dimensions and indicators. A poverty cut-off is set for each indicator and finally the multidimensional poverty cut-off is set by combining all the indicators based on the weight assigned to each indicator. There are several main features of MPI that can be used as important tools for a poverty analysis. First, MPI can be expressed as a product of the incidence of poverty (Headcount ratio H) and the intensity of poverty or the average deprivation score (A) among the poor. Second, the MPI measure can be decomposed across population sub-groups which can be geographic regions, ethnic or religious groups. We use this feature to create poverty measures for regions within a country. Third, MPI can be broken down into the indicators in which the poor people are deprived (Alkire and Foster 2011). In other words, it is possible to compute the contribution of each indicator to the overall poverty.

8.4 Data and Methodology

8.4.1 Data

Our research used the Ethiopian Demographic and Health Survey (EDHS) data. EDHS is conducted by the Ethiopia Central Statistical Agency (CSA) with support from the worldwide Demographic and Health Survey (DHS) project. DHS is a comprehensive dataset that consists of samples from all regions in the country (nine regional states and two city administrations) which represent the national population of Ethiopia.

DHS is cross-section data collected almost every five years. The first round was in 2000; the second in 2005; the third in 2011; and the most recent was in 2016. The data collected contains information on household characteristics, households' dwelling units such as the source of water, type of sanitation facilities, access to electricity, types of cooking fuel and others.

The DHS data for 2016 has not yet been released. Hence, as an alternative we used the Ethiopia Mini Demography and Health Survey (EMDHS) of 2014. However, in the Mini 2014 DHS, the variable 'types of cooking fuel' was not collected and the 2014 analysis does not include types of cooking fuel. We make necessary adjustments for that. In our research the unit of analysis is a household, a household has common resources and takes decisions that affect almost all its members.

8.4.1.1 Components of Multidimensional Poverty

There is no fixed list of what should be included in a MPI (Ravallion 2011). The list is open and the most important thing is the process through which the components are selected (Alkire et al. 2011). This must be agreed upon with a certain degree of consensus. Such a consensus may derive from participatory experiments, a legal basis, international agreements such as the MDGs or human rights and empirical evidence regarding people's values. Statistical relationships or the correlation between the variables must also be explored and understood.

We selected MPI's indicators after a thorough consultation process involving experts in all the three dimensions (Alkire et al. 2011). The ideal choices of indicators had to be reconciled with what was actually possible in terms of data availability. We used three dimensions and 10 indicators suggested by Alkire and Foster (2011)—health, education and living standard. The deprivation dimensions and indicators used in our multidimensional poverty analysis are listed in Table 8.1.

Table 8.1 MPI's dimensions and indicators

Dimensions	Indicators	A household is deprived of the indicator if:
Health	Child mortality	One or more child died in the household after the last survey
	Nutrition	There is child malnutrition in the household and/or adult malnutrition in the household after the last survey
Education	Highest grade obtained	No household member who is 13-years or older has completed six years of schooling
	School attendance	Any school age child in the household is not attending school in the academic year
Living standard	Electricity	The household has no access to electricity
	Sanitation	There is no facility/bush/field, or sanitation facilities are open to the public or shared with other households
	Sources of water	A household's source of water is an unprotected spring, well, river/dam/lake/pond/stream and others
	Floor materials	The floor material of the house is earth, sand, dung and others
	Cooking fuel	The cooking fuel used by a household is charcoal, firewood, straw, dung and others
	Asset ownership	A household has at most one asset in one of the three asset categories: access to information (phone mobile or fixed), radio, TV); asset for easy mobility (bicycle, motorbike, motorboat, car, truck or animal wheel cart); asset for livelihood (refrigerator, agricultural land or livestock (at least one cattle or at least one horse or at least two goats or at least two sheep, or at least 10 chicken)

8.4.1.2   The Weight of the Indicators

In a multidimensional poverty analysis, there is no general consensus not only on multidimensional poverty dimensions but also on relative weights of indicators and the substitution between attributes (Decancq and Lugo 2013; Maasoumi and Xu 2015; Ravallion 2011). Next to the identification of dimensions and indicators of multidimensional poverty, the crucial problem is assigning suitable weights to the indicators (Berenger and Verdire-Chouchane 2007). Weights play a crucial role in aggregating and determining the trade-off between the dimensions (Decancq and Lugo 2008). The equal weight approach has been used by different authors (Atkinson 2003; Alkire and Foster 2011; Dhongda et al. 2015; Salazar et al. 2013). However, this approach is controversial and it has its share of critics (Decancq and Lugo 2008). Most multidimensional poverty indictors are assumed to be correlated and the equal weight approach fails to consider these correlations and therefore multidimensional poverty dimensions cannot have similar importance or weight (Ravallion 2011). One of the options for an alternative method is to use individual preferences as a weighting scheme (Decancq et al. 2014; Takeuchi 2014). In this weighting scheme, the relative importance and trade-off among dimensions are left to the individual. The problem with this approach is that individuals may not reveal their real preferences (Takeuchi 2014). Following this criticism other weighting approaches such as parametric or statistical approaches have been used. Statistical techniques are widely used in designing poverty measures and in giving a weight to each indicator (Maggino and Zumbo 2012). Key techniques include descriptive and model based methods. Descriptive methods are the principle component analysis (PCA), the multiple correspondence analysis (MCA) and cluster analysis (CA). Model based methods are the latent class analysis (LCA), the structural equation model (SEM) and factor analysis (FA).

The main difference between PCA and MCA is the scale of the variables used. PCA is used when variables are of cardinal scale, while MCA is appropriate when variables are categorical or binary. The model-based methods are latent variable models and cover latent class analysis (LCA), factor analysis (FA) and more generally, structural equation models (SEMs). When the indicators are ordinal, binary or categorical, a more suitable multivariate technique for a lower-dimensional description of the data is a correspondence analysis (CA).

Like PCA, FA is also used as a data reduction method; however, there is a fundamental difference between the two methods. PCA is a descriptive method that attempts to interpret the underlying (latent) structure of a set of indicators on the basis of their total variations (common variation and unique variation), while FA is a model-based method that focuses on explaining the underlying common variance across indicators instead of total variance. The observed dimensions are a manifestation of the factors and have been used by different authors (Decancq and Lugo 2008; Noble et al. 2007). Since the factor analysis (FA) model makes no prior assumptions regarding the pattern of relationships among the observed indicators (Alkire et al. 2015), it can be used for cardinal and categorical data. Further, it considers the correlation between indicators and removes or reduces redundancy or duplication from a set of correlated variables. Our research uses the factor analysis model to determine the weight of the indicators.

In finding the weight of the indicators using factor analysis, if the observed variables are $X_1, X_2, \ldots, X_n$, the common factors are $F_1, F_2, \ldots, F_m$ and the unique factors are $e_1, e_2, \ldots, e_n$, the variables may be expressed as a linear function of the factors:

$$
\begin{aligned}
X_1 &= a_{11}F_1 + a_{12}F_2 + a_{13}F_3 + \cdots + a_{1m}F_m + a_1 e_1 \\
X_2 &= a_{21}F_1 + a_{22}F_2 + a_{23}F_3 + \cdots + a_{2m}F_m + a_2 e_2 \\
&\vdots \\
X_n &= a_{n1}F_1 + a_{n2}F_2 + a_{n3}F_3 + \cdots + a_{nm}F_m + a_n e_n
\end{aligned}
\tag{8.1}
$$

The model assumes that each observed variable is a linear function of these factors with a residual variable. The model produces the maximum correlation and seeks to find the coefficients $a_{11}, a_{12}, \ldots, a_{nm}$. The coefficients are weights or factor loadings in the same way as regression coefficients. The factor loadings give us the strength of the correlation between the variables and the factor.

It is possible to solve Eq. 8.1 for the factor score so as to obtain a score for each factor for each subject. The equation is of the form:

$$
\begin{aligned}
F_1 &= \lambda_{11}X_1 + \lambda_{12}X_2 + \lambda_{13}X_3 + \cdots + \lambda_{1m}X_m \\
F_2 &= \lambda_{21}X_1 + \lambda_{22}X_2 + \lambda_{23}X_3 + \cdots + \lambda_{2m}X_m \\
&\vdots \\
F_n &= \lambda_{n1}X_1 + \lambda_{n2}X_2 + \lambda_{n3}X_3 + \cdots + \lambda_{nm}X_m
\end{aligned}
\tag{8.2}
$$

In this model, each factor is a weighted combination of the input variables. The main idea behind this model is that the factor analysis seeks to find factors such that when these factors are extracted, there remain no correlations between variables as the factors account for the correlations.

8.4.2 Aggregation of MPI

We have n-households in each round representing the population of interest and d-indicators for selected dimensions for which $d \geq 2$. Once the data is available and the range of dimensions and indicators have been selected, we have achieved the level matrix of dimension (n × d) of n-households and d-indicators of the selected dimensions. Let $\sum Y = [Y_{ij}]$ denote the n × d matrix of achievement for i household across j dimension. The typical entry in the achievement $Y_{ij} \geq 0$ which represents individual i's achievement in indicators j. Each row vector

$Y_i = (Y_{i1}, Y_{i2}, \ldots, Y_{id})$ gives household i's achievements in the different dimensions j across individuals and the column vector $Y_j = (Y_{1j}, Y_{2j}, \ldots, Y_{nj})$ gives the achievements of all households in the sample on j indicator.

In MPI we have the deprivation cut-off and the poverty cut-off. A deprivation cut-off vector $z = (z_1, \ldots, z_d)$ (deprivation cut-offs for each dimension) is used to determine whether a household is deprived in that indicator. If a household's achievement level in a given dimension j falls short of the respective deprivation cut-off z_j, the household is said to be deprived in that indicator and will have a value of 1. If the household's level of achievement is at least as great as the deprivation cut-off, the household is not deprived in that indicator and will have a value of 0 in that indicator. Finally, we have a deprivation score matrix of $(n \times d)$ dimension with values of 0 and 1.

Following Nawaz and Iqbal (2016) each household is assigned a deprivation score (C_i) based on the weighted sum of the deprivations experienced in each indicator. The deprivation score of each household lies between 0 and 1.

The deprivation score of each household (C_i) is calculated by:

$$C_i = W_1 I_1 + W_2 I_2 + \cdots + W_d I_d \tag{8.3}$$

where, $I_i = 1$ if the household is deprived in indicator i and 0 otherwise, and W_i is the weight attached to indicator i with $\sum_{i=1}^{d} W_i = 1$.

A column vector $C = (C_1, \ldots, C_n)$ of the deprivation score reflects the breadth of each household's deprivation.

A second cut-off, which in the Alkire and Foster methodology is called the poverty cut-off, is the share of (weighted) deprivations that a household must have to be considered multidimensionally poor and is denoted by k. A household is considered poor if its deprivation score is equal to or greater than the poverty cut-off, $C_i \geq K$. In MPI, a household is identified as poor if it has a deprivation score greater than or equal to 1/3 (33%) (Alkire and Santos 2011; OPHI 2013).

MPI is an index designed to measure poverty. Following Alkire and Foster (2011), method the structure of the adjusted headcount measure of MPI combines two key pieces of information: the proportion or incidence of households whose share of weighted deprivations is k or more and the intensity of their deprivation: the average deprivation that poor households' experience. Formally, the first component is called the multidimensional headcount ratio (H):

$$H = \frac{q}{n} \tag{8.4}$$

Here q is the number of households that are multidimensionally poor and n is the total population. However, the headcount ratio (H) violates dimensional monotoncity (Bruck and Workneh 2013). To solve dimensional monotoncity of the headcount ratio, Alkire and Foster (2011) developed the second component of MPI called the intensity (breadth) of poverty (A). It is the average deprivation score of multidimensionally poor households and can be expressed as:

$$A = \frac{\sum_{i=1}^{n} C_i(k)}{q} \qquad (8.5)$$

where, $C_i(k)$ is the censored deprivation score of household i, and q is the number of households that are multidimensionally poor. MPI is the product of both incidence (H) and severity or depth (A) components:

$$MPI = H \times A \qquad (8.6)$$

8.4.2.1 Decomposition by Sub-groups

One good feature of MPI is that it can be decomposed by population sub-groups such as regions, zones, rural/urban or ethnic groups, depending on the sample design. For example, if there are n sub-groups by which the survey is represented, the decomposition is:

$$MPI_{country} = \frac{n_1}{N} MPI_{n_1} + \frac{n_2}{N} MPI_{n_2} + \cdots + \frac{n_n}{N} MPI_{n_n} \qquad (8.7)$$

where, n_i denotes the population sub-group (regions, zones or rural/urban) and N denotes the total population $(n_1 + n_2 + \cdots + n_n = N)$. This relationship can be extended for any number of groups, as long as their respective populations add up to the total population.

Given Eq. 8.7, we can easily compute the contribution of each sub-group to overall poverty by using the formula:

$$Contribution\ of\ sub-\text{group}\ (n_i)\ \text{to}\ \text{MPI} = \frac{\frac{n_i}{N}\text{MPI}_{n_i}}{\text{MPI}_{country}} \times 100 \qquad (8.8)$$

When a sub-group's contribution to poverty exceeds its population share, it suggests that there is a seriously unequal distribution of poverty in the country or the region with some regions/sub-regions/ethnic groups bearing a disproportionately high share of poverty.

The average annual absolute change of each indicator X can be computed by using the formula:

$$\Delta X_{t-s} = (X_t - X_s)/(t - s) \qquad (8.9)$$

where, X_t, denotes the performance or MPI of a country or a region in period t and X_s is the performance or MPI of a country or region in period s. The average annual change of each indictor X is:

$$\Delta\% X_{t-s} = ((X_t - X_s)/X_s)/t - s \tag{8.10}$$

The estimated percentage of absolute or relative changes for different sub-groups provide information about the effects of various policies aimed at reducing poverty. A change in MPI over time can provide information about changes in the incidence or intensity of poverty levels or their combined changes. Following Apablaza and Yalonetzky (2011) we decompose the change in MPI as:

$$\Delta\% MPI_{t-s} = \Delta\% H_{t-s} + \Delta\% A_{t-s} + (\Delta\% H_{t-s} * \Delta\% A_{t-s} * (t - s)) \tag{8.11}$$

8.4.2.2 Decomposition by Indicators

MPI can also be decomposed by indicators. An easy way of doing this is by computing the censored headcount ratio in each indicator. We can get the censored headcount ratio by adding up the number of people who are poor and deprived in that indicator and dividing this by the total population. Once all the censored headcount ratios have been computed, we can find the multidimensional poverty index of a country as:

$$MPI_{country} = W_1 CH_1 + W_2 CH_2 + \cdots + W_{10} CH_{10} \tag{8.12}$$

Here W_1 is the weight of indicator 1 and CH_1 is the censored headcount ratio of indicator 1, and so on for the other nine indicators, with $\sum_{i=1}^{d} W_i = 1$. From Eq. 8.12 one can compute the contribution of each indicator to overall poverty by:

$$Contribution\ of\ indicator\ i\ to\ MPI = \frac{W_i CH_i}{MPI_{country}} \times 100 \tag{8.13}$$

If a certain indicator's contribution to poverty widely exceeds its weight, it suggests that there is relatively high deprivation in this indicator as compared to the other indicators and this requires appropriate policy interventions.

8.4.3 Determinants of Multidimensional Poverty

Besides the extent of multidimensional poverty and its dynamics, we are also interested in identifying the determinants of multidimensional poverty. These are essential for reducing multidimensional poverty. There are different household characteristics that determine a household's poverty status (Adetola 2014; Berenger and Verdire-Chouchane 2007; Berisso 2016). We consider the variable family size of the household, number of children under 5-years, age of the household head and the education level of the household.

Because of differences in job opportunities and the uneven distribution of infrastructure across the country, people living in different places such as the capital city, small cities, towns, the countryside or rural areas are exposed to different levels of multidimensional poverty. Therefore, place of residence needs to be controlled for. Livestock are important assets for rural people as they are used as food, drought animals and a source of cash. We used a tropical livestock unit to represent livestock assets of the households.

In the AF method of multidimensional poverty, the households' deprivation score (c_i) is compared with the multidimensional poverty cut-offs (k). If the deprivation score is greater than or equal to the poverty cut-off $(c_i \geq k)$, a household is considered to be multidimensionally poor. This is represented by the binary variable (y_i) that takes the value 1 or 0 as:

$$y_i = \begin{cases} 1 \ \textit{if and only if } c_i \geq k \\ 0 \ \textit{otherwise} \end{cases} \tag{8.14}$$

The binary variable (y_i) occurs with probability p_i, which is conditional on the explanatory variables (x_i) and is represented as:

$$p_i = pr(y_i = 1) = pr(y_i = 1 | x_i) \tag{8.15}$$

The outcome variable has only two values (binary). Therefore, we use the logistic regression model which is a limited-dependent variable model. The logit of p_i is the natural logarithm of odds that the binary variable (y_i) takes a value 1 rather than 0 which is the relative probability of being multidimensionally poor. The logit model is a linear model for the natural logarithm of the odds Eq. 8.16:

$$\ln \frac{p_i}{1 - p_i} = \eta_i = \beta_0 + \beta_1 x_{i1} + \cdots + \beta_k x_{ik} \tag{8.16}$$

In our logistic model, y_i is the dependent variable, $y = 1$ indicates that a household is multidimensional poor, which is our variable of interest and p is probability of success. In this case the p-value indicates the probability that a household is multidimensionally poor, x is the independent variable and β is the coefficient to be estimated.

The coefficient β_j is the change in the logit due to a one-unit increase in x_j while holding all other explanatory variables in the model constant. e^{β_j} gives the odds ratio associated with a one-unit increase in x_j.

The logit model is also a multiplicative model for the odds as in:

$$\frac{p_i}{1 - p_i} = e^{\eta_i} = e^{\beta_0}(e^{\beta_1})^{x_{i1}} \cdots (e^{\beta_k})^{x_{ik}} \tag{8.17}$$

The conditional probability p_i is then given as:

$$p_i = \frac{1}{1+\mathrm{e}^{-\eta_i}} = \frac{1}{1+\mathrm{e}^{-\sum_{j=0}^{k}\beta_j x_{ij}}} \tag{8.18}$$

The logistic regression estimation results of determinants of multidimensional poverty for the three rounds of DHS data is presented in Table 8.2. We performed the model specifications, goodness of fit and multicollinearity tests.

8.5 Results and Discussion

Our multidimensional poverty analysis' results show that multidimensional poverty is high in Ethiopia in general and in rural Ethiopia in particular (Table 8.6). Because of the traditional farming system in rural Ethiopia and given that a bulk of the rural population derives its livelihood from agriculture, poverty is by and large a rural phenomenon (Alemayehu et al. 2014; GTP II 2016). In 2000, MPI in rural Ethiopia was very high (0.913) relative to urban Ethiopia (0.245). Over time, poverty in rural Ethiopia has been decreasing moderately (Fig. 8.1). But in urban Ethiopia multidimensional poverty has not been decreasing; instead it has been increasing over time. Ethiopia was committed to attaining the MDGs by 2015. It developed the first Growth and Transformation Plan (GTP-I) which was designed to maintain rapid and broad—based growth and eventually to end poverty. Despite all these steps, multidimensional poverty in Ethiopia has remained high. Our MPI estimation results are almost similar to UNDP's internationally comparable MPI measures (Tables 8.6 and 8.7).

Comparisons of regional multidimensional poverty show that even though there were some differences over years, the multidimensional poverty level was high in almost all the regions of the country. In particular, multidimensional poverty was the highest in Amhara, Afar, Somali and Tigary regions in 2000; in Afar, Tigray,

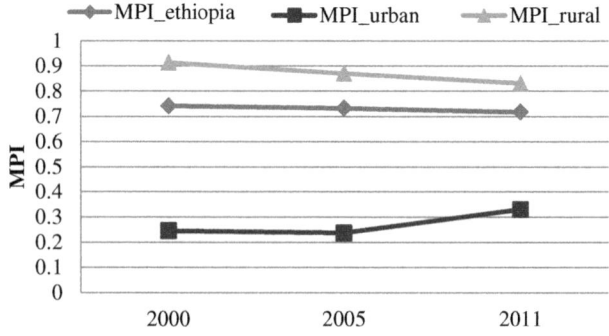

Fig. 8.1 MPI trends in rural and urban Ethiopia over the years, 2000–2011

Amhara and Somali regions in 2005; and in Somali, Benishangul and SNNP regions in 2011. Whereas Addis Ababa, Dire Dawa and Harari regions were among the regions where multidimensional poverty was relatively lower (Table 8.6).

Out of the nine regions in Ethiopia (excluding the two city administrations), Tigary, Amhara, Oromia and SNNP regions constituted about 90% of the total population of the country (CSA 2010). Hence, a poverty analysis of these regions can give us a good picture of multidimensional poverty in Ethiopia. Multidimensional poverty is very high in these regions; however, moderate reduction has been observed in Amhara, Oromia and Tigary regions, but in SNNP there is no such reduction in multidimensional poverty (Figs. 8.2 and 8.3).

One advantage of MPI is that it makes it possible to see the contribution of each region or sub-group to multidimensional poverty. The contributions of regions to overall (country) multidimensional poverty indicate that the regions contributed different shares to multidimensional poverty. For example, in 2000, 2005 and 2011,

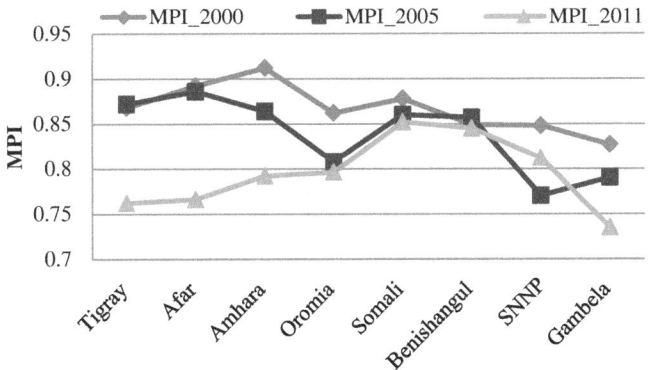

Fig. 8.2 Development of regional MPI in Ethiopia over the years, 2000–2011

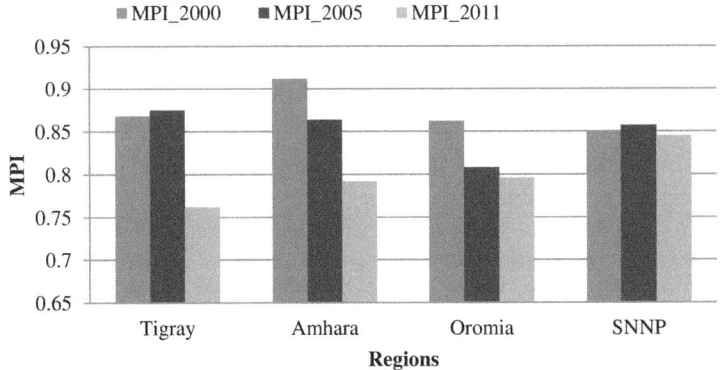

Fig. 8.3 Multidimensional poverty of selected regions over the years, 2000–2011

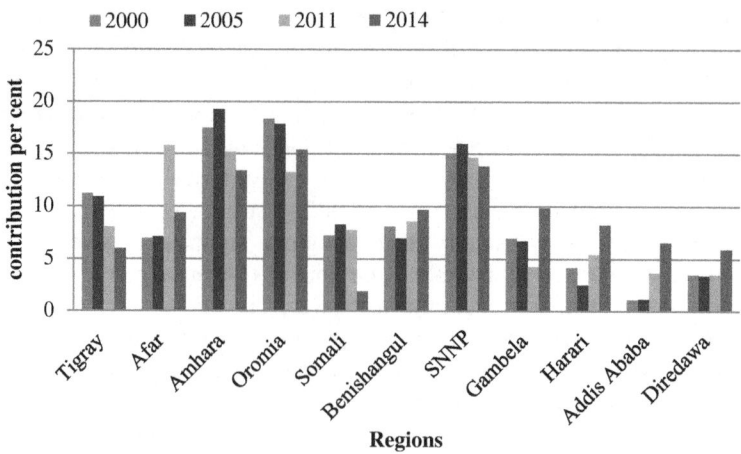

Fig. 8.4 Regions' contribution to MPI and its development over time, 2000–2014

Harari, Addis Ababa and Dire Dawa regions contributed less to multidimensional poverty as compared to their population shares, whereas Amhara and Oromia regions contributed more to multidimensional poverty (Table 8.11; Fig. 8.4). In 2014, Tigray, Somali, SNNP, Amhara, Dire Dawa and Addis Ababa contributed less to multidimensional poverty. Whenever a sub-group or region's contribution to poverty exceeds its population share, it suggests that there is a seriously unequal distribution of poverty in the country. This may be because of differences in policy and its implementation or both. If the same poverty reduction policy is implemented over years, the regions contribute differently to overall multidimensional poverty which implies that there are differences in the way in which the regions implement the policy or in the effects of the policy. Heterogeneity in region's ability to escape poverty can be used to design region specific poverty reduction policies to speed up regional equalities.

Tigray region's contribution to multidimensional poverty has been decreasing over time while Addis Ababa's contribution has been increasing over time (Figs. 8.4 and 8.6).

When we consider the contribution of different dimensions to multidimensional poverty, living standards contributed the most (more than 85%) followed by education (14%) and health (less than 1%) (Table 8.8).

Among the indicators used in our multidimensional poverty analysis, we found high deprivation in sanitation, cooking fuel, floor and electricity. Further, sanitation and cooking fuel deprivations increased over time, but education deprivation and school attendance deprivation decreased over time (Fig. 8.5). These results are in line with other recent studies, for example, Alemayehu et al. (2015), which indicate that the proportion of population deprived in multiple indicators has declined but deprivation in some indicators of multidimensional poverty are quite high in Ethiopia (Fig. 8.5).

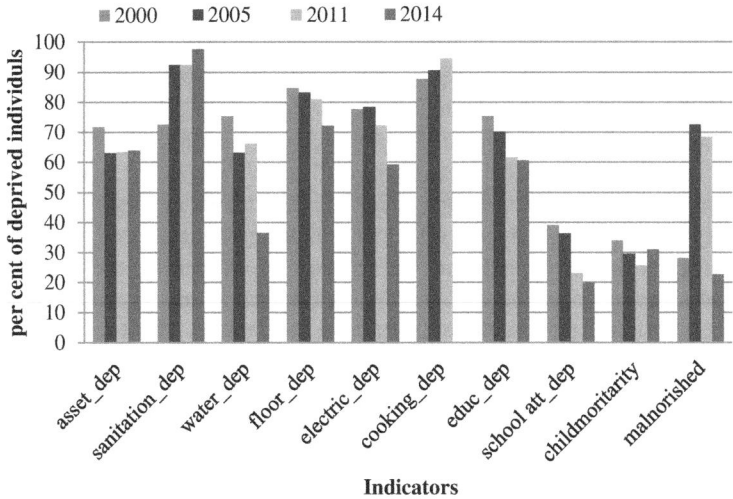

Fig. 8.5 Indicator-wise deprivation in the population

Our multidimensional poverty dynamic results show that in 2005, the highest annual MPI change was in Harari region (about a 3.7% reduction relative to 2000) whereas, in 2014 the highest annual MPI change was in Tigray region (about a 16% reduction). On the contrary, Addis Ababa's annual multidimensional poverty change increased from 3.4% in 2005 to 16% in 2014 relative to the previous survey year (see Table 8.10).

8.5.1 Econometric Model's Results

In addition to the computation of MPI and its decomposition by regions and indicators, it is very important to identify determinants of multidimensional poverty to identify areas of interventions in multidimensional poverty reduction efforts. Our logistic model estimation results show that the family size (fsize) coefficient was negative and significant (Table 8.2), which indicates that as the family size increased the likelihood of failing into multidimensional poverty decreased. This finding is different from other studies, for example, by Bruck and Workneh (2013) which shown that family size matters in consumption poverty (the larger the family size the higher is the probability that a household will fall into consumption poverty) but family size has no significant impact on multidimensional poverty. However, on the contrary, some studies indicate a direct relationship between poverty and family size (Adetola 2014; Berisso 2016). One possible reason for this is that most people in Ethiopia are living in rural areas and are engaged in traditional agriculture. Traditional agriculture, by its nature, is labor intensive. Hence, all working age (even under-age) rural household family members engage in family farm activities in one way or another. Therefore, households' with more family members who are actively involved in family farm activities can manage their family farms easily and the more economically active household members in a family, the less likely the family is to fall into poverty.

The number of children under 5-years-old (childrenunder5) and dependency ratio (depratio) were positive and significant, implying that as the number of children under-5 and number of dependent family members increased a household's probability of being poor also increased. As expected education of the household head (educ) was negative and significant because as people get more educated they become more productive and earn more which makes them less likely to be poor. This is also consistent with other findings (Adetola 2014; Berenger and Verdire-Chouchane 2007).

People usually like to invest in human capital at a young age as they have enough time to get returns. Earnings increase with age as new skills and knowledge are acquired through life and work experiences and also by investing in human capital (education). So, during young ages or economically active ages, households' probability of multidimensional poverty decreases as age increases. Adetola (2014) states that an increase in household age reduces the household's likelihood of being multidimensional poor initially at a threshold and then it increases.

The dummy variable—bank account—is negative; those households which had bank accounts were less poor as compared to those who did not have a bank account. We also considered place of residence as a variable in our analysis. In 2000 and 2005 households in the countryside, towns and small cities were poorer compared to households in large cities (the reference area) as their coefficients were positive and significant. Data on place of residence was not available for 2011, so as an alternative, we used residence (rural/urban). Households in the rural areas were poorer than those in urban areas.

Region is dummy variable and region1_Tigray is base or reference region. In 2005 and 2011 (except Afar in 2005), no region was significantly better than Tigray as far as multidimensional poverty is concerned and some regions like Afar, Amhara and Somali had intense multidimensional poverty.

8.5.2 Multidimensional Poverty Index Robustness to Change in Weight of Indicators

We estimated MPI using factor analysis weights which take into consideration the correlation among indicators. We also used the equal weight approach as an alternative. In this approach each dimension is equally weighted at one-third; each indicator within a dimension is also equally weighted. Then we verified if the rankings were stable using both approaches. We calculated the correlation coefficients using different ranking methods—Pearson's correlation coefficient,

Table 8.2 Logistic regression model estimation results of the determinants of multidimensional poverty-coefficients

Multidimensional poverty	Round1_2000	Round2_2005	Round3_2011
Fsize	−0.4993***	−0.3706***	−0.3079***
Childrenunder5	0.9074***	0.6536***	0.2082
Age (household head age)	−0.0040	−0.0159***	−0.0233***
Educ.	−1.1776***	−0.2134***	−0.0833*
TLU	0.9682***		−0.0151
Land for agriculture_1 (0 = No, 1 = yes)	0.6416***	0.8611***	0.5448
Sex_2dummy (1 = Male, 2 = female)	−0.1744	0.1169	−0.0451
Place of residence-dummy (capital or large city is the reference)			
Small city	1.9615***	0.2296*	
Town	4.7096***	2.4594***	
Countryside	8.9348***	6.6189**	
Regions dummy (Tigray_1 is the reference)			
Afar_2	−0.1526	−0.1543	0.9875***
Amhara_3	0.8522**	1.8270**	3.5669***
Oromia_4	0.9508***	0.6753	0.7255
Somali_5	0.4325	1.4830	2.0259***
Benishangul_6	2.1498***		
SNNP_7	−0.1742	1.0721*	0.1592
Gambela_12	2.2209***	0.6639	0.5866
Harari_13	−0.6238	0.4407	0.3575
Addis_14	(omitted)	(omitted)	0.4153
Dire Dawa_15	−1.2098***	0.2333	−0.1379
Depratio		0.2590**	0.6722***
Bankaccout_1dummy (0 = No, 1 = yes)		−2.0827***	−1.3829***
Hecland			−0.0016**
Residence_2 dummy (1 = urban, 2 = rural)			4.9809***
Cons.	0.8011***	−0.3451	2.4084***
N	13,811	5367	2335
Chi2	9653.8885	3131.1694	798.95555
Bic	2296.9858	1275.7274	803.5593

$*p < 0.1$; $**p < 0.5$; $***p < 0.01$

Spearman's rank correlation coefficient and Kendall's rank correlation coefficient (Tau-b). As a starting point, we estimated the correlation coefficient of the deprivation score of households' in the two weighting systems and found that the correlation in Ethiopia in general and in rural/urban Ethiopia in particular was large enough to conclude that there was a strong rank correlation of deprivation scores of households in the two weighing systems (Table 8.3).

Changing the indicators' weight affected the multidimensional poverty index. We compared the correlation coefficient of the multidimensional poverty index of regions in Ethiopia for a change in weights of indicators for 2000–2011. Interestingly, the correlation coefficient obtained between the two alternative weighting systems was high and the regions ranking remained quite stable, thus one region had higher poverty than the other regions regardless of the weighting system used (Table 8.4).

8.5.3 Sensitivity Analysis of MPI to Different Choices

A multidimensional poverty analysis is based on certain selected dimensions and indicators. Once we had identified the dimensions and indicators we aggregated them using weights and finally we categorized people or households into multidimensionally poor or non-poor based on an agreed poverty cut-off.

8.5.3.1 Sensitivity to Change in Weights of Indicators

We used a factor analysis to determine the weights of the indicators. We used a factor analysis and equal weight for comparison and sensitivity analysis purposes. Multidimensional headcount ratio and multidimensional poverty index (MPI) were different when equal weight and factor analysis weights were used (Tables 8.5, 8.6,

Table 8.3 Correlation of deprivation score (ci) of households using equal weight and factor analysis weight

Regions	Correlation coefficient measures used	Deprivation score Correlation coefficients for years, 2000–2011		
		2000	2005	2011
Ethiopia	Pearson	0.823	0.825	0.778
	Spearman	0.865	0.837	0.809
	Tau-b	0.744	0.695	0.553
Rural Ethiopia	Pearson	0.583	0.626	0.600
	Spearman	0.758	0.718	0.692
	Tau-b	0.646	0.580	0.553
Urban Ethiopia	Pearson	0.802	0.802	0.778
	Spearman	0.818	0.784	0.692
	Tau-b	0.661	0.644	0.659

Table 8.4 Regions' correlation coefficient of MPI using equal weight and factor analysis weight

Correlation coefficient measures used	MPI correlation coefficients for years, 2000–2011		
	2000	2005	2011
Pearson	0.9914	0.9880	0.9860
Spearman	0.9297	0.8678	0.9297
Tau-b	0.8242	0.7889	0.8242

8.7, 8.8, 8.9, 8.10, 8.11 and 8.12). The headcount ratio (H) using a factor analysis weight was greater than that of equal weight (except in 2005). Similarly, MPI using a factor analysis weight was greater than that of equal weight in each year. These differences are mainly because of the differences in weights given to the indicators. Thus, the multidimensional poverty analysis is sensitive to the weights attached to the indicators (Decancq and Lugo 2008).

8.5.3.2 Sensitivity to Change in Poverty Cut-offs (K)

The Alkire and Foster method of multidimensional poverty index which we used has two cut-offs: deprivation cut-off (z_i) and poverty cut-off (k). Poverty cut-off is used to identify those households as multidimensionally poor if their weighted deprivation score (c_i) is greater than or equal to the poverty cut-off $k (c_i \geq k)$. In the Alkire and Foster method, a household is multidimensionally poor if its deprivation score is greater than or equal to 33%. The change in multidimensional poverty for some selected poverty cut-offs $(k = 0.2, k = 0.5, k = 0.7)$, relative to the benchmark poverty cut-off $(k = 0.33(33\%))$, indicated that a decrease in multidimensional poverty was relatively higher for an increase in poverty cut-off compared to an increase in poverty when there was a decrease in the poverty cut-off. We found that the proportion of the multidimensional poor was less sensitive to downward as opposed to upward revisions of the poverty cut-off (Fig. 8.6).

Table 8.5 Multidimensional poverty: with equal weight and factor analysis weight

Years	H	A	MPI
Aggregation with equal weight			
2000	0.832	0.645	0.531
2005	0.877	0.667	0.585
2011	0.809	0.632	0.511
Aggregation with factor analysis weight			
2000	0.843	0.879	0.741
2005	0.872	0.839	0.732
2011	0.908	0.789	0.717

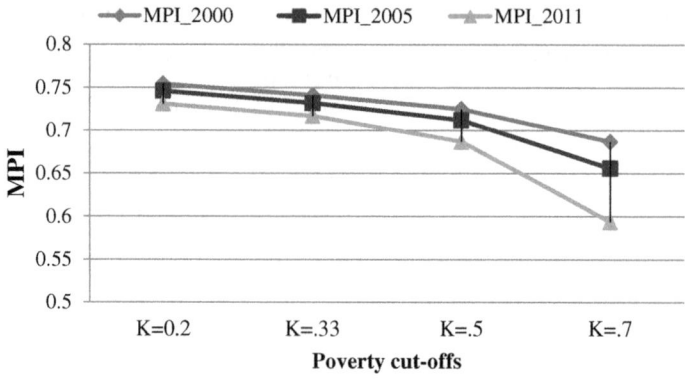

Fig. 8.6 Sensetivity of MPI to the change in poverty cut-off (K)

8.6   Conclusion and Recommendations

Despite efforts to reduce it, multidimensional poverty is still high in Ethiopia. Though urban multidimensional poverty is on the rise, poverty mainly remains a rural phenomenon. The dynamics of a multidimensional poverty analysis indicate that poverty in rural Ethiopia is decreasing, but this has not been observed in urban Ethiopia. Even though Ethiopia is an agrarian country and a majority of its population lives in rural areas, the poverty redaction policy of the country should also consider urban poverty (Fig. 8.7).

The intensity and depth of poverty is different in different regions of the country and level of multidimensional poverty reduction is not the same in all the regions. There is unequal distribution of poverty in the country with some regions bearing a disproportionately high share of the poverty. Regions in Ethiopia are different in social, cultural and resource endowments. Poverty reduction policies and implementation strategies need to consider these differences. Regional heterogeneity should be taken into consideration when designing region specific poverty reduction policies to speed up regional equalities. In some regions (for example, Afar, Somali and Bensihangul) multidimensional poverty is very high relative to the other regions. Poverty reduction policies in these regions do not seem to be as effective as in the other regions of the country. This results in regional differences in the prevalence and intensity of poverty within the country which raises the question of equity. Poverty reduction interventions require identifying determinants of multidimensional poverty. Level of education, having a bank account and more working family members in a household reduce multidimensional poverty. On the other hand, number of children under-5, number of dependent family members and households' engagement in agriculture increase multidimensional poverty. Multidimensional poverty is sensitive to the weight of the indicator and the poverty cut-offs used for the analysis.

Table 8.6 Multidimensional poverty index (MPI) and the 95% confidence interval for the 2000–14 (unequal weight)

	2000		2005		2011		2014	
	MPI	95% confidence interval	MPI	95% confidence interval	MPI	95% confidence interval	MPI	95% confidence interval
Ethiopia	0.741 (0.003)	(0.736, 0.746)	0.732 (0.004)	(0.725, 0.739)	0.717 (0.005)	(0.708, 0.726)	0.517 (0.017)	(0.483, 0.551)
Urban	0.245 (0.005)	(0.236, 0.254)	0.237 (0.007)	(0.224, 0.250)	0.330 (0.008)	(0.314, 0.346)	0.403 (0.020)	(0.334, 0.472)
Rural	0.913 (0.001)	(0.911, 0.915)	0.870 (0.018)	(0.866, 0.874)	0.831 (0.003)	(0.825, 0.837)	0.490 (0.035)	(0.451, 0.521)
Regions								
Tigray	0.868 (0.005)	(0.858, 0.878)	0.872 (0.006)	(0.860, 0.884)	0.762 (0.015)	(0.733, 0.791)	0.397 (0.053)	(0.293, 0.501)
Afar	0.892 (0.006)	(0.881, 0.903)	0.886 (0.008)	(0.870, 0.902)	0.766 (0.012)	(0.743, 0.789)	0.700 (0.061)	(0.581, 0.819)
Amhara	0.912 (0.003)	(0.905, 0.919)	0.864 (0.006)	(0.855, 0.873)	0.792 (0.009)	(0.774, 0.810)	0.501 (0.054)	(0.394, 0.608)
Oromia	0.862 (0.004)	(0.855, 0.869)	0.808 (0.006)	(0.797, 0.819)	0.796 (0.010)	(0.777, 0.815)	0.525 (0.041)	(0.444, 0.606)
Somali	0.878 (0.006)	(0.866, 0.890)	0.860 (0.010)	(0.841, 0.879)	0.852 (0.010)	(0.832, 0.872)	0.248 (0.065)	(0.121, 0.375)
Benishangul	0.849 (0.005)	(0.839, 0.859)	0.857 (0.006)	(0.845, 0.869)	0.845 (0.008)	(0.829, 0.861)	0.607 (0.062)	(0.485, 0.729)
SNNP	0.848 (0.004)	(0.840, 0.856)	0.770 (0.006)	(0.757, 0.783)	0.812 (0.008)	(0.797, 0.827)	0.501 (0.047)	(0.410, 0.592)
Gambela	0.827 (0.006)	(0.816, 0.838)	0.790 (0.010)	(0.770, 0.810)	0.735 (0.020)	(0.695, 0.775)	0.691 (0.068)	(0.559, 0.823)

(continued)

Table 8.6 (continued)

	2000		2005		2011		2014	
	MPI	95% confidence interval	MPI	95% confidence interval	MPI	95% confidence interval	MPI	95% confidence interval
Harari	0.498 (0.012)	(0.474, 0.522)	0.405 (0.019)	(0.368, 0.442)	0.604 (0.018)	(0.570, 0.638)	0.638 (0.060)	(0.520, 0.756)
Addis Ababa	0.083 (0.005)	(0.073, 0.093)	0.097 (0.007)	(0.083, 0.111)	0.251 (0.010)	(0.231, 0.271)	0.271 (0.055)	(0.164, 0.378)
Dire Dawa	0.401 (0.012)	(0.377, 0.425)	0.434 (0.019)	(0.397, 0.471)	0.580 (0.032)	(0.517, 0.643)	0.643 (0.056)	(0.534, 0.752)

Source Author's computations using DHS data

Table 8.7 Headcount (H), intensity (A) and multidimensional poverty index (MPI) of Ethiopia by regions for the 2000, 2005, 2011 and 2014 (equal weight)

Regions or residence	2000			2005			2011			2014		
	H	A	MPI	H	A	MPI	H	A	MPI	H	A	MPI
Ethiopia	0.823	0.645	0.531	0.877	0.667	0.585	0.809	0.632	0.511	0.658	0.523	0.344
Urban	0.386	0.476	0.184	0.494	0.472	0.233	0.374	0.499	0.187	0.463	0.449	0.208
Rural	0.974	0.668	0.651	0.877	0.666	0.585	0.944	0.645	0.612	0.718	0.538	0.386
Regions												
Tigray	0.943	0.655	0.618	0.978	0.692	0.677	0.847	0.614	0.520	0.462	0.449	0.208
Afar	0.945	0.699	0.661	0.974	0.733	0.714	0.874	0.693	0.606	0.875	0.569	0.498
Amhara	0.967	0.645	0.624	0.979	0.692	0.677	0.905	0.617	0.558	0.813	0.510	0.415
Oromia	0.929	0.645	0.599	0.942	0.667	0.628	0.894	0.660	0.590	0.686	0.519	0.356
Somali	0.949	0.681	0.639	0.943	0.719	0.678	0.977	0.684	0.668	0.445	0.533	0.234
Benishangul	0.938	0.639	0.600	0.972	0.681	0.662	0.954	0.632	0.603	0.789	0.560	0.442
SNNP	0.918	0.651	0.597	0.930	0.665	0.618	0.902	0.609	0.549	0.606	0.558	0.338
Gambela	0.911	0.602	0.549	0.957	0.630	0.603	0.830	0.596	0.494	0.647	0.533	0.345
Harari	0.599	0.599	0.359	0.596	0.577	0.344	0.740	0.556	0.412	0.625	0.547	0.342
Addis Ababa	0.229	0.422	0.097	0.363	0.426	0.155	0.264	0.476	0.126	0.429	0.367	0.157
Dire Dawa	0.535	0.589	0.315	0.654	0.613	0.401	0.600	0.673	0.404	0.667	0.553	0.369

Source Author's computations using DHS data

Table 8.8 Percentage contribution of multidimensional poverty dimensions to multidimensional poverty index, by years and regions (unequal weight)

Regions or residence	2000				2005				2011				2014			
	Living stand.	Educ.	Health	Total	Living stand	Educ.	Health	Total	Living stand.	Educ.	Health	Total	Living stand.	Educ.	Health	Total
Ethiopia	85.74	13.72	0.54	100	86.22	13.13	0.64	100	87.87	11.52	0.61	100	85.76	13.60	0.64	100
Urban	85.81	13.61	0.58	100	87.33	11.98	0.69	100	90.47	8.95	0.58	100	93.87	5.75	0.37	100
Rural	85.73	13.74	0.54	100	86.14	13.22	0.64	100	87.56	11.83	0.61	100	83.46	15.83	0.56	100
Regions																
Tigray	85.58	13.91	0.51	100	86.55	12.86	0.59	100	89.05	10.46	0.48	100	82.00	17.45	0.56	100
Afar	85.29	14.09	0.63	100	84.58	14.85	0.56	100	85.68	13.64	0.68	100	84.54	14.91	0.55	100
Amhara	85.71	13.79	0.50	100	86.21	13.13	0.66	100	88.66	10.72	0.63	100	82.08	17.03	0.89	100
Oromia	85.92	13.51	0.57	100	86.52	12.84	0.65	100	87.23	12.14	0.64	100	85.91	13.64	0.45	100
Somali	84.61	14.96	0.44	100	84.95	14.58	0.46	100	86.22	13.13	0.66	100	91.13	8.33	0.54	100
Benishangul	85.89	13.58	0.53	100	86.26	13.02	0.72	100	87.37	11.96	0.67	100	82.12	17.26	0.62	100
SNNP	86.32	13.12	0.56	100	86.39	12.87	0.72	100	89.88	9.55	0.57	100	86.42	12.91	0.67	100
Gambela	88.06	11.38	0.56	100	88.89	10.47	0.64	100	91.18	8.24	0.59	100	89.65	9.81	0.54	100
Harari	84.78	14.66	0.57	100	85.01	14.32	0.68	100	86.34	13.20	0.46	100	88.81	10.35	0.84	100
Addis Ababa	80.08	19.27	0.64	100	84.49	14.72	0.79	100	89.90	9.55	0.55	100	92.84	7.07	0.08	100
Dire Dawa	83.92	15.15	0.57	100	85.32	13.96	0.72	100	86.87	12.55	0.59	100	83.65	15.05	1.29	100

Source Author's computations using DHS data

Table 8.9 Percentage contribution of multidimensional poverty dimensions to multidimensional poverty index, by years and regions (equal weight)

Regions or Residence	2000 Living stand.	Educ.	Health	Total	2005 Living stand	Educ.	Health	Total	2011 Living stand.	Educ.	Health	Total	2014 Living stand.	Educ.	Health	Total
Ethiopia	46.68	34.79	18.53	100	43.00	30.00	27.00	100	45.99	26.33	27.68	100	46.08	31.19	22.73	100
Urban	39.02	33.14	27.83	100	35.84	24.90	39.30	100	44.50	18.57	36.93	100	65.80	14.66	19.54	100
Rural	47.43	34.45	17.62	100	43.47	30.00	26.00	100	46.17	27.29	26.53	100	42.95	33.82	23.23	100
Regions																
Tigray	47.58	35.47	16.95	100	44.3	29.6	26.10	100	48.87	24.64	26.49	100	48.60	32.71	18.69	100
Afar	45.24	34.18	20.58	100	42.0	34.56	23.41	100	42.09	28.75	29.16	100	47.37	31.58	21.05	100
Amhara	48.48	35.29	16.23	100	43.8	29.44	26.76	100	47.91	24.95	27.14	100	41.25	35.25	23.50	100
Oromia	47.13	34.76	18.12	100	43.52	29.80	26.67	100	44.43	29.17	26.40	100	44.75	33.15	22.10	100
Somali	45.66	38.26	16.08	100	42.91	34.43	22.66	100	43.63	29.75	26.63	100	21.87	39.06	39.06	100
Benishangul	47.52	34.22	18.26	100	43.76	28.01	28.23	100	47.26	25.46	27.29	100	43.44	33.94	22.62	100
SNNP	47.23	34.50	18.26	100	42.15	30.18	27.67	100	49.37	23.52	27.11	100	44.10	32.61	23.29	100
Gambela	50.25	28.30	21.44	100	46.57	23.94	29.50	100	50.91	18.37	30.72	100	57.83	24.10	18.07	100
Harari	44.84	34.83	20.32	100	39.21	29.41	31.38	100	45.49	29.91	24.59	100	51.22	24.39	24.39	100
Addis Ababa	24.37	38.71	36.93	100	26.55	26.48	46.97	100	42.55	19.88	37.58	100	74.75	15.15	10.10	100
Dire Dawa	40.85	36.48	22.67	100	37.9	30.73	31.34	100	44.89	28.70	26.41	100	39.76	30.12	30.12	100

Source Author's computations using DHS data

Table 8.10 Multidimensional poverty index (MPI), absolute annual change and relative annual change in MPI relative to the previous survey years in Ethiopia, by Rural/Urban and regions

Regions or residence	MPI_2000	MPI_2005	Annual change		MPI_2011	Annual change		MPI_2014	Annual change	
			Absolute	Relative (%)		Absolute	Relative (%)		Absolute	Relative (%)
Ethiopia	0.741 (0.003)	0.732 (0.004)	−0.002**	−0.24	0.717 (0.005)	−0.003**	−0.34	0.5 (0.017)	−0.067**	−9.30
Urban	0.245 (0.005)	0.237 (0.007)	−0.002	−0.65	0.33 (0.008)	0.016***	6.54	0.49 (0.020)	0.053**	16.16
Rural	0.913 (0.001)	0.87 (0.002)	−0.009***	−0.94	0.831 (0.003)	−0.007***	−0.75	0.403 (0.035)	−0.143**	−17.17
Regions										
Tigray	0.868 (0.005)	0.872 (0.006)	0.001	0.09	0.762 (0.015)	−0.018***	−2.10	0.397 (0.053)	−0.122**	−15.97
Afar	0.892 (0.006)	0.886 (0.008)	−0.001	−0.13	0.766 (0.012)	−0.020***	−2.26	0.7 (0.061)	−0.022	−2.87
Amhara	0.912 (0.003)	0.864 (0.005)	−0.010***	−1.05	0.792 (0.009)	−0.012***	−1.39	0.501 (0.054)	−0.097***	−12.25
Oromia	0.862 (0.004)	0.808 (0.006)	−0.011***	−1.25	0.796 (0.01)	−0.002	−0.25	0.525 (0.041)	−0.090**	−11.35
Somali	0.878 (0.006)	0.86 (0.01)	−0.004	−0.41	0.852 (0.01)	−0.001	−0.16	0.248 (0.065)	−0.201**	−23.63
Benishangul	0.849 (0.005)	0.857 (0.006)	0.002	0.19	0.845 (0.008)	−0.002	−0.23	0.607 (0.062)	−0.079**	−9.39
SNNP	0.848 (0.004)	0.77 (0.006)	−0.016***	−1.84	0.812 (0.008)	0.007***	0.91	0.501 (0.047)	−0.104**	−12.77
Gambela	0.827 (0.006)	0.79 (0.01)	−0.007***	−0.89	0.735 (0.02)	−0.009**	−1.16	0.691 (0.068)	−0.015	−2.00
Harari	0.498 (0.012)	0.405 (0.02)	−0.019***	−3.73	0.604 (0.018)	0.033***	8.19	0.614 (0.055)	0.003	0.55
Addis Ababa	0.083 (0.005)	0.097 (0.007)	0.003	3.37	0.251 (0.01)	0.026***	26.46	0.373 (0.056)	0.041	16.20
Dire Dawa	0.401 (0.012)	0.434 (0.019)	0.007	1.65	0.58 (0.032)	0.024***	5.61	0.471 (0.060)	−0.036	−6.26

Source Author's computation using DHS data, standard errors in parentheses, ***$p < 0.01$, **$p < 0.05$, *$p < 0.1$

Table 8.11 Population share and multidimensional poverty contribution of regions

Regions	2000			2005			2011			2014		
	%	Contr.	Diff.	%	Contr.	Diff.	%	Contr.	Diff.	%	Contr.	Diff.
Tigray	9.55	11.18	1.63	9.15	10.89	1.74	7.55	8.03	0.48	7.79	5.98	−1.81
Afar	5.79	6.96	1.17	5.87	7.10	1.23	14.77	15.78	1.01	6.98	9.35	2.37
Amhara	14.19	17.49	3.3	16.34	19.25	2.91	13.73	15.16	1.43	13.85	13.42	−0.43
Oromia	15.78	18.35	2.57	16.22	17.88	1.66	11.94	13.26	1.32	15.15	15.37	0.22
Somali	6.10	7.23	1.13	7.04	8.26	1.22	6.51	7.74	1.23	3.90	1.87	−2.03
Benishangul	6.96	8.08	1.12	5.96	6.96	1.00	7.25	8.55	1.30	8.23	9.65	1.42
SNNP	13.14	15.04	1.63	15.21	15.97	0.76	12.96	14.67	1.71	14.29	13.83	−0.46
Gambela	6.24	6.96	1.90	6.22	6.70	0.48	4.17	4.27	0.10	7.36	9.85	2.49
Harari	6.19	4.16	−2.03	4.50	2.49	−2.01	6.44	5.42	−1.02	6.98	8.21	1.23
Addis Ababa	9.66	1.08	−8.58	7.80	1.13	−6.49	10.42	3.66	−6.76	9.09	6.55	−2.54
Dire Dawa	6.41	3.46	−2.95	5.69	3.38	−2.31	4.28	3.47	−0.81	6.49	5.92	−0.57

Note %—population percentage share of the regions; *contr.*—region's multidimensional poverty contribution; *diff.*—difference between multidimensional poverty contribution and population percentage share

Table 8.12 Factor analysis/correlation

Factors	Eigen value	Difference	Proportion	Cumulative
Factor 1	4.00854	2.90402	0.4009	0.4009
Factor 2	1.10452	0.08387	0.1105	0.5113
Factor 3	1.02065	0.23047	0.1021	0.6934
Factor 4	0.79018	0.08903	0.0790	0.6924
Factor 5	0.70115	0.10428	0.0701	0.7625
Factor 6	0.59687	0.00881	0.0597	0.8222
Factor 7	0.58806	0.07026	0.0588	0.8810
Factor 8	0.51780	0.11043	0.0518	0.9328
Factor 9	0.40737	0.14251	0.0407	0.9735
Factor 10	0.26486	–	0.0265	1.0000

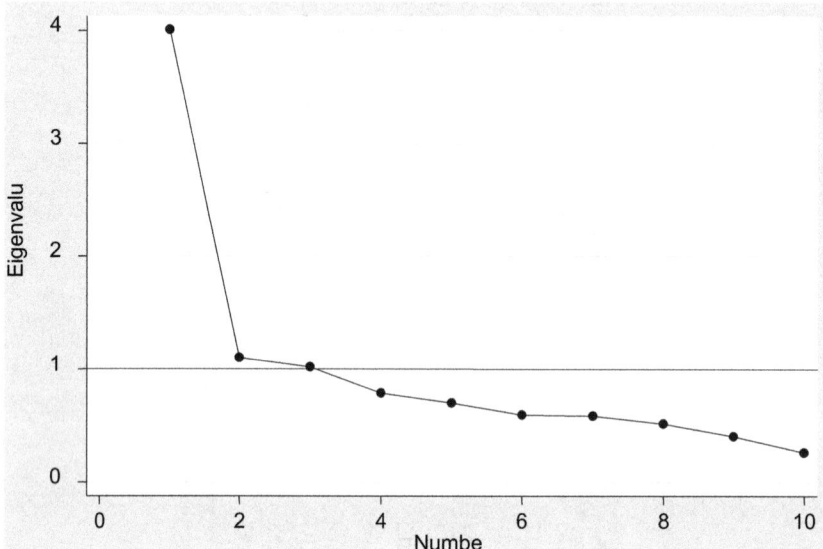

Fig. 8.7 Screen plot of eigenvalues after factor

Poverty reduction policies should focus on living standard indicators as these indicators contribute the most to multidimensional poverty in almost all regions in the country. There is high deprivation in sanitation, cooking fuel, floor and electricity in Ethiopia; thus, these indicators require careful interventions by federal and regional governments to reduce multidimensional poverty.

Poverty is multidimensional and thus a response to poverty should involve many sectors and stakeholders. Collective effort is the right approach and should be scaled up and practiced more extensively.

Our analysis used a household as the unit of analysis. However, in Ethiopia where there is high ethnic and cultural diversity, intra-household inequalities (between men and women, adults and children) may be severe. Our household multidimensional poverty analysis did not take into consideration intra-household inequalities because of unavailability of data at an individual level. A multidimensional poverty analysis at the individual level provides potential for future research when individual level data is available. Multidimensional issues such as an analysis of child poverty and nutrition based poverty are also potential research areas.

References

Adetola, A. 2014. Trend and determinants of multidimensional poverty in rural Nigeria. *Journal of Development and Agricultural Economics* 6 (5): 220–231.

Alemayehu, A., M. Parend, and Y. Biratu. 2015. Multidimensional poverty in Ethiopia, change in overlapping deprivations. Poverty Research Working Paper, 7417. The World Bank Group.

Alemayehu, G., and Y. Addis. 2014. *Growth, poverty and inequality in Ethiopia, 2000–2013: A macroeconomic appraisal.* A chapter in a Book to be published by Forum for Social studies, FSC, Department of Economics, Addis Ababa University.

Alkire, S., and J. Foster. 2011. *Understandings and misunderstandings of multidimensional poverty measurement.* Berlin: Springer Science+Business Media.

Alkire, S., and M.E. Santos. 2010. Acute multidimensional poverty: A new index for developing countries. OPHI Working Paper, 38.

Alkire, S., and M.E. Santos. 2011. The multidimensional poverty index. OPHI Research in Progress.

Alkire, S., J. Foster, and M.E. Santos. 2011. Where did identification go? *Journal of Economic Inequality* 9 (3): 501–505.

Alkire, S., J.E. Foster, S. Seth, M.E. Santos, J.M. Roche, and P. Ballon. 2015. Multidimensional poverty measurement and analysis: Overview of methods for multidimensional poverty assessment. OPHI Working Papers, 84.

Ambel. A, P. Mebta, and B. Yigezu. 2015. Multidimensional poverty in Ethiopia: Change in overlapping deprivations. Policy Research Working Paper 7417. The World Bank Group.

Apablaza, M., and G. Yalonetzky. 2011. Measuring the dynamics of multiple deprivations among children: The cases of Andhra Pradesh, Ethiopia, Peru and Vietnam. Paper submitted to CSAE conference, March.

Atkinson, A.B. 2003. Multidimensional deprivation: Contrasting social welfare and counting approaches. *Journal of Economic Inequality* 1: 51–65.

Bersisa, M., and A. Heshmati. 2016. Multidimensional measure of poverty in Ethiopia: Factor and stochastic dominance analysis, in A. Heshmati A. (ed.), *Poverty and well-being in East Africa. Economic studies in inequality, social exclusion and well-being.* Cham: Springer.

Berisso, O. 2016. Determinants of consumption expenditure and poverty dynamics in Urban Ethiopia: Evidence from panel data, in A. Heshmati (ed.), *Poverty and well-being in East Africa. Economic studies in inequality, social exclusion and well-being.* Cham: Springer.

Berenger, V., and A. Verdire-Chouchane. 2007. Multidimensional measures of well-being: Standard of living and quality of life across countries. *World Development* 35 (7): 1259–1279.

Bourguignon, F., and S. Chakravarty. 2003. The measurement of multidimensional poverty. *Journal of Economic Inequality* 1 (1): 25–49.

Bruck, T., and S. Workneh. 2013. Dynamics and drivers of consumption and multidimensional poverty: Evidence from Rural Ethiopia. Discussion Paper No. 7364.

Chen, S., and M. Ravallion. 2008. China is poorer than we thought but no less successful in the fight against poverty. Policy Research Working Paper WPS4621.

CSA (Central Statistical Agency). 2009. *The 2007 population and housing census of Ethiopia: National statistical summary report*. Addis Ababa, Ethiopia: CSA.

CSA (Central Statistical Agency). 2010. *The 2007 population and housing census of Ethiopia: National statistical summary report*. Addis Ababa, Ethiopia: CSA.

Dhongda, S., Y. Li, P. Pattanaik, and Y. Xu. 2015. Binary data, hierarchy of attributes, and multidimensional deprivation. *Journal of Economic Inequality* 14: 363–378.

Decancq, K., M. Fleurbaey, and F. Maniquet. 2014. *Multidimensional poverty measurement with individual preferences*. Princeton: Princeton University Williams, Economic Theory Center Research Paper.

Decancq, K., and M.A. Lugo. 2013. Weights in multidimensional indices of wellbeing: An overview. *Econometric Reviews* 32 (1): 7–34.

Decancq, K., and M.A. Lugo. 2008. Setting weights in multidimensional indices of well-being. Working Paper, University of Oxford, Department of Economics.

Dercon, S., D. Gilligan, J. Hoddinott, and T. Woldehanna. 2009. The impact of roads and agricultural extension on consumption growth and poverty in fifteen Ethiopian villages. *American Journal of Agricultural Economics* 91 (4): 1007–1021.

Duclos, D.S., and S. Younger. 2006. Robust multidimensional poverty comparisons. *Economic Journal* 116 (514): 943–968.

Foster, J., S. Seth, M. Lokshin, and Z. Sajaia. 2013. *A unified approach to measuring poverty and inequality: Theory and practice*. The World Bank. https://doi.org/10.1596/978-0-8213-8461-9.

GTP II. 2016. *Growth and Transformation plan II (GTPII) (2015/16–2019/20)* (vol. 1). Addis Ababa: Federal Democratic Republic of Ethiopia, National planning commission, main text.

Hishe Gebreslassie, G. 2013. Multidimensional measures of poverty analysis in urban areas of Afar regional state. *International Journal of Science and Research (IJSR)*, 6.

Hulme, D., and A. McKay. 2008. Identifying and measuring chronic poverty: Beyond monetary measures? In *The many dimensions of poverty*, ed. N. Kakwani, and J. Silber, 187–214. Palgrave: Macmillan.

Maasoumi, E., and T. Xu. 2015. Weights and substitution degree in multidimensional well-being in China. *Journal of Economic Studies* 42 (1): 4–19.

Maggino, F., and B.D. Zumbo. 2012. *Measuring the quality of life and the construction of social indicators, Handbook of social indicators and quality of life research*. Springer Science +Business Media, pp. 201–238.

Ministry of Finance and Economic Development (MOFED). 2010. *Growth and transformation plan, 2010/11–2014/15*. Addis Ababa, Ethiopia: Ministry of Finance and Economic Development.

Nawaz, S., and N. Iqbal. 2016. Education poverty in Pakistan: A spatial analysis at district level. *Indian Journal of Human Development* 10: 270–287. https://doi.org/10.1177/0973703016674081.

Noble, M., D. McLennan, K. Wilkinson, A. Whitworth, H. Barnes, and C. Dibben. 2007. *The English indices of deprivation 2007. Communities and local government*. London.

OPHI (Oxford Poverty and Human Development Initiative). 2013. *How multidimensional poverty went down: Dynamics and comparison*. Oxford: University of Oxford.

Ravallion M. 2011. On multidimensional indices of poverty. The World Bank Development Research Group. Policy Research Working Paper 5580.

Salazar, R., B. Duaz, and R. Pinzon. 2013. *Multidimensional poverty in Colombia, 1997–2013*. Institute for Social and Economic Research, ISER working paper series.

Sen, A.K. 1992. *Inequality re-examined*. New York: Russell Sage Foundation.

Stewait, F., R. Saith, and B. Harriss White. 2007. *Defining poverty in the developing world*. Basingstoke: Palgrave Macmillan.

Stiglitz, J.E., A. Sen, and J.P. Filtoussi. 2009. Report by the Commission on the Measurement of Economic Performance and Social Progress, Mimeo.

Takeuchi, L.R. 2014. Incorporating people's value in development: Weighting alternatives. Development progress, World Bank Photo Collection.

The World Bank. 2014. *The World Bank Annual Report 2014*. Washington, DC: The World Bank. Available at: https://openknowledge.worldbank.org/handle/10986/2009.

The World Bank. 2016. *The World Bank Annual Report 2016*. Washington, DC: The World Bank. Available at: https://openknowledge.worldbank.org/handle/10986/24985.

Thorbecke, E. 2008. Multidimensional poverty: Conceptual and measurement issues. In *The many dimensions of poverty*, ed. N. Kakwani, and J. Silber. New York: Palgrave Macmillan.

Tran, V., S. Alkire, and S. Klasen. 2015. Static and dynamic disparities between monetary and multidimensional poverty measurement: Evidence from Vietnam, Oxford Poverty & Human Development Initiative (OPHI), Working Paper, No. 97.

Tsui, K.Y. 2002. Multidimensional poverty indices. *Social Choice and Welfare* 19 (1): 69–93.

UNDP. 2013. *Human development report 2013. The Rise of the South: Human progress in a diverse world*. United Nations Development Programme.

Woldehanna, T., and A. Hagos. 2013. Dynamics of welfare and poverty in rural and urban communities of Ethiopia. An International Study of Child poverty, *Yongs Lives*, Working Paper 109.

Part IV
Human Capital and Firm Growth

Chapter 9
Returns to Education in Ethiopia

Yonatan Desalegn

Abstract Previous studies on returns to education in Ethiopia have been fraught with endogeneity. Moreover, the non-linearity of returns to education has not been established on a national scale. Hence, this study measures the marginal private returns to education in Ethiopia using the latest National Labor Force Survey (NLFS) in 2013. It also examines the presence of non-linearity in the returns to education, particularly if sheepskin effects are evident at different levels of education. To address these objectives the study uses a Heckman selection model on adaptations of a Mincerian type earnings function. It finds that the average marginal returns to a year of schooling is 14.43%. The average marginal returns to a year of experience is 0.5%. The study also finds that schooling has increasing marginal returns whereas experience has decreasing marginal returns. Non-linearity in the returns to education is found to be a character of the returns to education profile in Ethiopia. A sheepskin effect of the returns to education is also established at different levels of education in Ethiopia. The highest rate of return to education is for basic education (completing Grade 4). However, the biggest dip in the rate of returns occurs for general primary education (completing Grade 8). These findings suggest that investing in education is still a profitable venture for private citizens as it exhibits increasing marginal returns.

Keywords Returns to education · Non-linearity · Mincerian earnings function

JEL Classification Codes J01 · J08 · J24

Y. Desalegn (✉)
Economics Department, Addis Ababa University, Addis Ababa, Ethiopia
e-mail: yambs4@yahoo.com

9.1 Introduction

Spanning an area of 1,127,127 km², Ethiopia is the second most populous country in Africa. About 43% of its population is below the age of 15 years (CSA 2007). Agriculture is the mainstay of the Ethiopian economy and is practiced in the rural parts of the country. It employs 80% of the workforce and accounts for 52% of the gross domestic product. According to the CSA Welfare Monitoring Survey Report (2000), the share of the population living below the poverty line fell from 46 to 44% between 1995 and 2000; in rural areas, the rate declined from 48 to 45% while the rate in the urban areas increased from 33 to 37% (The World Bank 2005). In 2002 Ethiopia's adult literacy rate was 41.5% and its gross primary enrolment rate was 66%, which was worse than the average for low-income countries (63.9% and 98.6% respectively) (Tassew et al. 2009). Though enrolments have shown remarkable improvements, variations by regional states, rural-urban divide and gender beg for more improvements (Tassew et al. 2009). The Government of Ethiopia declared universal primary education (the first six years of schooling) in the country in 2004. Literacy rates have since improved mainly reflecting gains in rural areas. However, the gap between urban and rural areas remains huge (Joshi and Verspoor 2013; The World Bank 2005).

Between 1962 and 1994, the education system had a 6-2-4 structure: six years of primary schooling, two years of junior secondary education and four years of senior secondary education with national examinations certifying students and determining selection to the next cycle. Students screened into the tertiary level were eligible to join a highly-subsidized college or university level education. In 1995 a 4-4-2-2 structure was introduced. It consists of an eight-year primary education cycle (divided into a basic education cycle covering Grades 1–4 and general primary cycle covering Grades 5–8, followed by two years of general secondary education (Grades 9–10), and two years of preparatory secondary education (Grades 11–12). National examinations are now administered only at the end of Grades 10 and 12; regional examinations have replaced those at the end of Grade 8 and certification at Grade 6 has been abandoned (The World Bank 2005). A preparatory freshman year has also been left out and students are admitted to a specific undergraduate field of study. Technical and vocational education and training (TVET) and teachers' training (TT) programs were also introduced as an alternative on completion of Grade 10 aside from the general education scheme (Education Sector Development Program III (ESDP III).

The dramatic improvements in access, relevance and quality of education in Ethiopia has seen a parallel explosion in growth. Between 2000 and 2010, the country saw an average 10% growth in GDP. According to the National Labor Force Survey reports the share of employed individuals spiked. Participation rates and activity rates also increased. Unemployment steadily declined since 1999 and reached 4.5% in June 2013. However, urban unemployment remained very high with the unemployment rate standing at 20.6% in 2005 and 16.5% in 2013. Rural unemployment remained low for the duration of our study period—it was 2% in

2009. However, matching the level of education in rural areas, the employment activities are in low paying jobs that require mostly no schooling or some primary education or at most a certificate in diploma level education. Self-employment and unpaid family employment still dominate the rural employment landscape. The national mean work week involves 33 work hours per person. The urban hours of work week average at 41 while the rural work week stands at 31 h (or 10 h less) (CSA 2014).

Understanding the returns to investment in education is relevant for informing economic growth and development. And this is more so for a developing country. It is now established in economics literature that human capital is no less important than physical capital, labor or land in an individual's productivity (Becker 1993). Labor market employment benefits the most from schooling in the form of increased wages for more years of schooling (Byron and Manaloto 1990; Lang 1993). Some studies claim that education is of little use in non-market employment of labor. In traditional agriculture, for example, farming methods and knowledge are readily passed on from parents to children and there is compelling evidence of the link between human capital and technology in rural non-market activities as well (Becker 1993). For example, the more educated a farmer, the easier it is for him to embrace new technologies such as new high yield seeds or a new plough tool, a fertilizer or even such seemingly mundane innovations as row seeding (Banerjee and Dufalo 2011). Education is also known to improve one's standing in her or his community. Therefore, accumulating human capital will not only have pecuniary benefits realized in the form of increased earnings potential, but also non-pecuniary external effects that spill beyond those who directly receive schooling. Education will not only increase her (his) productivity but also the productivity of those around her (him). Therefore, understanding the mechanism in which education translates into increased earnings potential is useful for informing policy and development efforts.

Previous studies have put the average returns to a year of schooling in Ethiopia at 15.6% (The World Bank 2005). However, most of these studies are fraught with endogeneity problems. As a result, the coefficients of earnings regressions usually understate the magnitude of returns to education. Moreover, they use age as a proxy variable to gauge experience. This proxy usually overstates experience as it is prone to include the time that an individual is out of work after completing school or when transitioning between jobs or is unemployed. Previous studies on Ethiopia have also been based on a relatively small samples (The World Bank 2005; Verwimp 1996; Weir 1999). Our study aims to address these shortfalls in the returns to schooling literature on Ethiopia. It employs econometric techniques to rectify endogeneity. It uses actual experience of workers instead of potential experience as proxied by age, thereby identifying a more accurate link between experience and labor market earnings. Our study thus offers a larger sample size than that used in previous studies as it employs the NLFS dataset. By addressing these gaps in the returns to education literature in Ethiopia, our study generates a more reliable estimate of the private returns to investing in education. In addition to addressing the concerns mentioned earlier, our study makes a detailed analysis of the non-linearity in the returns to education in Ethiopia. Unlike previous studies, our study tests for both general non-linearity and the presence of sheepskin effects in the education system. Our study also explores what variables, other than schooling and experience, have a bearing on labor market outcomes in the form of increments in earnings.

Our study measures the returns to investment in education by means of a Mincerian (Mincer 1974) type modeling of the relationship between education and earnings. It focuses on that part of the labor force that receives a stream of monthly earnings from labor market employment. Specifically, we address the following objectives:

- Measuring the average marginal returns to education in Ethiopia, and
- Testing the presence of a sheepskin effect of the returns to education.

9.2 Literature Review

Dissemination of knowledge can take different forms. It can be provided in the form of an organized institution where students are admitted and made to fall in line with a set of subjects introduced in the form of an organized curriculum. These institutions—schools, colleges or universities—grant certificates to those who meet minimum standards. These institutions add value to the labor that individuals who pass through the system possess. Imparting knowledge can also occur outside schools, especially on jobs. Graduates are not well prepared for the labor market when they leave school and they are fitted into their jobs through formal and informal training programs called on-the-job training. The amount of on-the-job training ranges from an hour or so at simple jobs like dishwashing or weeding a farm to several years at complicated tasks like performing a surgical procedure on a patient or doing engineering in an auto plant or modeling economic phenomena. The limited information available indicates that on-the-job training is an important reason for the very large increase in earnings as workers gain greater experience at work (Becker 1993).

Education, in its different forms, is among the key events that are attributed to improvements in labor productivity. This productivity role of education can be thought of as an investment with market returns. These returns to education can take on private and socials forms. The private returns to investment in education are pecuniary and non-pecuniary accruals to an individual or household investing in education. These accruals usually take the form of differential earnings which is increased wage and salary net of costs that one makes to get through school. The less tangible private returns include higher prestige in the community and perhaps a better shot at one's ability to solve personal problems. Social returns, on the other hand, are broader in concept and concern the gains that society makes out of educating its citizens such as going to the moon (Ashenfelter et al. 1999).

It is very common in economics to use household based choice models to simulate the pattern of individual and group-decision behaviors. Modeling of the returns to education is no different. There are two popular approaches to modeling the returns to education in terms of pecuniary earnings. The first approach has been popularized by Becker (1993). It analyzes the relationship between earnings and education as a temporal investment decision with expected returns and costs. A rational individual decides to invest in a level of schooling when the wage rate is above the discount rate. The second approach was introduced by Mincer (1974, 1996). It skillfully avoids the complications of the tedious task of incremental explicit and implicit cost and benefit streams resulting from schooling and takes a shortcut specifying a semi-log earnings function. This Mincer type earning function originally specified log earnings as a function of completed years of formal schooling, experience and the square of experience. A third wheel approach fits a production function where education is introduced as an input variable. This approach is more common in studies that measure labor productivity in agriculture.

The first two approaches have been married and reformulated to an empirically tractable form in Card (1995). Our study follows a modification of Card's theoretical formulation to study the relationship between earnings and education. Card reduced the dynamic life-cycle comparison of earnings and costs of schooling into a static model focused on completed schooling and average returns over the life-cycle. This abstraction comes at the cost of restricting the analysis to individuals who enter the labor market after completing their formal schooling. A key assumption made here is that the returns to education are linear. Another, rather less restricting assumption is the separability of the effects of schooling on log earnings from the effect of experience, which is the case in standard human capital earnings functions (Ashenfelter et al. 1999). This modeling approach has become so popular that it has been replicated over time and different spatial contexts. Psacharopoulos and Patrinos (2004) give a summary of the replications.

Due to the nature of the bidirectional causal relationship between education and earnings, an analysis of the earnings function is fraught with potential problems. Endogeneity, selection bias and measurement problems all cause OLS estimation of the coefficients on schooling to be biased. Fortunately, a couple of statistical routes have been taken to address these problems. The instrumental variable approach is one. Some studies have implemented the Heckman two-step procedure for correcting self-selection biases. Another problem in gauging returns to schooling concerns data on education. Data on schooling and experience is usually far from ideal. Schooling data usually omits repetition rates. Likewise, experience data is either proxied by age and does not fully capture the experience one gains by being at work. These shortcomings in measuring schooling and experience result in measurement problems. And such problems result in biased coefficient estimates (Card 1995, 2001; Psacharopoulos 1985). This is more difficult to correct since it relates to the instruments of data collection.

It does not, however, always mean that earnings functions suffer from endogeneity. Lang (1993) re-examined various methods for correcting for bias in estimates of the returns to schooling. He found that adding ability to the wage equation may not be informative about the importance of bias and that variables correlated with the discount rate will generally not be suitable instruments for education.

Discount rate variations may generate a downward bias of OLS estimates instead of the theoretically expected upward bias. Literature on ability bias ignores complications implicit in theoretical formulations of the choice of human capital. A more selective rate of returns estimate focusing on the causality debate between schooling and earnings concludes that ability and related unobserved factors account for no more than 10 percent of the estimated schooling coefficients (Psacharopoulos and Patrinos 2004).

Another important methodological debate in a study of the returns to schooling is concerned with the linearity of the returns to schooling. For example, Card (1995) argues that there is a log linear relationship between earnings and schooling in cross-sectional data. This view is supported by other empirical work (such as Angrist and Krueger 1991). On the other hand, Trostel (2005) argues that non-linearity was evident in his examination of cross-section data for 12 OECD countries. In particular, he found that the marginal returns increased significantly at low levels of education and decreased significantly at higher levels. Our study addresses the presence of such non-linearity in the labor market in rural Ethiopia.

In many low-income countries, strong empirical regularities exist with respect to the relationship between educational attainments of the population and their productivity and performance in both market and non-market (home) production activities. In general, more educated men and women receive more earnings and produce more output than the less educated in a wide range of activities. These regularities were presented as a set of stylized facts by Becker (1993) and later by Psacharopoulos and Patrinos (2004). However, the specifics of returns to education vary by geography, time of study and the nature of the sampling methodology used. Existing evidence on the impact of education on agricultural productivity in Africa is mixed with estimates usually insignificant and generating large and significant coefficients in other studies.

Following a production function approach Appleton and Balihuta's (1996) study in Uganda using a nationally representative household survey gives an estimate of the impact of household primary schooling on crop production comparable to the developing country average at 13% for primary education and 18% for secondary education. Babatunde (2015) found that in Nigeria education improved one's participation in off-farm activities. It also found that the level of schooling of the household head was significantly and positively related to the level of farm output. Weir (1999) found that education did not significantly affect agricultural productivity in rural Ethiopia. However, when educational attainments were specified in terms of dummy variables, the regression estimates indicated that farmers with four to six years of primary schooling were more productive than those who were either illiterate or had three or fewer years of schooling. With respect to mean earnings, those with higher education earned 93% more than those with secondary education; those with secondary education earned 47% more than those with only Grades 5–8 of primary education; those with Grades 5–8 education, in turn, earned about 76% more than those with only Grades 1–4 education; and the latter earned about 72%

more than workers who were illiterate. This increase in earnings with educational attainments is a pattern found among men and women workers as well as among those in urban and rural areas.

According to Welday's (1997) study the average marginal returns to schooling for one year of schooling was 5% in the public sector. Private sector average marginal returns for a year of schooling calculated by the same author was 8%. These figures, however, were generated using a straightforward OLS estimate. A study by Verwimp (1996) estimated that an extra year of schooling yielded an estimated return of 15% based on a sample 422 male workers employed in public and private sectors in 1994 using a Mincer type earnings function. Krishnan et al. (1998) estimated separate earnings' functions for urban men and women aged 14–65 years by sector of employment. For men employed in the public sector, the study estimated a return of 10.6% for primary education and 15% for both secondary and higher education. For those working in the private sector, the returns were virtually zero for primary education, while they were estimated at 8.2% a year for secondary education and 21.5% for higher education.

As stated earlier, an estimation of returns to education is faced with theoretical difficulties, unresolved methodological issues and inevitable data collection and measurement issues that pose challenges. Empirical literature on Africa in particular does not seem to have reached a level of richness that is capable of identifying concrete empirical regularities. Using more up-to-date data that has a nationally representative sample design, our study answers some of the issues discussed in this section.

9.3 Methodology

9.3.1 Data and Variables

Our study uses data from the latest National Labor Force Survey (NLFS) collected in 2013. This data is representative of Ethiopia.

The variables used for our study are identified based on Card (2001) and Carneiro et al. (2011).

Earnings (y_i): earnings are the returns to investing in education to augment the productivity of one's labor. Literature indicates a clear preference for measuring earnings as log of wages (Ashenfelter et al. 1999). In our study, the monthly earnings of a worker employed in the labor market is taken in its natural logarithm.

Education (s_i): there are different ways of measuring the education that an individual accumulates. One could count the years of schooling that an individual spent in school or the maximum level of education that one has achieved. We employ both the approaches. The number of years of schooling are used under the assumption that the returns from any one given additional schooling is equal. However, this is not true since returns to schooling between graduation years and a year before graduation show significantly different earning margins (Hungerford and Solon 1987; Trostel 2005). To address this non-linearity, we introduce dummy variables for the different levels of education attained by a sampled labor market employee.

Experience (E_i): is the accumulated knowledge of the study subject obtained through learning by doing. Experience is usually proxied by age of the study subject which is considered as potential experience. In our study, however, actual experience in months is used as the National Labour Force Survey of 2013 collects data on actual experience.

Other control variables (x_{ik}): it is common to include additional covariates in the standard Mincerian earnings function; these include individual characteristics, household characteristics and community level characteristics. The k covariates used in our study are sex, marital status, major occupation, household size, highest completed years of school of worker's mother, highest completed years of school of worker's father, number of children (male, female and total) in worker's household, monthly earnings of the worker's household head (in ln), monthly pooled earnings of worker's household members and the regional state to which the worker belongs.

A list of the variables used along with their measurements, reference categories for dummies and expected signs of regression coefficients are given in Tables 9.1 and 9.2.

Table 9.1 Continuous variables used in the study, their units of measure and expected signs

Variable	Measurement units	Expected signs
Monthly earnings of worker from employment (in ln)	Birr per month	
Monthly earnings of worker from employment (levels)	Birr per month	
Household size	Number	−
Age	Years	+
Actual experience (E)	Months	+
Potential experience (A)	Years	+
Highest completed years of school of worker (S)	Years	+
Highest completed years of school worker's mother	Years	+
Highest completed years of school of worker's father	Years	+
Number of children in worker's household	Number	−
Number of male children in worker's household	Number	−
Number of female children in worker's household	Number	−
Monthly earnings of worker's household head (in ln)	Birr per month	+
Monthly pooled earnings of worker's household members	Birr per month	+

Table 9.2 Selected categorical variables used in the study, reference categories and coding

Variable	Category (code)	Reference category
Regional state	All 9 regional states and two city administrations: Tigray (1), Afar (2), Amhara (3), Oromia (4), Somalia (5), Benishangul (6), SNNP (7), Gambella (8), Harari (9), Addis Ababa (10), Dire Dawa (11)	Tigray
Sex	Male (0), Female (1)	Male
Marital status	Married, Single Spouse (1), Single (2), Divorced (3), Widowed (4)	Single
Major occupation	Managers (1), Professionals (2), Technicians and associate professionals (3), Clerical support workers (4), Service and sales workers (5) Skilled agricultural, forestry and fish (6) Craft and related trades workers (7) Plant and machine operators (8) Elementary occupations (9)	Managers
Level of education	No schooling, $L0$ (0), Basic primary education, $L1$ (1), General primary cycle, $L2$ (2), General secondary cycle, $L3$ (3), Preparatory education, $L4$ (4), Undergraduate education, $L5$ (5) and Graduate level education, $L6$ (6)	No schooling (illiterate)
Age category	Pre-school age: 0–6 years (0), school age: 7–21 years (1), post school working age: >21 years (2)	–

9.3.2 Theoretical and Analytic Framework

The empirical relationship between wages and schooling is conceptualized as a life-cycle regularity or as an age-wage profile with the wage increasing first in the cross-section with the age of the worker and then decreasing beyond some age at which depreciation of productive skills outweighs new investments in human capital. In other words, returns to education can be modeled using micro-equilibrium investment approaches. This per se means that the value of education is seen as primarily determined in the marketplace (Chenery and Srinivasan 1986). Following this equilibrium based approach, there is a view in literature that a decision to invest in a certain level of education is driven by the rate of returns to that investment vis-à-vis one's discount rate (Becker 1993). This method proceeds to produce an internal rate of returns that will equate the marginal benefits with the marginal cost of investment in one's education (the theoretical underpinning of this approach is explored in reasonable detail in Ashenfelter et al. (1999)). Another alternative specification is one proposed by Jacob Mincer (1974) in his seminal work *Schooling, Experience and Earnings*. This is the simplest presentation of the relationship between earnings and education but remains the most versatile and widely used. Our study uses the Mincerian route to analyze the causal relationship between education and its returns in Ethiopia.

The challenges in addressing the returns to education can be seen from three different perspectives—functional form, measurement and causal modeling. The earnings equation has a simple but parsimonious mathematical presentation of the relationship. The simplicity of its functional form has begged for much questioning chief among which is a doubt on the linearity of the schooling and earnings relationship. In addressing this problem, literature takes Mincer's equation as an approximation of the general production function form given as:

$$\log y_i = f(s, A) + e \tag{9.1}$$

where, s is the years of schooling and A is the age of the laborer,[1] where age is used as a proxy for experience. One functional form developed for $f(s, A)$ is to introduce higher order polynomials to the experience variable. A third and fourth order polynomial of the age variable produces the maximum improvement in fit of the earnings function relative to Mincer's original specification. Another suggestion is the use of interactions between education (s) and experience (A) to better capture the relationship. A common theme surfacing in the discussion on the functional form is that there is a linear relationship between education and the log of wages (Card 1995; Psacharopoulos and Patrinos 2002).

Another challenge discussed in economics literature is the issue of measuring education. The imposition of a linear relationship between education and log wages means that on the one hand, the correct measure of education is the number of years of completed education and on the other, that each additional year of schooling has the same proportional effect on earnings. The latter problem has been addressed by introducing additional variables to adjust for non-linearity caused by the sheepskin effect observed at the 8, 12 and 16 years of education (Ashenfelter et al. 1999). Log transformed earnings as a measure of returns is the most popular measure of returns to education. This popularity stems from the fact that the distribution of log earnings has a close to normal distribution. Moreover, the success of the semi-log earnings function has motivated many to adopt log wages as a measure of earnings and it remains the best measure (Psacharopoulos and Patrinos 2004). Another measurement issue relates to the problem with the instruments used for collecting data on education and experience. In particular, data on education does not account for repetitions, level of performance in a given grade and on-the-job training. These shortfalls in data are suspected for possible measurement errors in the education variable.

Modeling the earnings function to examine a causal relationship in an analytically tractable way is another key challenge. Card (1995, 2001) and Kling (2001) have developed a simple static model. Within an optimization framework, their model assumes that each individual faces a market opportunity locus that gives the level of earnings associated with alternative schooling choices. An additional assumption is that people finish their formal schooling before supplying their labor in the market. Further, it is also assumed that the effect of schooling on log earnings is separable from the effect of experience. The latter two assumptions enable an abstraction of the dynamic nature of the schooling-earnings relationship into a static

---

[1]This age is measured as the age of the laborer after completing his or her stated maximum level of educational achievement (Ashenfelter et al. 1999).

one. Let $y(S)$ denote the average level of earnings that an individual receives per year if she receives S years of schooling and let $h(s)$ denote the cost of schooling. Consider a maximization problem where an individual maximizes a utility function $U(S,y)$ where [2]:

$$U(S,y) = \log[y(s)] - h(s) \tag{9.2}$$

An optimal schooling choice should satisfy the first-order condition of Eq. 9.1:

$$\frac{y'(s)}{y'(s)} = h'(s) \tag{9.3}$$

Given the empirically supported linear relationship between log earnings and schooling, the marginal benefits (b_i) that influence an individual's optimal schooling choice can be parameterized as functions of observable characteristics, X, and unobservable components, η_1:

$$\frac{y'(s)}{y(s)} = b_i = X_i \pi_1 + \eta_{1i} \tag{9.4}$$

We can do the same for the marginal costs of education to obtain:

$$h'(s) = r_i + ks; r_i = X_i \pi_2 + Z_i \varphi_{2i} + \eta_{2i} \tag{9.5}$$

where, the marginal cost, $h'(s)$, has an individual specific discount rate (r_i) and a component that is increasing at a constant positive rate (k) in the amount of schooling. The parameter φ_{2i} is a random coefficient to allow for individual differences in response to the instrument, Z_i.

Substituting Eqs. 9.4 and 9.5 back into Eq. 9.3 will give the individual's optimal schooling, s_i^*,[3]

$$\frac{b_i - r_i}{k} = s_i^* = X_i \pi_3 + Z_i \varphi_{3i} + \eta_{3i} \tag{9.6}$$

Integrating Eq. 9.4 and substituting the results in the equation for earnings, we get:

$$\int_0^{s_i} \frac{y'(s)}{y(s)} ds = \log(y_i) = a_i + b_i s_i = X_i \beta + S_i \rho_i + \varepsilon_i \tag{9.7}$$

---

[2]This function generalizes the discounted present value objective function which is given by, $\int_s^\infty y(s)e^{rt}dt = y(s)\frac{e^{rs}}{r}$ where h is some increasing convex function of s.

[3]The instrument, Z_i, is assumed not to decrease schooling $(\gamma_{i3} \geq 0)$.

where, X_i is vector of observable covariates, including experience (A), ε_i captures the unobservable effects on log earnings and ρ_i is a random coefficient that is given as the measure of market returns to investments in education.

9.3.3 Econometric Strategy

We used a variation of the earnings function in Card (2001) and Kling (2001) to study the relationship between schooling and wages. In tandem with the standard log earnings function our econometric model is stated as:

$$\ln y = E\alpha + s\rho + X\gamma + \epsilon \tag{9.8}$$

where, s is a vector of schooling variables containing up to fourth power of the number of years of school attended to accommodate for the possibility of a non-linear relationship between education and earnings following Card (1995). Alternatively, a set of dummy variables for the different levels of education where certification is given is introduced to examine the presence of a sheepskin effect. E stands for the experience vector and like education with up to fourth order powers to form a polynomial function of experience to capture the possibility of a non-linear relationship between earnings and experience. X represents vectors of observed covariates that include individual, household and community level characteristics. ϵ is the error term that captures all unobserved variables as the error term.

Equation 9.8 can be restated in the following form:

$$\ln y_i = \gamma + \sum_{l=1}^{4} \rho_l s_i^l \sum_{m=1}^{2} \alpha_m E_l^m + \sum_{k=1}^{n} \alpha_k x_{ki} + \varepsilon_i \tag{9.9}$$

where, i stands for the ith worker in the regression, γ is a constant; education polynomial runs up to the fourth order and the experience polynomial runs up to the second order. Note that we have separated experience (E) from the matrix of observed covariates, X.

In addressing the stated objectives of our study variations we used the basic Mincerian equation. The standard Mincerian earnings function is extracted from the general specification given in Eq. 9.9 for $l = 1$, $m = 2$ and $n = 0$. This formulation produces average marginal returns to a year of schooling. To test the non-linearity hypothesis in the returns to education, two sets of earnings functions are formulated. The first formulation has schooling and experience variables introduced into the model as polynomials of up to four orders and second order respectively such that modifying Eq. 9.9 will be done for $l = 4$, $m = 2$ and $n = 0$. In the second formulation, instead of polynomials of schooling, a set of six dummies are introduced corresponding to the different points of certification in the schooling system in Ethiopia. In this case, years of schooling, s_i^l, is replaced by the level of education at which certification of a certain kind is conferred upon completion, c_{li}, where l now stands for the level of education instead of the order of the polynomial. To study the influence of other individual, household level and community level covariates, an extension of the standard Mincerian function is adopted by including these covariates such that Eq. 9.9 will now have $l = 4$, $m = 2$ and $n = $ the number of additional covariates used. Because of the oversampling and under-sampling of primary sampling units to better understand certain features of the labor force, a survey sampling design was used to gather information. And to correct for over- and under-sampling, probability weights were introduced as sampling correction when computing statistics. Following the same logic of correction, the survey regression techniques were used.

9.4 Results and Discussion

9.4.1 Descriptive Statistics

Our study employed a rich cross-sectional data on the labor force. The Central Statistics Agency of Ethiopia collects information on the participation of the population in the economic and social development process in the country. It is collected every five years as a cross-sectional dataset with a nationally representative sample. Our study used the latest instalment of the NLFS collected for 2013. The survey provides data on key demographic variables, economic activity status, characteristics of the employed population and characteristics of the unemployed population. Our study used data from the 2013 cross-sectional survey particularly relying on data on demographic characteristics and characteristics of the employed population.

NLFS is a household based sample survey. Hence, information on individuals is collected within the context of the household. Therefore, it was possible to generate characteristics at the individual laborer level, household to which he/she belonged and various levels of communal hierarchy. National Labour Force Survey of 2013 was collected using a stratified two-stage cluster sampling design. The primary sampling units (PSUs) were enumeration areas (EAs). Households were used as secondary sampling units (SSUs). The survey covered 240,656 individuals divided among 52,059 households. The data is collected to represent the whole country with the exception of parts which are nomadic. All the nine regional states and the two city administrations are included in the sampling. Twenty-two (22) zonal administrations, 25 woredas, 55 kebeles and 68 enumeration areas were included in the sample. This survey was restricted to a sub-sample of employed individuals within the monthly earnings stream. This form of earning is associated with formal employment and the most common form of payment frequency (Table 9.3). This sub-sample constituted 23,355 individuals with monthly earnings streams

Table 9.3 Descriptive statistics for ratio scaled variables

Variable	Obs.	Mean	Std. dev.	Min	Max
Monthly earnings (in natural logarithms)	23,200	6.938	0.919	0.0	11.513
Monthly earnings (in levels)	23,200	1540.303	2111.328	1.0	99,997.000
Completed years of schooling	21,372	11.086	3.964	0.0	17.000
Age	23,355	32.498	11.609	7.0	97.000
Potential experience (years)	21,372	15.371	11.421	−3.0	83.000
Actual experience (months)	22,039	95.665	105.279	0.0	744.000
Head's monthly earning (in natural logarithms)	16,903	0.118	0.169	0.0	4.615
Household's monthly earnings (in natural logarithms)	23,235	0.183	0.293	0.0	9.304
Number of children in household	23,355	1.808	1.774	0.0	12.000
Number of male children in household	21,254	1.031	1.179	0.0	8.000
Number of female children in household	20,831	0.976	1.099	0.0	7.000
Household size	23,355	4.289	2.427	1.0	27.000

Refers to the number of individuals with non-missing observations used in computing a statistic for the specified variable. We refer to Obs. in a similar manner in all subsequent tables
Source Author's calculations using National Labour Force Survey of 2013

distributed among 14,919 households. This sub-sample was spread over all nine regional states and the two city administrations. A total of 68 enumeration areas, spread over 22 woredas were covered in the sub-sample.

Descriptive statistics of the sub-sample are given in Tables 9.3 and 9.4. Table 9.3 gives basic statistics of continuous variables while Table 9.4 gives statistics of the categorical variables.

In addition to earnings, schooling and experience, which are the variables of concern in the original Mincer equation, our study includes additional variables to see their implications on earnings. Studies have repeatedly shown that an individual's earning is influenced by the household conditions of the worker. Household characteristics included in our study are household's pooled monthly earnings, household head's monthly earnings, number of children (male, female and total) in the household and household size. An average household had a pooled monthly income of 0.18 (in natural logs) and the head earned 0.12 (in natural logs) per month. The same average household, from which our worker of interest comes had 1.81[4] children where 1.03 were male and 0.97 were female and the total number of members of such a household was 4.29.

In addition to the variables measured on a ratio scale, our study also explored the significance of categorical variables in the context of a Mincerian earnings function. Forty-three per cent of the individuals included in the sub-sample were female.

---

[4]Male and female children's averages do not add up because there are households with male children only and other households with female children only.

Table 9.4 Summary of categorical variables (with selected categories)

Variable	Category	Freq.	Percent	Total
Sex	Male	13,211	57	23,355
	Female	10,144	43	
Relationship to household head	Head of household	12,148	52.01	23,355
	Spouse	3160	13.53	
	Son/daughter of head and spouse	4144	17.75	
	Mother/father of head/spouse	48	0.21	
	Sister/brother of head/spouse	703	3.01	
	Domestic workers	1686	7.22	
	Other-relatives and non-relatives	1466	6.27	
Marital status	Never married	9646	41.32	23,347
	Married/living together	11,523	49.35	
	Widowed	674	2.89	
	Divorced/separated	1504	6.44	
Region	Tigray	1376	5.89	23,355
	Afar	903	3.87	
	Amhara	3118	13.35	
	Oromia	3938	16.86	
	Somalie	545	2.33	
	Benishangul-Gumuz	806	3.45	
	SNNP	3148	13.48	
	Gambella	852	3.65	
	Harari	770	3.3	
	Addis Ababa	7130	30.53	
	Dire Dawa	769	3.29	
Major occupation group	Managers	1108	4.76	23.258
	Professionals	3622	15.57	
	Technicians and associate professionals	4233	18.2	
	Clerical support workers	1755	7.55	
	Service and sales workers	4411	18.97	
	Craft and related trades workers	1709	7.35	
	Plant and machine operators	1865	8.02	
	Elementary occupations	4303	18.5	

(continued)

Table 9.4 (continued)

Variable	Category	Freq.	Percent	Total
Education level (by certification at different levels)	No schooling	41	0.19	21.372
	Basic primary education (1–4 years)	1744	8.16	
	General primary cycle (5–8 years)	3873	18.12	
	General secondary cycle (9–10 years)	3195	14.95	
	Preparatory education (11–12 years)	3402	15.92	
	Undergraduate education (13–16 years)	8515	39.84	
	Graduate level education (>16 years)	602	2.82	

The construction of this variable is based on ESDP IV (MoE 2010)
Source Author's calculations using National Labour Force Survey of 2013

This is typical of labor market employment indicating lower participation of females in the labor force. In a relational context of the household, about 52% of the sampled workers were household heads followed by children (17.75%), spouses of the heads (15.53%), domestic workers in the household (7.22%), other relatives and non-relatives (6.27%), siblings of the head or his/ her spouse (3.01%) and parent of the spouse (0.21%) respectively.

With respect to marital status, about half (49.35%) of the workers in the sub-sample were either married or living together as couples. Another 41.32% workers had never been married. The remaining workers had been in a marital relationship earlier but were single at the time of the survey. A big chunk of the sampled respondents came from Addis Ababa (30.53%), Oromia (16.86%), SNNP (13.48%) and Amhara (13.35%). These regional states were the source of employment because of either size or concentration of population. Concerning occupation groups, service and sales workers (18.97%) had the largest share among the different major occupational groups while managers had the smallest share (4.76%). Of salaried workers, undergraduate degree holders had the largest share (39.48%) followed by general primary cycle completion (18.12%), preparatory education completion (15.92%), general secondary cycle completion (14.95%), basic primary education completion (8.16) and graduate degree holders (2.82%). A small percentage of the sample (0.19%) was without any education.

There was a marked variation in the mean earnings among the different levels of education (Table 9.5). The level of monthly earnings steadily increased with increasing levels of education, the increase being more rapid for higher levels of education. This is an early indication that more education pays better. Table 9.5 also shows that the earnings gap between male and female workers narrowed down

Table 9.5 Mean earnings differential by level of education

Level of education	Mean monthly earnings		
	Overall	Male	Female
No schooling (L0)	455.3	676.1	274.5
Basic primary education (L1)	581.5	777.9	411.2
General primary cycle (L2)	847.9	1117.3	516.9
General secondary cycle (L3)	1037.4	1238.6	761.6
Preparatory education (L4)	1477.4	1722.9	1143.0
Undergraduate education (L5)	2275.5	2536.3	1866.8
Graduate level education (L6)	4686.0	4723.2	4475.2

Source Author's calculation using National Labour Force Survey of 2013

Table 9.6 Mean comparison of monthly earnings, age, actual experience and schooling by sex of worker

Variable	Diff	p-value	Std. err.	Sample size
	(Male–Female)	(for $H_0! = 0$)		
Monthly earnings (in levels)	798.6768	0.0000	27.4629	23,200
Monthly earnings (in natural logarithms)	0.6224	0.0000	0.0115	23,200
Completed years of schooling	0.9949	0.0000	0.0546	21,372
Actual experience	39.2743	0.0000	1.4062	22,039
Potential experience	5.0430	0.0000	0.1548	21,372

Source Author's calculation using National Labour Force Survey of 2013

as the level of education increased. One explanation for this is that jobs that require little or no education tend to be highly segregated by gender (Siphambe 2000).

The sub-sample of workers used for our study, and also the whole National Labour Force Survey of 2013 has marked variations when segregated further by categories such as sex, disability, marital status and regional state.[5] Table 9.6 shows that there is a statistically significant difference in the monthly earnings, completed years of schooling and experience (actual or potential). Men's monthly earnings were ETB 798.68 in excess of women on average. Men also had more completed years of schooling (close to one more year than women), and more experience (3.27 years of actual experience or 5.04 years of potential experience) than women. Such results are a precursor to a detailed disaggregated analysis of the returns to schooling by gender. However, such an analysis is beyond the scope of our research.

---

[5]ANOVA tables of the variations by marital status, regional state, relationship to the household head, age category and major occupation are included as an Appendix for reference.

Table 9.7 Pairwise correlation of selected variables (with list-wise deletion)

ln (Monthly earning)	1.0000						
Schooling	0.5869**	1.0000					
Actualexperience	0.2390** (0.0000)	0.1146* (0.0116)	1.0000				
Ln (head's monthly earning)	0.1519** (0.0008)	0.1190** (0.0088)	−0.0138 (0.7628)	1.0000			
Father's schooling	0.3200** (0.0000)	0.3754** (0.0000)	0.0016 (0.9725)	0.1383** (0.0023)	1.0000		
Mother's schooling	0.3135** (0.0000)	0.4021** (0.0000)	−0.0183 (0.6873)	0.1108* (0.0147)	0.6468** (0.0000)	1.0000	
Aggregated parent's schooling	0.1969** (0.0000)	0.2305** (0.0000)	0.0525 (0.2489)	0.0084 (0.8532)	0.5238** (0.0000)	0.4783** (0.0000)	1.0000

Note *Indicates a 5% significance level and **indicates a 1% significance level
Source Author's calculations using National Labour Force Survey of 2013

The scope of our study is limited to measuring the average marginal returns to schooling, the presence of non-linearity in such returns to education with increasing number of completed years of schooling and identifying the additional determinants of monthly earnings in the context of a Mincer type earnings function. However, before investigating a causal relationship between schooling and earnings it is imperative to see the extent of correlations between the different ratio scaled indicators. Table 9.7 gives pairwise correlation coefficients for the study sub-sample. Monthly earnings are significantly correlated with both completed years of schooling (58.69%) and actual experience (23.9%). This is an early indication of a relationship between earnings and schooling and earnings and experience. However, further statistical investigation is needed to establish a causal relationship between schooling and earnings. Another important result of the pairwise correlation is the small correlation coefficient (11.46%) between actual experience and schooling. This affirms our assumption of separability between schooling and experience. In other words, the small correlation coefficient suggests that only 11% of the movement in schooling and experience is common to the two variables.

9.4.2 Econometric Modeling Results

Before measuring the returns to education in the form of marginal increments to a worker's earnings, it is proper to explore the distributional pattern of the data under consideration. Two observations with zero monthly earnings were dropped as there is no rational incentive to go for more years of schooling for zero compensation. Since our study uses survey regression techniques, our estimation results are robust to violations of normality, multicollinearity and heteroscedasticity assumptions. A survey regression bases its inference on the sample design, that is, stratification and variations between primary sampling units (Deaton 1997).

In accordance with the objectives of our research, we first measured the average marginal returns to education. Then, a formal test of the existence of non-linearity was done. Finally, additional variables were introduced into the regression model to identify determinants of earnings other than education and experience.

9.4.2.1 Average Private Marginal Returns to Education

Following Mincer's (1974) pioneering work, the returns to education can be measured as the coefficient of the schooling variable after regressing the natural log of earnings on completed years of schooling and experience. This approach assumes a relationship between the natural log of earnings and completed years of schooling as linear. This implies that the rate of returns to different levels of schooling is fairly constant. Table 9.8 gives the regression coefficients of the basic Mincerian earnings function; the coefficients reported are for three different regression approaches. The first coefficients are obtained from an OLS regression. However, literature on returns to education agrees that the completed years of schooling variable is plagued with endogeneity problems. This may render the OLS coefficients inconsistent and hence uninterpretable. Further, such OLS coefficients usually understate the average marginal returns to a year of schooling (Card 2001). To correct for endogeneity, an instrument or a set of instruments are substituted for the endogenous variable, in this case completed years of schooling. The instruments used must qualify for both inclusion and exclusion criteria (Greene 1990). The common instruments used in literature include parents' schooling, distance to school (Humphreys 2013) and season of birth (Card 1995).

Another way to look at endogeneity of schooling is to think of schooling as the observed variable determining the probability of employment of a worker but also that there are other unobserved variables that determine both schooling and the probability of employment. If a certain individual is unemployed, then we cannot know what his potential earnings will be as we cannot observe her earnings. Heckman (Greene 1990; Gujarati 2004) devised a method of constructing the probability of employment using a probit regression[6] that includes the inverse of the mills ratio (also called the non-selection hazard ratio) obtained in the second stage regression (also called the outcome regression) to correct for the selection bias that may result due to unobserved earnings of the unemployed.

---

[6]This equation is called the selection regression. The second stage estimation is called the outcome regression.

Table 9.8 Average marginal returns from schooling (OLS, Heckman and 2SLS regressions) (Dependent variable: natural log of monthly earnings)

Variables	Regression coefficients (standard errors)		
	OLS	Heckman	2SLS
Schooling (S)	0.1343** (0.0027)	0.1346** (0.0028)	0.1809864** (0.0221582)
Actual experience (E)	0.0051** (0.0002)	0.0051** (0.0002)	0.0060** (0.0012)
E^2	−0.0217** (0.0048)	−0.0217** (0.0048)	0.0000** (0.0048)
Constant	5.2086** (0.0378)	5.2008** (0.0408)	4.7148** (0.2855)
Sample size	20,094	23,621	1065
F-statistic	960.95**	856.83**	41.36**
R-squared	0.5249	–	0.3594

Note *indicates a 5% significance level and **indicates a 1% significance level
Source Author's calculations using National Labour Force Survey of 2013

Table 9.8 gives the regression results for both cases of endogeneity. Of the three regressions, we interpret the coefficients of the selection based modeling as the instruments used in the 2SLS approach were deemed weak.

The private average marginal returns to one more year of schooling is 14.43[7]%. This result is slightly above the OLS based value of 14.37%. The marginal return to experience is 0.5% for every additional year of experience. The coefficient of the square of experience variable (E^2) indicates that the returns to experience have diminishing returns. This result agrees with literature that with increasing age additional experience becomes less valuable since a worker ages both mentally and physically (Byron and Manaloto 1990; Carneiro et al. 2011; Dagsvik et al. 2011; Lang 1993; Renshaw 1960; Varga 1995; Welday 1997). The regression coefficients of the earnings function are all statistically significant. The F-test rejects the joint insignificance of the explanatory variables. The model explains 52% of the variations in log earnings. This is quite a robust result for an earnings function given the usually low R^2 result reported in studies. The 2SLS approach is not pursued further because parents' (father, mother and both parents) education was found to be a weak instrument for substituting schooling in the standard earnings function.

---

[7]To change from ln(monthly earnings) to annual percentage returns we applied the following operation: marginal returns = $\left(e^{coefficient} - 1\right) * 100\%$. For coefficient values below 0.1, this correction is not necessary.

9.4.2.2 Non-linearity in the Private Marginal Returns to Education

Literature on the non-linearity of schooling approaches the non-linearity investigation from two viewpoints. The first approach is to include up to fourth order polynomials of the schooling variable and test the inclusion of these powers of education to improve the goodness-of-fit of the extended Mincerian earnings equation (Ashenfelter et al. 1999; Trostel 2005). A more specific approach for testing non-linearity is investigating for the presence of the sheepskin effect (Hungerford and Solon 1987; Psacharopoulos and Patrinos 2004). A sheepskin effect is a term coined for the difference in marginal earnings before and after completing a certain level of education and getting a certificate or diploma for it. For example, it is intuitive to expect that for a three-year undergraduate program, an individual who completes all the three years and gets a diploma will earn marginally higher monthly earnings relative to an individual who drops out before completing the final year thereby failing to earn her diploma. To identify this a set of education dummies were constructed for six different levels of education and each of these was interacted with schooling. The coefficients of the interaction variables were then interpreted as the marginal returns to education for the different levels where illiteracy (no schooling) serves as a base category.

In the first approach, a regression (OLS and selection model) is run by incrementally introducing higher order polynomials into the standard Mincer regression. Then a likelihood ratio (LR) test is implemented to check if introducing a schooling variable with one more power to the regression equation produces an increase in the goodness-of-fit of the model. The results indicate that introducing schooling variables up to the fourth power in the schooling polynomial will improve the model's goodness-of-fit (see Table 9.9). Alternatively, implementing the Akaike Information Criteria (AIC), the regression equation with a higher order polynomial of schooling will give a better goodness-of-fit. This result is robust whether an OLS regression is implemented or a Heckman selection model is implemented.

These robust results indicate that there is a general non-linearity in the returns to schooling. Specifically taking the extended Mincerian regression where schooling is introduced as a second order polynomial it is easy to see that the returns to education are increasing since the coefficient of the square of the schooling variable (E^2) is positive (refer to Appendix for the regressions table with order of polynomial (OP) = 2).

The regression with levels of education introduced as dummies is given in Table 9.10. The education dummy is constructed so that illiteracy is the reference category and the other six levels are those where certification is given as a recognition of completion. The coefficients at each level of education are given as coefficients of the interaction of schooling with the level of education.

The results indicate that the returns to education have a spine structure at different levels of certification. A closer look at the regression coefficients of the interaction variables reveals that the returns to schooling fall from a high level and

Table 9.9 Likelihood ratio tests and Akaike Information Criterion for Mincerian equations with different orders of polynomials for schooling (Dependent variable: natural log of monthly earnings)

Null hypothesis	OLS			Selection model (Heckman)		
	LR statistic	AIC (with h equal to model no.)		LR statistic	AIC (with h equal to model no.)	
		Model h	Model $h + 1$		Model h	Model $h + 1$
Model 1 is nested in 2	368.94**	37067.99	36701.05	435.94**	55001.89	54569.95
Model 2 is nested in 3	33.37**	36701.05	36669.68	55.38**	54569.95	54518.58
Model 3 is nested in 4	36.9**	36669.68	36634.78	70.99**	54518.58	54451.58

The models can be generalized as

$\ln(W) = \alpha + \sum_{i=1}^{k} \beta_i S^i + \sum_{j=1}^{l} \beta_j E^j + \varepsilon_i$

Model 1 (k = 1, l = 2); Model 2 (k = 2, l = 2); Model 3 (k = 3, l = 2); and Model 4 (k = 4, l = 2)

Note *Indicates a 5% significance level and **indicates a 1% significance level
Source Author's calculations using National Labour Force Survey of 2013

rise back again. This result confirms the earlier finding of a general non-linearity in the returns to schooling and to increasing returns to schooling in particular. Restricting our interpretation to the selection model, a closer look at the regression coefficients reveals the following. Acquiring basic primary education (Grades 1–4) has a 13.92% marginal increment in the monthly earnings of a worker relative to not having completed any schooling, ceteris paribus. The education premium for acquiring a certificate for a general primary cycle (Grades 5–8) completion is 12.64% given no schooling as a reference category, ceteris paribus. Completing the general secondary cycle, that is, getting a Grade 10 completion certificate will increase an individual's monthly earnings by 12.34% against a reference category of no schooling, ceteris paribus. The education premium for preparatory education is 12.93%, ceteris paribus. Beyond high school, the education premiums for completing undergraduate and graduate level schooling stand at 13.78% and 15.23% respectively. Clearly, the highest return to education occurs with graduate level certification while the lowest is with completing the general secondary cycle. It is possible to analyze private returns to education as a rate of returns by taking the immediately preceding category as the reference category for a given level of education.[8] Figure 9.1 gives a plot of the rate of returns to different levels of education.

---

[8] Arithmetically the private rate of return (r_l) to education is given as $r_l = \frac{e^{(\beta_l - \beta_{l-1})} - 1}{S_l - S_{l-1}}$, where l is the level of education for which the private rate of return is being calculated.

Table 9.10 Regression with non-linearity introduced at six different points of certification (Dependent variable: natural log of monthly earnings)

Explanatory variables	Coefficients (standard error)	
	OLS	Heckman
Level of education (no schooling is the reference category)		
Basic primary education (*L1**S)	0.1303** (0.0180)	0.1303** (0.0180)
General primary cycle (*L2**S)	0.1191** (0.0082)	0.1191** (0.0081)
General secondary cycle (*L3**S)	0.1163** (0.0064)	0.1164** (0.0064)
Preparatory education (*L4**S)	0.1216** (0.0051)	0.1217** (0.0052)
Undergraduate education (*L5**S)	0.1291** (0.0041)	0.1292** (0.0041)
Graduate level education (*L6**S)	0.1418** (0.0042)	0.1418** (0.0042)
Actual experience (*E*)	0.0051** (0.0002)	0.0051** (0.0002)
E^2	−0.0216** (0.0048)	−0.0216** (0.0048)
Constant	5.3068** (0.0599)	5.3057** (0.0592)
F-statistic	520.31**	526.01**
R-squared	0.5296	–
Sample size	20,094	23,631

Note *Indicates a 5% significance level and **indicates a 1% significance level
Source Author's calculations using National Labour Force Survey of 2013

As the graph in Fig. 9.1 shows, the highest rate of return to education occurs with acquiring basic primary education. This indicates a clear incentive to invest in basic education. The biggest slump in the rate of return occurs with general primary education, that is, continuing past Grade 4 through Grade 8. Such a dipping in the rate of returns to general primary cycle education may be one of the reasons why dropouts are still a challenge at this level of education (MoE 2010). The resolve to sustain progression from *L*1 to *L*2 in the ESDP IV (MoE 2010) is a plan in the right direction in this respect. Graduate level education boasts the second highest rate of returns to schooling. The overall shape of the rate of returns graph displays similar results to a World Bank study (The World Bank 2005). Another important finding that proceeds from the rate of returns line graph is that sheepskin effects are evident in the rate of returns to education in Ethiopia. This result is in agreement with the increasingly supported, and empirically tested, view of spined returns to education at different points of certification (Afzal 2011; Carneiro et al. 2011; Kimenyi et al. 2006; Laveesh and Mridusmita 2006; Psacharopoulos and Patrinos 2004;

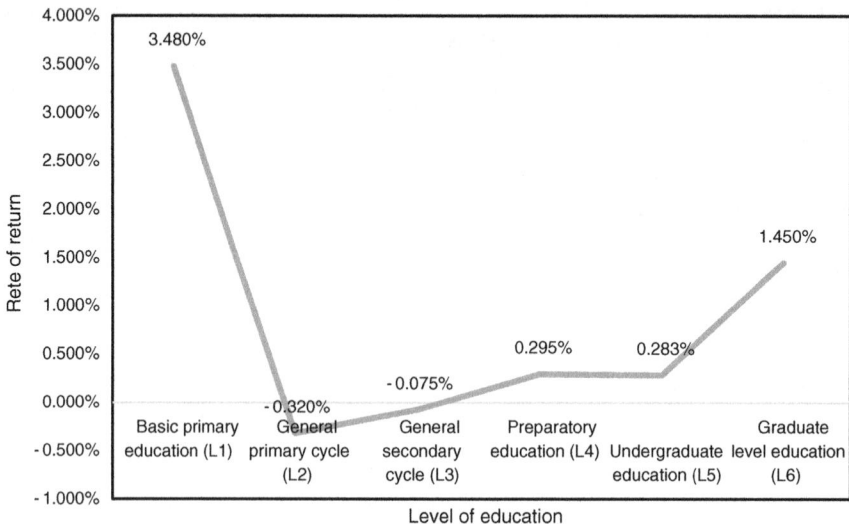

Fig. 9.1 The rate of returns to different levels of education

Trostel 2005). The rate of returns at any level of education, however, are below the cost of borrowing.[9] This implies that investing in education is not worthwhile. This could explain why Ethiopia remains below sub-Saharan levels in a number of educational attainment indicators (Joshi and Verspoor 2013; The World Bank 2005).

9.5 Conclusion and Recommendations

Our study explored the returns to education in Ethiopia. It used variations of the earnings function popularized by Jacob Mincer to address its research objectives. The variations deployed were implemented as per the works of Card (2001) and Kling (2001). First a straightforward standard Mincerian regression was run to determine the average marginal returns to a year of schooling. After correcting for endogeneity caused by a selection bias, the results indicated that the returns to education for a year of schooling was 14.43%. Our study went further to explore if this result remained the same at every level of schooling or that the returns to schooling varied with increased years of schooling. Fitting a schooling polynomial up to a fourth order revealed an improvement in the goodness-of-fit using the likelihood ratio test of the earnings function. An alternative approach was pursued

---

[9]The cost of borrowing currently stands at 5% as issued by the National Bank of Ethiopia. Available at: http://www.nbe.gov.et/aboutus/faq.html.

to determine if the returns to education exhibited spines at different levels of certification in the education system. To answer this question, a set of education dummies were interacted with the completed years of schooling variable. Each of the coefficients of the interaction variables were positive and significant confirming that the sheepskin effect was prevalent in the returns to education in Ethiopia. The returns to education for basic primary education (Grades 1–4), general primary cycle (Grades 5–8), general secondary cycle (Grades 9–10), preparatory education (Grades 11–12), undergraduate education and graduate level education were 13.92, 12.64, 12.34, 12.93, 13.78 and 15.23% respectively. Following both approaches of investigating non-linearity in education revealed that education had increasing returns. In this respect, the use of education dummies shed further light on the non-linearity of education. It revealed that the highest returns to education were at the primary level. The largest fall in the rate of returns to education was when an individual transitioned from basic primary (Grades 1–4) to general primary (Grades 5–8) education. These results could perhaps explain why moving past universal basic education has remained difficult.

On the experience front, we found that the average marginal returns to a year of experience was 0.5%. However, the returns to education from experience diminished with higher years of experience as the coefficient of the square of the experience variable was negative and significant.

Our study found a sheepskin effect at different levels of education. This throws light on where the government should focus on facilitating access to education. Our study also found that universal primary education was a right education policy. Also, the government's commitment to improving access to higher education should be a key priority. In this regard, the current expansion in tertiary level education is commendable. Regarding student progression, the lowest private incentive is in pursuing Grades 5 through 8. This is a big hurdle for progressing towards levels of education with high returns such as the graduate level. Hence, it is recommended that the government subsidy for basic primary education should be expanded to the second cycle of primary education and the first cycle of secondary education.

Appendix

Table of regressions on ln of monthly earnings with different order polynomials (OP) for schooling

Variables	Regression coefficients (standard error)							
	OLS				Heckman selection model			
	OP=1	OP=2	OP=3	OP=4	OP=1	OP=2	OP=3	OP=4
Schooling (S)	0.134454**	0.037724**	0.122026**	−0.05992	0.1367406**	0.0360557**	0.121273**	−0.0690712**
	(−0.001212)	(−0.00576)	(−0.017951)	(−0.03893)	(−0.0015278)	(−0.0052363)	(−0.0155708)	(−0.033933)
S^2		0.004841**	−0.00513**	0.033844**		0.0048777**	−0.005257**	0.0354546**
		(−0.000272)	(−0.001955)	(−0.007462)		(−0.0002513)	(−0.0017653)	(−0.0066831)
S^3			0.000343**	−0.0028**			0.0003489**	−0.0029349**
			(−6.48E-05)	(−0.000572)			(−0.0000601)	(−0.0005241)
S^4				8.51E-05**				0.0000888**
				(−1.51E-05)				(−0.0000141)
Experience (E)	0.004696**	0.004623**	0.004622**	0.004639**	0.0047186**	0.0046147**	0.0046104**	0.0046276**
	(−0.000137)	(−0.000135)	(−0.000135)	(−0.000135)	(−0.0001209)	(−0.0001196)	(−0.0001195)	(−0.0001194)
E^2	−7.83E-06**	−7.78E-06**	−7.80E-06**	−7.81E-06**	−7.83E-06**	−7.78E-06**	−7.81E-06**	−7.81E-06**
	(−3.61E-07)	(−3.57E-07)	(−3.56E-07)	(−3.56E-07)	(−3.02E-07)	(−2.99E-07)	(−2.98E-07)	(−2.98E-07)
Constant	5.243302**	5.650761**	5.462976**	5.705263**	5.199808**	5.670704**	5.489547**	5.743415**
	(−0.015151)	(−0.029414)	(−0.049497)	(−0.068567)	(−0.0239129)	(−0.0304367)	(−0.0429867)	(−0.0595346)
F-stat.	5984.9**	5049.01**	4082.38**	3416.7**				
R^2	0.5062	0.5152	0.516	0.5169				
Obs.	20089	20089	20089	20089	23621	23621	23621	23621
Censored					3532	3532	3532	3532
Wald stat.					10663.05**	12192.02**	12739.89**	13128.06**

OP stands for the Order of Polynomial

References

Afzal, M. 2011. Microeconometric analysis of private returns to education and determinants of earnings. *Pakistan Economic and Social Review* 49 (1): 39–68.

Angrist, J.D., and A.B. Krueger. 1991. Does compulsory school attendance affect schooling and earnings? *Quarterly Journal of Economics* 979–1014.

Appleton, S., and A. Balihuta. 1996. Education and agricultural productivity: evidence from Uganda. *Journal of International Development* 8 (3): 415–444.

Ashenfelter, O., R. Layard, and D. Card. 1999. *Handbook of Labor Economics*, vol. 3. North Holland: Elsevier.

Babatunde, R.O. 2015. On-Farm and Off-Farm Works: Complement or Substitute? Evidence from Nigeria. Working Paper. Department of Agricultural Economics and Farm Management, University of Ilorin. Mastricht School of Management.

Banerjee, A.V., and E. Dufalo. 2011. *Poor economics: a radical rethinking of the way to fight poverty*. New York: Public Affairs.

Becker, G.S. 1993. *Human Capital: a Theoretical and Empirical Analysis with Special Reference to Education*. Chicago: NBER.

Byron, R.P., and E.Q. Manaloto. 1990. Returns to education in China. *Economic Development and Cultural Change* 38 (4): 783–796.

Card, D. 1995. Earnings, schooling and ability revisited. *Research in labor economics* 14: 23–48.

Card, D. 2001. Estimating the return to schooling: progress on some persistent econometric problems. *Econometrica* 69 (5): 1127–1160.

Carneiro, P., J.J. Heckman, and E.J. Vytlacil. 2011. Estimating marginal returns to education. *The American Economic Review* 101 (6): 2754–2781.

Chenery, H., and T.N. Srinivasan. 1986. *Handbook of Development Economics*, vol. 2. Boston: Esevier.

CSA. 2007. *Population and Housing Census Report*. Addis Ababa.

CSA. 2014. *Key Findings on the 2013 National Labour Force Survey.*

Dagsvik, J.K., T. Hægeland, and A. Raknerud. 2011. Estimating the returns to schooling: a likelihood approach based on normal mixtures. *Journal of Applied Econometrics* 26(4): 613–640.

Deaton, A. 1997. *The Analysis of Household Surveys, a Microeconometric Approach to Development Policy*. Baltimore, London: John Hopkins University.

Greene, W. 1990. *Econometric Analysis*. New York: Elsevier.

Gujarati, D. 2004. *Basic Econometrics, 4th ed.* New York: The McGraw—Hill Companies.

Humphreys, J. 2013. *An alternative to the Mincer model of education*. Australia: University of Queensland.

Hungerford, T., and G. Solon. 1987. Sheepskin effects in the returns to education. *The Review of Economics and Statistics* 69 (1): 175–177.

Joshi, R.D., and A. Verspoor. 2013. *Secondary Education in Ethiopia, Supporting Growth and Transformation*. Washington, DC: The World Bank.

Kimenyi, M.S., G. Mwabu, and D.K. Manda. 2006. Human capital externalities and private returns to education in kenya. *Eastern Economic Journal* 32 (3): 493–513.

Kling, J.R. 2001. Interpreting instrumental variables estimates of the returns to schooling. *Journal of Business and Economic Statistics.* 19 (3): 358–364.

Krishnan, P., T. Selassie, and S. Dercon. 1998. *The urban labour market during structural adjustment: Ethiopia 1990–1997*. Centre for the Study of African Economies, Institute of Economics and Statistics, University of Oxford. Worksing Paper Series, 1998:9.

Lang, K. 1993. *Ability Bias, Discount Rate Bias, and the Return to Education*. Research Article. Department of Economics. Boston, MA: Boston University.

Laveesh, B., and B. Mridusmita. 2006. Income differentials and returns to education. *Economic and Political Weekly* 41 (36): 3893–3900.

Mincer, J. 1974. *Schooling, experience and earnings*. Chicago: NBER.

Mincer, J. 1996. Economic development, growth of human capital, and the dynamics of the wage structure. *Journal of Economic Growth* 1 (1): 29–48.

MoE. 2010. *Education Sector Development Program IV (ESDP IV), 2010/2011–2014/2015*. Addis Ababa: Federal Ministry of Education (MoE), FDRE.

Psacharopoulos, G. 1985. Returns to education: a further international update and implications. *The Journal of Human Resources* 20 (4): 583–604.

Psacharopoulos, G. and H.A. Patrinos. 2002. Returns to investment in education: a further update. *Policy research working paper.*

Psacharopoulos, G., and H.A. Patrinos. 2004. Returns to investment in education: a further update. *Education Economics* 12 (2): 111–134. https://doi.org/10.1080/0964529042000239140.

Renshaw, E.F. 1960. Estimating the returns to education. *The Review of Economics and Statistics* 42 (3): 318–324.

Siphambe, H.K. 2000. Rates of return to education in Botswana. *Economics of Education Review* 19: 291–300.

Tassew, W., M. Alemu, and N. Jones. 2009. Education choices in Ethiopia: what determines whether poor households send their children to school? *Ethiopian Journal of Economics* 1 (17): 43–80.

The World Bank. 2005. *Education in Ethiopia: Strengthening the Foundation for Sustainable Development*. Washington DC: The World Bank.

Trostel, P.A. 2005. Non linearity in the return to education. *Journal of Applied Economics VIII*(1): 191–202.

Varga, J. 1995. Returns to education in hungary. *Acta Oeconomica* 47 (1/2): 203–215.

Verwimp, P. 1996. Estimating returns to education in Off-Farm activities in rural Ethiopia. *Ethiopian Journal of Economics* 5 (2): 27–56.

Weir, S. 1999. The Effect of Education on Farmer Productivity in Rural Ethiopia. Working Paper. Centre for the Study of African Economies. Oxford University.

Welday, A. 1997. Return to schooling in Ethiopia: the case of the formal sector. *Ethiopian Journal of Economics,* VI(1), 87–104.

Chapter 10
An Analysis of Firm Growth in Ethiopia: An Exploration of High-Growth Firms

Guta Legesse

Abstract This study identifies the incidence of high-growth firms (HGFs) in Ethiopia with their corresponding business obstacles and growth determinants. The research is based on data from the World Bank's Enterprise Survey dataset (World Bank Enterprise Survey. The World Bank, Washington, DC, 2015). The survey covered 848 firms distributed over six major regions in the country—Addis Ababa, Oromia, Amhara, SNNP, Tigray and Dire Dawa. The analysis was done using OLS and QR. HGFs were concentrated in the capital city and in the services sector while medium-sized firms dominated the HGFs. Like non-HGFs, access to finance was the biggest perceived obstacle for HGFs followed by tax rates as compared to the informal sector's activities for non-HGFs. Region-wise, access to finance was the key problem only for firms operating in Addis Ababa and Tigray while the informal sector dominated in Oromia region. In Amhara region, corruption was the most significant obstacle. The econometric estimation results show that firm growth was negatively related to firm size. Growth were associated positively with firms' products and process innovations, resources and firms website. The research fails to show any significant difference among firms' growth based on gender of ownership, competition, capacity utilization and nationality of ownership. The heterogeneity in business obstacles across regions and performance of firms can be taken as important lessons for policy interventions.

Keywords High-growth firms · Business obstacles · Quantile regression

10.1 Introduction

The process of firms' growth has attracted the attention of economists for long. According to Sutton (1997) Robert Gibrat's work was the first formal model dealing with the dynamics of firm size and industry structure. According to Gibrat,

G. Legesse (✉)
Department of Economics, Addis Ababa University, Addis Ababa, Ethiopia
e-mail: gutalegesse@gmail.com

© Springer Nature Singapore Pte Ltd. 2018
A. Heshmati and H. Yoon (eds.), *Economic Growth and Development in Ethiopia*, Perspectives on Development in the Middle East and North Africa (MENA) Region, https://doi.org/10.1007/978-981-10-8126-2_10

the rate of firm growth is independent of its size and is framed as the law of proportionate effect (LPE) (Gibrat 1931, cited in Sutton 1997). This law stipulates that the capacity to grow is the same for all firms, regardless of their initial size. There are several empirical works on this with somewhat inconclusive findings.

Following the well-documented role of entrepreneurial firms in creating employment and generating wealth, more recent studies have turned their attention to the prevalence and determinants of high-growth firms (HGFs) in addition to measurement and definition issues. Researchers have suggested several alternative measures to classify firms as high-growth firms with employment being the most studied output variable although productivity, sales, wages and revenue have also been used as indicators (Daunfeldt et al. 2013a).

Attempts to identify the prevalence of HGFs in different countries and industries have shown that HGFs are only a small percentage of all firms and are found in all countries across all industries. A meta-analysis by Henrekson and Johansson (2010), for instance, fails to show any evidence in support of the view that HGFs are over-represented in high-technology industries. They note that there were more HGFs in service industries relative to sectors such as manufacturing. Daunfeldt et al. (2013a) updated Henrekson and Johansson's (2010) work by incorporating nine additional studies published after 2009 on HGFs. One of their key findings is the significant difference in characteristics of HGFs depending on the growth indicator used and how it is measured. They found that absolute and relative measures of HGFs led to 'most pronounced difference between HGFs' with HGFs defined in relative terms as being younger and smaller than HGFs defined in absolute terms for most of the indicators.

Further, understanding the persistence and incidence of HGFs has become an important task for policymakers as better insights into the existence, characteristics and stimulating factors of high-growth firms could be a key breakthrough in sustainable economic growth. The shareholders are concerned about knowing what stimulates the growth of their firm while for policymakers it is the issue of sustaining firm growth and capitalizing on the incidence of HGFs.

A new research initiative has been undertaken to know if HGFs can be sustained. The aim of this initiative is to find out if firm growth can be sustained for a long period of time and whether firm growth is a random process. The initiative also seeks to find out whether the probability of repeating high-growth rates was high. We know that governments spend considerable amounts of money to support specific types of firms based on either size and/or industry type to encourage them to grow. It is difficult to target policies towards certain groups of firms if growth is unsustainable. A dominant empirical work in this regard is by Daunfeldt and Halvarsson (2014) who argue that high-growth firms are one hit wonders and the probability of repeating high-growth rates is very low. Despite such findings, the role played by HGFs is well documented.

Studies have shown that high-growth firms play an important role in creating jobs and fostering innovative behavior. Bravo-Biosca (2010), for instance, shows that a small number of high-growth firms accounted for a disproportionate 35–50%

of all jobs created by all firms with ten or more employees in a large number of countries that they considered.

The role of business environment in deterring firm performance is not well-studied. Firms have heterogeneous abilities and entrepreneurs could perceive environmental challenges differently. For firms operating in different regions and sectors, the effects of the obstacles could vary and this is another dimension of our study.

The purpose of our study is to provide an insight into the incidence of HGFs in Ethiopia by firm characteristics (such as size, age, location, ownership and industry type). Further, our study also explores perceived obstacles in a firm's performance and the firm's growth determinants.

In general, HGFs have attracted considerable attention from researchers, policymakers and practitioners. Our research adds to literature by investigating the incidence of high-growth firms and business obstacles by region, industry type and the relationship between size and growth using the Enterprise Survey (ES) database on Ethiopia. Ours is perhaps the first research of its kind in Ethiopia.

10.2 Literature Review

Firms have long been recognized as one of the determinants of economic growth and the factors affecting their performance have attracted lots of researchers among which Robert Gibrat's work is recognized as the first formal model dealing with the dynamics of firm size and industry structure (Sutton 1997). His work has been called Gibrat's Law which states that the rate of a firm's growth is independent of its size although empirical studies conducted later have predominantly rejected this.

Firm growth is viewed as a result of continuous discovery and use of productive knowledge which requires an institutional framework that determines the incentives to acquire and utilize knowledge (Henrekson and Johansson 2010).

10.2.1 The Role and Prevalence of High-Growth Firms

There is an increased interest among academicians and policymakers in the prevalence of HGFs in an economy. Some of the questions that they have tried to address include size, age, industry type and region of HGFs.

The role of HGFs in the job creation process has been examined in a number of empirical studies most of which have showed that job creation is accounted for by a few firms. Several recent researchers have verified the role played by HGFs in job creation (Acs et al. 2008; Anyadike-Danes et al. 2013; Autio et al. 2000; Coad et al. 2014; Davidsson and Henrekson 2002; Daunfeldt et al. 2013b; Delmar et al. 2003; Henrekson and Johansson 2010; Moreno and Coad 2015; Nesta 2009; Schreyer 2000; Storey 1994).

Coad et al. (2014), for instance, presents HGFs' disproportionate job creating role as a stylized fact. Daunfeldt et al. (2013b) show that 6% of the fastest growing firms in the Swedish economy contributed 42% of the jobs in Sweden during 2005–08. Nesta (2009) documents that 6% HGFs in UK generated 49.5% of all new jobs created by operational firms in UK during 2002–08 while Storey (1994) found that 4% firms created 50% of the jobs. Although the roles of HGFs may depend on how they are measured, Daunfeldt et al. (2013a) found that they play a key role in the economy as sources of economic growth, employment growth and sales and productivity growth.

10.2.2 Determinants of Firm Growth

Several researches have been done to address the question of what determines firm growth. Moreno and Coad (2015) give two types of theoretical explanations of the determinants of firm growth where one relates to dynamic strategic choices within the firm while the other considers growth as purely random. Other recent studies have tried to classify determinants of firm growth as firm size, firm age, firm innovation and capabilities, entrepreneurship characteristics and resources.

Proponents of the strategic choice theory argue that a firm's output will depend on the owner's behavior, which is determined by knowledge, skills and ability to access and capitalize on key resources. This theory relates to the contribution of human capital in the form of formal education and experience (industry, managerial and/or prior business experience). The theory proposes that human capital and firm resources together with entrepreneur-specific capabilities allow some entrepreneurs to enter profitable niches and enjoy sustained superior performance compared to others (Moreno and Coad 2015). According to this explanation, HGFs can be seen as skilled firms with the ability to identify entrepreneurial opportunities to create a competitive advantage.

The second argument about determinant of firm growth argues that growth is a product of random events. It argues that patterns that are identified in stochastic methods are confused and used to fit a specific theory of convenience. Hence, it argues that it would be difficult to fully understand the systematic drivers of sustained superior performance unless the effect of randomness is known in a large population of firms (Henderson et al. 2012).

10.2.3 Business Environment and Firm Performance

Policymakers and entrepreneurs have also been interested in the role of a business environment for firm growth and improved performance. The World Bank's publication Doing Business has been widely used to give a general picture about the business environment in an economy and policymakers have been advocating reforms that will improve their country's ranking.

Nguimkeu (2013) investigated the main barriers of doing business in Cameroon using 2009 ES data on retailing firms. His findings show that taxation, illicit trade, lack of infrastructure, lack of access to credit, administrative delays and an incompetent labor were the major obstacles for retailing firms in Cameroon. Using a structural econometric analysis, the author shows that factors related to the business climate reduced domestic traders' annual gross margins significantly.

Using their study on the prevalence and determinants of high-growth enterprises in 11 SSA countries, Goedhuys and Sleuwaegen (2009) show that electricity and access to finance were the major constraints in all surveyed countries among the listed elements of a business environment.

Hallward-Driemeir and Aterido (2007) did a comprehensive study on the role of business environment in sub-Saharan Africa relative to the rest of the developing world using the World Bank's ES data for 2001. They found that employment growth in the region was relatively concentrated in the smallest firms. According to their findings, medium and large firms grew less rapidly as compared to other parts of the world. This could be due to the fact that firms in Africa faced greater challenges in accessing finance, reliable infrastructure services and other public services deemed crucial for growth which may have hindered the growth of large firms relative to small firms.

10.3   Methods

10.3.1   Defining and Measuring High-Growth Firms

It is difficult to do an analysis of the prevalence and determinants of HGFs without setting out working definitions of HGFs. Several approaches have been used for this although the following four and their derivatives are widely used in literature:

 i. Top 1 or 5% firms in terms of revenue, employment, profit and labor productivity as measured in growth rates, absolute change, log changes, index etc.
 ii. Firms with 20 or more employees for the period under investigation (Autio 2007).
 iii. Firms with annualized growth rates of at least 20% over a 3-year period and at least ten employees (Eurostat-OECD 2007).
 iv. Establishments which have achieved a minimum of 20% sales growth each year over the interval starting from a base-year revenue of at least $100,000 (Birch 1987).

In literature earlier estimates of high-growth firms defined HGFs as the share of firms with the highest growth during a particular period, for instance, the 1 or 5% of firms with the highest growth rate. The problem with this approach is it is difficult to create consistent time series data of high-growth firms because the threshold that defines the top firms is higher during the expansion phase of the business cycle than during the contraction phase. It is also inconvenient to compare the share of HGFs across time or across countries.

Later, Birch's original proposition was dropped and a new index called the Birch Index was introduced as an alternative measure of firm growth (Coad et al. 2014; Hölzl 2011; Schreyer 2000). The Birch Index corrects the inherent bias of using absolute and relative measures of growth since several studies have documented that small firms exhibit larger relative growth rates of employment while bigger firms show larger absolute growth rates. The Birch Index considers both the relative and absolute employment growth rates and is based on a multiplicative combination of the absolute growth rate and the relative growth rate. The value of this index for our study is calculated as (Coad et al. 2014; Hölzl 2011):

$$\text{BI} = [\text{Employ}'\, t\, 2014 - \text{Employ}'\, t\, 2010][\frac{\text{Employ}'\, t\, 2014}{\text{Employ}'\, t\, 2010}] \quad (10.1)$$

Under this index, firms can be classified as HGFs by deciding on the cut-off point to be used like firms with BI values of top 1, 5 and 10%. Some studies define 10% of the firms with the highest Birch Index as high-growth firms (Lopez-Garcia and Puente 2012; Schreyer 2000).

For our study although we can use one or a combination of these approaches, customizing the criteria is required due to availability of data and the economic situation of the country under investigation. Application of the GEM approach does not show firms' potential for growth since it ignores the number of years required to reach the threshold employment level. On the other hand, threshold levels of growth rates and initial employment recommended by OECD need to be adjusted by considering that there are limited numbers of entrepreneurial firms in Ethiopia. According to Daunfeldt et al. (2013a, b) findings the OECD criteria will exclude close to 95% of all surviving firms in Sweden over the period 2005–08 and about 40% of all created private jobs. Similarly, based on the ES data for Ethiopia, the standard Eurostat-OECD definition of HGFs will exclude more than 95% of the firms in the sample.

Based on Goedhuys and Sleuwaegen (2009), the threshold level of the initial size of firms was at least five employees and the growth rate is calculated for four years owing to data availability problem from 2010 to 2014 while the threshold is set to be a minimum of 10% average growth rate per annum. Accordingly, high-growth firms are firms with annualized growth rate in excess of 10% over the period 2010–14 and with at least five employees in 2010.

In our study, owing to the low incidence of HGFs in Ethiopia and in order to generate comparable number of HGFs to the Eurostat-OECD for the Birch Index measure of HGFs, we used the top 20% firms.

The World Bank's ES reports sales data for all firms only for two years (2012 and 2014) leading to too narrow a measurement of firm growth in terms of sales. Therefore, we ignore growth of an establishment measured by sales growth as the survey does not report sales data for 2010.

Using the relative measure of growth, 137 firms were classified as HGFs while there were only 109 HGFs using BI. The number of HGFs further decreased to 86 and 56 if one adopted the top 15 and 10% cut-off points in BI. Like Eurostat-OECD, a 10% cut-off point on BI will exclude 90% of the sample firms.

In our analysis, we selected fast-growing firms with the modified Eurostat-OECD definition as HGFs and firms selected on the basis of the modified Birch Index as BHGF.

10.3.2   Measuring Business Obstacles

The questionnaire gives two groups of questions on business obstacles. The first group asks about the severity of an obstacle in a Likert scale question format by listing each obstacle separately. Establishments are asked to express their perceptions about the magnitude of the obstacle caused by elements of the business environment with a 0 score implying that it is not an obstacle and a score of 5 implying that it is a very severe obstacle. The second type of questions ask firms to select the single most important obstacle among a list of possible challenges. In the second approach, firms are expected to compare obstacles and select the one they believe to be the biggest obstacle relative to all listed obstacles while in the first approach they are exposed to one challenge at a time and asked to state if it is an obstacle or not.

Since the sampling design for the World Bank Enterprise Survey is a stratified random sampling, individual observations should be properly weighted when making inferences about the population. Under stratified random sampling, unweighted estimates are biased unless sample sizes are proportional to the size of each stratum. This is important because individual observations may not represent equal shares of the population.

To identify key business obstacles, our analysis is based on the percentage of firms that reported the listed elements as a major or severe obstacle (score of 3 or 4) from the first group of questions. To identify the most important perceived obstacles among the given list of challenges, the frequency with which a given obstacle was selected by firms as its biggest obstacle was computed.

10.3.3   Modeling Determinants of Firm Growth

We used both descriptive and econometric techniques in our data analysis. The descriptive analysis was used to explore the distribution of HGFs in Ethiopia using firm characteristics and other relevant factors.

Although several researchers have modeled the determinants of firm growth differently, the empirical model for our research is based on Goedhuys and Sleuwaegen (2009) who modeled firm growth as a function of firm age and size after controlling for other relevant factors which they classified into three major categories as firm characteristics, technological characteristics and firm resources. Firm characteristics refer to variables such as firm age and size, sex of the entrepreneur and education levels of the top management while resources refer to firm level resources to deal with constraints arising from poor infrastructure, insecurities and financial constraints. Further, we used the nature of a firm concerning export status, licensing technology from foreign-owned companies, ownership of a website and delivery of training as a proxy for a firm's technological characteristics.

Owing to poor data availability and the high rate of non-responses in some of these variables, some of these characteristics were dropped and other new variables were included (see Eq. 10.4 for the model):

$$
\text{Firm growth} = \text{f(firm age, firm size \& firm resources, technological \&} \\ \text{market characteristics \& other dummies)} \tag{10.2}
$$

$$
\begin{aligned}
\text{GROWTH4} = {}& a_0 + a_1(\text{Employment 2010}) + a_2(\text{Employment 2010})^2 \\
& + a_3(\text{Firm age}) + a_4(\text{Firm age})^2 + a_5(\text{Employment 2010}) * (\text{Firm age}) \\
& + \sum b(\text{Entrepreneur characteristics}) + \sum c(\text{Technological \& Market characteristics}) \\
& + \sum d(\text{Resources}) + \sum f(\text{Industry dummies}) + \varepsilon_i
\end{aligned}
$$

$$(10.3)$$

Given that there are several approaches for measuring HGFs we used the two most frequently used ones. These are the modified Eurostat-OECD definition and the modified Birch Index.

To measure firm growth using the modified Eurostat-OECD definition we used the logarithmic difference in the number of employees over a 4-year period:

$$
\text{GROWTH4} = \ln(S_{i,2014}) - \ln(S_{i,2010}) \tag{10.4}
$$

where, GROWTH4 is the growth rate for firm i, and $S_{i,2014}$ and $S_{i,2010}$ are firm sizes measured by the number of employees in 2014 and 2010 respectively.

We prefer quantile regression (QR) to OLS for estimating the results because OLS estimates how the mean of the (conditional) distribution of firm growth rates changes systematically with its covariates assuming a well-shaped normal distribution of growth around the mean. In other words, it provides the marginal effect of the explanatory variables at the mean of the growth distribution (Goedhuys and Sleuwaegen 2009).

QR, on the other hand, estimates the effects of the different explanatory variables at different quantiles of the growth distribution. Since the HGFs are located in the extreme tail of the conditional growth distributions, factors that affect the upper deciles can be considered as factors that generate a significant number of high-growth firms. Using quantile regression avoids regression to the mean and shows the marginal effects at various deciles of growth distribution.

10.4 Data

10.4.1 Data Source

Our research is based on the World Bank's Enterprise Survey (ES) data on Ethiopia for 2015 which was a sample survey conducted using stratified random sampling with industry, establishment size and region representing the three levels of stratification. The survey covered 848 firms including micro, small, medium and large firms. For our study the 26 micro firms were excluded owing to their insufficient representation with the result that we had 822 firms. Further cleaning of the data by considering firms with positive employment history in 2010 (to calculate growth rates over four years), dropping firms with no/error response to employment size and defining outliers in employment data as observations that were more than three standard deviations away from the mean in 2014 to purge out the effects of a few outliers left us with 547 firms. After removing the outliers, nearly 97% of the enterprises had 5–290 employees.

A number of questions were asked in the questionnaire to capture important dimensions of a firm's performance, infrastructure availability and business obstacles. The questionnaire has 14 major components with relevant sub-sections for each. It starts by getting control information (biography) on firm size, size of locality, industry classification and region of operations. The general information section asks questions related to ownership type and sex of the top manager while the next section asks questions related to infrastructure and services. Questions related to sales and supplies, degree of competition, innovation, capacity utilization, land and permits, incidence and cost of crimes, sources of finance, business-government relations, labor, business environment and firm performance are all integral part of the questionnaire. The questionnaire distributed to manufacturing firms and service sectors had comparable contents with some minor differences.

The survey covered firms operating in the six major geographic regions in the country—Addis Ababa, Oromia, Amhara, SNNP, Tigray and Dire Dawa—while the size stratification was defined as small if the employment was between 5 and 19 employees, medium if employment was between 20 and 99 employees and large if a firm had more than 99 employees. Half of the sample firms were operational in Addis Ababa with Oromia and Tigray hosting 15% of the sampled firms each. Dire Dawa represented the smallest number of firms while Amhara and SNNP accounted for about 8% of the sampled firms each.

The survey was conducted for all categories of businesses. Two questionnaires were used in the survey (one for manufacturing and the other for the services sector) with common questions (core module) and additional questions to capture sector specific issues. The distribution of the sample by industry classification shows that the highest number of enterprises were in wholesale (16%) followed by the food industry (11%). The retail trade sector accounted for the third highest number of firms in the sample (11%). In terms of gross classification in services and manufacturing, 56% of the firms were from the services sector while the remaining

Table 10.1 Distribution of the sample establishments by region and size

Sampling region	Screener size			
	Small	Medium	Large	Total
Addis Ababa	101	117	58	276
Amhara	24	17	4	45
Dire Dawa	8	6	2	16
Oromia	54	14	16	84
SNNP	26	13	4	43
Tigray	64	16	3	83
Total	277	183	87	547

Source The World Bank Enterprise Survey (2015)

44% were from the manufacturing sector. Small firms accounted for just over half (51%) while the remaining half was accounted for by medium (33%) and large (16%) firms (Tables 10.1 and 10.2).

10.5 Empirical Results

10.5.1 The Prevalence of HGFs

Using the two measures we identified two cohorts of HGFs. The Eurostat-OECD classified 137 firms as HGFs while from BI there were 109 HGFs. Compared to BI, the Eurostat-OECD measure identified 25% of the surveyed firms as HGFs while the BI showed that 20% of the firms can be considered as HGFs in Ethiopia (Table 10.3). The relaxation of assumptions in the Eurostat-OECD measure could lead to different levels and types of HGFs. Using the standard Eurostat-OECD definition of a 20% annualized growth rate and a minimum of ten employees at the start of the study period, only 6% of the sampled firms were HGFs. These results are consistent with Petersen and Ahmad (2007), Goedhuys and Sleuwaegen (2009).

Irrespective of the type of measurement, 369 firms (over two-third of the establishments) were non-HGFs. On the other hand, more than 50% of the HGFs identified through the relative criteria remained HGFs when evaluated using the Birch Index while 86% of the HGFs identified using the Birch Index remained in the same category when the Eurostat-OECD measure was used. This result is consistent with previous research findings which show that different HGF measures lead to different firms being selected as high-growth firms.

The two cohorts of HGFs identified in Ethiopia in our study had similar features. In terms of age, for example, the mean age was around 12 years compared to the mean age of the non-HGFs which was close to 15 years (14 years for all the firms). Under both the measures, HGFs were found to be younger by 3 years on average than non-HGFs. Concerning ownership structure, the Eurostat-OECD measure identified around 53% HGFs as the sole ownership type while 25% were

Table 10.2 Distribution of the sample by industry and firm size

Industry screener	Screener size			
	Small	Medium	Large	Total
Food	19	26	19	64
Textiles	1	1	4	6
Garments	11	7	1	19
Leather	4	4	5	13
Wood	1	3	2	6
Paper	0	1	1	2
Publishing, printing	4	13	2	19
Chemicals	1	1	3	5
Plastic and rubber	1	10	8	19
Non-metallic minerals	24	12	2	38
Basic metals	3	4	1	8
Fabricated metal prods	6	5	1	12
Machinery and equipment	3	0	1	4
Electronics (31 and 32)	0	1	0	1
Precision instruments	1	1	0	2
Transport machines (3)	1	2	1	4
Furniture	12	5	3	20
Construction section	12	13	5	30
Services for motor vehicles	17	11	3	31
Wholesale	48	29	10	87
Retail	49	8	5	62
Hotels and restaurants	28	16	6	50
Transport section I	29	9	4	42
It	2	1	0	3
Total	277	183	87	547

Source The World Bank Enterprise Survey (2015)

operational under the limited partnership form of ownership. The Birch Index, on the other hand, showed that 70% of the BHGFs were sole ownership and limited partnerships with each contributing half of the proportion. All these results were found to be statistically significant. The search for gazelles, firms which were HGFs and younger than 5 years was unsuccessful as there were no such firms in the economy (Table 10.4).

Persistence of high-growth firms was not studied due to data problems. Since most of the firms in Ethiopia are small sized firms, there is a high tendency for firms to fall below the threshold level of employment. Ayenew (2015) study based on CSA data of large and medium sized manufacturing firms showed that on average 22% of the firms were new entrants while 19% of them left the category in the same year with the exit level reaching as high as 46%. This makes it difficult to analyze persistent of HGFs.

Table 10.3 Comparison of high-growth firms by measurement type (%)

HGF	BHGF		
	0	1	Total
0	67.45	2.72	70.17
1	13.04	16.79	29.83
Total	80.49	19.51	100

Source The World Bank Enterprise Survey (2015)

Table 10.4 Distribution of HGFs by sector and by growth measures

Distribution of HGFs by sector and by growth measure			
Sector	Industry screener sector	Proportion of HGFs (%)	Proportion of BHGFs (%)
Services sector	Services of motor vehicles (G)	26.92	22.13
	Construction section (F)	20.57	21.60
	Wholesale (G)	19.08	29.10
	Retail (G)	15.07	3.42
	Transport section I: (60–64)	6.48	5.49
	Hotels and restaurants (H)	5.30	5.00
	Sub-total	93.41	86.75
Manufacturing sector	Non-metallic mineral products (D)	1.71	2.25
	Food products and beverages (D)	1.32	4.01
	Plastics and rubber (D)	1.04	1.97
	Sub-total	4.07	8.23
The rest of the sectors		2.50	5.02

Source The World Bank Enterprise Survey (2015)

Looking at industry type, the two measures refer to nearly the same types of firms where the services sector is over-represented in the HGF classification with a share of over 90 and 85% under the Eurostat-OECD and Birch Index measures respectively. The Eurostat-OECD measure shows that services in motor vehicles (section G) had the highest incidence of HGFs (around 27%) followed by the construction sector (around 21%) with both belonging to the services sector while under BI, wholesale businesses represented the highest incidence of HGFs (29%) followed by services in motor vehicles (section G) at 22% of BHGFs. Under the two measures, services in motor vehicles, wholesale businesses and the construction sector represented the top-3 dominant sources of HGFs. In the manufacturing sector, only food, non-metallic mineral products and plastics and rubber accounted for a noticeable proportion of HGFs as they accounted for 4% of the HGFs using the Eurostat-OECD measure while the percentage doubled to 8% using BI. The domination of HGFs in the services sector in Ethiopia is consistent with the findings

Table 10.5 Distribution of HGFs by firm size and by growth measures

Size screener	Proportion of HGFs using Eurostat-OECD measure (%)	Proportion of HGFs using BI score (%)
Small	9.46	0.78
Medium	17.93	14.74
Large	2.44	3.99
Total	29.83	19.51

Source The World Bank Enterprise Survey (2015)

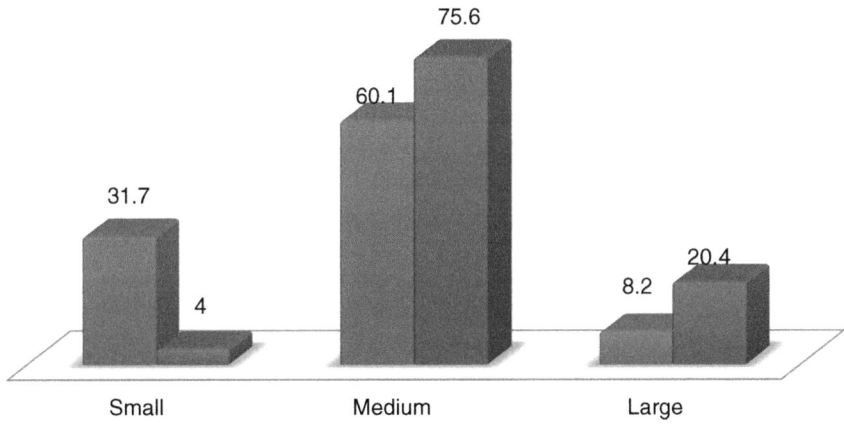

Fig. 10.1 Incidence of HGFs by firm size

of Henrekson and Johansson (2010) who did a meta-analysis of the role of HGFs. The incidence of high-growth firms in the manufacturing sector was very low in Ethiopia with only 4–8% of the HGFs in this sector (Table 10.5; Fig. 10.1).

Coming to the size of firms, both the measures showed somewhat similar cohorts of HGFs since medium sized firms (with 20–99 employees) dominated the proportion of HGFs. Under the Eurostat-OECD measure they constituted 60% of the HGFs while in BI they accounted for 75.5% of the HGFs. The essential difference between the two measures is that the Eurostat-OECD measure showed that the incidence of HGFs tended to be the least for large firms (only 2.4%) while it was the least in small firms under BI (less than 1%). This finding could be due to the inherent bias of relative growth measures such as the Eurostat-OECD measure towards small firms while BI controls for such a bias (Coad et al. 2014; Hölzl 2011).

Table 10.6 Distribution of HGFs by region and by growth measures

HGFs in Ethiopia by firm, region and measurement type		
Sampling region	Percent of HGFs (%)	Percent of BHGFs (%)
Addis Ababa	93.9	89.9
Amhara	0.6	1.5
Dire Dawa	0.2	0.2
Oromia	2.4	4.5
SNNP	1.3	2.7
Tigray	1.6	1.5
Total	100.0	100

Source The World Bank Enterprise Survey (2015)

Another indicator of the prevalence of HGFs that we used is their regional distribution. Nearly all the HGFs were concentrated in Addis Ababa regardless of the type of measurement used (over 90%) while Oromia region was the second largest host of HGFs (around 4.5%) under BI and 2.4% under the Eurostat-OECD measure. The regions showed a higher share of HGFs when BI was used relative to the Eurostat-OECD measure. This result is not surprising as Addis Ababa accounted for over 80% of the sampled establishments with a significant percentage of them being medium sized firms (35%) with high incidence of HGFs in the survey; the differences were found to be statistically significant (Table 10.6).

Table 10.7 gives average statistics on firm performance for the two cohorts of firms. It shows that HGFs had a growth rate which, on average, was three times that of non-HGFs under the two measures. HGFs also showed a higher number of employees on average with nearly twice the number of employees as the non-HGFs using BI. They also had a higher proportion of export engagement and a significantly large proportion of firms were owned by foreigners.

10.5.2 Perceived Business Obstacles by Establishments

An analysis of business obstacles was done based on the two inter-related groups of questions asked in the questionnaire. Measuring the proportion of firms that reported the business environment as a major obstacle or a very severe obstacle, 33% of all the firms reported supply of electricity as a major or severe obstacle making it the top obstacle in doing business followed by corruption and tax rates. Corruption was perceived to be a top obstacle by around 29% of the establishments while 28% of them ranked tax rates either as a major or very severe obstacle. Problems related to tax administration and informal sector competition were found to be the 4th and 5th major or severe obstacle to doing business in Ethiopia. Hence, tax rates and their administration posed a severe threat to doing business. Figure 10.2 gives details of the perceived obstacles by firms.

Table 10.7 Descriptive statistics (average values) in 2014 for HGFs and non-HGFs

Static	HGFs in terms of Eurostat-OECD	Non-HGFs in terms of Eurostat-OECD	HGFs measured as top 20% on BI score (i.e. BHGF)	Non-HGFs measured using BI score
Employee growth in 2010–14 (%)	22.3	7.2	26.5	8.1
Sales growth in 2012–14 (%)	12.4	13.5	18.5	12
Firm size	11 employees	9 employees	17 employees	9 employees
R&D engagement (%)	4.8	2.6	6.5	2.5
Export engagement (%)	4.5	2.6	6.5	2.5
Innovation activity (%)	45	55	32.5	67.5
Domestic ownership (%)	27.6	72.4	15.9	84.1
Foreign ownership (%)	60.5	39.5	70.5	29.5
Female ownership (%)	38	62	20.8	79.2

Source The World Bank Enterprise Survey (2015)

The World Bank Enterprise Survey which covers 139 countries and over 125,000 firms (The World Bank 2015) presents an excellent opportunity to do a global comparison of the business environments in which firms operate. Figure 10.3 gives the global picture of business obstacles that firms believe hinder their growth. It locates Ethiopia close to the center next to the high-income OECD countries using most of the indicators which shows that firms in Ethiopia work under a better environment relative to most of the countries surveyed. For example, compared to SSA, Ethiopia was better in nearly all the indicators.

Further, the Bank also asks establishments to identify the biggest obstacle among a given list of 15 obstacles. Over 40% of the establishments selected access to finance as the number one problem while customs and trade regulations and electricity supply were rated as the biggest obstacle by 12 and 10% of the establishments respectively. Tax administration and the practices of the informal sector were reported as the biggest obstacles by approximately 8 and 6% of the establishments respectively. Figure 10.4 gives the details.

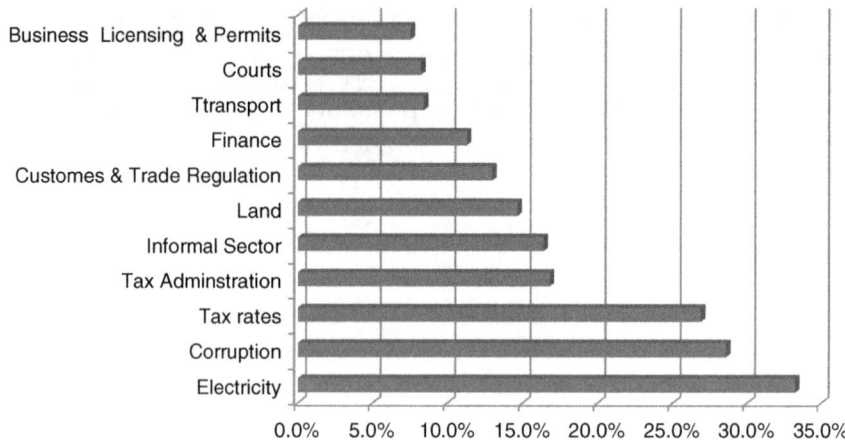

Fig. 10.2 Percentage of firms reporting business obstacles as a major or very severe obstacle. *Source* The World Bank Enterprise Survey (2015)

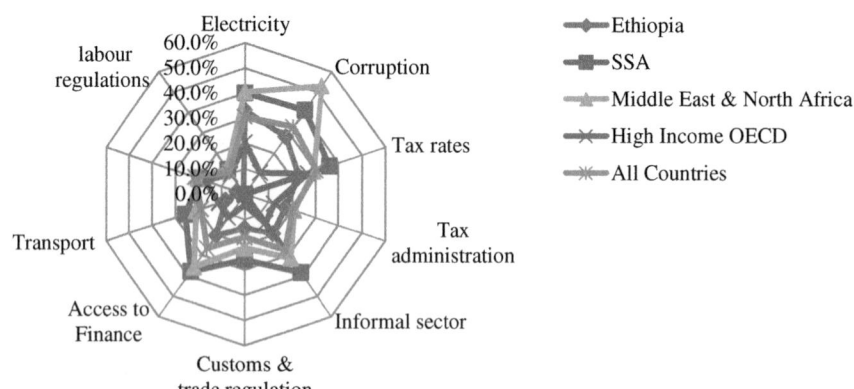

Fig. 10.3 Global picture of perception about business obstacles by firms. *Source* The World Bank Enterprise Survey (2015)

Taken together, the two types of questions reveal that access to finance and shortage of electricity were the two most important obstacles which were followed by customs and trade regulations and corruption with tax rates emerging as other important obstacles.

A decomposition of the analysis on the biggest obstacles using firm growth achievements shows that perceived business obstacles were not the same for the two cohorts of firms. Access to finance was perceived as the biggest obstacle by both cohorts of firms with the problem being more severe for non-HGFs. For HGFs, tax rates and customs and trade regulations represent the 2nd and 3rd biggest obstacles while electricity and corruption completed the list of the top-5obstacles.

Business Environment (biggest obstacle among the list in %)

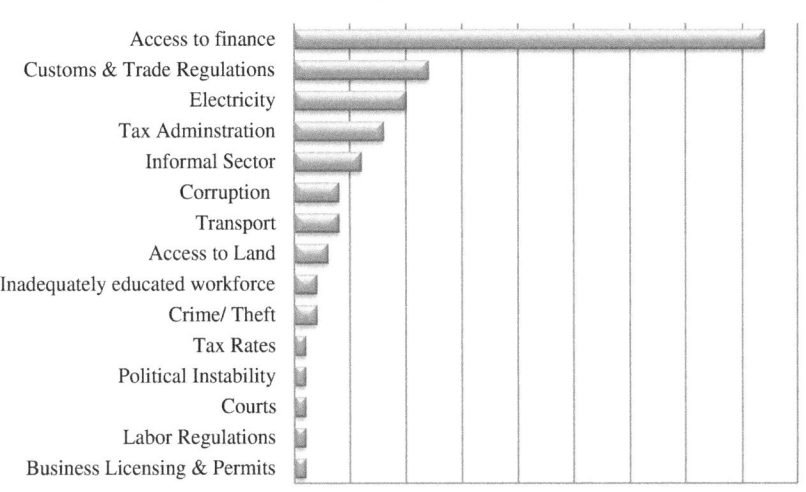

Fig. 10.4 Single most important obstacle to doing business in Ethiopia (%). *Source* The World Bank Enterprise Survey (2015)

For non-HGFs, informal sector, electricity, tax administration and customs and trade regulations were among the top-5obstacles in order of importance (see Fig. 10.5 for details). These findings show that access to finance was the dominant challenge affecting a significant number of firms irrespective of their nature of

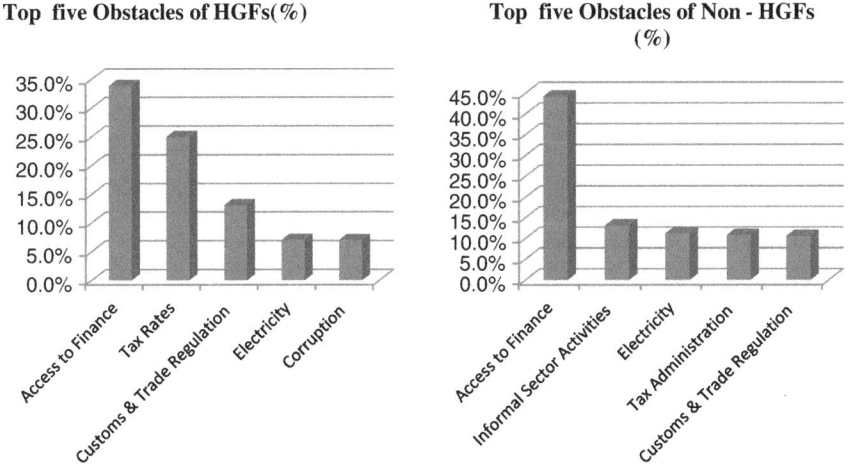

Fig. 10.5 Top-five obstacles in Ethiopia by firm growth category. *Source* The World Bank Enterprise Survey (2015)

growth. The differences in perceived obstacles by the two groups of firms was tested using Chi-2 test of independence and the results confirm the presence of statistically significant differences at the 5% significance level.

An analysis of business obstacles using region of operation as a reference point reveals that there was a systematic difference among regions (Fig. 10.6). Looking at these problems from a regional perspective, firms operating in different regions perceived different obstacles and these differences were found to be statistically significant. For example, 45% of the firms in Addis Ababa believed that the biggest obstacle was access to finance while only 21% firms operating in Oromia considered finance as the biggest obstacle and it was not reported in the list of top-3 problems for firms operating in the Amhara region and SNNP. For firms in these regions, corruption topped the list in Amhara while electricity was reported as the biggest obstacle in SNNP. Establishments in Oromia reported informal sector activities as their biggest obstacle (29%) while those operating in Tigray reported finance as a key problem (42%). The implication of this finding is that regions should take into account these differences when improving their business environments.

Regrouping the obstacles into five major categories (Fig. 10.7), as infrastructure (comprising of electricity and transport), access to finance, institutions (composed of business licensing and permits, labor regulations, crime/theft, courts, customs and trade regulations, corruption, tax administration, tax rates and the informal sector), access to land and other obstacles including political instability and an inadequately educated workforce generated three dominant obstacles. According to this classification, institutions were the second biggest obstacle with 34% of the establishments reporting it as the biggest obstacle next to finance (42%). Further,

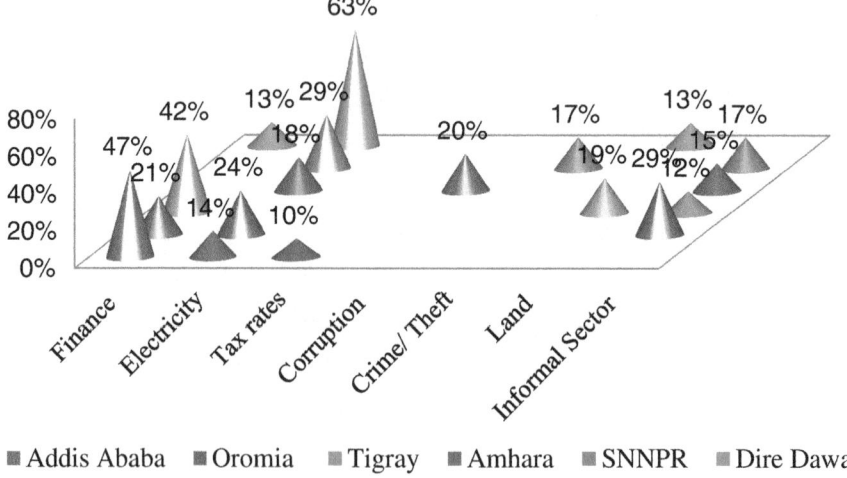

Fig. 10.6 Top business obstacles by region of establishment. *Source* The World Bank Enterprise Survey (2015)

Key business obstacles faced by firms (%)

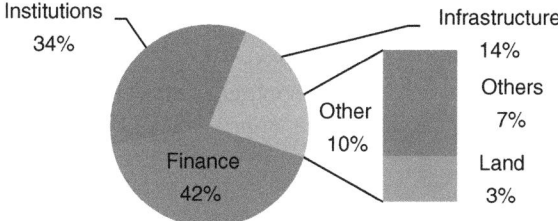

Fig. 10.7 Top business obstacles classified into five major segments. *Source* The World Bank Enterprise Survey (2015)

14% of the firms reported infrastructure as the biggest obstacle with these three obstacles being reported by nearly 90% of the establishments.

10.5.3   A Test of Gibrat's Law

Gibrat's Law of proportionate effect proposes that firm growth is independent of its size. This law can be easily tested by plotting the log size of a firm at a point. In Fig. 10.8, the normal line is presented by the dashed line while the unbroken line represents the kernel density curve. Looking at Fig. 10.8, the natural logarithm of size does not follow a normal distribution. The distribution has a peak around 8 employees and is skewed to the right. This is indirect proof against the law because small firms (as presented by the high density around 8 employees) grew faster than their medium and large counterparts.

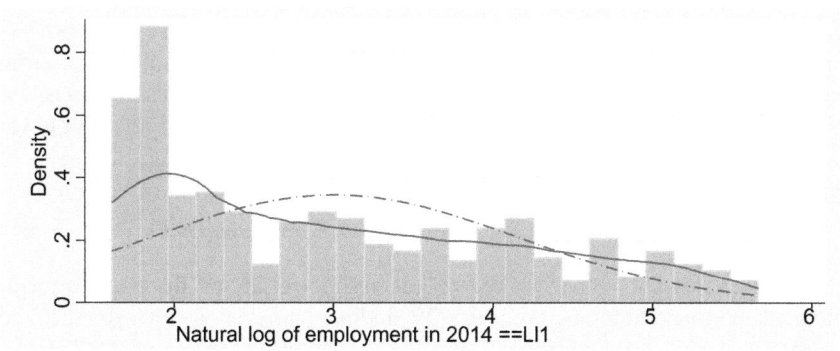

Fig. 10.8 Log normality plot of firm size using number of employees in 2014. *Source* The World Bank Enterprise Survey (2015)

10.5.4 An Econometrics Analysis

We did an econometric estimation using OLS and QR and the results are given in Table 10.8. The first column gives the results of the OLS estimation while columns 2–10 give the QR results which show the marginal effects at various deciles of the distribution. The reference group consists of firms in Addis Ababa active in hotels and restaurants solely owned by male domestic entrepreneurs.

An analysis of the results from the OLS estimation shows that firm growth was negatively related to firm size and positively related to the squared term. The average marginal effect was found to be negative and significant implying a convex relationship between size and firm growth. The QR results also support the OLS estimation. From QR, the size effect was highly significant and negatively related to firm growth at each decile. The negative relationship shown here suggests that small firms grew faster than larger firms and this result is consistent with many global studies on the nexus between firm size and growth. The log normality plot of firm size introduced earlier is also in line with this finding. Using CSA data on Ethiopian manufacturing firms, Bigsten and Gebreeyesus (2007) found similar results.

Our analysis shows that there was a negative and convex relationship between age and growth under the OLS estimation. QR also shows a similar relationship between the two but the relationship was found to be significant only at the 60th, 70th and 80th growth deciles. For HGFs which would normally be located in the 90th decile, age was no more significant.

Other important variables of interest in the analysis are the role played by the gender and nationality of the owners of the establishments on firm growth. From the OLS regression, there was no statistically significant difference in the growth of firms based on the gender and nationality of the owner. This result is generally the same when evaluated using QR except for the 30th and 40th growth deciles for which female ownership had a statistically significant negative effect on growth at the conventional significance level.

Concerning technological and market factors that were hypothesized to determine growth, the OLS regression showed that firm level product and process innovations and ownership of a website had a positive and significant effect on firm growth. A unit increase in ownership of a website or product innovation led to 4% point increase in employment while the effect of process innovation was a bit lower (close to 3% points). Other explanatory variables in this category such as degree of competition, experience of the top management, training, degree of capacity utilization and export engagement were found to have an insignificant effect on firm growth.

An analysis of QR conveys more or less similar results on the effect of technological and market factors. From the QR findings, innovation (both product and process) positively and significantly affected growth at all deciles of the distribution. Both process innovation and product innovation could contribute a maximum of a 5% point increase in firm growth. Previous export engagement had a positive and significant effect on firms in the 90th decile. For most of the growth

Table 10.8 OLS and QR estimation results

Variables	OLS	QR10	QR20	QR30	QR40	QR50	QR60	QR70	QR80	QR90
Size	-0.152***	-0.130***	-0.146***	-0.146***	-0.156***	-0.156***	-0.161***	-0.159***	-0.157***	-0.133***
	(0.016)	(0.027)	(0.022)	(0.014)	(0.017)	(0.018)	(0.017)	(0.018)	(0.025)	(0.033)
Size2	0.017***	0.015***	0.016***	0.018***	0.019***	0.020***	0.021***	0.019***	0.017***	0.011*
	(0.003)	(0.005)	(0.004)	(0.002)	(0.003)	(0.003)	(0.003)	(0.003)	(0.005)	(0.006)
Age	-0.005***	-0.002	-0.001	-0.001	-0.000	-0.001	-0.004**	-0.004**	-0.006**	-0.006
	(0.002)	(0.003)	(0.002)	(0.001)	(0.002)	(0.002)	(0.002)	(0.002)	(0.003)	(0.003)
Age2	0.001***	0.001*	0.001	0.001	0.001	0.001	0.001**	0.001**	0.001*	0.001
	(0.000)	(0.000)	(0.000)	(0.000)	(0.000)	(0.000)	(0.000)	(0.000)	(0.000)	(0.000)
Agesize	-0.001	-0.001*	-0.001	-0.001	-0.001	-0.001	-0.001*	-0.001	-0.001	-0.001
	(0.000)	(0.001)	(0.001)	(0.000)	(0.000)	(0.000)	(0.000)	(0.000)	(0.001)	(0.001)
Firm ownership dummies with male as a reference group										
Female	-0.012	-0.001	-0.016	-0.022*	-0.025*	-0.022	-0.017	-0.017	-0.018	0.003
	(0.013)	(0.022)	(0.017)	(0.011)	(0.014)	(0.015)	(0.014)	(0.015)	(0.021)	(0.027)
Foreign	-0.017	0.037	0.029	0.007	-0.001	0.004	-0.013	-0.021	-0.027	-0.007
	(0.018)	(0.030)	(0.023)	(0.015)	(0.019)	(0.020)	(0.019)	(0.020)	(0.028)	(0.036)
Technological and market dummies										
Competition	-0.025	-0.049	-0.036	-0.016	-0.018	-0.029	-0.027	-0.030	-0.001	-0.022
	(0.021)	(0.035)	(0.028)	(0.018)	(0.022)	(0.024)	(0.023)	(0.024)	(0.033)	(0.043)
Capacity	0.013	-0.008	-0.010	0.004	0.003	0.012	0.011	0.002	0.016	0.028
	(0.016)	(0.027)	(0.021)	(0.014)	(0.017)	(0.018)	(0.017)	(0.018)	(0.025)	(0.032)
LEXP	-0.003	0.004	-0.014	-0.018**	-0.019**	-0.015*	-0.010	-0.008	-0.002	-0.009
	(0.008)	(0.013)	(0.011)	(0.007)	(0.008)	(0.009)	(0.008)	(0.009)	(0.012)	(0.016)
DEXPO	-0.027	-0.013	-0.038	-0.038**	-0.033*	-0.036*	-0.048**	-0.048**	-0.020	0.100***
	(0.019)	(0.031)	(0.025)	(0.016)	(0.020)	(0.021)	(0.020)	(0.021)	(0.029)	(0.038)

(continued)

Table 10.8 (continued)

Variables	OLS	QR10	QR20	QR30	QR40	QR50	QR60	QR70	QR80	QR90
Train	0.012	0.044*	0.021	0.016	0.009	0.000	0.012	0.012	0.005	0.007
	(0.015)	(0.025)	(0.020)	(0.013)	(0.016)	(0.017)	(0.016)	(0.017)	(0.023)	(0.030)
Web	0.044***	0.037*	0.039**	0.030***	0.033***	0.023*	0.024*	0.044***	0.047**	0.037
	(0.012)	(0.020)	(0.016)	(0.011)	(0.013)	(0.014)	(0.013)	(0.014)	(0.019)	(0.025)
PINNO	0.040***	0.039***	0.026*	0.019*	0.021*	0.030**	0.041***	0.037***	0.039**	0.050**
	(0.011)	(0.019)	(0.015)	(0.010)	(0.012)	(0.013)	(0.012)	(0.013)	(0.018)	(0.023)
PROCINNO	0.029**	0.009	0.040***	0.042***	0.046***	0.032**	0.06**	0.026**	0.025	0.050**
	(0.012)	(0.019)	(0.015)	(0.010)	(0.012)	(0.013)	(0.012)	(0.013)	(0.018)	(0.023)
Resource dummies										
Power	0.022**	−0.012	0.004	0.008	0.006	0.020	0.029**	0.026**	0.027	0.023
	(0.011)	(0.018)	(0.014)	(0.009)	(0.011)	(0.012)	(0.011)	(0.012)	(0.017)	(0.022)
ODRAFT	0.032***	0.018	0.014	0.021**	0.013	0.015	0.011	0.015	0.027	0.061**
	(0.012)	(0.020)	(0.016)	(0.010)	(0.013)	(0.014)	(0.013)	(0.014)	(0.019)	(0.024)
Regional dummies										
AmhD	−0.003	0.016	−0.006	−0.017	−0.004	−0.008	−0.005	0.005	0.019	−0.011
	(0.019)	(0.032)	(0.026)	(0.017)	(0.020)	(0.022)	(0.021)	(0.022)	(0.030)	(0.039)
OroD	−0.038**	−0.037	−0.047**	−0.044***	−0.039**	−0.036**	−0.032**	−0.032*	−0.024	−0.050
	(0.015)	(0.026)	(0.020)	(0.013)	(0.016)	(0.017)	(0.016)	(0.017)	(0.024)	(0.031)
SNNP	−0.045**	−0.001	−0.061**	−0.068***	−0.063***	−0.054**	−0.052**	−0.028	−0.028	−0.034
	(0.020)	(0.034)	(0.027)	(0.018)	(0.021)	(0.023)	(0.022)	(0.023)	(0.031)	(0.041)
TigD	−0.051***	−0.022	−0.041*	−0.047***	−0.043***	−0.055***	−0.050***	−0.051***	−0.048*	−0.048
	(0.016)	(0.026)	(0.021)	(0.014)	(0.016)	(0.018)	(0.017)	(0.018)	(0.024)	(0.032)
DDD	−0.005	−0.002	0.007	0.002	−0.012	−0.010	−0.020	0.016	−0.005	−0.048
	(0.031)	(0.052)	(0.041)	(0.027)	(0.032)	(0.035)	(0.033)	(0.035)	(0.048)	(0.063)

(continued)

Table 10.8 (continued)

Variables	OLS	QR10	QR20	QR30	QR40	QR50	QR60	QR70	QR80	QR90
Ownership dummies (sole ownership is the reference group)										
Share	0.019	0.001	−0.064	−0.069***	−0.040	0.009	0.027	0.022	0.077*	0.046
	(0.03)	(0.050)	(0.040)	(0.026)	(0.031)	(0.034)	(0.032)	(0.034)	(0.047)	(0.060)
Partner	−0.008	−0.017	−0.026	−0.023**	−0.011	−0.003	0.005	0.001	−0.004	−0.010
	(0.013)	(0.021)	(0.017)	(0.011)	(0.013)	(0.014)	(0.014)	(0.014)	(0.020)	(0.026)
Otherowner	−0.021	−0.025	−0.046**	−0.031**	−0.028	−0.028	−0.022	−0.021	−0.023	−0.050
	(0.017)	(0.028)	(0.022)	(0.015)	(0.017)	(0.019)	(0.018)	(0.019)	(0.026)	(0.034)
Industry dummies (hotel and restaurant is the reference group)										
Wholesale	−0.002	−0.039	−0.020	0.003	−0.013	−0.012	0.009	0.019	0.023	0.011
	(0.022)	(0.037)	(0.029)	(0.019)	(0.023)	(0.025)	(0.024)	(0.025)	(0.034)	(0.045)
Food	0.029	0.031	0.024	0.020	0.010	0.012	0.027	0.042	0.031	0.044
	(0.030)	(0.050)	(0.039)	(0.026)	(0.031)	(0.034)	(0.032)	(0.034)	(0.046)	(0.060)
Retail	−0.030	−0.039	−0.019	−0.014	−0.037	−0.039	−0.022	−0.024	−0.034	−0.011
	(0.023)	(0.039)	(0.030)	(0.020)	(0.024)	(0.026)	(0.024)	(0.026)	(0.036)	(0.047)
Transport	0.009	−0.055	−0.027	−0.026	−0.021	−0.014	−0.001	0.034	0.028	0.061
	(0.025)	(0.042)	(0.033)	(0.022)	(0.026)	(0.029)	(0.027)	(0.029)	(0.039)	(0.051)
Mineral	0.025	0.038	0.028	−0.001	−0.015	0.045	0.039	0.054	0.019	0.026
	(0.035)	(0.058)	(0.046)	(0.030)	(0.036)	(0.039)	(0.037)	(0.039)	(0.054)	(0.070)
Vehicles	0.004	0.006	0.017	0.006	−0.001	−0.009	−0.002	−0.001	0.014	−0.003
	(0.027)	(0.044)	(0.035)	(0.023)	(0.028)	(0.030)	(0.028)	(0.030)	(0.041)	(0.054)
Construction	0.059**	0.032	0.037	0.048**	0.058**	0.055*	0.077***	0.068**	0.068	0.115**
	(0.03)	(0.04)	(0.04)	(0.02)	(0.03)	(0.03)	(0.03)	(0.03)	(0.04)	(0.05)
GARTEX	0.035	−0.041	0.005	−0.010	−0.023	−0.017	−0.006	0.014	0.061	0.157**
	(0.04)	(0.06)	(0.05)	(0.03)	(0.04)	(0.04)	(0.04)	(0.04)	(0.06)	(0.07)

(continued)

Table 10.8 (continued)

Variables	OLS	QR10	QR20	QR30	QR40	QR50	QR60	QR70	QR80	QR90
WOODFUR	0.026	0.020	0.040	0.015	0.013	0.034	0.034	0.043	0.022	0.036
	(0.04)	(0.06)	(0.05)	(0.03)	(0.04)	(0.04)	(0.04)	(0.04)	(0.06)	(0.07)
OtherSEC	0.030	0.016	0.052	0.030	0.016	0.027	0.038	0.046	0.026	0.041
	(0.030)	(0.050)	(0.040)	(0.026)	(0.031)	(0.034)	(0.032)	(0.034)	(0.047)	(0.061)
Constant	0.385***	0.234***	0.315***	0.327***	0.366***	0.386***	0.404***	0.420***	0.448***	0.480***
	(−0.035)	(−0.057)	(−0.045)	(−0.030)	(−0.036)	(−0.039)	(−0.037)	(−0.039)	(−0.053)	(−0.070)
Observations	536	536	536	536	536	536	536	536	536	536
(Pseudo) R2	0.428									

Note Standard errors in parentheses; ***$p < 0.01$, **$p < 0.05$, *$p < 0.1$

distribution, exporting firms had lower growth rates using QR. These results are significant for most of the growth deciles. Exporting firms' growth might be better measured by other measures of growth such as sales or revenue growth. Goedhuys and Sleuwaegen (2009) also found similar relationships in their study. All the other technology and market factors were found to be insignificant in affecting HGFs.

From the resource dummies used in the regression, the OLS regression showed a positive relationship between ownership of generator and access to overdraft facility with growth. The mean growth is predicted to grow by 2 and 3% points for firms with generator and access to overdraft facility respectively. QR shows that the role of these resources was not the same for all firms. Ownership of generator enhanced growth for firms that fell in the 60th and 70th growth percentile while access to overdraft facility could increase firm growth by 6% points for the top growing firms.

An analysis of ownership type and region of operation dummies provides an interesting insight. Sole ownership had the upper hand in growth performance for some of the growth deciles against all other forms of ownership although the OLS estimation found it to be insignificant. Hence, the role of ownership on firm growth is not well established. Similarly, establishments whose business operations were located in the capital, as expected, were found to outperform others. The differences were found to be significant for firms in Oromia, SNNP and Tigray regions under the OLS estimation. The QR estimates confirm these findings although the top growing firms (firms in the 90th percentile) did not show statistically significant differences across regions. For firms in the Amhara and Dire Dawa regions, both estimation techniques failed to show any statistically significant difference from firms in Addis Ababa.

Concerning the relationship between sector of establishment and growth, the OLS estimation showed that there was no significant difference among firms except for the construction sector in which firms had a statistically significant superior growth performance relative to those in hotels and tourism. From QR, firms in the construction sector had a higher growth performance across most of the growth distribution with the exception of the fastest growing firms from the garment and textile industry. These firms outperformed the reference group in the 90th decile.

10.6 Summary, Conclusion and Recommendations

Our study was done with the aim of identifying the incidence of high growth firms with their corresponding growth determinants in Ethiopia using the World Bank's ES database for Ethiopia collected in 2015. The survey covered 848 firms distributed over six major regions—Addis Ababa, Oromia, Amhara, SNNP, Tigray and Dire Dawa. Firm growth was measured by employment size over four years (2010–14). We also identified if these firms' perceived challenges were different from those for non-HGFs. We discussed the incidence of high-growth firms and their perceived business obstacles and identified the drivers of firm growth across different growth distributions and econometric estimations using OLS and Quantile regression.

The Eurostat-OECD classified 137 (25%) firms as HGFs while from BI only classified 109 (20%) of the firms as HGFs. Compared to BI, the Eurostat-OECD measure identified a higher number of firms as HGFs. Regardless of the type of measure used, 369 firms (over two-third of the establishments) were non-HGFs. These percentages could have been significantly higher if the standard Eurostat-OECD definition was used.

Our study also showed that the HGFs were mostly located in the capital city and in the services sector and that the medium sized firms dominated HGFs in Ethiopia. Nearly all the HGFs were concentrated in Addis Ababa regardless of the type of measurement used (over 90%) while Oromia region was the second largest host of HGFs (around 4.5%) under BHGF and 2.4% under the Eurostat-OECD measure.

HGFs were found to be younger by 3 years on average than non-HGFs under both measures. In terms of ownership structure, a majority of these firms were sole ownerships followed by limited partnerships. Looking at the industry type, the two measures referred to nearly the same type of firms where the services sector was over-represented in the HGFs' classification with a share of over 90 and 85% under the Eurostat-OECD and the Birch Index measure respectively. The domination of HGFs in the services sector in Ethiopia is consistent with the findings of Henrekson and Johansson (2010) who did a meta-analysis of the role of HGFs.

High-growth firms were also found to have growth rates which were on average over three-fold of those of non-HGFs under the two measures. HGFs also hired nearly twice the number of employees compared to non-HGFs. They also had a high proportion of export engagement and a significantly large proportion of foreign ownership.

Thirty-three percent of all the firms reported supply of electricity as a major or severe obstacle followed by corruption and tax rates. Corruption was perceived to be a top obstacle by around 29% of the establishments while 28% of them ranked tax rates either as a major or a very severe obstacle. Compared to other countries in the region such as SSA, the Middle East and North Africa which are also surveyed by the World Bank, firms in Ethiopia operated under a better environment.

Over 40% of the establishments reported access to finance as their number one problem while customs and trade regulations and electricity supply were rated as the biggest obstacles by 12 and 10% of the establishments respectively. Regrouping the obstacles into five major categories, institutional factors emerged as the second top obstacle next to access to finance.

An analysis of business obstacles using region of operation as a reference point showed that there was a systematic difference among the regions. For establishments in Addis Ababa and Tigray, the biggest obstacle was access to finance while it was the informal sector for firms operating in Oromia. Corruption topped the list for firms in Amhara while electricity was reported as the biggest obstacle by firms in SNNP and Dire Dawa. The implication of this is that regions should take into account these differences for improving their business environments.

Coming to sectoral aspects, although finance and electricity were reported as key problems by a significant number of firms from all industries showing a need for addressing these problems before resolving industry specific problems such as land (for leather, wood and furniture, metal products and other manufacturing), informal sector (for food, textiles and garments, leather, hotels), tax rates (for retail businesses) and corruption (construction sector and transport).

Considering perceptions about elements of a business environment and firm growth performance, like the non-HGFs even HGFs stated access to finance as the biggest perceived obstacle to growth. The key difference is that for HGFs tax rates were found to be the next biggest obstacle compared to informal sector activities for non-HGFs. Hence, the policy implication is giving priority to problems related to access to finance and tax rates for promoting HGFs.

We also discussed the determinants of firm growth. Firm growth was associated positively with firms' product and process innovations and ownership of a website. Our research failed to show any significant difference among firms' growth based on gender, degree of competition, capacity utilization and nationality of ownership. Export engagement, on the other hand, was found to have a negative relationship with growth. Facilitating innovation activities and technology acquisition such as website ownership and access to financial alternatives might be taken as policy tools.

When it comes to future research, alternative measures of firm growth could improve our research outcomes. Another concern is the persistence of HGFs. Daunfeldt and Halvarsson (2014) show that high-growth firms are one hit wonders and the probability of repeating high-growth rates is very low. This issue is more complicated in Ethiopia due to high entry and exit rates of firms in the manufacturing industry.

Acknowledgements The researcher would like to thank the World Bank Enterprise Survey team for granting access to the data.

The researcher would like to thank Seid Ali (Ph.D.) for his comments and supervision.

References

Acs, Z., W. Parsons, and S. Tracy. 2008. *High-Impact Firms: Gazelles Revisited*. Washington, DC: Office of Advocacy of the US Small Business Administration (SBA).

Anyadike-Danes, M., M. Hart, and J. Du. 2013. Firm Dynamics and Job Creation in the UK Taking Stock and Developing New Perspectives. *ERC-White-Paper-No_6*.

Autio, E. 2007. *GEM's Report 2007: Global Report on High Growth Entrepreneurship*. London: Mazars/London Business School/Babson College.

Autio, E., P. Arenius, and H. Wallenius. 2000. Economic impact of gazelle firms in Finland. Helsinki University of Technology, Institute of Strategy and International Business. Working Paper Series 2000:3.

Ayenew, T. 2015. Essays on Firm Heterogeneity and Export: Productivity, Quality and Access to Finance. A dissertation submitted to the doctoral school of economics and management in partial fulfillment of the requirements for the Doctoral degree (Ph.D.) in Economics and Management.

Bigsten, A., and M. Gebreeyesus. 2007. The small, the young and the productive: Determinants of manufacturing firm growth in Ethiopia. *Economic Development and Cultural Change* 55: 813–840.

Birch, D. 1987. *Job Creation in America: How Our Smallest Companies Put the Most People to Work*. New York, NY: Free Press.

Bravo-Biosca, A. 2010. *Growth Dynamics: Exploring business Growth and Contraction in Europe and the US*. London, UK: NESTA Research report, November.

Coad, A., S.O. Daunfeldt, W. Hölzl, D. Johansson, and P. Nightingale. 2014. High-growth firms: Introduction to the special section. *Journal of Industrial and Corporate Change* 23 (1): 11–91.

Daunfeldt, S.O., N. Elert, and D. Johansson. 2013a. The economic contribution of high-growth firms: Do policy implications depend on the choice of growth indicator? *Journal of Industry, Competition and Trade* 14 (3): 337–365.

Daunfeldt, S.O., D. Halvarsson, and D. Johansson. 2013b. *A cautionary note on using the Eurostat-OECD definition of high-growth firms*. Sweden: HUI Research.

Daunfeldt, S.O., and D. Halvarsson. 2014. Are high-growth firms one-hit wonders? Evidence from Sweden. *Journal of Small Business Economics* 44 (2): 361–383.

Davidsson, P., and M. Henrekson. 2002. Determinants of the prevalence of startups and high-growth firms. *Small Business Economics* 19 (2): 81–104.

Delmar, F., P. Davidsson, and W. Gartner. 2003. Arriving at the high-growth firm. *Journal of Business Venturing* 18 (2): 189–216.

Eurostat, O.E.C.D. 2007. *Eurostat-OECD Manual on Business Demography Statistics*. Paris: OECD.

Goedhuys, M., and L. Sleuwaegen. 2009. High-growth entrepreneurial firms in Africa: A quantile regression. *Small Business Economics* 34: 31–51.

Hallward-Driemeier, M., and R. Aterido. 2007. *Impact of Access to Finance*. Corruption and Infrastructure on Employment Growth: Putting Africa in a Global Context. Unpublished.

Henderson, A., M. Raynor, and M. Ahmed. 2012. How long must a firm be great to rule out chance? Benchmarking sustained superior performance without being fooled by randomness. *Strategic Management Journal* 33: 387–406.

Henrekson, M., and D. Johansson. 2010. Gazelles as job creators: A survey and interpretation of the evidence. *Small Business Economics* 35 (2): 227–244.

Hölzl, W. 2011. *Persistence, Survival and Growth: A Closer Look at 20 years of High Growth Firms and Firm Dynamics in Austria*. Vienna: Austrian Institute of Economic Research.

Lopez-Garcia, P., and S. Puente. 2012. What makes a high-growth firm? A dynamic probit analysis using Spanish firm-level data. *Small Business Economics* 39 (4): 1029–1041.

Moreno, F., and A. Coad. 2015. *High-Growth Firms: Stylized Facts and Conflicting Results*. England: University of Sussex.

Nesta, 2009. *The vital 6 per cent How high-growth innovative businesses generate prosperity and jobs*. NESTA: Research summary.

Nguimkeu, P. 2013. *Business Environment and Firm performance: The Case of Retailing Firms in Cameroon*. Georgia: Andrew Young School of Policy Studies.

Petersen, D.R., and N. Ahmad. 2007. *High-growth enterprises and gazelles: Preliminary and summary sensitivity analysis*. Paris: OECD.

Schreyer, P. 2000. *High-growth firms and employment. OECD STI Working Paper 2000 3*. Paris: OECD.

Storey, J. 1994. *Understanding the Small Business Sector*. London: Routledge.

Sutton, J. 1997. Gibrat's legacy. *Journal of Economic Literature* 35: 40–59.

The World Bank. 2015. *World Bank Enterprise Survey*. Washington, DC: The World Bank.

Chapter 11
An Analysis of the Effects of Aging and Experience on Firms' Performance

Guta Legesse

Abstract This study identifies the effects of a firm's age on its performance as measured by labor productivity and total value of sales using survey based panel data of large and medium scale manufacturing firms in Ethiopia. The analysis is based on 6370 firms and 10,231 firm-years during 2010–15 distributed all over the nation with Addis Ababa, Oromia, SNNP, Amhara and Tigray regions hosting over 90% of these firms. The results of the fixed-effects (unbalanced) panel data estimation technique fail to show a statistically significant relationship between a firm's age and its performance irrespective of the choice of the dependent variable and different model specifications. The coefficient of the average marginal effect of age is negative, but insignificant, for both measures of a firm's performance. The study also shows that the effect of a firm's size on its performance depends on the choice of the dependent variable. Firm size is predominantly associated with lower labor productivity but higher sales value. When it comes to the role of other control variables capital intensity and wage expenditure have a positive and significant effect on a firm's performance and the result is invariant to the method of estimation. The effect of a change in the gender composition of the owner on a firm's performance is found to be negative and significant for the OLS regression but insignificant for the fixed-effects model. Finally, the role of region of operation on a firm's performance is significant and positive only in the labor productivity regression. The lack of empirical support for the effect of a firm's age on its performance shows that the 'learning by doing' affect is weak and improving this could be a possible option for reducing the high rates of firms' entries and exits observed in the survey.

Keywords Firm age · Firm performance · Fixed-effects

G. Legesse (✉)
Department of Economics, Addis Ababa University, Addis Ababa, Ethiopia
e-mail: gutalegesse@gmail.com

© Springer Nature Singapore Pte Ltd. 2018
A. Heshmati and H. Yoon (eds.), *Economic Growth and Development in Ethiopia*, Perspectives on Development in the Middle East and North Africa (MENA) Region, https://doi.org/10.1007/978-981-10-8126-2_11

11.1   Introduction

The Ethiopian economy has experienced strong and broad-based growth over the past decade with an average GDP growth rate of 10.1% per year between 2006–07 and 2016–17 (NBE 2016). This is relatively high compared to the growth rate in the region as a whole. Ethiopian manufacturing sector's export performance was also below the average performance of firms in sub-Saharan African countries.

The services sector has emerged as the top contributor with a share of slightly over 45% over the last six years while the role of agriculture is on a decline from 45% in 2010–11 to 37% in 2016. Similarly, the industrial sector has shown modest progress over the past decade with a maximum share of 16.7% registered in 2016–17 (NBE 2016).

The manufacturing sector plays a key role in developing the Ethiopian economy. In 2016–17, the manufacturing sector represented over 32% of the total production of the industrial sector; the construction sector accounted for more than 50%. In 2015 the number of persons employed in the manufacturing was reported to be more than 329,000 and the total wages and salaries were over Birr 9 million. Further, the total gross value of production in 2014–15 was about Birr 142 billion (CSA 2016).

The Government of Ethiopia is implementing the second phase of its five-year growth and transformation plan (GTP II) to transform the economy and achieve lower-middle-income status by 2025. Under GTP II, which started in 2015–16, the government aims to continue investing in physical infrastructure through public investment projects and transform the country into a manufacturing hub. The government has also embarked on the development of industrial parks to enhance the transformation process.

A study on the dynamics of a firm's performance is essential to sustain the promising performance of the Ethiopian economy. Our research studies how a firm's performance changes over time. It is important to study this because there are two contradictory findings about the effects of a firm's age on its performance. Some researchers argue that age increases a firm's performance while for others age lowers a firm's performance.

Most of the literature on firm growth talks about the determinants of firm growth. Early work on firm dynamics focused almost exclusively on how firm size was related to firm growth, whereas firm age received little attention. It is only recently that we have started seeing studies on the role of a firm's age on its performance. These researches draw an analogy between aging of living organisms and a firm's performance. It is known that aging leads to deterioration in the performance of organisms and researchers want to know if firms also face a decline in their capacity to compete as they get older (Loderer and Waelchli 2010).

There is a large literature suggesting a negative relationship between firm age and growth rates. One dominant line of thinking is that since firms are organizations that can be restructured if the need arises there is no reason why they should age. This hypothesis suggests that firms should be able to learn by doing or by investing in research and development; they can hire human capital and train their employees; and they can learn from other firms. Hence, older firms should enjoy higher profits and value. Others argue that due to organizational rigidities and rent-seeking behavior, old firms face a higher probability of failure and exit.

Some researchers argue that both the young and old firms face corresponding liabilities. New entrants face what is now commonly called the 'liability of newness' (Hannan and Freeman 1984; Stinchcombe 1965). This hypothesis claims that new firms have higher failure rates. On the other hand, Bruderl and Schussler (1990) have introduced another relationship between age and a firm's performance termed 'liability of adolescence.' Barron et al. (1994) introduced a third term, 'liability of obsolescence.' The liability of adolescence and obsolescence argue that aging firms might have lower performance as they do not adapt to changing business environments. It is difficult to know which of these arguments dominates firms at work without doing a survey. Since these liabilities suggest conflicting roles of a firm's age on its performance and with both being at work simultaneously, the net effect of age could vary from firm to firm and from place to place.

11.2 Literature Review

11.2.1 Theoretical Review

There are competing theories that explain how the age of a firm is related to its performance. Some of them suggest a positive relationship between the two while others argue that the opposite is true. Young firms might, for example, have higher growth rates but also more erratic growth paths as compared to older firms. This concept is termed liability of newness (Hannan and Freeman 1984; Stinchcombe 1965). According to this argument young firms might achieve minimum efficient scale as they struggle to overcome their liability of newness but once they have survived the first few years and have settled into their new organizational routines, growth will lose its momentum. It also argues that older firms may have more experience and foresight regarding their business environment and hence a smoother growth path with fewer bumps and surprises.

Barron et al. (1994) provide a supporting argument for the role that inertia plays in a firm's performance. They argue that old firms suffer from a liability of obsolescence and also a liability of senescence. According to the liability of senescence, firms become accustomed to the existing rules, routines and organizational structures which generate inflexibility and hence inferior performance.

Coad et al. (2013) give three inter-related theories that explain how firm age affects its performance—selection affects, learning by doing affects and inertia affects. According to them, selection effects occur when an early exit of the weakest firms in the industry leads to an increase in average productivity of the remaining firms, irrespective of the nature of their individual performance over time. Learning by doing proposes that older firms have better financial performance because they are more experienced and benefit from learning by doing. This idea is discussed by Arrow (1962) and Chang et al. (2002). Firms' tendency to learn and apply new production techniques increases with time. Third, aging can have a negative impact on firms' performance through inertia affects leading firms to become inflexible and face difficulties in fitting into the rapidly changing business environment in which they operate.

11.2.2 Empirical Review

In early studies on the nexus between firm age and performance, researches treated a firm's age and size as measures of the same phenomenon since younger firms tended to be smaller and vice versa. Later studies introduced firm age as an independent variable in the model (Coad et al. 2013).

Evans (1987) studied the relationship among firm age, size and growth using a sample of all firms operating in 100 manufacturing industries in the US. His results show that firm growth and the probability that a firm will fail decrease with its age. He also found that a firm's growth decreased at a diminishing rate with firm size even after controlling for the exit of slow-growing firms from the sample.

Huergo and Jaumandreu (2003) did a study on the impact of firms' age and (process) innovations on productivity growth using semiparametric methods. They show the impact of productivity growth on the process innovations introduced by firms along their different ages using (unbalanced) panel data on the ages of more than 2300 Spanish manufacturing firms and their process innovations during 1990–98. Their results indicate that new firm's productivity increased more rapidly while productivity growth of surviving firms converged to common (activity-specific) growth rates.

The relationship between a firm's age and the level and growth rate of productivity has also been studied by Brouwer et al. (2005) in the Dutch manufacturing industry. Their study covers all enterprises with at least 20 employees and with at least 10 years of existence during 1994–99. Their study shows that young firms either caught up with the more mature firms or they exited resulting in an above average growth rate of productivity in the early stages. In general, they found very few indications of a relationship between age and productivity for the Dutch manufacturing industry. They also found no or little indication that sector-specific level of productivity and productivity growth rate were related to firm age.

Palangkaraya et al.'s (2006) study on the relationship between productivity, size and age of large Australian firms employing more than 100 employees found that there was an inverse relationship between firm productivity and age. They found that larger and older firms were on average less productive. They used the World Bank database on large manufacturing firms in Australia.

Another important study on the role of aging on a firm's performance is by Loderer and Waelchli (2010). Their study was undertaken to investigate the relationship between firm age and performance using a dataset consisting of 10,930 listed US firms and covering the years between 1978 and 2004. Their empirical results show that as firms got older, all measures of their profitability declined. They also found that return on assets, profit margins, and Tobin's Q ratios all deteriorated with age suggesting aging of firms.

Coad et al. (2013) verified the performance of firms over time using a panel of Spanish manufacturing firms' active between 1998 and 2006. They found mixed results depending on how performance was measured. Using the ratio of profits to sales as a proxy for performance, they found that older firms enjoyed higher productivity and profits. They thus provide evidence of firms improving with age. Further, they also show that older firms were better able to convert sales growth into subsequent growth in profits and productivity. Using other measures of a firm's performance such as expected growth rates in sales, profits and productivity, they show that a firm's performance deteriorated with age and it appeared to be less capable of converting employment growth into growth in sales, profits and productivity.

Coad et al. (2014) present new evidence on the relationship between firm age and performance by using firms from Sweden during 1997–2010. Using autocorrelation methods, they found that sales growth for new firms was characterized by positive autocorrelation while it showed a negative autocorrelation for older firms. The implication is that older firms were distracted by the environmental turbulence that they worked in while new firms needed to grow to achieve a minimum efficient scale.

Akben-Seluck (2016) did a study on the effect of a firm's age on its productivity using Turkish firms covering the period between 2005 and 2014. They used a fixed-effects model with robust standard errors. Using multiple measures of profitability such as returns on assets, returns on equity or gross profit margins, they showed that there was a negative and convex relationship between a firm's age and profitability which suggests that firms face decline in profitability over time.

Heshmati and Rashidghalam (2016) did an analysis of labor productivity and its determinants in the manufacturing and services sectors in Kenya using the World Bank's Enterprise Survey database for 2013. Using OLS with robust standard errors they show that capital intensity and wage significantly and positively affected labor productivity while a higher female share in the labor force reduced labor productivity. Training and education of workers were found to have positive effects on labor productivity. In their study, the managerial experience of CEOs was also associated with higher labor productivity. Regarding the role of the business environment, as expected access and use of utilities and infrastructure tended to discourage labor productivity.

According to a study by Heshmati and Su (2014) the source of labor productivity and its evolution in China during the period of 2000–09 varied across provinces. They estimated determinants of labor productivity in China using the fixed-effects panel data model with time and province-specific affects and robust standard errors where labor productivity was measured both in level and in growth rates. They found that labor productivity was positively associated with industry output, investments in fixed assets and telecommunications, total volume of the business post-profits of the enterprises and the average wage for labor both in level and growth rates. Although the share of urban labor had an ambiguous affect, investments in education had positive and significant affects only in the formulation of the growth rate model.

Rijkers et al. (2010) did a study on the role of location and the characteristics of the investment climate on a firm's performance. They used data on urban firms from the Ethiopia Enterprise Survey (EES) carried out by the Ethiopian Development Research Institute (EDRI). They found that urban firms were larger, more capital intensive and had higher labor productivity than rural firms, although there was no strong evidence of increasing returns to scale. They also did not get sufficient evidence to reject the hypothesis of same average total factor productivity of firms irrespective of their location of operations. However, according to their results rural firms grew less quickly than urban firms.

11.3   Methods

11.3.1   Measuring Firm Performance

We measure firm performance by two inter-related variables to check the robustness of the results to the choice of the variables. We use labor productivity and total sales as a proxy for a firm's performance. These variables are converted to logarithmic forms.

We measure labor productivity (LPLABORD) as the ratio of total value of production to total number of employees. The total number of employees includes both permanent and temporary workers. Similarly, total sales value in log form is presented as (LSALED). To control for sector specific affects, industry median of sales and labor productivity are subtracted from a firm's value. Hence, the dependent variables are given as deviations from the median value for industry as defined by the two-digit international standard industry classification (ISIC).

Some firms were excluded during the data cleaning process due to missing values for these proposed measures of the dependent variable. Forty-six firms had missing sales values; six had missing total value of production while 284 had missing values of employment for June and March.

11.3.2   Measuring Firm Age and Other Control Variables

Firm age is measured as the difference between the survey period (2015) and the year the firm started its business operations. To capture non-linearity aspects, a squared term of firm age is also included. Both age and the squared term were transformed to log forms (LAGE and LAGESQ). The squared term of firm age was introduced as a factor variable in the regression equation to show that they are related variables.

Table 11.1 and Fig. 11.1 present statistics on the age of eligible firms. In the survey, the oldest firm had an age of 115 years while the youngest firm had an age of eight years. The fact that the minimum age is above zero shows that new entrants are not new to the industry but are graduates from the small and medium enterprises categories. On average, firm age was around 22 years with a median age of 17 years. The mean was above the median age for all years. The distribution of firm age (as measured by mean and median values) declined over the sample period with a narrowing gap between the two measures over time. This shows that most firms had ages below the mean age and were younger which could be due to high rates of firm entry and exit.

Other control variables used in the analysis include capital intensity, firm size, wage expenditure, investments in fixed assets, region of operation and year dummies.

Table 11.1 Firm age statistics by year of survey for manufacturing firms in Ethiopia (2010–15)

Year	Mean	Median	P10	P25	P75	Max	Min	St. dev.	N
2010–2015	21.83	17	11	14	25	115	8	13.66	10,017
2010	24.84	19	15	16	27	101	13	14.05	1610
2011	24.47	19	14	16	26	101	12	14.53	1267
2012	22.82	18	12	14	26	115	11	14.09	1658
2013	21.08	17	11	13	23	101	10	12.76	1880
2014	20.55	16	11	13	23	109	9	13.37	1820
2015	18.43	15	9	11	20	109	8	12.43	1782

Source Author's computation from the CSA survey data

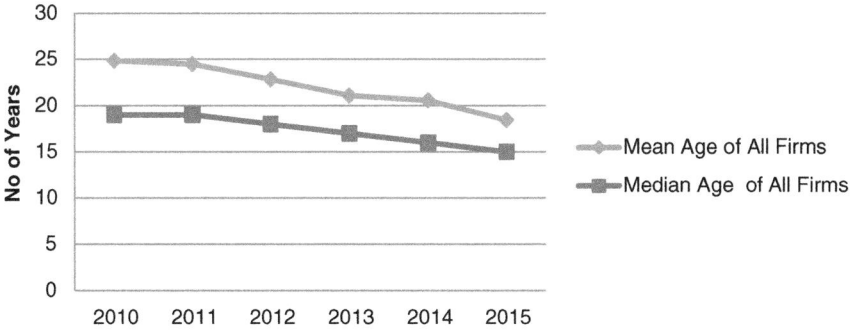

Fig. 11.1 Mean and median age of firms by year

Capital intensity (LCAPINT) is measured as the total amount of working capital divided by the number of employees in natural logarithm. Firm size (LSIZE) is measured as natural logarithm of total employees for June. The total number of employees is the sum of male and female Ethiopian workers and foreigners in June. For missing values, the number of employees who reported for March was taken as equivalent, if it was not missing, otherwise zero value was recorded. A squared term (LSIZESQ) and its alternative specification as a factor variable was used for size to capture non-linearity. Wage expenditure (LWAGE) is measured as the natural logarithm of total wages. LINVST shows natural logarithm of total investments in fixed assets.

Finally, region and time dummy variables were introduced to control for region and year specific affects. A test for the importance of time fixed-effects in the model was done and the results suggested the need for year dummies in the model. The proportion of female owners (FEMPROP) shows the number of female owners in the total firm owners while the number of months a firm was in operation per year is presented as (NMONTH). Region dummies for the major regions were also created (AA for firms operating in Addis Ababa, ORO for firms operating in Oromia region, AMH for firms operational in Amhara region, TIG for Tigray region, SNNP for Sothern Nations Nationalities and People, OTHEREG for firms operational in the rest of the regions (Dire Dawa, Somale, Benishangul, Gambela, Afar and Harai) which accounted for a smaller fraction of firms.

11.3.3 Modeling the Nexus Between Firm Age and Firm Performance

Our empirical model to show the nexus between firm performance and aging is the fixed- effects panel data model which was based on a suggestion from the Hausman test. Two separate regressions were run depending on the proxy used for measuring firm performance. The starting point was labor productivity as a proxy followed by total sales:

$$LPLABOR_{i,t} = f\{AGE_{i,t}, AGESQ_{i,t}, X_{i,t}, \varepsilon_{i,t}\} \tag{11.1}$$

$$LSALE_{i,t} = f\{AGE_{i,t}, AGESQ_{i,t}, X_{i,t}, \varepsilon_{i,t}\} \tag{11.2}$$

$$LPLABORD_{i,t} = \omega_i + \beta_1 AGE_{i,t} + \beta_2 AGESQ_{i,t} + \beta_3 LSIZE_{i,t} + \beta_4 LSIZESQ_{i,t} + \beta_5 LCAPINT_{i,t} + \beta_6 LINVST_{i,t} + \beta_7 LWAGE_{i,t} + \beta_8 FEMPROP + \beta_9 NMONTH + \varepsilon_{i,t}\} \tag{11.3}$$

$$LSALED_{i,t} = \omega_i + \beta_1 AGE_{i,t} + \beta_2 AGESQ_{i,t} + \beta_3 LSIZE_{i,t} + \beta_4 LSIZESQ_{i,t} + \beta_5 LCAPINT_{i,t} + \beta_6 LINVST_{i,t} + \beta_7 LWAGE_{i,t} + \beta_8 FEMPROP + \beta_9 NMONTH + \varepsilon_{i,t}\} \tag{11.4}$$

where,

$LPLABORD_{i,t}$ is labor productivity as an indicator of firm performance for firm i in year t,

$LSALED_{i,t}$ is the natural logarithm of the total value of sales,

$LAGE_{i,t}$ is the age of the firm i in year t,

$LSIZE_{i,t}$ is the size of the enterprise, and

$X_{i,t}$ is a set of control variables.

$\omega_i, \beta_1, \beta_2, \beta_3, \ldots \beta_9$, are vectors of parameters to be estimated, $\varepsilon_{i,t}$ is the error term. To control for potential heteroscedasticity, robust standard errors are reported.

11.4   Data: Survey Description

The data used in our research is survey based panel data collected by the Central Statistical Agency (CSA) of Ethiopia on a yearly basis for large and medium scale manufacturing industries (LMMIS) in the country. For our study, all manufacturing firms in operation between 2010 and 2015 with minimum employment of 10 people who used power driven machinery were included. The survey covered both public and private industries in all regions of the country.

Panel data was constructed using the latest six years data of the survey leading to 8248 firms and 13,534 firm-years. The data cleaning process included excluding firms with no data on employment and sales records in the 3rd and 4th quarters of the year (March and June), firms with no region indicated, and firms with no wage data and firms with less than 10 employees. In addition, outliers on employment, sales and labor productivity data were excluded. Outliers are defined as scores outside three standard deviations from the mean score. Accordingly, we had 6370 firms and 10,231 firm-years for the analysis.

A number of questions were asked in the questionnaire to capture important dimensions of firm performance, availability of infrastructure and the business obstacles that a firm faced. The questionnaire had eight major components with relevant sub-sections for each. It started by asking a firm's background information on firm location and region of operations, industry classification and issues related to ownership type and sex of the top manager while the next section raised questions related to paid-up capital, business obstacles and the number of employees with their corresponding wages and salaries. Cost of raw materials, infrastructure costs, sales and supplies and capacity utilization are all a part of the questionnaire.

The survey covered firms operating in all the nine geographic regions in the country (Oromia, Amhara, SNNP, Tigray, Harari, Afar, Benishangul, Gambela and Somale) and two city administrations of Addis Ababa and Dire Dawa.

Looking at the firm entry-exit dynamics we see that there was high firm turnover in Ethiopia. After cleaning the data, we had 1635 firms in 2010 and 1820 firms in 2015.

Table 11.2 Statistics on entry and exit dynamics of firms in the survey period

Year	Entry	Exit
2010	1635	672
2011	488	1218
2012	1591	356
2013	710	758
2014	612	1077
2015	1048	1820
Total	6084	5901

Source Author's computation using CSA survey data

Within the study period (2010–14), 6084 firms entered while 4081 firms left and 1820 firms were active in 2015 so we had data for 10,321 firm-years. The data shows very high firm turnover over such a short period of time. The high number of exits can be due to a lower median for number of employees (19). Firms in which the number of employees fell below 10 were excluded from the survey (Table 11.2).

11.5 Empirical Results

11.5.1 Descriptive Statistics

This part of the analysis presents results from both the descriptive statistics and empirical estimations.

Table 11.3 gives the descriptive statistics of the variables included in the analysis. Labor productivity, on average, is Birr 124,119 while the median value is Birr 138,012. Similarly, mean sales value is around Birr 4.6 million and the median

Table 11.3 Descriptive statistics of manufacturing firms in Ethiopia (2010–16)

Variable	Mean	Median	Max	Min	St. dev.	N
Dependent variables: performance measures						
Labor productivity	124,119	138,012	17,200,345	800	5.15	10,232
Sales	4,576,568	4,327,584	2,599,383,140	2782	10.15	10,232
Independent variables: control variables						
Capital intensity	117,008	21,218	41,050,763	28.9	5.109	9917
Size	75.56	26	1029	9	130.28	10,232
Wage expenses	358,613	300,875	772,343,533	178	5.71	10,105
Proportion of female owners (%)	35	33	100	0	33	5779
Number of month operated per year	10.5	12	13	2	2.53	10,075
Investments in fixed assets	233,603	250,000	1,332,922,850	0	17.25	6060

Source Author's computation using CSA survey data

sales value is Birr 4.3 million. After controlling for outliers, we still see that the maximum total sales were around Birr 2.6 billion. Concerning firm size, the mean size was 76 employees while the median was 26 employees. The discrepancy between mean and median sizes shows that there were too many small firms. This could be one of the reasons why a large number of firms exited from the survey each year since the minimum number should be 10 employees to be eligible for the survey. On average, the number of months that a firm was operational was 10.5 months showing that firms on average were not operational for more than a month. The proportion of female owners varied from the smallest value of no female owners (0%) to the maximum of only female owners (100%) with mean and median proportions of 35 and 33% respectively.

Figures 11.2 and 11.3 summarize the movement in mean values of labor productivity and total value of sales relative to the median over years. Both labor productivity and total sales value increased with time with nearly identical mean and median values. The average and median firm size dynamics over the six years (Fig. 11.4) show that employment growth was stable with a huge difference in the median and mean values. Average employment was more than twice the median employment showing that most of the firms were medium sized.

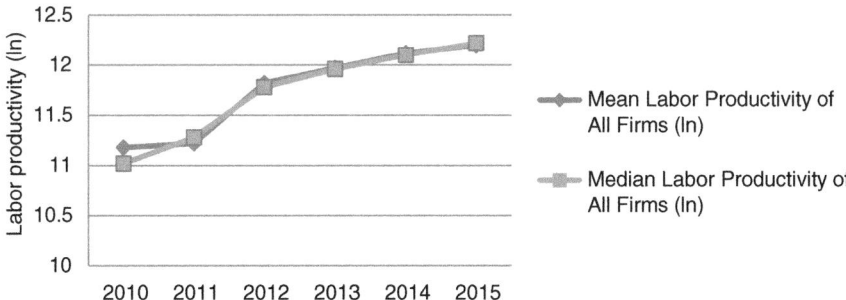

Fig. 11.2 Mean and median labor productivity of firms (by year)

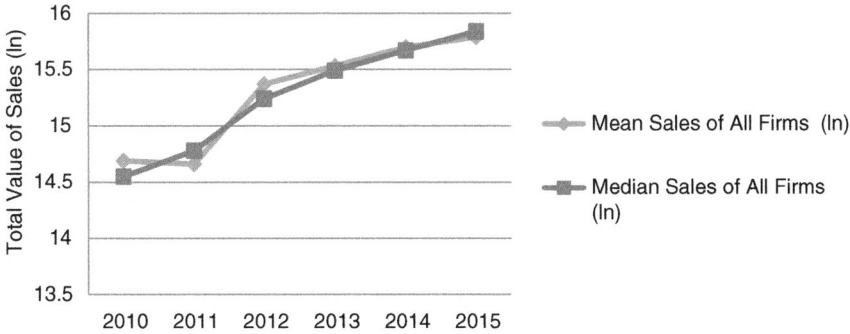

Fig. 11.3 Mean and median of total sales value of firms

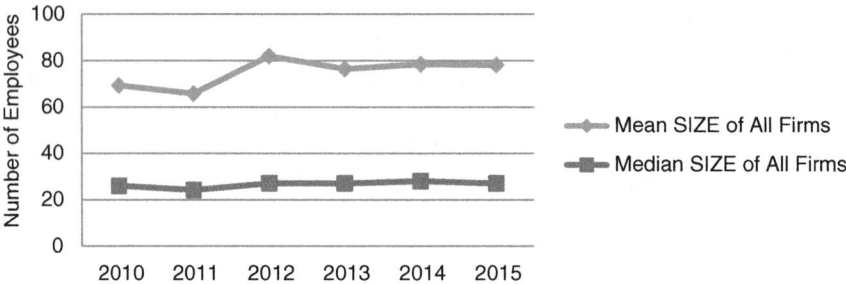

Fig. 11.4 Mean and median firm size (by year)

   A matrix of correlation coefficients among the explanatory variables was generated to check for collinearity among them (Table 11.4). Only wage expenditure
and firm size show a correlation higher than 0.70 indicating multicollinearity. The
remaining pairs were low correlated with each other and did not show any signs of
serious multicollinearity. The size and age of a firm, capital intensity and wages
were positively correlated with investments in fixed asset. The variance inflation
factor (VIF), also supplements the relationship of no multicollinearity.

11.5.2 Business Challenges Faced by Firms

Concerning elements of the business environment, firms were asked to state the
single most important obstacle for not operating at full capacity. The most
important business obstacle hindering full capacity operations was also decomposed by the firm's age category to see if there were systematic differences based on
the age of the firm. Figures 11.5 and 11.6 give the comparisons.
   The results show that older firms whose age was above the median year reported
similar problems as their younger counterparts. This is contrary to the expectation
that older firms had better information about the market and resource availability
and higher probability of generating their own financial resources. Manufacturing
firms in Ethiopia were not operating at full capacity predominantly due to a
shortage of raw materials, lack of electricity and water and lack of a market irrespective of the difference in their age.
   Shortage of raw materials was reported as a major obstacle to full capacity
operations by 30% of the young firms which reported any kind of obstacles while
this percentage increased to around 40% for older firms. The severity of raw
material shortage increased with a firm's age. Moreover, 20% of both the younger
and older firms ranked shortage of electricity and water as their number one
problem. Older firms had a relative advantage over the younger ones in terms of
access to markets and customers since only 11% of them reported access to markets

Table 11.4 Matrix of correlation of coefficients

	LAGE	LAGESQ[b]	LSIZE	LSIZESQ	LWAGE[a]	LCAPINT	LINVST	NMONTH	FEMPROP	AA	ORO	SNNP	AMH	OTHERREG
LAGE	1													
LAGESQ[b]	1	1												
LSIZE	0.23	0.23	1											
LSIZESQ	0.22	0.22	0.99	1										
LWAGE[a]	0.25	0.25	0.80	0.78	1									
LCAPINT	0.06	0.06	0.24	0.22	0.46	1								
LINVST	0.04	0.04	0.57	0.55	0.58	0.47	1							
NMONTH	0.19	0.19	0.21	0.21	0.27	0.16	0.10	1						
FEMPROP	0.12	0.12	-0.09	-0.09	-0.13	-0.06	-0.09	0.00	1					
AA	0.39	0.39	0.15	0.13	0.18	0.06	0.07	0.15	0.14	1				
ORO	-0.22	-0.22	0.15	0.14	0.14	0.17	0.19	-0.05	-0.06	-0.58	1			
SNNPR	-0.10	-0.10	-0.23	-0.20	-0.22	-0.13	-0.21	-0.03	-0.05	-0.26	-0.23	1		
AMH	-0.10	-0.10	-0.16	-0.15	-0.21	-0.21	-0.17	-0.11	-0.05	-0.24	-0.21	-0.10	1	
OTHERREG	-0.04	-0.04	-0.07	-0.06	-0.03	-0.04	-0.05	0.04	-0.05	-0.16	-0.14	-0.06	0.06	1

[a]Wage expenditure shows a strong correlation with size and its squared term but the result is generally the same if wage is dropped from the regression. [b]The squared term of age and size were replaced by the factor variable in the estimation

Source Author's computation using CSA survey data

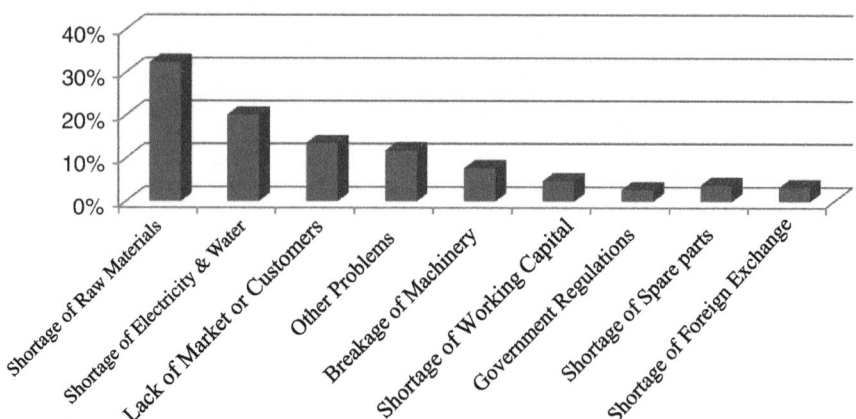

Fig. 11.5 First major obstacle hindering full capacity operations of young firms (below median age). *Source* Author's computation using CSA survey data

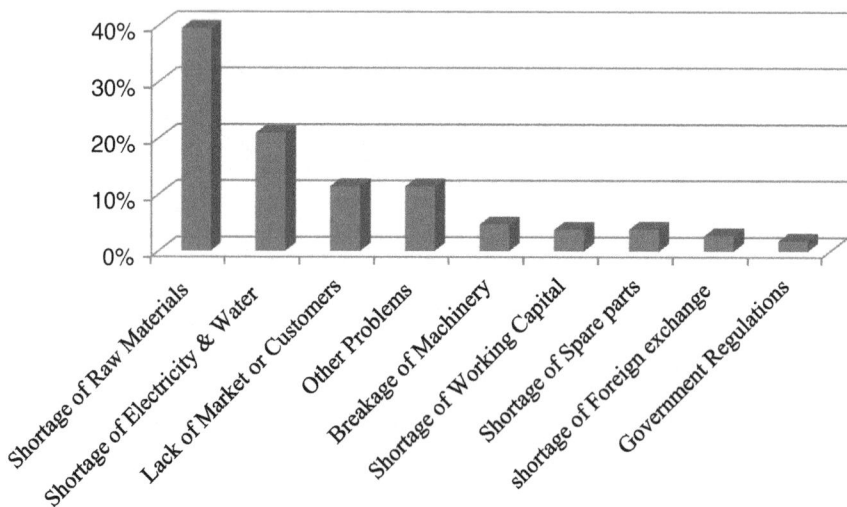

Fig. 11.6 First major obstacle hindering full capacity operation of old firms (above median age)

and customers as a major problem as opposed to 14% of the younger firms. This shows that market related problems improved with a firm's experience.

When firms were asked to reflect on the top business obstacles that they currently faced, a similar list of challenges emerged among older and younger firms. For older firms, shortage of raw materials (41%), access to markets (14%) and shortage of working capital (6%) were the top major problems. On the other hand, 32% of the younger firms said that shortages of raw materials was their number one problem, while 15% of them rated access to markets as their top problem followed by shortage of working capital (8%). About 18% of the firms from both age categories did not report any problem.

11.5.3   Results from Econometric Estimations

To assess whether there is a relation between firm age and its performance an OLS and a fixed effect panel data model with robust standard errors was estimated. The first two regressions present pooled OLS estimations with age and its squared term as the only explanatory variables using labor productivity and sales as a proxy for a firm's performance. The evidence suggests that age was negatively related to a firm's performance while the squared term was positively associated with firm performance. Firm age had a non-linear relationship with performance. The average marginal effect of firm age on labor productivity was found to be negative and significant at the 10% significance level supporting the aging argument for a firm's performance. Using sales as a measure of firm performance, the average marginal affect shows that age had a positive and significant effect on firm performance. Hence, how a firm age relates to its productivity depends on our choice of the left-hand side variable.

By including other control variables in the OLS regression analysis, we get a slightly different result. The average marginal affect, which is significant at the 1% significance level, presents a positive association between sales value and firm age. The effect of firm age on firm performance under the pooled OLS regression becomes significant for the sales regression but insignificant for the labor productivity equation.

Concerning the effect of firm size on its performance, labor productivity was negatively related to firm size and positively to its squared term. The average marginal effect of firm size on labor productivity was negative and significant. Using total sales value, we also see that size had a non-linear relationship with performance and under this specification the average marginal effect of size was positive and significant.

Capital intensity and total wages also had a significant positive affect on a firm's performance at the 1% significance level. Higher capital intensity implies more capital per worker and hence higher productivity. Higher wage expenditure could imply a high proportion of skilled and quality employees which are essential for a firm's performance. Like the number of months that a firm had been operational, total investments in fixed assets were found to have an insignificant effect on both the sales and productivity of a firm at the 1 and 5% significance levels. Another result of the OLS estimation is that the proportion of female owners was related to firm performance. The proportion of female owners was found to be associated with lower performance of firms. After controlling for other factors, firms with a higher number of female owners tended to have a lower performance. Concerning the region of operation, the OLS estimation shows some significant differences among firms. Firms in SNNP and smaller regions had superior performance relative to the reference region.

An alternative, and more appropriate approach, is to use the fixed-effects panel data model recommended by the Hausman test. The fixed-effects are selected over random-effects due to rejection of the null hypothesis of no systematic differences between coefficients in the Hausman test. The FE estimation was done with and without a control variable for time effects. The important variable of interest is to know how a firm's age relates to its performance. The results of the FE model estimation show that our study failed to show any significant relationship between firm age and firm performance at the conventional significance levels. This finding is in line with Brouwer et al. (2005). Looking at the average marginal effects the result was still insignificant. The total elasticities with respect to age for both measures of firm performance are reported in Tables 11.5 and 11.6 and they are insignificant.

Our research findings fail to support the 'learning by doing' hypothesis. This could be one of the reasons why a large number of firms exited and there were lower levels of industrialization in Ethiopia as firms were unable to excel in performance with experience. Moreover, a significant proportion of new entrants each year had graduated from small and medium sized firms as the minimum age of firms in the analysis was eight years.

Table 11.5 Summary of elasticities (dependent variable: sales value)

Variable name	Elasticities (%)	$P > |z|$
LAGE	−0.13	0.489
LSIZE	0.55	0.000
LWAGE	0.24	0.000
LCAPINT	0.27	0.000
LINVST	−0.00	0.871
NMONTH	3.05	0.133
FEMPROP	−36.34	0.192

Source Author's computation using CSA data

Table 11.6 Summary of elasticities (dependent variable: labor productivity)

Variable name	Elasticities (%)	$P > |z|$
LAGE	−0.19	0.314
LSIZE	−0.42	0.000
LWAGE	0.21	0.001
LCAPINT	0.29	0.000
LINVST	0.01	0.557
NMONTH	3.05	0.197
FEMPROP	−32.31	0.159

Source Author's computation using CSA data

Further, the effect of firm size on firm performance depended on our choice of the dependent variable. When labor productivity was used, the role of size and its squared term became insignificant. The average marginal effect of size, however, was associated with lower performance and the result was found to be statistically significant at the 1% significance level. There seems to be a convex relationship between labor productivity and firm size. In terms of elasticity, a 1% increase in firm size resulted in a 0.42% decline in labor productivity. On the contrary, firm size was associated with higher sales although the effect of the squared term was insignificant. The average marginal effect of size was found to be positive and statistically significant when performance was measured in terms of the total value of sales. A 1% increase in firm size was associated with a 0.55% increase in sales value. Therefore, the issue of how size relates to a firm's performance depends on our choice of the dependent variable. Hence, firm size was predominantly associated with lower labor productivity but higher sales value.

The effect of capital intensity and wage expenditure on a firm's performance was consistent with the pooled OLS estimation showing positive and significant affects irrespective of the choice of the dependent variable and hence robust results. A 1% increase in wage expenditure is associated with an over 0.20% increase in firm performance for both measures of firm performance. Similarly, a 1% increase in capital intensity is associated with around a 0.30% increase in a firm's performance as measured by the values of sales and labor productivity.

Concerning the role of the number of months that a firm was in operation during a survey year, our study fails to show a significant relationship. The results of the effect of investments in fixed assets was also found to be inconclusive. Finally, the effect of change in gender composition of owners on firms' performance was estimated by using a proportion of female owners (FEMPROP) and the results are insignificant under the fixed-effects model specifications although the pooled OLS estimation showed an inverse relationship between firm performance and the proportion of female owners.

Region specific affects were captured using regional dummies. Compared to the reference group (firms operating in region 1), firms in all the other regions showed better performance as measured by labor productivity. However, using sales as a proxy for firm productivity, our study fails to show statistically significant differences among firms based in different regions except for the two smaller regions of SNNP and OTHEREG which showed better performance. This could be due to too much concentration of firms in a few industries such as manufacturing of furniture and grain mill products.

We also did relevant post-estimation tests. The results of the multicollinearity test show that there was no multicollinearity problem as indicated by the low VIF and the correlation matrix among the coefficients (Table 11.7). The heteroskedasticity test led to a rejection of the null hypothesis of homoscedasticity. Hence, robust standard errors are reported in the regression (Table 11.8).

Table 11.7 Test of
multicollinearity

Variable	VIF	1/VIF
AGE	13.11	0.076279
AGESQ	12.32	0.081198
SIZE	11.22	0.089106
SIZESQ	7.84	0.127592
AA	5.32	0.187927
ORO	4.93	0.202990
LWAGE	3.08	0.324752
SNNPR	2.55	0.392133
AMH	2.33	0.428409
LINVST	1.81	0.551969
OTHERREG	1.64	0.610389
LCAPINT	1.59	0.630692
NMONTH	1.12	0.891250
FEMPROP	1.07	0.936500
Mean VIF	4.99	

11.6   Conclusion and Recommendations

Our research showed how a firm's age was related to its performance using a survey based panel data on large and medium scale manufacturing firms in Ethiopia with a minimum of 10 employees. Due to high exit and entry rates of firms, the analysis was done for the latest available data collected over the period 2010–15.

Firm age was measured by the number of years since a firm started operations while firm performance was measured by labor productivity and total sales value. Concerning the main research question, our results failed to show a statistically significant and conclusive relationship between firm age and its performance irrespective of our choice of the dependent variable and different model specifications. The average marginal effect of age was also statistically insignificant. The lack of a statistically significant relationship between firm age and its performance provides grounds to question the learning by doing hypothesis.

The issue of how size relates to a firm's performance depended on our choice of the dependent variable. When labor productivity was used, size tended to limit productivity while firm size was associated with improved sales. Total sales tended to grow with firm size until a certain threshold was achieved after which the effect of size became insignificant. The average marginal effect of size on labor productivity was associated with lower performance and the result was found to be statistically significant at the 1% significance level while it was found to be positive and statistically significant when the performance was measured in terms of the total sales value. Thus, firm size was predominantly associated with lower labor productivity but with higher sales value.

Concerning the role of other control variables, our results show that the effect of capital intensity and wage expenditure on a firm's performance was invariant to the

Table 11.8 Regression estimations

Variables	Pooled OLS				Fixed-effects model			
	LPLABORD	LSALED	LPLABORD	LSALED	LPLABORD	LPLABORDt	LSALED	LSALEDt
	Labor productivity	(Sales)	Labor productivity	(Sales)	Labor productivity	Labor productivity	(Sales)	(Sales)
LAGE	-0.915***	-2.477***	0.546	0.803*	-1.462	-1.738	-0.828	-0.969
	(0.319)	(0.407)	(0.379)	(0.471)	(1.205)	(1.226)	(1.174)	(1.199)
LAGESQ	0.129***	0.462***	-0.0873	-0.115	0.226	0.267	0.122	0.144
	(0.050)	(0.064)	(0.060)	(0.074)	(0.184)	(0.187)	(0.176)	(0.180)
LSIZE			-0.553***	0.273*	0.121	0.0827	0.612*	0.613*
			(0.129)	(0.152)	(0.367)	(0.367)	(0.358)	(0.360)
LSIZESQ			0.026*	0.036**	-0.071	-0.068	-0.006	-0.009
			(0.014)	(0.017)	(0.047)	(0.047)	(0.046)	(0.047)
LWAGE			0.262***	0.273***	0.217***	0.211***	0.260***	0.241***
			(0.034)	(0.035)	(0.060)	(0.061)	(0.058)	(0.060)
LCAPINT			0.489***	0.439***	0.287***	0.292***	0.274***	0.274***
			(0.021)	(0.022)	(0.054)	(0.054)	(0.052)	(0.053)
LINVST			-0.0015	-0.017	0.010	0.009	-0.002	-0.002
			(0.009)	(0.011)	(0.015)	(0.015)	(0.014)	(0.014)
NMONTH			-0.0084	-0.018	0.021	0.025	0.026	0.027
			(0.010)	(0.011)	(0.019)	(0.020)	(0.018)	(0.018)
FEMPROP			-0.327***	-0.410***	-1.462	-0.282	-0.339	-0.308
			(0.065)	(0.075)	(1.21)	(0.200)	(0.230)	(0.236)
AA			0.076	-0.082	1.58***	1.59***	0.228	0.288
			(0.083)	(0.094)	(0.344)	(0.331)	(0.737)	(0.743)
ORO			0.071	-0.042	2.032***	2.049***	1.014	1.044

(continued)

Table 11.8 (continued)

Variables	Pooled OLS				Fixed-effects model			
	LPLABORD	LSALED	LPLABORD	LSALED	LPLABORD	LPLABORDt	LSALED	LSALEDt
	Labor productivity	(Sales)	Labor productivity	(Sales)	Labor productivity	Labor productivity	(Sales)	(Sales)
SNNP			0.346***	0.489***	3.302***	3.048***	1.928**	1.725*
			(0.092)	(0.104)	(0.471)	(0.698)	(0.844)	(0.923)
AMH			0.112	0.339***	2.475***	2.549***	1.178	1.267
			(0.097)	(0.108)	(0.484)	(0.465)	(0.851)	(0.823)
OTHERREG			0.402***	0.393**	1.746***	1.781***	3.331***	3.321***
			(0.137)	(0.164)	(0.430)	(0.422)	(0.765)	(0.775)
Year dummy			NO	NO	NO	YES	NO	YES
Constant	1.557***	3.233***	-8.356***	-11.15***	-5.236**	-4.632**	-8.015***	-7.566***
	(0.500)	(0.639)	(0.652)	(0.807)	(2.141)	(2.240)	(2.179)	(2.277)
Observations	10,017	10,017	3406	3406	3406	3406	3406	3406
R-squared	0.001	0.018	0.443	0.559	0.220	0.232	0.291	0.232
Number of firms					2624	2624	2624	2624

Note Robust standard errors in parentheses

***$p<0.01$, **$p<0.05$, *$p<0.1$

method of estimation showing a positive and significant affect irrespective of the choice of the dependent variable. In addition, the role of investments in fixed assets and the number of months that a firm had been operational during a survey year were found to be insignificant. The effect of change in the gender composition of owners on firms' performance showed that firms with a higher number of female owners tended to have inferior performance from the OLS regression although the affect became insignificant under the FE model. Finally, the role of region of operation on a firm's performance was significant and positive for the labor productivity regression.

An investigation of the elements of the business environment revealed that the business obstacles reported by older firms were the same as the one reported by the younger firms showing that both cohorts of firms generally operated in similar environments. Both the young and old firms reported shortage of raw materials, infrastructure problems and lack of markets as their top business obstacles inhibiting full capacity operations. Concerning current challenges faced by firms, shortage of raw materials, access to markets and shortage of working capital emerged as top challenges for both cohorts of firms.

Some useful policy implications emerge from the findings of our study. Business outcomes can be improved if policymakers work on enhancing the learning and absorptive capacities of older firms. This is because we found firm age to be insignificant in affecting a firm's performance. The business obstacles reported by older firms were the same as ones reported by the younger firms showing that both cohorts of firms generally operated in a similar environment. Solving the generic problems of shortage of raw materials, insufficient infrastructure (electricity and water), lack of markets and shortage of working capital are expected to improve a firm's performance. Firm turnover could also be reduced by giving more support to younger firms by addressing their top challenges. Capital intensity was found to promote a firm's performance. Thus improving access to finance could be useful in sustaining a firm's performance.

The results obtained from our research can be improved through a number of interventions related to measurement of variables and model specifications. Measuring labor productivity using value added, for instance, could improve the results. Measuring firm performance using total factor productivity and its growth rate could also enhance the results. Other issues not addressed in our research include simultaneity and endogeneity problems among variables and reverse causation problems. Firm performance may affect firm age, for example, since productive firms face a high probability of survival and hence higher age. The effects of the lagged values of some of the explanatory variables could be important in resolving the conflicting results observed in our analysis. Firm size, for instance, could be affected by the lagged values of labor productivity showing reverse causation.

References

Akben-Selcuk, E. 2016. Does firm age affect profitability? Evidence from Turkey. *International Journal of Economic Sciences* 3 (3): 1–9.

Arrow, K.J. 1962. The economic implications of learning by doing. *Review of Economic Studies* 29: 155–173.

Barron, D.N., E. West, and M.T. Hannan. 1994. A time to grow and a time to die: Growth and mortality of credit unions in New York City, 1914–1990. *The American Journal of Sociology* 100: 381–421.

Brouwer, P., J. Kok, and P. Fris. 2005. Can firm age account for productivity differences? A study into the relationship between productivity and firm age for mature firms. *Scientific Analysis of Entrepreneurship and SMEs (SCALES), Paper No. 200421.*

Brüderl, J., and R. Schüssler. 1990. Organizational mortality: The liabilities of newness and adolescence. *Administrative Science Quarterly* 35: 530–547.

Chang, Y., J.F. Gomes, and F. Schorfheide. 2002. Learning-by-doing as a propagation mechanism. *American Economic Review* 92: 1498–1520.

Coad, A., A. Segarra, and M. Teruel. 2013. Like milk or wine: Does firm performance improve with age? *Structural Change and Economic Dynamics* 24: 173–189. https://doi.org/10.1016/j.strueco.2012.07.002.

Coad, A., S.O. Daunfeldt, and D. Halvarsson. 2014. Firm age and growth persistence. *Conference: Innovation forum VI-2014. Crisis, innovation and transition.* 1–3 October 2014, University of Paris.

CSA (Central Statistical Agency of Ethiopia). 2016 (Various years). *The survey of manufacturing and electricity industries.* Addis Ababa: Central Statistical Agency of Ethiopia.

Evans, D.S. 1987. The relationship between firm growth, size, and age: Estimates for 100 manufacturing industries. *Journal of Industrial Economics* 35: 567–581.

Hannan, M.T., and J. Freeman. 1984. Structural inertia and organizational change. *American Sociological Review* 49: 149–164.

Heshmati, A., and B. Su. 2014. Development and sources of labor productivity in Chinese provinces. *IZA Discussion Paper No. 9923.*

Heshmati, A., and M. Rashidghalam. 2016. Labour productivity in Kenyan manufacturing and service industries. *IZA Discussion Paper No. 9923.*

Huergoa, E., and J. Jaumandreu. 2003. Firms' age, process innovation and productivity growth. *International Journal of Industrial Organization* 22: 541–559.

Loderer, C., and U. Waelchli. 2010. Firm age and performance, Munich personal RePEc archive. University of Bern, ECGI European Corporate Governance Institute. *MPRA Working Paper No. 26450.*

NBE (National bank of Ethiopia). 2016. *Annual Report 2015/16.*

Palangkaraya, A., A. Stierwald, and J. Yong. 2006. *Is firm productivity related to size and age? The case of large Australian firms.* Melbourne Institute of Applied Economic and Social Research, The University of Melbourne.

Rijkers, B., M. Soderbom, and J.L. Loenin. 2010. A rural-urban comparison of manufacturing enterprise performance in Ethiopia. *World Development* 38 (9): 1278–1296.

Stinchcombe, A.L. 1965. Social structure and organizations. *Handbook of organizations*, 142–193. Chicago: Rand McNally.

Printed by Printforce, the Netherlands